GOD'S CHOICE

GOD'S CHOICE

The Total World of a Fundamentalist Christian School

Alan Peshkin

The University of Chicago Press
Chicago and London

Alan Peshkin is professor of education at the University of Illinois, Urbana-Champaign. *God's Choice* is the third in his series of studies exploring American communities and their schools. The other books in the series, *Growing Up American* and *The Imperfect Union*, were also published by the University of Chicago Press.

The University of Chicago Press, Chicago 60637
The University of Chicago Press, Ltd., London
© 1986 by The University of Chicago
All rights reserved. Published 1986
Printed in the United States of America

95 94 93 92 91 90 89 88 87 86   54321

Library of Congress Cataloging-in-Publication Data
Peshkin, Alan.
   God's choice.

   Bibliography: p.
   Includes index.
   1. Christian schools—United States—Case studies.
2. Fundamentalism—Case studies.   I. Title.
LC562.P47   1986   377'.0973   85-24524
ISBN 0-226-66198-9

For my parents, Harriet Peshkin and Simon Rotberg

Contents

Preface

Given the range of objective realities that characterize a school, the number of questions that can be raised about these realities, and the diverse perspectives created by the personal biographies of different researchers, it is clear that no story told about any school can be everyone's story. Obviously, the story in this book is mine. In one way or another, it is about Bethany Baptist Church and its school, about the pseudonymous Pastor Muller and Headmaster McGraw, about my Christian landlady and several other Bethany families, about a school faculty and several hundred students—and, unavoidably, about me. It is not a story about the gifts of cooperation, warmth, and hospitality that I received in such abundance, but it is a story I could never have told without these gifts. It hardly suffices to express gratitude for the largesse one receives. I do so, anyway, to Barb, her dad, and Tim, for my home away from home, and to all those students and teachers who were unfailingly polite.

To all Bethanyites I am grateful for giving as they did, and to no one more than Pastor Muller and Headmaster McGraw. They permitted me and my gifted research assistants, Corrine Glesne and Rich Franz, to become participants and observers in their world, and to remain there long enough to complete my study. They gave me numerous hours of their time, good, unrushed, patient time. As did Pastor Carter Hill, an official of the American Association of Christian Schools, and each of the teachers with whom we completed our interview schedules. I hope I have included a sufficient selection of their words to convey their world as they would want it conveyed. I meant to do so, just as I meant to indicate how I perceive it and them. We are worlds apart, Bethany and I. I say this neither sadly nor defiantly. It's just the way things are. If they are right—and I do not think they are—then I am forever doomed, but that's another story, more challenging to tell than the one that follows.

Before I begin my story, I happily express my gratitude to those others who have helped me at various times. The Reverend David Housholder literally led me to this study of a fundamentalist school, and thereafter informed, advised, and critiqued everything I did in a most wonderful and valuable way. His wife, Linda, provided helpful moral support. When this study was no more than an idea, I wrote proposal drafts that benefited from the criticism of Steven Asher, Eric Bredo, Ed Bruner, Walter Feinberg, Maryann Peshkin, and Bob Stake. My study was funded by the Spencer Foundation, and it was a pleasure to work for three years with its always supportive and encouraging president, Tom James. Further essential financial support was provided by the University of Illinois's Center for Advanced Study, Research Board, and College of Education. For their fine work in the development of my questionnaire and the analysis and presentation of the data, I thank Sandra Mathison, Hans Wagemaker, and Colleen Bell. When my manuscript was in draft form, the following friends and colleagues read various chapters—some of them, all eleven: Gordon Cohn, Walter Feinberg, Corrine Glesne, Maryann Peshkin, Jim Raths, Bob Stake, Nancy Weinberg, and Barbara Yates. Each made a contribution that put me in their debt, but none more so than David Housholder and Hank Browne, who criticized and challenged each chapter in the most exceptional way. Finally, I extend thanks to Patti Peterson for transcribing my tapes, and to June Chambliss and her patient, persistent operators, who with the help of a word processor produced clean drafts from my mess of revised pages.

1

Introduction
The Setting, the Author,
the Times

The Pastor Speaks: From inside the Fold

"Bless this interview, Lord. Let it be helpful for Christian education, but as well, Lord, for the community at large, and, Lord, for the testimony of Jesus Christ, our Savior, in whose name we pray. Amen."

Pastor William Muller,[1] spiritual and academic leader of Bethany Baptist Church and Bethany Baptist Academy (BBA), usually opened our interview sessions with a prayer like this one. This dynamic and committed man has established a large, thriving church and school in the fundamentalist independent Baptist tradition. He is a Christian, which is to say a born-again Christian, and in this book, unless stated otherwise, "Christian" will always refer to "born-again Christians,"[2] as Pastor Muller uses the term. To such Christians, all men are born once of the flesh; if they accept Jesus Christ as their personal savior, they are born once again, but the second time as new men in him. The basic condition for becoming a fundamentalist Christian is being born again.

I spent eighteen months as a participant in, and observer of, the life of his church community located in "Hartney," an Illinois city of approximately fifty thousand persons. It was more than long enough to learn that Pastor Muller is the key to his church community's growth and its national prominence. Consequently, his own words provide the best possible introduction to the world of Bethany. In the informal setting of our interview, he speaks with all the ease, forthrightness, authority, and eloquence that characterize his presentations delivered

1

from any platform to any audience. Given that he is involved at the highest levels in both the state and national educational organizations to which Independent Baptist schools belong, his views and perspectives, more than being those of just another local church leader, are those of a respected insider.

The time is several months before the Reagan-Carter presidential election. Pastor Muller and I sit in his comfortable, well-decorated office. Our matching chairs are separated by a large, black, bearskin rug, one of the many trophies of Pastor Muller's hunting prowess that adorn the room's walls and floors. His silver-colored miniature schnauzer is never far from him throughout our conversations, which stretch over many weeks. Indeed, this very busy man has been exceptionally generous with his time, never showing the least sign of impatience to get on with the next of his numerous scheduled activities. His willing cooperation has been matched by that of his teachers, administrators, and students, who opened their classrooms and lives for the purposes of my study.

Pastor Muller epitomizes the new type of pastor that was described at a meeting of his fellow Christian educators: "Independent, fundamentalist, Baptist pastors don't speak ungrammatical English anymore; their socks now match their suits, as well as each other; and they don't meet in store-front churches. They are on the move in the United States." And his church, Bethany Baptist Church, fulfills each condition that Dean Hoge has identified as necessary for church growth during the past several decades: "(1) a demand for high commitment from their members . . . (2) discipline over both beliefs and life style . . . (3) missionary zeal . . . (4) absolutistic about beliefs . . . (5) conformity in life style" (1979: 180–81).

Pastor Muller begins his first-person account with reference to his youth and continues with observations about the establishment of his school and about Christians and politics.[3]

> My dad still lives in my hometown. He's out of the pastorate now, but he still oversees the seminary which he founded. When I was growing up, I knew that my parents prayed I'd be a preacher. I went away to a Christian college knowing that the Lord had called me to be a preacher, but I hadn't fully submitted. There was still some apprehension in my mind. When I was a freshman, probably a month and a half in college, I can remember cutting classes and going to my dormitory and praying by the old, underslung metal

bed. I asked the Lord to show me that day. For sure, I wanted some peace in my heart. By the end of a day filled with bringing Scripture and prayers to my mind, I had submitted and the burden was off.

I finished up my seminary in 1960 and by November I became pastor of the First Baptist Church in a small Wisconsin city. I spent the next four years there as the pastor, choir director, and youth pastor. My wife did my secretarial work. When I went there, there were 26 people. When I left we had a consistently high attendance of 140 or 150 and over $10,000 in the bank.

I started here at Bethany in 1964 on the Sunday before Christmas. I loved it: a nice little building, a good opportunity, and a progressive area that I felt really wanted to grow. Some time around 1968 we had established several goals in our church. They were, one, to buy a new bus. Two, we felt the Lord leading to start a Christian radio station in town. And three was the Christian school.

The Christian school—we threw it out as one of the matters to pray about. "We'll wait until the Lord leads us," is what we thought. My own children had started public school. I remember their kindergarten teacher still had grace before crackers and milk. I went over to speak a couple times a year. And they still had baccalaureate services over at the high school. All those things seemed to say to me, "Hey, we're not quite as bad as Chicago." Well, around 1970, when the Vietnam War was on, I saw the American flag being insulted. I saw colleges opening up their dormitories to coed living. I saw the products of the schools of education, who were going to be the teachers in the public schools. Anyway, my wife went over to my kids' school during National Education Week in 1971. There was a new teacher in my son's second-grade class. When my wife walked in, a rock and roll record was on, the kids were jiving, and the teacher was standing there. She said, "I don't know what to do with these kids. I can't control them." My wife came home burned up about it. This, I felt, was the new crop of teachers. Then, there was some evolution being given to my daughter. I went over there at parent visitation time and I saw the stuff around the walls. When I saw these things, I said that this is the time. We took a survey among our church members and it revealed that we could start our own school, a K-6 program, with sixty-five students. In fact, the first year we had about eighty-eight students, with four teachers, and we made $3,000. That was the beginning of our Christian school.

At first, right here in our church, we found our teachers—experienced and certified women who agreed to help us get started. After a while, we were able to look for teachers from outside. I was pretty much directly involved in hiring all the teachers in the early years. I guess the first thing I'd look at in a teacher candidate is if they have it academically; we look at the academic end of things immediately and then we look to make sure that they're spiritually born-again people, know Christ as their savior, and want to walk with the Lord and experience fellowship with him. They also have to show that they're willing to be subservient to the local church because our school is a ministry of our church.

Well, we got started, and most everything was going along just fine. It wasn't too long before we got involved with other Christian schools like our own, building upon the statewide organization that began in Florida. Eventually, we got our own state organization together and also built a national association, the American Association of Christian Schools, under the umbrella of Dr. Al Janney, who was president of the Florida Association of Christian Schools.

Dr. Janney got involved in national politics because there were so many issues that affected our churches and schools. Soon, many others of us also got involved. In 1976, a presidential election year you remember, a bunch of Christians, a good number of fundamental pastors, most of them Independent Baptists, and evangelists got together in Texas with a strong, conservative congressman. I was at the meeting. What happened was basically this: Christian schools were producing patriotic young people who had good character, a real difference from what public schools of the country were producing.

At that meeting in Texas, we discussed the possibility of Christians having a voice. Christians had been too silent, too long; we'd put our heads in the sand. We had condemned the National Council of Churches for getting politically involved, and we hadn't even encouraged our own people to get out and vote. So we leaders formed an organization called CALL—Concerned Americans for Life and Liberty. Remember, just one vote more per precinct across the country would have elected Goldwater in '64. And yet so many Christians didn't vote. It's not because we're not patriotic; see, we feel that our citizenship is in heaven and consequently we're more involved with spiritual entities. It's too easy for us to get the idea that, well, the Lord is coming one of these days and we're on our way to heaven, and just forget about this whole world. Here's the way we finally began to think: We've got leaders that have caused our problems, and governments that have created difficulties for us in the operation of our ministries. So, as leaders we got together and said, "We've got to do something about this."

Now, I think there are probably some politicians who look at our power and think that if they befriend the Christian school movement, it'll help them to get reelected. We're used to action and I think government people see that. We can crank up our people to write letters and do some things. Recently, when I said to my churchfolk, "Go write a letter to your congressman about ERA," a lot of people said they'd write a letter. The latest one we cranked up in about two days. We had to hurry because Congress was voting on the continuation of the Ashbrook and Dornan amendments to the treasury bill. We got on the phone Saturday and Sunday, and got our people to send telegrams and make phone calls immediately to our state representatives and congressman. I asked people Sunday night, "How many of you will write a letter or send a telegram by Tuesday night?" We must have got sixty-five or seventy hands. I checked the following Wednesday night and asked how many did it. I must have got fifty of them.

Fundamentalists are a small group in this country. As long as we're a minority, society has no problem with us. But if Christians begin to effect some change . . . For example, we're draining off a few dollars of support from public schools. As long as it isn't too much, there won't be too many rules against us, but as soon as it begins to affect pocketbooks, you can rest assured that there will be suppression. There will be laws and there will be regulations. I guess the point is that if we're to have enough power and clout to withstand, then we must get more involved in political issues. We're not asking for anything other than our freedom.

Several organizations, one a group called Freedom Foundation, have been going about the country trying to organize Christians into precinct-level politics. That's what we've tried to do here in Hartney. Because our church has tax-exempt status, we must not get involved politically toward the election of those candidates the church prefers, but we can always get involved in that which threatens our existence. IRS issues are a clear matter where we can speak out all we wish. When the Lord said, "Render to Caesar that which is Caesar's and render to God that which is God's," I don't think he necessarily meant that we should stick our heads into the sand about this world. Somebody has said, "If you don't fight to defend your freedom, you don't deserve to have your freedom." That means for us to take on some of the issues. If we don't, the end result is godlessness or Communism or socialism, and then your missionary activity would be outlawed. I think that when it gets right down to the point of being able to preach the gospel, at that point I'm to obey God, rather than man or governments of men. If they [state government] passed laws and said they'd forbid Christian schools from operating until they were accredited by the state standard of accreditation for public schools, they'd have to haul me to jail. I wouldn't close down Bethany Baptist Academy based on that reason. Our school is a ministry of the church and we have a right.

I have a message I preached back in 1964 called "Extremism: A Vice or a Virtue?" "Extremism in the defense of liberty is no vice; moderation in the defense of justice is no virtue." That's what Barry Goldwater said. We *are* extreme in our belief. In essence, we negate all the other religions of the world. OK. They're wrong. There is no way of getting in to heaven except through Jesus Christ. Fewer and fewer people believe in the fact that Jesus was God. You're extreme if you do, and I point out in this speech that we are extreme in our belief of the Virgin Birth. We are extreme in believing that Jesus is coming again, we are extreme in believing in salvation by faith, and we are extreme in witnessing to others.

What I'm saying is that Christians are extremist in the eyes of the world. I don't look at myself as a conservative. I can see kooky people to the right of me, but if somebody else looks at me from their perspective, and if they're outside the fold of Christ, they'd look at me as a conservative. I see myself as obeying the Bible. Our belief has got to affect our behavior; if we're Christians, our behavior is going to be conservative politically.

We look around us and see Satan. He's prince and power of this age and he has stronger involvement with this world than Christians do. With all the governmental involvement in the school system today, there's no longer parent control.

Ronald Reagan, I think, is the best choice for president, but no way are things going to be much better under any administration. He's going to try to make a stand, and there will be a few areas whereby we'll get some satisfaction, but it won't last long and you'll soon discover that his administration will be corrupted. I hate to be a doomsday prophet because I enjoy life, but I want to face reality just as much as I can. I guess the bright side is the coming again of Jesus Christ. Young persons find it hard to put themselves in that great hope. Christian as they are, they don't wake up in the morning and say, "Praise the Lord, Jesus may come today." What they're thinking is, "I can't wait till I get my driver's license." Well, those are the things that motivate kids. They motivated me. I remember thinking, "Boy, I sure hope the Lord doesn't come until I'm sixteen and have a car."

Today, Christian schools are a necessity. Without them we can't rightfully accent our biblical commitment. Salvation was not the purpose for starting this school, and it's not a primary goal for when people enroll kids in our school. Our primary goal is to educate and edify the Lord in students' lives. Public institutions tolerate everything. You say anything you want to the teacher, you treat that teacher like dirt, call them any name in the book. I don't know anything that's restricted anymore.

In comparison to the public schools, our kids get a better education. The public schools have more kids with higher IQs, so they get more kids who go on to higher academic achievement, but we'll provide a good or better education for a greater percentage of our kids. Likewise, we'll lose less of a percentage than they will and provide fewer people for the welfare rolls of America. The Christian schools, I think, are the only way we'll be able to have missionaries to send out to the world, provide preachers, and train schoolteachers for the Christian school movement. They're a continuation of our total effort. Primarily, we're pushing kids to go to Christian colleges and then to go out and serve the Lord. It would be a great thing if you could read in the papers that a kid from our academy wins a scholarship to Harvard, but all along he's been hearing, "Go off to a Christian school—go to Bob Jones, or go to Maranatha."

You know, there are some very real differences between us and a public school. The primary distinction is going to be character. We develop character. Just as long as we feel we're fulfilling our commitment to the Lord and to our children, and, likewise, that the Lord feels this is where our kids ought to be, who cares what distinction others may see? And Christian teachers come at the subject matter from a different point of view. They come with a basic understanding that God exists, that God has created, and that God has left us with revelations, whereas the non-Christian teacher perhaps comes with a strong desire maybe to know truth, but wonders if he ever arrives at it. The non-Christian teacher, subconsciously, has accepted a philosophy which may not be organized in his mind, but it's there. It is humanism. The public school system—we are just naturally in competition with it.

Most Christian schools that I know of do what we do: we take the parents' pledge and the students' pledge and the commitment is basically to those pledges. We say this: We feel like we are wasting time if we teach a kid all day, and then he goes out and leads his own life. If we're not touching his life, if we're just touching his academics, we don't care to have him. We're not running that kind of a school. I think most Christian schools have discovered that just having a bunch of kids enrolled to help them make financial gain is not at all worth it. So, you know, you're left with a twenty-four hour school. We can deal with the moral aspects of life. A public school doesn't do that. We deal with the morals of the faith and we can touch our students' total behavior pattern. That's what makes this a twenty-four hour school.

For us, this is a total life. I'm talking about the academy, the church, the families. We see each other several times a week; there's a chance for more rapport with students. When students are here in the academy, we involve ourselves a little bit more in their lives. With most students, our work affects their social lives. It involves their Friday and Saturday nights, it involves their work life, and it involves their religious life. They're here on Wednesday nights and on Sundays for church. My life is the same way. My friends are church people. I just don't have any people I socialize with outside the church. You know, birds of a feather flock together.

I believe Christian schools try to teach that in the total society of mankind, young people must abide by God's structures and God's system of order. That's why they learn to say "Yes, sir" and "Yes, ma'am" down here. We come at it from an authoritarian point of view. The very first verse in the Bible doesn't endeavor to prove that God exists; it just assumes that God exists. It begins with, "In the beginning

God created the heaven and the earth." So we come to these young people with a background of authority. Humanism elevates man and his reasoning. I'd put it this way: Without authority and without structure, we do a disservice to our total educational program. If there's a doubting of authority, you're going to waste a good measure of time. Our faith is *not* based upon reason, but our faith is not unreasonable. We're for structure. I'm a friend of the policeman because I believe that he is needed and he is God's minister. I'm a friend of the real politician, because I know that he is necessary. All of God's part and structure I'm for because it's God's way. Why doubt those things? To me, it's just ridiculous.

The Bible says that we are in the world, but not to be of the world. All that is of the world—the lust of the flesh, the lust of the eyes, and the pride of life—is not of the Father. We try to teach principles whereby our young people will have enough sense by the time they graduate to realize that there is reasoning behind it all. We want to present the fact that here we are, as the Bible says we are, the salt of the earth. Therefore, we must do what we can to influence the world, and yet to know the breaking point at which we say, "I want to reach the world, but I don't want to be identified as necessarily part of the world." See, here is the darkness and here is the light: we're the light of the world. Let's have no fellowship with those who live in darkness. We're not to be in partnership or relationship with the untruthful works of darkness. We are to reprove them or we are to convict them. One way the Bible teaches us to convict them is by not having any fellowship with them.

We want our boys and girls when they get out of school to want to have this Christian life. We want to give these young people the ability to make rational choices, and to be able to make them because they've come to school here. This is not a place where there are alternative world views, competing and confronting cosmologies. Christianity claims to be the only way, and I guess if we were noncompetitive we would say, "Well, you can choose the way you want to go." But we put ourselves in a position of being the first and only among the religions of the world. There is one truth. Truth, as we see it, is singular.

By the same token, I don't think it's anything other than by design that the public school system does not have an alternative to humanism. I think there are just two systems, ours and the public school's. I'm not at all advocating prayer and Bible reading in the public school as the answer. I think that we're too far down the road to believe that's the answer. We need doctors and lawyers, and we need all the various categories of persons that Christian schools aren't able to provide. So, I don't necessarily write public schools off. I'm just more enthusiastic about the Christian school movement.

Pastor Muller and I spoke of these and many other things. When, two years earlier, we had met for the first time, he asked if I was a Christian. Hearing that I was not, he smiled and said we would have to talk about that some time. And so we did. During our last meeting, he explored what kind of a Jew I was, if I knew any Jewish believers in Christ, and if during the past eighteen months I'd ever felt compelled to become a believer. A man of force and fire from the pulpit, he ended this proselytizing effort quietly and gently.

I only pray and hope that you would become a believer in Jesus Christ and that you would understand that Jesus would be the answer to the need in your life as a person and that somewhere along the way you would believe. Jewish folk—there are not many of them that turn to Christ as Christians. I don't think less of Jews because they're not Christians. All I have in Christ is built upon the fact that Jesus Christ was himself a Jew. Many of the warnings of the Old Testament concerning the Jewish faith were probably realized. In fact, one of the great concerns was that their faith would become reduced, and their people would be scattered about the earth, not only in a physical realm but also in a spiritual realm. There isn't much of the real Jewish religious faith left any longer.

There is little that is gray in Pastor Muller's outlook; uncertainty does not plague him. The true believer's sharp, dichotomous distinctions are to his taste and in his manner. I see in his articulate characterizations of church and school every major aspect of Bethany's world that had caught my attention and provoked my reactions—their belief in the "total life," a "twenty-four hour school," "the light of the world," "one truth," and their "position of being first and only among the religions of the world." Not for a moment did I believe that Pastor Muller was presenting a case tailor-made for the benefit of his long-term visitor. The man I heard in the privacy of his chambers was the man I heard address his devoted congregation each Wednesday night, Sunday morning, and Sunday night. As befits the partisan of a divine, absolutist doctrine, he spoke always with one voice, as did the educators his school employed, whether it was in behalf of the rightness of the fundamentalist Christian's political activism or of the warrant for unrestrained proselytizing.

Coming to a Christian School

By means of an event which my Christian friends would call providential, and everyone else I know would call coincidental, I came to my present study. The event: a midwinter blizzard, an evening class, and a student in need of a ride home. The student was the Reverend David Housholder, whose son attended a local Christian school and who assured me, when I expressed a fascination with religious schools, that he would help in every way he could to arrange for me to study his son's school. My impatience with the blizzard and its inevitable constraint on mobility for the next several days was moderated by the joy that the prospect of a new study always produces.

At this time I knew very little about parochial schools, a designation I then thought encompassed all full-time religious schools below the university level. What I thought I knew assured me that at least one of their signal attributes—community maintenance—linked them to the inquiry I had been pursuing since 1972. I reasoned that as the creature of a Roman Catholic, Lutheran, or Jewish community the parochial school would be expected to function as a community-maintenance institution. This function was a central point in a study I had done in the Midwestern village of Mansfield,[4] and in one I was in the process of completing concerning a school district embroiled in a school-closing struggle. This struggle dramatized a community's perception of the contribution its local school made to the survival of that community.[5]

My fortuitous cross-town drive that winter's night occurred in 1978. I devoted the following spring to gaining access to the school David Housholder's son attended (I failed in 1978 and again in 1979) and to learning about the guardedness of at least one Christian school. No public school administrators and no public school board members ever probed more incisively into my research intentions. One board member of this Christian school wondered what I would say if a student in a class I was observing asked me, "Do you love Jesus?" Her litmus-test query was a powerful reminder of my outsideness. This fact was reinforced by the experiences of my pilot study in 1978–79, during which time I sought entry to a variety of religious schools.

The pilot study was designed to introduce me to the world of Christian education. This was the explanation I offered to all the gatekeepers I encountered (usually either the principal or pastor of the church who established the school), and it was a true one. At this time, I did not intend to collect data for a study of any sort; learning about religious schools was primary. A hoped-for dividend was the identification of a school that would allow my entry for year-long, intensive fieldwork in 1979–80. Roman Catholic, Lutheran, and Seventh-Day Adventist schools readily welcomed me and my research assistants. These schools were easy, comfortable, fruitful observation sites, and they were in sharp contrast to what I learned to call "Christian" as opposed to "parochial" schools. So-called "Christian" schools, although neither more nor less religiously established and connected than parochial schools, use the term "Christian" to describe their class of institutions and only that class. This distinction between "Christian" and parochial schools was one of the earliest I learned. The second distinction related to gaining access: parochial schools are easy to enter; "Christian" schools are not. In the course of this pilot year, we were allowed entry to one, only to be asked later to leave; allowed entry to another for "two weeks only, that's all, no bargaining"; and absolutely refused entry to a third.

The refusing pastor spurned me with a flourish. To my innocent statement that we wanted merely to learn about the world of a Christian day school, he replied:

> You're like a Russian who says he wants to attend meetings at the Pentagon—just to learn. . . . No matter how good a person you are, you will misrepresent my school because you don't have the Holy Spirit in you. First, become a child of the King, and then you can pursue your study of Christian schools.

"Do I love Jesus?" "First, become a child of the King." I doubted that I would ever be allowed to conduct a study in the fundamentalist Christian setting that I had determined was the best place to be to continue my school-community research. From what I had seen, parochial schools neither claimed to be, nor acted as though they were, fully committed to establishing a school suffused with doctrinal orientation. In contrast, Christian schools were.

The pilot study had been agonizing, instructive, and absolutely essential. Long before it was over, I felt I'd been attempting an assault on treasures within a stronghold. I sensed moats, steep, slick walls, and alert guards, all placed to prevent menacing non-Christians from entering. At Bethany Baptist Academy, the last pilot site we approached for permission to enter as observers, we were able to obtain the consent of Pastor Muller and headmaster Tom McGraw to return the next fall. This consent freed me to focus on the next year's work and what I hoped to accomplish.

The Objects of My Assault

In his fine study of the impact of Mennonite schools, Donald Kraybill wrote that "new members of a [Mennonite] society acquire the knowledge, skills and dispositions that enable them to participate as effective members of their group" (1977:1), and that his Mennonite community schools contribute to that acquisition. As mentioned earlier, it was this community-maintenance function that first attracted me to the Christian school; it remains as a focal point and thereby connects this study to my previous ones. Survival in this instance was not tied to a geographically or politically circumscribed community, but to the group established by Bethany Baptist Church members and, as well, by their brethren, the body of kindred believers throughout the world. Accordingly, survival has both a near and a distant object. Like Kraybill, I was interested in the impact of Bethany Baptist Academy (hereafter often referred to as BBA) on its students. The most meaningful impact of schooling is best measured when students have left school and settled into those activities (work, marriage, postschool friendships, child rearing, etc.) which will characterize their life as adults, but BBA is too new to support such measurement. Nonetheless, I will try to suggest what appears to be the contribution of the BBA experience to its students.

As a result of the year of pilot study, the objects or purposes of my research expanded. From what I had seen at several Christian schools, including BBA, I decided to examine the relationship between religious doctrine and educational practice. BBA's doctrine, derived from Scripture, is viewed as the absolute, unvarying, eternal Word of God. BBA, accordingly, is based upon Truth. A challenge for my research, then, was to compare the "God-centered" Christian school with the "man-centered" public school.

My interest in the relationship between doctrine and practice meant that I would have to show what a Christian school is really like. To date, most scholarly studies of religious schools have emphasized their impact.[6] What these studies do not emphasize is the nature of the school whose impact is being investigated. Although assessing the impact of years of schooling undoubtedly has merit, it does not establish what a year of schooling encompasses. This is a major intent of my study. I will make clear what an "exemplary" Christian school is like, of the variety that is Independent Baptist and affiliated with the one-thousand-member American Association of Christian Schools (AACS). In my portrayal, I intend to identify the most typical characteristics of such a school so there is no mistaking whether a particular school is or is not a fundamentalist Christian school. I intend, further, to establish what it is that makes such schools attractive to many Americans.

If a school is founded on absolute truth, it must follow that its doctrine is not subject to critical scrutiny. For its adherents, the only proper response to such doctrine is belief and obedience, and the best means of establishing this response is the total institution,[7] as in Pastor Muller's twenty-four hour school. Impressed by the applicability of the total-institution concept to the Bethany setting, I was guided by it as I made my observations and conducted my interviews and, eventually, organized and analyzed my data.

With its basis in Scripture interpreted literally, the Christian school is directed by its educators as an institution with one doctrine, one truth, one way. Thus, this setting provides an opportunity to learn about parents and a school which agree in rejecting the diversity that is not only allowed but often celebrated in the public school. I will consider whether a single outlook prevails at Bethany and, if it does, ascertain whether it manifests itself in the "true believer's" style of lauding one's own faith as orthodox, while rejecting all others as heterodox.

If logic tells us that Y should follow X, experience tells us that Ys often have a way of striking off in their own directions, especially when those Ys are Christian youth growing up not only in a singular school but also in an incredibly diverse society whose pervasive reach leaves no one untouched. Notwithstanding my assumption of BBA's singularity and of its organization as a total institution, BBA is a day school. Its students, away from school each night, weekend, and holiday, have ample time to be caught by the barbs of ecclesiastically unsanctioned persons in unsanctioned places. Thus, to record that all but a handful of BBA students are born-again Christians is to suggest a uniformity that denies the probability of adolescent variability. Notwithstanding the immutability of its doctrine and the ubiquity of its application, Bethany's students may be no more alike than trees: if you have seen one, you have not seen them all. Given this perspective, I will examine the question of student diversity, not in order to praise it but to identify the strains and tensions that affect Bethany's socialization process.

A final purpose, one that moves beyond the more descriptive one of portrayal, is drawn from the fact that BBA, like its counterparts nationwide, is an alternative school. Since the late 1960s, alternative schools from within the public domain have attracted thousands of parents and their children. These efforts to educate children join those of the older, more established alternative private independent and parochial schools. Parents with financial means have long had a choice of schooling; today, more choices than ever before are available. A Supreme Court decision of 1925, *Pierce vs. Society of Sisters* (See Fellman 1969:3–5), established the legality of the religious educational alternative. Thus, the legality of BBA is not in question, nor, indeed, is the wisdom of the judgment that established the legality. There remain, however, the question of what kind of alternative the fundamentalist Christian school offers and the highly pertinent question of what consequences the Christian schools hold for American education and American society.

These past few pages describe my public research agenda, the one I share with colleagues, funders, and friends. In every sense it is a true agenda. In addition to one's public agenda there may often exist a private agenda, one that includes gaining recognition, promotion, money, etc. The latter aims may or may not be primary and, indeed, they may be the natural outcome of the public agenda. In my case, however, there always is at least one more. Having sought a professional career that involves cross-cultural studies, I have found great personal satisfaction in the excitement of South Asia and West Africa. Today, I find no less excitement in the terra exotica of American subgroups that are a substantial cultural distance from the Peshkin family home. For me to embark on a journey of discovery (I always conceive of fieldwork this way) in the realm of a fundamentalist Christian school and church is to begin an adventure like that of the writer Paul Theroux. With infectious delight, he has traveled by train across the breadth of Asia (1975), and from his home in Boston to Argentina's Patagonia (1979).

The field researcher assumes the license to gawk and poke about in the name of scholarship. Of course, I hope always that respectable scholarly ends will emerge in the course of the gawking and poking about in places that, while not necessarily far-flung, may be farfetched for me to be in. Perhaps it is unseemly to parade in public one's private joy in doing what is supposed to be done for exalted reasons. However, as I increasingly come under conviction (an expression I owe to this study) about the relationship between who I am, what I see, and what I conclude about what I see, I feel increasingly inclined to reveal enough about myself so that readers can make their own judgments about what I saw, what I missed, and what I misconstrued.

To speak of personal joy and adventure is merely to state that I savored being where I would not ordinarily be, subjecting myself to the hazards, indignities, and fun of abiding as an outsider. These rewards are the common province of fieldworkers. That there is nothing new under the sun seldom precludes one from remarking on this aspect of one's experience. Furthermore, and not incidentally, I did take seriously the people and the institution I had come to learn about, though not from the perspective they would have liked—that of a born-again Christian. To "take seriously" in my terms is committing oneself to understand other people in their own terms; to respect their values and decisions; to be as patient and comprehensive in the gathering of data as I can manage; and, ultimately, to consider the meaning of the phenomena I have experienced and to assess and report their implications for myself, for education, and for American society. I share the anthropologist Robert Jay's view that fieldwork is not "two unrelated things— reportable knowledge and personal adventure" (1974:380), and his view that the two can be joined "consciously" and "publicly" without damaging either.

The Natural Man

> But the natural man receiveth not the things of the spirit of God: for they are foolishness to him: neither can he know them, because they are spiritually discerned.
>
> 1 Corinthians 2:14

> "Are you a Catholic?" one priest asked her. "Good," he answered, "now I can speak freely."
>
> Joan Brothers

In jargon-laden advertisements designed to trap health faddists, "natural" is a positive term, an eye-opener that announces, "Read on. Good things ahead." To the fundamentalist, the term signals caution, reservation, possibly danger, since the natural man is the non-Christian, his life unredeemed by Jesus Christ.

To refer in passing to the fact that I am a natural man, a non-Christian who studied a Christian school, is insufficient. Such brief acknowledgment does not amply forewarn the reader who the ego is in this study. Researchers as outsiders often are distinguished by traits that truly will influence their perception. The anthropologist Barbara Myerhoff studied aged working-class Jews, but she, though Jewish herself, was comparatively young and a college professor, anything but aged and working-class. And so it goes.

At Bethany, I felt I resided in a world totally unlike any other I had ever known. For example, integral to almost each day's activities at BBA was the invitation to everyone present to consider whether they were saved, right with the Lord, in the Word, etc. This regular calling of attention to one's relationship with the Lord was accompanied by daily, frequent prayers of gratitude to Jesus for blessings from him. For almost everyone at Bethany, with the exception of me and my two research assistants, no events were as significant as Jesus' death and Resurrection, and no relationship with a living person as significant as their relationship with him. The virtual uniformity of Bethany's social environment showed us in sharp relief.

One day in chapel during the first week of school Headmaster McGraw adressed all seventh- to twelfth-graders. After a brief greeting, he developed at length the idea of BBA as being different on purpose, as befits a truly alternative school designed for the new creature that man becomes when, after accepting Jesus Christ as his personal savior, he is born again. To fulfill its "different" purpose, Bethany, I learned, employs only born-again Christians; no others will do for any position in the entire Bethany organization. This insures that students will be influenced by nearly invariant models of right belief and behavior. For eighteen months, the one regular exception to this carefully calculated model was me.

I am a Jew—which is to say that I was born of Jewish parents and grandparents (and Jewish forebears as far back as anyone knows); I grew up in an overwhelmingly Jewish neighborhood in Chicago, became a bar mitzvah at the appropriate time (as did my son), married a Jewish girl, joined a temple, and sent my children to Sunday school. I have mostly Jews as best friends, and fast on Yom Kippur. This is the person I was in the winter of 1978 when I began nearly three years of contact with Christian schools. I have been born only once, and though I have received numerous invitations to be born again, I remain as I was: I am a Jew.

I did not enter the world of Bethany as a potential postulant. Though frequently moved by the force and sincerity of the school's chapel messages and the church's sermons, I never felt stirred to make that leap of faith which would lead me to abandon my lifetime identity. I cannot conceive of attempting this leap. Trying on the belief in Jesus Christ as my Redeemer is not comparable to trying some other novel thing, like tasting bleu cheese, for example, in order to give it a chance, and then tasting it again and again in the hope that if I persist, I will acquire a taste for it. I cannot be tentative about who I am in order to test the desirability of becoming someone else—which is how I perceive becoming a born-again Christian. I am what I am.

The same pastor who during my pilot year refused access to his school admonished me with 1 Corinthians 2:14, saying that because I do not have spiritual discernment, I will not understand his Christian school. He concluded that if I do not understand, as decent as I may be and however hard I try, I will confuse and distort. This admonition is fresh in mind. Having resisted evangelistic efforts conducted by dint of reason, love, fear, and cajolery, and thereby having remained beyond the pale of spiritual discernment, I know there are several aspects of the world of Bethany that I fail to grasp or that I grasp incompletely.[8] They relate mostly to experiences rooted in believing in God, in general, and in accepting the Bible as the precise Word of God, in particular. I understand, though I cannot completely feel, what it means to believe in an actual heaven and hell, and what it means that because one is saved, one has the "blessed assurance" of spending eternity in heaven.

If my comprehension suffers limitations, these also exist for those who approach Bethany from other perspectives. I have not had the opportunities to know and to feel as does, say the Christian apostate who once believed and therefore experienced the spiritual as a true believer. However, the apostate as observer-writer on Bethany faces special problems associated with once having believed and believing no longer. The apostate may be bitter and angry. Yet who does not approach a phenomenon with limitations of some sort resulting from their personal life history? Christian true believer, apostate, nonbeliever, believer in some other doctrine—all are marked by the idiosyncracies of their particular form of profession. All are subject to the claim of having blind spots, of not realizing when they fail to know because the darkness of ignorance obscures. If I acknowledge, as I do, the probability of constraints from my own background—and thus to the limits of my understanding—I must at once add that at no time did I encounter unfathomable mysteries. At no time did I feel unable to make out what was happening, astounded and confused by the seemingly inexplicable. It is absurd to think that only insiders can truly understand. Within not necessarily severe limits, I believe outsiders can know that which they have not undergone; if their interpretations and conclusions differ from those of the insider, it is not necessarily due to a failure of understanding but to the likelihood of using other values as the basis for judgment. We may stand together in what we see in and understand about Bethany, and then quite properly part company when we consider what we make of what we see.

The Fellowship of Darkness with Light

> Be ye not unequally yoked together with unbelievers: for
> what fellowship hath righteousness with unrighteousness?
> and what communion hath light with darkness?
>
> 2 Corinthians 6:14

Is it possible to write a book about human beings in their social capacities without that book also being about its author? I think not. By calling attention to myself here and elsewhere I mean to communicate that I was very conscious of my identity throughout my association with Bethany. This self-consciousness was heightened during my second semester there, when I became the target of many proselytizing efforts, usually, but not always, by teachers during our extended interview sessions.

Not only the proselytizing but the entire experience at Bethany compelled my almost continuous awareness of the differences between me and most persons I saw all day in Bethany's world. Though I intend that the people and the social situations under study will dominate this book, yet the writer may hover here and there, now unseen, now a shadow, now a lurking presence. As I read my own pages, I almost expect to see myself peering out from around the pages, a Kilroy-like interloping specter.[9]

At Bethany I learned about a world which, if I knew in some abstract sense that it existed, still was not tangible to me. It is like learning about hunger by seeing it portrayed in words and pictures. By living within the orbit of Bethany Baptist Church, my words and images were fleshed out in the forms of actual believers who greeted me in the morning, asked after my family when I returned from a visit home, and shook my hand when I arrived for the Wednesday evening service.

Never before had I known true believers, possessors of Truth, who are convinced beyond my imagination of the certainty of God, heaven, hell, Jesus Christ, and salvation, and of the unqualified authenticity of the Bible as God's word. Since the things I believe I do not believe with such certainty, I had difficulty knowing what to make of the stories the Christian school educator Reverend Lowden used to illustrate that "No blessing can come when impurities are present and not rooted out" (1980:4). God refused to bless the school Lowden administered until "God brought hidden sin out in the open in the form of a male coach who was carrying on homosexual conduct with five male students."

When the coach was fired, blessings began. At another time, blessings stopped until "God revealed the sin in the camp": eighth-grade girls smoking at a miniature golf course. (p. 5).

I was perplexed by John Cline. In his fourth year as a BBA teacher, and earning a salary that is strikingly less than that of public school teachers anywhere in the country, Cline works occasionally at a part-time job. He was apologetic about his extra job because he felt it demonstrated that he lacked complete trust in the Lord's promise to provide. Knowing that the Lord never failed his faithful believers, he realized his faith was not yet as total as it should be.

I also was perplexed by Art Swanson. This BBA teacher of Bible also drives a school bus. When he was shopping for a house, he knew beyond question when he had found the right one, and he knew that he faced no risk from other prospective buyers who might make a higher offer. Pastor Muller told him that because of the proximity of the house to the school, Swanson could complete his after-school bus run and then keep the bus at home each night so he would be ready for the morning run. "Wow! When I heard that, I knew the house was mine," said Swanson. Did I hear the story right? Had I missed something? Yes, I had heard right, and, yes, I had missed something—the implications for Swanson of his pastor's comment. Swanson became convinced that acquiring the house in question was part of God's plan for him when he not only felt at ease about the decision to buy it, but also when things began to fall into place, when obstacles were removed. Being able to keep his bus at home overnight—an obstacle removed—was a sign from God manifest in Pastor Muller's words.

Perhaps it is a measure of my insularity that Lowden's, Cline's, and Swanson's stories stirred me. Perhaps I should have been able to anticipate such events. After all, their belief in God and God's will is not esoteric. Nothing they said was new to me; I knew people believed as they did. What struck me was that I had never really known a Lowden, Cline, or Swanson before, let alone an entire building full of them. I was the strange one here at Bethany, where God is no more than a whisper away, a God who intervenes actively in the mundane and the glorious affairs of man, in both beneficent and dreadful ways.

At Bethany I heard a great deal about God's signs from many others than Art Swanson, and never in the joking or semi-joking manner non-Christians use. I wonder what interpretation Bethanyites would have given to the following experience. One day I returned to my rooms in the home of my Christian family after hours of observation and interviewing. I felt most annoyed because I had been subject to evangelizing by a person I thought would not do that to me. (Only later did I appreciate that it was being done *for* me and, moreover, that the obedient Christian sees everyone as a candidate for salvation.) I made a quick dinner, brought it to my kitchen table, and was cheered by the sight of the book I had been reading at breakfast—Max Dimont's *The Indestructible Jews*.

Other mealtime books unintentionally reminded me of who and where I was. For example, seeing John Updike's *Couples* on my table seldom failed to elicit a twinge; it was the sort of book, and Updike the sort of writer, that the Christian is enjoined from reading. *Couples* made me feel neither sinful nor guilty, just uneasy, as did the lurid advertisement for a drive-in theater's twin bill I passed on the road into Hartney; it invited all passers-by to see "Vampire Playgirls" and "Cemetery Girls." I was becoming sensitive to the things of this world that Bethany scorned and was committed to staying separated from.

One mealtime book elicited a different feeling. It was Myerhoff's *Number Our Days* (1978), an enviably fine study and enviable to me in one more way. She writes of a meeting early in her fieldwork:

> "Faegl, Faegl, come here!" Basha shouted to a friend across the room. Faegl picked her way neatly over to where we were sitting. . . ."Faegl, sit down. Faegl, this here is—What did you say your name was? Barbara? This is Barbara. She is a professor and wants to study us. What do you think of that?" "Why not? I wouldn't object. She could learn a lot. Are you Jewish?" Faegl leaned past Basha and carefully peered at me over her bifocals. [p. 15]

At least momentarily I wished I was doing research in a Jewish setting where I could say yes to a similar question some Faegl asked me, and then enjoy the warm, intimate acceptance I imagined would follow my affirmative.

I savored the thought because never had I felt so alien so geographically close to home. I was the outsider; by my own choice, I would remain one in this setting where all students could rattle off the warning, "Be ye not unequally yoked together with unbelievers," and all heard every day how they should behave in order to be an acceptable Christian human being. Notwithstanding their fullest cooperation, Bethanyites could never fully accept me because I lacked the credentials they recognized for acceptability.

To them, I am wanting as I am. By denying Christ as my savior, I remain always wanting, a part of the world of darkness Christians are forever urged to reject. Of course, we are not of different species. Christians are like me and I am like them, a fact which serves to accentuate our profound dissimilarities. But, to paraphrase F. Scott Fitzgerald's famous remark about the very rich, "Let me tell you about the born-again Christians. They are different from you and me." As Peter Bertocci says, "the God they feel in their bones" (1971:5) is the basis for significant differentiation. As a Jew, I am the perpetual out-sider. "So," my grandmother might have said, "what else is new?"

This personal exposition is not meant to insinuate myself into a study of others, in the manner of bit-part actors who insist on stepping out from the periphery of the stage where they belong, to the center where they do not, or of children who can not bear to have their mother's attention diverted from themselves. Given my perception of self in Bethany, it follows that in the conduct of this study I pondered not only the usual, "Who are these people and what are they doing?", but also the unusual, "Who are these people and what are they doing to me?"

In this book I want to portray some part of the realities I observed at Bethany in a way that graphically communicates to others the feeling of being there. The "there" I present is my Bethany, not mine in the possessive sense anthropologists use when referring to the village they labored in and learned to love, but mine in the perceptual sense; it is the one I saw with the help of Bethany's adults and students. I have used no sleight of hand to conjure up the images of Bethany that follow, though it is only fair to say I took the pictures with my own camera.

In the I of the Observer

> To take the role of the other impels us to look at how the other constructs his world.
>
> Charles Bosk

BBA was not unchanged by my presence during the three semesters I was there on a daily basis, but I doubt that it was perceptibly different after the first month even to those who knew it best. Despite our externality, I believe my research assistants and I became appropriately unobtrusive throughout the period of our observations of classrooms and attendance at school activities, so that events and people "were present without presenting themselves" (Rosenberg 1976:12). When, after six months, we began our interviews, we then called attention to ourselves (that is, to our non-fundamentalist-Christian selves), and

unwittingly invited an extended period of student and teacher proselytizing (or "witnessing," as Bethany people call it and as I will hereafter).

For the nine months of their work at BBA, my research assistants
Rich Franz (a nonpracticing Roman Catholic) and Corrine Glesne (a
nonpracticing Lutheran) were at BBA for two days each week.[10] Like
me, they observed, interviewed, and attended meetings and activities.
After about a month of sitting empty-handed wherever we were, we
began to use a pocket-size notebook sporadically and ended up taking
full, running notes of everything we saw and heard except during lunch
and in other informal settings. Our interviews, conducted with a continuously evolving interview schedule, ranged in time from about four
to twelve hours; all were taped and later transcribed.

Unlike me, Franz and Glesne did not live in Hartney. I found an
apartment in the home of a charter-member family of Bethany Baptist
Church. I lived there throughout my field work, commuting to my own
home one full day each week on a schedule that insured I would be in
Hartney to attend all church services. Bethany members are advised to
be in church "whenever the doors are open." As a participant in the
church side of Bethany's world, I tried to follow this advice, being as
faithful as I could in attending Sunday school, Sunday morning and
evening services, and Wednesday evening services followed by the
men's prayer group, and in reading the Bible daily. Appearing to be a
faithful Christian was much easier to manage than appearing to be a
spiritual Christian, although, in connection with "proper behavior," it
was easy to avoid drinking, smoking, gambling, swearing, and going to
the movies. It did prove difficult to avoid uttering "minced oaths,"
which are the blasphemous "gee," "gee whiz," and "gosh" that most
everyone other than born-again Christians blurt out with astonishing
and unintentional frequency.

When I came to Bethany to live and work in August 1978, I was a
stranger there in almost every sense, as the people of Bethany were to
me. When I left I was still largely a stranger to everyone, a consequence
of the curious way that fieldworkers have of being present without
really being present. The "natives" take for granted your naturally
unlimited interest in them and their naturally superficial interest in you.
Unsurprisingly, Bethanyites were strongly interested in my (and everyone's) relationship to Christ, as well as in my behavior, since they are
careful guardians of the adult models their students will experience.
Although the reserve of the researcher's role, combined with my ordinary reserve, left me somewhat on the edge of their consciousness, I still

hoped to participate in their lives as if I were a Christian. My intent was to moderate and minimize their they-ness so that I could move beyond being the visitor-at-a-zoo type of observer to being one who revels in their joys and empathizes with their pains. Visitor I might be in both instances, but, in the latter case, possibly one who views with some sense of identification.[11] I wanted to feel close enough so that I could be as one human puzzling over the efforts of other humans to manage their lives, rather than as one peeking at the antics of others. Ideally, through my participation, they would lose enough of their they-ness so I could perceive them as a part of my we, a part, to be sure, with a profound difference.

In my fourth and final semester at BBA, by which time I was spending most of each week at home, I completed my collection of data by administering a questionnaire to all students and teachers, and to one parent of each student. During the first semester we observed the world of Bethany largely unaided by the views and perceptions of Bethany's participants; in the second and third semesters we concentrated on acquiring their views and perceptions by means of interviews; and in the fourth semester we used a questionnaire in order to get systematic data of the sort necessary both to describe and to verify what we had learned earlier by other means.

When on that blizzardy winter night I casually expressed to David Housholder my interest in some day studying a Christian school, I did not realize I was focusing on a type of school I would soon see represented as the fastest growing segment of American education. By the time I commenced my study, they were reputed to be opening at the rate of two and then three and four new schools per day. As the media made clear, they were an expression of the resurgent fundamentalist Christian movement, with robust counterparts in the political and religious realms as well. It was not just a case of, say, buying a 1948 green Hudson and suddenly discovering the streets filled with previously unnoticed 1948 green Hudsons. Admittedly, a substantial investment will focus one's vision in the direction of that investment. But in fact growth was occurring at such a pace that even a cursory review of the media would reveal the range of fundamentalist activity in America.

The Times

The doings of religious groups and individuals tend to be ordinary fare to Americans who, even when they are not faithful members of a church, think of themselves as being religious in some sense. Local churches advertise their Sunday services and revivals on their community newspaper's religion page; national church organizations meet and pass resolutions that get duly reported. Such goings-on usually do not generate either high interest or alarm, except, perhaps, when they are associated with scandal in the vestry or with the exceptionally success-ful revivals of Billy Graham. When there is a sustained pattern of religiously inspired activity, the impact of which clearly transcends the locality of its origins, the events assume a different character: they become candidates for attention in the nation's media. This is such a time. Religious activity does not constantly claim the headlines, elicit editorials, or dominate the covers of *Time* and *Newsweek*, but we have ceased to be surprised when it does.

My own community's now-defunct newspaper, the *Morning Courier*, carried a small story entitled "Religious Awakening Found across America" (August 2, 1978). Three years later, readers of Los Angeles's *Herald Examiner* were asked, "Has American Religion Begun Its Fourth Great Awakening?" (April 17, 1981). This headline was stimulated by the findings of a Connecticut Mutual Life Insurance survey indicating "that religion is emerging as the dominant force in U.S. culture." Historians and others use the term "awakening" to characterize those grand, sweeping periods in our past which, seen in retrospect, were shaped by the powerful force of religion. Some scholars have begun to see in the past twenty years or so the makings of a fourth awakening (McLoughlin 1978). It is premature to attach a label to our contemporary religious stirrings, and to affirm what the consequences of these stir-rings will be. Nonetheless, one need not be a practicing prophet to know that evidence of activity inspired by religion abounds, attesting to a robustness that one day may well warrant the "awakening" des-ignation. The robustness is beyond dispute, as is the tenor of the present religious movement.[12]

The movement, for the sake of my narrative, is bounded by the actions of the conservative churches in the United States. A central fact of this movement is the growth of conservative churches and the decline of the comparatively more liberal mainline churches. Perhaps the most telling mark of this success is the victory of the fundamentalist side in the Southern Baptist's 1980 election. Already considered con-servative, this largest of all Protestant church groups in the country voted its own right wing into office, with the soon-to-be notorious Reverend Bailey Smith assuming the convention's presidency.

In theological and other ideological terms, conservatives do not constitute a single group predictably united behind the same leaders and causes, but they do share a common view of biblical inerrancy that joins them together as fundamentalists. This view holds that " every word in the Bible is spiritually, historically and scientifically true, without contradiction of error" (Mattingly 1980:A10). It is this view which undergirds the world of Bethany and which has engendered the fundamentalist's organized opposition to homosexuals, the Equal Rights Amendment, abortion, and Communism. It has merged with other factors—academic, racial, social—to form a bill of particulars against public schools.

Whatever justice there was in the charges of permissiveness, physical danger, and debased learning, a growing disenchantment with the public schools enhanced the attractiveness of the private school. An issue of *Newsweek* announced, "Why Public Schools Fail," a "Three-part Special Report on the crisis of confidence in the American public-school system" (April 20, 1981). The case against the public school was aided by the Christian's accusation that it was a "humanist" institution, a godless place that ignores, if not scorns, the Word of God.

Simultaneous with the expansion of conservative, fundamentalist churches has been the impressive growth of new Christian schools sponsored by these churches.[13] To begin with, private schools of all sorts claim approximately 12 percent (5.3 million) of the nation's 48 million or so school children.[14] As of 1976, churches sponsored 85 percent of these private schools and Roman Catholic schools composed 75 percent of this 85 percent; by 1981, the Catholic percentage had decreased to 65 percent, stabilizing after fifteen years of decline (Heard 1981). So the impressive expansion of Christian schools must be seen in context: their pupils compose a tiny segment of what at best is a small portion of all school-aged children. From 1965 to 1975, Catholic school enrollments plummeted from 5.5 to 3.4 million, a loss of 38.7 percent. At the same time, the number of most other types of religious schools increased, perhaps none more impressively than those associated with the two largest of the conservative national Christian education groups—the Association of Christian Schools International and the American Association of Christian Schools. BBA belongs to the latter group. Since many Christian schools remain unaffiliated and all resist state accreditation, it is difficult to keep precise tract of Christian school growth.[15] Erickson et al. estimated that as of 1975 there were about 400,000 students in such schools (1978:84); Nordin and Turner claim 350,000 in 1977 (1982:391); *Time* writers put the total at 450,000 in 1981 (up from 140,000 in 1971), or 1 percent of all school-age children (June 8, 1981). When these figures, modest in absolute terms, are seen in the light of public school enrollment declines—"11 percent in the West while private enrollment [largely but not exclusively in Christian schools] climbed 19 percent. In the South. . . public schools declined 6 percent while private enrollment increased by 31 percent" (*Newsweek*, April 20, 1981)—then we understand the hyperbolic language of "dramatic" growth, "resurgence," and "boom." Such language is most typically used to characterize what invariably is referred to as "the most rapidly expanding segment of American education."

From all indications, the claim is true: the Christian school is a rising star.[16] The vitality of these schools is evident in the increasingly comprehensive services their national organizations provide to members (see chapter 2), and in the increasing availability of textbook and instructional materials from Christian publishers. Christian schools constitute a market upon which some publishers have banked their success. The schools have grown despite their tuition costs and the shrinking pool of school-aged children. Can it be denied that they are perceived to be doing something very right? Have they found a formula for success in their blend of emphasis on the basics, dress codes, strong discipline, patriotism, and God? "Many parents," observes Christian writer Dorothy Rose, "have become weary of 'innovative' teaching activities. Movies, rap sessions, open classrooms and the 'nongraded' school" (1979:48) are among the innovations she lists. Based both on what they offer and on what they reject, Christian schools have attained a degree of success that cannot be explained, as it has in some places, by racism alone. They are not just *The Schools that Fear Built* (Nevin and Bills 1976). Indeed Christian schools open and thrive in communities where there are no black families.

If many American adults find comfort in the alternative opportunity Christian schools provide, many more have been attracted to the politics of Jesse Helms, Republican senator from North Carolina, the religion of Jerry Falwell, and "an interlocking set of organizations out to change the politics [and the morals!] of the nation" (Drew 1981:82). Given the "perfect candidate" in Ronald Reagan, Americans in 1980, and again in 1984, heard a great deal about conservatives, right-wing politics, a rejection of our liberal past, the new right, and God and politics. Arthur Schlesinger, Jr., contested this "illusion of conservatism," and postelection polls found that rejection of Carter accounted more for Reagan's victory than a "conservative tide" (Gallup 1980). The defeat in 1980 of congressmen whose voting records had earned them a place on conservative "hit lists," and the burst of attention from the media to this successful juncture of religion and politics, stimulated a reaction against each of the three major domains of conservative effort—education, religion, and politics, although in education and religion the signs of "fighting back" have been apparent for some time.

Theologians and church scholars who place the mainline churches in a pivotal position in American society view the decline of these churches as signifying changes of great and negative consequence. The distinguished historian Martin E. Marty articulates this concern when he laments the decline of the religious center which contained

> theologians and artists, pastors and literary figures, doers and thinkers, who construed reality in light of faith in Christ but who were critically open to the idea of using that faith to transform (not merely to judge) the culture. . . . The collapse of the middle has . . . and will have fateful consequences for religious communication in a pluralistic culture. [1979:12]

Smylie is less temperate when he describes electronic evangelists such as Oral Roberts, Pat Robertson, Jim Bakker, and Jerry Falwell, who epitomize the success of conservative Christian leaders and their mastery of television. "In the American ethos," Smylie writes, "these are the leaders by whom many members of the Protestant congregations measure ministerial effectiveness; at the same time, others suspect them of being manipulative and panderers of 'cheap grace'" (1979:84).

The clergy whose churches have been most negatively affected by the turn toward religious conservatism—Lutherans, Episcopalians, United Methodists, Presbyterians—have struggled to devise a response which keeps their churches faithful to social issues and somehow manages to stop the loss of members. For example, liberal and moderate evangelicals organized the Evangelicals for Social Action. This group is supported by Kenneth Kantzer, the editor of *Christianity Today*, who said he "doesn't like 'to see evangelicalism identified with the extreme right'" (Larson 1980:48). And a strong response to the fundamentalists appeared in the *New Republic*, a journal not ordinarily given to theological stances. Charles Krauthammer denounced the fundamentalists' resort to "secular humanism" as a club to attack everything about American society that violates their sense of propriety. Krauthammer does not reject a place for religion, he rejects this place being dominated by what he calls simplistic "lunacy" (1980:20–25).

After the 1980 defeat of Gaylord Nelson, Birch Bayh, George McGovern, and Edmund Muskie, the political reaction to conservative success also became evident. McGovern established Americans for Common Sense in order to build a "counterforce" (Weissmann 1981:8–9). His colleague Senator Edward Kennedy wrote the liberal faithful in 1981 requesting money for the Fund for a Democratic Majority to be used during the 1982 congressional election. Norman Lear, producer of

"All in the Family" and other television shows, created People for the American Way, a "coalition of laymen and ministers" to oppose the conservatives who mix religion and politics.

Reactions in the public school domain relate to but are not invariably caused by Christian school success. Public schools, always easy targets for criticism, have been attacked by many, including Christian fundamentalists. The latter, paradoxically, condemn public schools as centers of secular humanism, and thus unfit for Christian children, at the same time that they concentrate on several issues which, if corrected, might make public schools more acceptable places for Christian children. For example, they criticize the public schools' use of "unacceptable" books like *The Catcher in the Rye, Go Ask Alice, The Diary of Anne Frank*, and dictionaries that contain words like "bed" used as a verb for sexual intercourse. Their cause is advanced by Mel and Norma Gablers' Educational Research Associates and the Reverend Jack Gambill's Decency in Education Committee. A measure of the prominence of the censorship issue in American life and the role of the Gablers in it can be seen in *People* magazine's three-page article devoted to them. The article, with its pictures of the smiling, determined, praying Gablers, quotes a National School Board Association editor: "What they [the Gablers] are trying to do is purge the schools of all views other than their own. They are trying to kill the concept of pluralism, and that is a danger to our democracy" (Demaret 1981:86).

Fundamentalist-supported censorship relates to the public school's sex-education courses, but more prominently to the creationist-evolution controversy. The creationists want public schools to label evolution a theory, not a fact, and to give equal time to creationist theory so that children are not "misled" by teachers and textbooks which ignore any but the evolutionists' position. This issue has moved well beyond a textbook-control issue to the involvement of concerned professionals on both sides of the controversy,[17] and ultimately to the critical judicial arena of states (California and Arkansas) where antagonists clash in updated versions of the famous 1925 trial of John Scopes, the Tennessee science teacher who taught evolution in his classroom. It also has involved the American Civil Liberties Union, which brought suit against "religious indoctrination [creationism] in the public schools" of Arkansas, and informed its members of its concerns about daily prayer permitted in Louisiana schools; silent prayer permitted in Massachusetts, Arizona, and Connecticut schools; *all* theories of creation being taught in Columbus, Ohio; and school-district approval of the distribution of Bibles in Houston classrooms.

Defenders of the much-maligned, beleaguered public schools have both voice and platform, but defense, in this case, lacks the pizzazz of attack. Throughout the 1970s and lasting until about 1983, when the inquiries of federal government and foundation-supported groups inspired a frenzy of state-led educational reforms, initiative and attack had been seized by the public school antagonists. Nonetheless, the reaction from the education profession was apparent. President Shanker of the American Federation of Teachers cited Gallup poll data to verify that 64 percent of the American public and 84 percent of public school parents gave public schools either an A, B, or C rating. He criticized those who make "unfair targets" of the public schools (1979:8). The National Education Association dramatically established its position with a front-page picture in its *Reporter* of a bulldozer about to engulf a little red school and the headline, "As Attacks on Public Education Multiply . . . NEA FIGHTS—To protect *freedom to teach*" (*NEA Reporter* March 1981:1). Newspaper editorialists reminded readers that though the growth of private schools demonstrates flaws in public education, "public schools must get full and generous public support before any expansion of that public support is considered for 'schools of choice'" (Bloomington [Ill.] *Daily Pantagraph*, May 14, 1980:4). And the American Jewish Committee, ever sensitive to maintaining the separation of church and state, opposed tuition tax credits for private schools while linking viable public schools to the cardinal principle of an "open pluralistic society" (*Jewish Community Journal*, November 1981:5).[18]

The foregoing brief survey presents a contemporary context within which to see the world of Bethany. Their flourishing church and school are an example of local success, but they are significantly more than that. My impression of the fundamentalists is of energetic, driven, committed, aspiring, and successful groups; my impression of the fundamentalists' antagonists is of fragmented, defensive, and only incipiently aroused individuals and groups. In any event, Americans today are aware of fundamentalists as a result of Bailey Smith's comment about the funny noses of Jews and God's unwillingness to hear their prayers, the proliferation of Christian schools, and headlines about Jerry Falwell and the Moral Majority. Who the fundamentalists are, where they are going, and what their success may mean are some of the questions many Americans ask with admiration, curiosity, and agitation.

Fundamentalist Christian enterprise is manifest in three-pronged religious, political, and educational institution building. The success of each prong supports the work of the others. I would not expect, however, that the Christian school movement would necessarily have suffered if, for example, Senator Helms had been defeated in his 1984 campaign for reelection, for Helms's tenacity and political skills have been matched by his ecclesiastical and educational counterparts, as seen in the growth of conservative churches and fundamentalist schools. These successes and their apparent consequences are a matter either of newfound joy or nagging fear, depending on the nature of one's theological or political outlook. Whatever the case, the history of this period cannot be written in ignorance of the fruits of Christian enterprise. Many of our society's issues in the last decades of this century are likely to be shaped by the actions and reactions of fundamentalist Christians and their contenders.

The signs of confrontation between fundamentalists and their opponents are seen in local communities over the use of certain books, in the courts over the place of creationism, and in national politics over the vying doctrines and policies of legislators and political action groups. In many states, the signs of conflict between Christian schools and state education authorities are seen over issues relating to certification of teachers, accreditation, and requests for data which Christian schools believe are unwarranted. Although Bethany Baptist Academy fully endorses the efforts of its sister institutions to fend off what it sees as the "encroachments" of state authority, BBA itself enjoys a relatively peaceful status quo. Neither the state of Illinois nor the city of Hartney are hostile to Christian schools. Accordingly, BBA is relatively free to grow and prosper in keeping with the competencies of its educational leaders, their conception of the Word of God, and the implications of this conception for educational practice.

2

"Blessed Assurance"
The Dictates of Doctrine

In Pastor Muller's account of his church and school we got some idea of the centrality of a rigid theological system. And indeed, as a more detailed picture of Bethany emerges, each chapter of this book will unavoidably relate to the dictates of doctrine, since this is what Christian schooling truly is about.

Bethany Baptist Academy

On the face of it, the academy is a school much like any other. Of course, it is a voluntary school, a private school, required by the state of Illinois only to register,[1] but as with any school the conventional imperatives regarding the provision of space, instruction, scheduling, and the like, operate.

BBA contains about 350 boys and girls in its kindergarten through twelfth grade. The school building is split, its K–6 section occupying the south wing, built in 1976, and its 7–12 section occupying the north wing, built in 1973. Between stands the gymnasium connecting the two wings. This was built in 1970 as a church activity center. For several years it provided space for religious services as church membership rose from about 130 to about 1,500 in eighteen years. Physical facilities expanded to keep pace with student enrollments, which increased from 88 in 1972, the school's first year, to 358 in 1980. In recent years, enrollments have shown no appreciable change. This pleases Bethany because it suggests a stability won in the face of economic hard times and declining numbers of school-aged children in the local population.

The academy's building is separated from the church by a parking lot that also is used for recess activity and for physical education. In terms of space use and program, the entire church-school complex operates as an organic whole. This is consonant with Bethany's belief that church and school are one: the school is simply the academic expression of the church and no less integral to the church, as Pastor Muller has said, than its Sunday morning services. Bethanyites assume, accordingly, that the autonomy enjoyed by churches under our traditional separation of church and state precludes any level of government having jurisdiction over the school, beyond safety requirements.

BBA's remarkably clean hallways are the pride of Headmaster McGraw. The airy, spacious elementary classrooms have the stimuli-cluttered look of elementary classrooms anywhere. By contrast, the secondary classes are relatively dreary, though livened somewhat by bulletin boards displaying pinned and stapled pictures and good thoughts, an administration requirement. The gym, with a stage built at one side, doubles as an assembly hall. Opposite the stage is a small kitchen. To buy lunch, children line up against the gym wall, pick up their trays of food, and enter the lunchroom. The school library and the administrative quarters are in the elementary wing. Headmaster McGraw's well-decorated office is behind that of his secretary, who acts also as a factotum for the entire school—nurse, cheerleader consultant, piano accompanist for vocal soloists, and upholder of school rules. A decorative bookcase containing several books on Abraham Lincoln held in place by Lincoln bookends stands against the office wall; above it are two pictures of Lincoln and the Gettysburg Address framed. A waist-high barrier separates the visitor's sitting area from the offices. On the wall behind the visitor's couch hangs a picture of Theodore Roosevelt with "Thoughts of T.R." printed beneath. Surrounding this picture are plaques: the William Muller Award for high school students; the Anne Muller Award for the senior girl whose life best exemplifies the principles of the founder; the National School Choral Award; etc.

BBA's day begins at 8:00 A.M., when McGraw presides over the daily teachers' meeting. All non-bus-driving, off-duty, K–12 teachers come to hear him read and explicate a brief verse of Scripture. This is followed by announcements and by a prayer offered by a different teacher each day. McGraw always invites prayer requests, and these intentions are incorporated in the daily prayers, which also include, along with the general hope for an effective day in the Lord's service, specific prayers for needy members of the school and church community, as well as thanks for blessings received. After 8:00 A.M., students begin arriving by foot, car, or bus and must go at once to the lunchroom.

At 8:25, they begin a ten-minute locker break followed by a ten-minute daily homeroom period. Thereafter, classes begin; each one is forty-three minutes long. Two extracurricular activities—the student newspaper and the yearbook—are incorporated into the school day. Others begin after 3:10 P.M., when classes are done for the day; they are cheerleading and volleyball for girls, and soccer, basketball, baseball, track and field, and wrestling for boys.

BBA's curriculum (see appendix A) approximates that of most small public high schools. Students must take four years of English and physical education, three years of social studies, two years each of math and science, and one year of speech; they may take a foreign language, typing, band, choir, journalism, office practice, and drafting. Subjects peculiar to BBA as a Christian school are a required four-year Bible course and an optional soul-winning course; the school also requires attendance at chapel three times a week by all students in grades 7–12.

The rhythm of the school year, as manifest in BBA's scheduled events, also is not far removed from that of public schools. State and national holidays provide respite from the school routine. Summer vacations coincide exactly with Hartney's public schools. In fall, soccer rather than football brings spirit and high hopes to BBA's students, to whom victory means no less than it does to their public school counterparts; wrestling and basketball in winter and baseball and track and field in spring remove students from class for out-of-town games and keep the school buses rolling throughout the state. There are organized competitions and special tournaments aplenty to provide unlimited lunchtime, locker-room, and class-lull chatter. Each season has its special assembly program. Since 1978 BBA has had a yearly graduating class. Now each year is marked by seniors leaving, with all the accompanying ritual of that occasion. And like the public school, BBA's year is marked by days of no school when teachers attend workshops and conventions devoted to in-service training. The single event with no public school counterpart is the week-long evangelistic meetings held each fall and spring.

On principle, BBA does not now—and means never to—receive government funds.[2] To Christian educators, government money connotes government control. Accordingly, they depend completely on other means to finance their enterprise. Bethany Baptist Church covers the school's large, nonrecurring costs. Of the four separate construction projects that went to make up the school's present building, church funds meet the mortgage payments for three of the projects, while BBA pays for the fourth. Tuition fees are the largest source of income in its budget, which amounted to $310,000 in 1981–82. Annual high school fees that year were $900 (up from $750 in 1979–80 and $800 in 1980–81).[3] Approximately 75 percent of the budget goes for teacher salaries. Pastor Muller estimated that BBA's per pupil costs in 1980–81 were $738, compared to the public school's $1,500 to $2,000. Funds are received from four other sources: candy sales—the 1980 sale produced a profit of $10,000 from a gross of $25,000; gifts; matching funds; and monthly donations from members of the Builders Club.

By readily measurable indicators, BBA is a success. It collects sufficient revenue to stay in or near the black. Stable student enrollments maintain the flow of tuition-fee revenues. Staff turnover is minimal. And the school's space and physical facilities accommodate its present student body and instructional program. Whether BBA succeeds by the measure of its most fundamental goal—serving the glory of God— remains to be discussed.

The American Association of Christian Schools

BBA is part of America's fundamentalist Christian school movement. More particularly, it belongs to the nationwide American Association of Christian Schools (AACS) and to its state branch, the Illinois Association of Christian Schools (IACS).

The AACS began with approximately 125 member schools and 25,000 students in 1972 and grew to more than 1,000 schools and 150,000 students by 1982. It has become a full-service organization for its affiliated schools who must "subscribe without reservation" to the AACS Statement of Faith. This statement (see appendix B) holds to the Bible's inerrancy, and emphasizes, among other doctrines, Christ's Virgin Birth and Second Coming, salvation only "by grace through faith," and the necessity of the "New Birth." Mindful of the denominational independence of the churches sponsoring their member schools, the AACS does not establish a large, central bureaucracy, or prescribe standards (beyond its doctrinal statement) for its member schools.

As the AACS has matured, it has expanded the range and adequacy of its services to members, as well as to pastors aspiring to open new schools. To help start a new school, AACS consultants offer specific financial and curricular suggestions.

An AACS flyer, distributed when A. C. Janney, the founder, directed the organization from Hialeah, Florida, clarifies why Christians should avoid public schools. The flyer describes these as institutions that may transport children long distances from their homes; that may hire teachers who are atheists, cultists, or addicts; and that may teach children to be "revolutionists." An undated letter sent from

Janney's office to "Christian Friends" aspiring to start a Christian school said:

> There are two major things we must do if our country is to continue as a free nation. . . . Christians must join hands in stopping the floodtide of socialistic-communistic legislation that is now being introduced and we must rescue our Christian youth from the brain-washing socialistic, amoral, and often atheistic public school system to educate them in a Biblical philosophy of life. We welcome you to the ranks of the Christian School Movement.

After a member school has been in operation for at least three years, it may seek AACS accreditation by completion of a long self-evaluation instrument and the visit of an accreditation team. While scorning the legitimation that state offices of education offer through their accreditation process, the AACS lauds its own accreditation process for verifying that proper biblical and academic standards are upheld. "It is time," Janney writes in an AACS tract called "Accreditation," "that we establish God's standards and leave the world out. Accreditation can be a blessing—if it's accreditation by God's people, for God's people . . . with God's stamp of approval on it."

The AACS literature makes clear that the association intends to provide Christian schools with the Christian counterpart of those events and opportunities available to public school educators and students: health insurance and retirement programs; academic, religious, and athletic competition, organized at regional, state, and national levels; a Christian Honor Society; regional, state, and national clinics and conferences; and publications, including *The Administrator*, a quarterly journal; the monthly *AACS Newsletter* (which announces meetings and forthcoming events, news from member schools and states, and legislative alerts); and the infrequent *Christian School Communicator*, a single-page statement on topics such as "Christian Education: Reaching the Heart" and "Christian Education Begins at Home."

Finally, and quite exactly like the national organizations that serve public school teachers, administrators, and school board members, the AACS has an office in Washington and a full-time staff member to monitor legislation and to activate, when necessary, their legislative-alert network. More than this, the AACS is committed to promoting the sensitivity and competence of its "pastors, administrators, and Christian school leaders" to deal with issues in the political domain. To this end, it has sponsored an annual Washington conference since 1974. In

1980 the conference featured Senator Jesse Helms (R., North Carolina) and the two representatives, John Ashbrook (R., Ohio) and Robert Dornan (R., California), who led the fight against the Internal Revenue Service's effort to tax Christian schools. Participants were informed that their meeting in the Senate Office Building would cover "the critical issues facing our movement that need to be communicated to our Congressmen." In 1981 the conference featured Senator William Armstrong (R., Colorado), "a real friend to Christian education"; Senator Charles Grassley (R., Iowa), "a consistent conservative in Congress" and a "Baptist lay preacher"; and Representative Carrol Campbell (R., South Carolina), "one of the real bright young conservative leaders."

A brief survey of commentary in the monthly *AACS Newsletter* will suggest the scope and nature of issues that animate Christian school leadership:

September, 1979
Rejoicing over a Senate decision that precludes the Internal Revenue Service from taking action against private schools which allegedly practice racial discrimination, the *Newsletter* announces the first-ever victory in "Congress by fundamentalist Christians. AACS is dedicated to expand the political clout demonstrated in these recent days."

November, 1979
Readers are informed of a major threat in antifamily legislation, including the Child Health Assurance Act, the Domestic Violence Act, and the Childsnatching Act. "Conclusion: get more facts—oppose federal intervention in family affairs."

September, 1980
On the eve of the 1980 presidential election, the *Newsletter* derides the guile of the Democrat-controlled Senate and warns that "the coming election is extremely important for the cause of liberty. . . . All Bible-believing Christians should get to the polls and vote."

November, 1980
Ronald Reagan's victory leads the *Newsletter* to exult over the promise of reduced federal harassment. "An analysis of the returns indicates that we can prevail in the new Congress."

May, 1981
Readers learn that since five members of the Supreme Court

are seventy-two or older, it is timely "for Christians to start organizing and communicating to their Senators and the President that the nation cannot stand the appointment of any more Supreme Court justices who will perpetuate the present philosophy of the Supreme Court."

September, 1981
The Friends of Free China are sponsoring a freedom speech and freedom essay contest. The Friends will reward the essay contest winner and an approved chaperon with a six-day, all-expense-paid trip to Taiwan.

February, 1982
Because of its substantive connection to the sense of the previous items, I include here an AACS alert, sent as a telegram to all AACS members; because of its importance, I quote from it at length.

"Urgent! Because of recent developments concerning the Bob Jones University case [relating to whether a school can discriminate against black Americans and still maintain tax exempt status] . . . we are at the most crucial point in the history of Christian education. *Freedom is threatened.* The press has been spewing out lies and distortions. All knowledgeable Christians in Washington agree that *the President's proposed legislation is disastrous.* We need you in Washington this month to *help us stop* the Reagan administration and Congress from selling out Christian schools. . . . If we do not get a large group of people to Washington to lobby for liberty, you must realize that the liberals will have a free hand to pass legislation that could destroy Christian schools."

With Reagan fallen from grace, at least temporarily, the AACS demonstrates that it has no permanent friends, only its permanent interest in doctrinally based institutions.

BBA's Doctrinal Orientation

God's School

If most public school statements of philosophy and goals are misleading guides to what actually happens in classrooms, and therefore best deposited in the least accessible fastnesses of the files, the converse is true at BBA. What this school's educators say and write about their philosophy and goals is the basis of today's lesson and tomorrow's lesson plan.

There is no better starting point for a discussion of the foundation of Bethany's educational enterprise than the fact that its educators believe that their school is God's school and that they are doing God's work, fulfilling his plan for themselves and their students. Repeatedly one hears at meetings of Christian educators and one reads in their documents that they are not merely good men doing good work.[4] Immeasurably more than this, they are godly men doing God's work! Lester Roloff,[5] a Texas pastor and subject of attention in the media for his controversial treatment of the runaway, orphaned, abandoned wards of his school, literally screams while addressing his AACS brethren in a chandeliered Hilton hotel ballroom: "We're going to win Texas [for Christ] because God says we're going to win. Oh, we've lost some skirmishes, but God will take us to victory. . . . Folks, my work is like shooting chickens in the yard."

In the same glittering Hilton ballroom, at the same meeting, Pastor Jerry Prevo of the Anchorage Baptist Temple faces a large, silent, attentive audience while standing under a three-foot-high red, white, and blue banner that reads, "Christian Education is the Foundation for America's Future." Pastor Prevo's words are as confidently assertive as that of the banner hanging overhead: "Don't get discouraged [when one's state enacts or enforces legislation that threatens the autonomy of Christian schools]. Keep making sacrifices because it is the work of God and he wants us to give our all."

In God's school, taught by God's teachers, it must follow that God's truth is the beginning and end of instruction. The presence of Scripture is not detectable in every moment of classroom activity. In mathematics or physical education or driver training, for example, one often listens in vain for the sound of an overtly religious comment. Nonetheless, whenever knowledge is present, so is God, because "All avenues of knowledge stem from God," as Paul W. Cates writes in an AACS pamphlet. He continues:

> Since God is central in the universe and is the source of all truth, it follows that all subject matter is related to God. . . . The Bible itself becomes the central subject in the school's curriculum. . . . This is not to imply that the Bible is a textbook on anything and everything; but rather that the Bible is to be the point of reference from which we can evaluate all areas and sources of knowledge (1975:3–4).

Headmaster McGraw is fond of saying that "the heart of Christian education is the education of the heart."[6] He and his fellow educators hold that students know neither their own hearts nor what is good for them. Students, like all of God's children, are depraved. Born with a "sin nature," they need no help to do wrong, but they must be taught how to do right, and that is why, as McGraw informed his teachers one morning, Christian schools are so important. "Christian kids," he said, "get what *we* think they need and want them to have. Our center doesn't change; it is Christianity. When kids are at the center, things always change." In Bethany's view, the Bible is not amenable to new evidence or higher criticism. For these Baptists, the letter and spirit of belief are one, notwithstanding the vicissitudes of changing times. Thus there is no scope for any change in the basics of BBA's pedagogical orientation. This does not mean, however, that the *process* of schooling is fixed, because new books, new instructional materials, and new technologies can alter this.

The "we" McGraw refers to above is himself and his BBA staff. Yet he is the first to acknowledge that the responsibility for educating children belongs through God to parents. Thus, Christian schools do the bidding of God and of Christian parents; they are second in importance to the Christian home for a child's spiritual training. Since parents may not always know their obligations, or, being products of public schools, may not always understand the mission of Christian schools, McGraw uses the occasions when he addresses BBA parents to instruct them. The formal "graduation" of the kindergarten class, held in the spacious Bethany Baptist Church auditorium, was one such occasion. The white robes of the children contrasted with the black academic gowns worn by Pastor Muller and Headmaster McGraw. The tots marched up one at a time midst popping flash bulbs; they entertained with "Pop Goes the Weasel," the "Alphabet Song," and "Little Peter Rabbit Had a Fly upon His Nose;" and they heard McGraw extol them as their parents' securest asset, the only one that can accompany them to heaven. The moment was the children's, but McGraw's message was for their parents:

> As parents, we have a holy calling of God that our kids should be taught in God's way. God's blessing will be upon you if they have a Christian education. There's a clear commandment that kids should not be taught through secular humanism that rejects absolutes, that believes there is no absolute truth. There's a battle for their minds. We have no problem declaring our tradition—the Bible, authority, patriotism. Learn not the way of the heathen.

And neither parents nor anyone else could doubt that his words are meant to be father to the deeds of BBA's students, for later in the year when Brother Hall came to conduct a full week of revival meetings in the church and school, BBA canceled basketball practice and homework and postponed the already scheduled nine-week tests so that students would not miss a moment of Brother Hall's revival.

The Vocabulary of Belief

No high school student at Bethany could be there more than a week without knowing that there are terms and expressions he or she hears repeatedly, more frequently in some settings than in others, but occasionlly anywhere in the entire school and at any time. These terms and expressions, italicized on the next several pages, constitute the elements of religious belief that BBA continuously reinforces. Bethany's Statement of Faith, closely reflecting the *American Association of Christian School's* creed (Appendix B), is a starting point. BBA's Bible class and chapel services accord with students' Sunday school lessons and the pastor's Sunday morning sermons in exploring the Bible chapter by chapter and verse by verse. In addition to these more structured occasions, students also acquire their vocabulary of belief during classes, homeroom devotions, and chats with teachers and friends. The academy's general socializing thrust emerges from the particulars of its salient terms.

I begin this vocabulary of belief with *God*, but for logical more than theological reasons. In fact, God the Father seems to be mentioned less often than *Jesus Christ*, who is identified both as the Son of God and also as God the Son. Though prayers are directed to God the heavenly Father, they always are closed "in Jesus' name, Amen." Otherwise, student attention is directed to the sacrificing Jesus, of exemplary perfection, the model for mankind, whose love for us compelled him to shed his blood and take our sins upon his shoulders so that we might join his Father in *Heaven* (see Hebrews 9:22 and 1 Peter 2:24).

Pastor Muller provided Bethany's perspective on Jesus Christ during a preschool, in-service week for teachers: "Our school's commitment is to the fact that Jesus Christ is the center. 'No man cometh to the father except by me.' We try to get kids to put Christ at their center—work, school, church, home, etc."

Our *sin nature*,[7] the consequence of Adam and Eve's disobedience (Romans 5:12), is powerfully attracted to the *world's* temptations. To fundamentalist Christians, the world encompasses all that is outside their realm in Satan's non-Christian domain. All of us who are not born again are of the world. If, however, we become *saved*, that is, if we are *born again* by confessing our sins and accepting Jesus Christ as our personal savior, then God has assured us of spending *eternity* with him in heaven. Heaven and hell exist as characterized in various biblical references, interpreted literally, with real fire in hell and golden thrones in heaven. Once saved by acknowledging one's faith in Jesus Christ (Acts 4:12), no good works need be done and no further requirements need be fulfilled to enter heaven. In fact, fundamentalist doctrine assures the born-again Christian that salvation is never lost.

Once saved, we have the choice either to follow Christ or to forsake him and behave disreputably. In the latter case, God still receives us but he discriminates between his rewards to the fallen and to the *faithful* Christian. When both stand before the Lord in heaven, the fallen will experience shame and less happiness. While the loving Lord is patient, his patience and love know limits. To persist in disobedience, to flaunt sinful behavior repeatedly without repentance, is to court his wrath. God teaches lessons in artful ways, strewing our paths with obstacles in the hope that we may learn and obey, but if thwarted he may use pain and suffering—indeed, even death—to accomplish his purposes.

Because most students at BBA are saved, the school focuses its lessons on their proper Christian conduct. At BBA there is no great need to warn of hell, except as an impetus to rescue unsaved friends, since hell is not in prospect for the overwhelming majority of students. These already born-again Christians hear incessantly about their obligations to the unsaved. These obligations are a matter of *Scripture*, embracing both the Old and the New Testaments (in the King James Version), and is held to be, in its entirety, the actual, literal, nonallegorical *Word of God*. Regarding the nature of the Bible, Pastor Muller reminded his congregation during a Sunday evening service that

> the Bible is a supernatural book, the inspiration of God, a book from God to man. If you reject the story of Jonah and the fish, you have to reject much of the Bible. Fundamentalists accept all of it. If you don't understand something in the Bible, it's no reflection on God but on man's puny, finite mind.

When Independent Baptists refer to their "literal" view of the Bible, they mean, explained Pastor Carter Hill, an AACS officer

> within the context of the historical, grammatical, and theo-

logical. When the Psalms say of David that he waters his couch with tears, it doesn't mean he cried a swimming pool's worth. We accept that as a figure of speech. Take the Grace Brethren; they see foot washing as a church ordinance. We say it's no big thing. In Bible times, it was dusty and people wore open-toed shoes. On the big things of doctrine, we're together.

In order to live a Christlike life students are exhorted to get *in the Word*, that is, in God's word, by the daily prayer and Bible reading that is referred to as *holding one's devotions*; by faithful attendance at church where the Word of God, the spiritual food that nourishes the heart, is preached; by reflecting on the Scripture that one reads and hears; and by obeying the Word of God. The Word of God operates as a bulwark against sin (Ephesians 6:13 reads: "Wherefore take unto you the whole armour of God, that ye may be able to withstand in the evil day," and the following four verses enlarge the concept), encasing the Christian with a mighty, protective shield. Yet sin enters our lives like sand seeping into a summer home on a storm-whipped beach. The inevitability of sin, on the one hand, and the need for constant vigilance to ward it off, on the other, is a matter for repeated exhortation. Assistant Headmaster Warren addresses students in chapel:

> Look at Isaiah 53:3 and see how people treat Christ. He is despised and rejected of men. . . . If you aren't saved, you've rejected him. What have you done today to help put Jesus on the cross? Your sins, my sins, helped put Jesus on the cross.

Obedience is extraordinarily important. The teachers readily find support for it: "Obey them that have the rule over you, and submit yourselves" (Hebrews 13:17); "Children, obey your parents in the Lord" (Ephesians 6:1); "to obey is better than sacrifice" (1 Samuel 15:22). Alternately, disobedience is a sin. Questioning often is construed as rebellion, and rebellion is anathema, for it "is as the sin of witchcraft" (1 Samuel 15:23). And God punishes sinners: "Whosoever he be that doth rebel against thy commandment . . . he shall be put to death" (Joshua 1:18); "An evil man seeketh only rebellion: therefore a cruel messenger shall be sent against him" (Proverbs 17:11). In this regard, a teacher spoke of her own adolescent experience with an unsaved boy her mother had strongly advised against dating. She persisted for one month until finally she realized:

It just hit me that if I didn't do what the Lord wanted me to do, I really don't think I'd be here now. I think he would have said, "Girl, I don't know how much more I can take." I always had a fear of the Lord, and then it dawned on me, "Wow, I don't want to die."

As much as teachers exalt obedience—"the whole Christian life centers around obedience"—many feel obliged to give questioning its due, hoping to avoid, as they said, the impression of "brainwashing" or of Christians as "dumb sheep." Questioning is acceptable if done in the right spirit, recalling 2 Timothy 2:15, that the Christian must test doctrines in order to "shew thyself approved unto God." Students can question if they do not rebel. They can discuss differences of view, as long as there "is proper respect, they don't question authority," and they realize that obedience always is first. Children can even question the "settled" matters because "they might wonder," says McGraw, "why did God set it up that way?" Although questioning was deemed "healthy," teachers also felt students need not always know the why of something. The Bible does not say understanding must precede obedience, but, rather, that if one obeys, understanding will follow (John 7:17). All teachers agree that obedience to parents and teachers, the tangible authorities, is critical for acquiring the habit of obedience to the Lord, the intangible authority. Yet discernment must temper obedience to all earthly authorities, since obedience to them must cease whenever they encourage behavior that violates Scripture.

For all that God's word is plainly inscribed in the Bible, *his will* for each of us is not transparently clear. Since he would have us do this rather than that, we must plumb the depths of our own will to ascertain which act, among a set of alternatives, in fact bears God's stamp of approval. Each BBA teacher told a personal story to illustrate the working of God's will.

How did you know you should not buy that house? "I had the check ready and the contract signed, but I couldn't go to sleep. I said, 'OK, Lord, if you don't want us to go ahead with this house, don't let me go to sleep. I couldn't sleep, and I prayed some more. Now I said, 'OK, Lord, if you don't want us to get it, let me fall asleep.' I was asleep in like one minute."

How did you decide to become a teacher? "I heard Jack Hyles preach about Christian schools fighting Communism and how they were better than public schools, and I just felt that was what I could do for the Lord." How did you happen to come to Hartney? "Well, the decision came down to whether we could sell our house in Colorado. It didn't sell for four months; we'd borrowed money from my dad, and I kept asking, 'Lord, is it this, or isn't it?' One night a guy visited our house, said he liked it, and came back with the $10,000 to assume our loan."

Why do you go around to other churches giving talks? "My husband had been urging me to do this for some time. I didn't think I knew enough Bible, theology, etc. One day I was listening to the radio and I heard this song, 'The King Is Coming,' a powerful song about the Second Coming of Christ. I got so thrilled thinking about this that I felt the Lord had just spoke to me. He wanted me to speak publicly, laid it upon my heart. Right out loud I said, 'OK, Lord, if you want me to speak publicly, I will.'"

Decisions made in God's will bring a sense of peace; they are enabled by God's removal of obstacles, since he never asks you to do something you cannot do; the contrary is true for decisions he does not approve. You never are made to do his bidding; the choice remains yours. But if you willingly do whatever he asks, "He uses circumstances, advice people give you, a verse you read, something" to inform you that he is opening this rather that that door for you to enter. "If the door is open, you need never fear the consequences of entering," because "God is not a fool. For example, God would not call somebody with a speech impediment to be a preacher."

Students are exhorted to know and obey what God enjoins them to do. In this way, the *Holy Spirit* will encompass them and enable them to live a *spiritual* life, a life whose actions communicate a resolve to reject the world, Satan's enticing domain in which *secular humanism* extols man rather than God as the measure of all things. Christians must be and must remain *separate from the world—in it but not of it*. Until one has been called home to Christ, there is no escaping the world in physical terms; one lives and works there and, accordingly, one must be involved in it. However, one's entire way of life should demonstrate resolve to be no part of the ways of the world. Separateness in dress, language, belief, and general conduct should be strikingly clear.

The concept of separation is extremely important in the Christian world view. It refers, primarily, to being "separate unto God" and, secondarily, to separation from the world. McGraw acknowledges that separation from the world sometimes takes the Christian into gray zones, like what is acceptable on Sunday, the Lord's day. Now that most commercial and recreational activities are available on Sunday, Christians must wend their way through a vast array of choices.

McGraw keeps Sunday as a day of worship and rest, although he has Christian friends who attend football games and chaff him for not accompanying them. Since he watches Sunday football games on TV, they wonder what the difference is. Though separation is an invariable principle of Bethany's Christians, it does not constrain participation in all activities the world finds enjoyable. They are not ascetics, but the imperatives of separation mean they must resist, for example, the testimony-blemishing enticement of popular music and entertainment.

The Word of God is sacred, to be known and revered, to be understood and obeyed. In this way, one can live in the only way that is proper for Christians—in God's will, according to his plan for each of us. This is not an unattainable, exalted status, available only to an elite; it is the ideal state for all Christians. The rewards of being in God's will are immense, for he has promised never to forsake those who trust him, heed his admonitions, and conduct their lives in a manner that will be an inspiring *testimony* for him to Christians and non-Christians alike. Students constantly hear that their lives must be a fitting testimony to their status as Christians. As McGraw is fond of stating: "If you were on trial for being a Christian, would there be enough evidence to convict you?" The Christian is reminded to have a godly conscience that will direct him to keep pure his own testimony and that of his church and school.

An obligatory contact with the world, enjoined by God, is the *witnessing* of one's faith in Jesus Christ to the unsaved whenever and wherever the opportunity arises. Like proselytizing and evangelizing, the act of witnessing relates to the duty of trying to convert others to the fundamentalist Baptist faith. At Bethany, these different terms refer to a single process. One's obligation to the unsaved is matched by one's obligation to backslid brethren who need help to see the error of their ways so they can *get right with the Lord* or, if they have strayed seriously from God's will, *rededicate* their lives to the Lord. The need to get right with the Lord arises when one has been disobedient. It involves realigning one's life so it is in perfect relationship to what the spirit of God would have one do. To be unaligned is to vitiate the impact of one's prayers. When the prayers of the unaligned are uttered, it is "like they would hit the ceiling and come right down," explained a teacher. It is no small matter to be denied the comfort of prayer.

> Nothing in the world can make you feel as good as when
> you pray and ask the Lord to forgive you. How good it is to
> feel that it's all taken care of and you don't have to worry

about it. Even in eternity the Lord will never say "Remember when you did this?"

When students internalize this vocabulary of belief, they will naturally endeavor to promote the *glory of God* by living their lives at least as *full-time Christians* or, ideally, dedicating their lives to *full-time Christian service*, which embraces those careers—preacher, evangelist, missionary, employee of a Christian organization (such as a church or school)—directed entirely to the Lord's work. When full-time in the Lord's work, the Christian says to his Lord, "I am yours to command, prepared to go where you wish and do as you want me to do." Bethany's young Christians learn that to be worthy of him is to confirm, "Lord, I am yours." Relatively few Christians enter full-time Christian service. Many work in factories or department stores or gas stations. They are not fully immersed in his service in the way that preachers, missionaries, and teachers are, or those who are employed in any capacity by Christian radio stations, publishing firms, or other Christian organizations whose sole function is serving the Lord.

Few schools are as explicit and forceful as the Christian school in directing students' vocational decisions. Students are urged to listen carefully for the possibility that the Holy Spirit is calling them into full-time Christian service, and, of course, to be obedient if they are called. Teachers do not denigrate other work; they pay it no attention. In contrast, they give the Lord's service constant encouragement: in the optional, after-school, Preacher Boy's Class—"Many young people seek to become preachers, but first they must be chosen;" at baccalaureate exercises—"May they [the graduates] be leaders in churches wherever they go and serve the Lord as preachers, teachers, and evangelists"; in chapel—"Have you said, 'I don't care, Lord, if you send me to the deepest, darkest jungles of Africa. I don't care about my body. I'll go anywhere'"; in English class—"How many of you boys feel called to be preachers? [Three raise their hands.] Doesn't it make you feel good to do something for the Lord?"; and in Bible class—"Now turn with me to Mark 10:43. What is the Lord telling us? He's telling us he wants us to be his ministers and servants."

It is not farfetched to conceive of BBA as a vocational school directed to work in the Lord's service. To be sure, it does not consider itself to be such a school. And no teacher ranked bringing students into full-time Christian service as BBA's major goal. Nonetheless, such service is the pride and joy of all teachers; when a student dedicates his life to the Lord it is a cause for celebration of a sort no other occupational decision receives; and it is the one career area most fully endorsed by the entire Bethany experience, from physical education to English.

Christian Behavior for Students

If it is true that a Christian school is built upon the Word of God and not upon the inclinations of mere men and women, it is nonetheless true that even the well-based school requires human agents to insure its success. A Christian school is an organization; to succeed, it needs more than a good idea. Headmaster McGraw embodies the Word in everything he does, but he is a first-rate administrator as well. Second only to Pastor Muller in the formal structure of BBA, he in fact, runs the school. He does so with a skilled, firm, informal hand, and always with humor, patience, and a sensitive understanding of people. He is uncompromisingly committed to BBA as a ministry of Bethany Baptist Church and, of course, as God's school. To be sure, Pastor Muller is the uncontested doctrinal authority for the world of Bethany; Headmaster McGraw, however, as the daily arbiter of things doctrinal at BBA, is a trusted spokesman for fundamentalist Christianity and for Christian education.

Addressing a meeting of the Illinois Association of Christian School administrators, McGraw reminded them that "the goal of our Christian education is to get the kids out serving the Lord. Think about that when you admit a boy. I didn't admit a boy yesterday because I couldn't see any point down the road when he would ever serve the Lord." This is McGraw speaking of his philosophy in operation. If, as his school's informational brochure claims, BBA admits students "of any race, color, and national or ethnic origin," it applies other yardsticks for admission and exclusion drawn from the central facts of its scriptural underpinning. McGraw's rejection of the boy squares with his view that Christian schools should be open to all persons only if these persons are, or can become, open to Christ. He will risk accepting students with a "questionable" past if they show promise of receptivity to the school's outlook. Though his judgment proves mistaken at times, he refuses to adopt the more stringent policy of some other Christian schools, which admit only confirmed born-again applicants.

Serving the Lord is BBA's ultimate goal for each student. Sending each of its graduates to a Christian college is a lesser goal, but McGraw is adamant on the causal connection between these two points: "If a kid does not go to a Christian college, he probably will not serve the Lord." Thus for him the indicator of a Christian school's success is the percentage of its graduates who enroll in a Christian college. "I just got a call,"

McGraw continues, "from a recent graduate. Her dad's a drunk. She needs encouragement. I think she needs a good Christian husband to make a good Christian home. And where else would she meet a good Christian husband?" For McGraw this is not a rhetorical question.

Again, we hear McGraw addressing his high school students in their first chapel meeting of the school year; it is a time for getting things off to a good start. Once students have assembled in the old church auditorium, each grade seated together, with the girls and boys usually in separate rows, McGraw's music teacher walks to the center of the two-step-high rostrum and says, "Let's start the year off right by standing and singing the Academy Hymn" (see Appendix C). Its words refer to important ideas—God can't be denied, man's knowledge is insufficient, freedom comes from proclaiming God. Then Headmaster McGraw takes his place at the lectern. Though he will smile and joke, no one present doubts his serious intent. His is not a religious message of the sort students usually hear during their thrice-weekly chapel meetings. To all but the new students, his points are redundant. Redundancy, however, is the norm for presenting the school's essential ideas. Shuffling feet and nodding heads are not tolerated in chapel meetings. McGraw's smooth tones soon dominate the small room:

> General instructions first of all for the new students—a reminder to bring your Bible to chapel every day. That is standard operating procedure. Second, bring your Bible to every class in this school with the exception of physical education. I'll ask your teachers to check on that. I want it followed. I want it done. We believe that the Word of God is central to the curriculum of a Christian school and for that reason a teacher in any one of his classes might want the Word of Scripture about some point or another. I want to talk to you today about that very thing as a way of emphasizing our philosophy.
>
> I was on a trip recently and came across an excellent phrase that I thought describes the philosophy of a Christian school: "We are different—different on purpose." That's the philosophy of a Christian school. When we began this school, and this is our ninth year of operation, we didn't start it because Hartney needed just another school. We're not just another school that teaches math, science, history, and so on. We try to be different in everything we do. We make no apology for that. I've made this pledge to students every year: If you can find any of our stands that aren't based upon the Word of God, I wish you'd come tell us and we'll bring them in line with the Word of God.

Our classes here reflect the Word of God. We believe that history, for example, is *his* story, the unfolding of the word of Jesus Christ on the center stage of the world. A man trying to write a history textbook that presents Jesus Christ as just another historical figure has no concept of real truth. We don't teach that way in our history classes. Math is a study of orderliness. The Word of God says, "Let everything be done decently and in order." Try to keep a checkbook sometimes without using some order and organization. Science is an understanding of God's handiwork. Men deny the Word of God and try to make us believe that all that we see about us has come about just through a series of events. Sometimes, the general term of evolution is used to apply to all this, but the Word of God is different on that. It clearly teaches that man was created from nothing: "Out of nothing," God states. The evolutionist says that the dinosaur and man were epochs of time apart, but Dr. Henry Morris, a born-again man, a Christian man, has a picture in one of his books you won't find in the average, secular high school biology book. It shows in the same petrified stream bed a footprint of a man and a footprint of a large dinosaur. So these creatures were on earth the same time as man. The evolutionists deny that, but here's a photograph that clearly shows the untruth of the evolutionary position. You'll get that kind of information in our school; you'll see that kind of thing emphasized.

Now, we don't have Christian textbooks in every area; they aren't available. But the textbook is not the key. The teacher is the key. So we insist that you respect your teachers, learn a proper attitude toward authority. Your teacher is the key for you getting the truth here, not the textbook but your teacher.

We are different. We are different on purpose and we don't make any apology about that. This is in line with the Word of God in 2 Corinthians 5:17. Notice what it says, a verse that should be memorized: "Therefore if any man be in Christ, he is a new creature: old things are passed away; behold, all things are become new." That's a simple way of stating what I've just told you. There are a lot of ways we work at being different. One of them is how we insist you young people conduct yourselves.

We believe that we are sensible and fair in what we require of a student. For example, when you're a student here, you are *known* as a student at Bethany Baptist Academy, and for that reason we have what we call an umbrella policy. It means that you'll be disciplined if you do something against our rules and regulations on Saturday night just as you would if it happened on Thursday night. Some people might say, "Well, school is not in effect on Saturday night." We won't argue that point. Obviously, it isn't. But the fact is that you're known in the community as a student at Bethany Baptist Academy whatever night it is. You are a student all the way through here, through the week, through the month, whatever. Not that we are trying to tell our students how to breathe and when to breathe. But we've got standards to maintain, and we are trying to be different on purpose, in a reasonable way.

The Word of God tells us here in 2 Corinthians 5:17, "Therefore if. . . " Many times the verses that begin with "therefore" are important because they conclude a whole line of reasoning, and that is what Paul is doing here. "Therefore if any man be in Christ"—in other words, if you've been born again by the spirit of God, you are saved today. If you've never trusted Jesus Christ as your personal savior, God says that you are lost. And if you die, you will go to hell. God makes that plain. If everybody, every reprobate, every heroin user, and every drunk out on the street, just automatically went to heaven, that wouldn't be much of a place. God has standards, too, you see.

If you are saved today, this verse applies to you where it goes on to explain that "if any man be in Christ, he is a new creature." Remember that when you think about the rules here, because these rules are to apply to new creatures, new creatures in Christ Jesus. If you just don't want to accept the rules, then you better ask God to remove whatever's in your heart that prevents you from accepting them, and accepting them with understanding.

New creatures, that's what this school is all about. We take new creatures in, blood-washed Christian young people, and teach them a way of life and have them go out and serve the Lord. We insist that boys look like boys, with manly-looking haircuts. Mr. Swanson and I will look at your hair right after chapel today. We do it at the beginning of school and we do it about every two or three weeks. The barbers in town love us. We insist you meet the standard. We won't have rules here that nobody obeys. That would be silly.

This year, teachers are going to be able to give homework every evening except Wednesday. No athletic practice on Wednesday evening—what are we saying? We're saying we want you to go to midweek service, we want you to go to visitation [a time when students and teachers visit homes for the purpose of proselytizing]. We want to do everything we can to make it easy for you to serve the Lord and to do the right thing.

Some of you who have been here in the past need to determine in your heart that you're going to have the best year you've ever had. You're going to raise that average, you're going to make that honor roll, you're going to attain some things for the glory of God. A Christian, you see, is to do everything up to a standard. It hurts me to see a student late all the time. That's the reason we have demerits for being tardy. And let me tell you, when you are tardy, those demerits really add up. We think it's important that you be everywhere on time. Don't you be out in these halls without a pass in your hand. Don't you come into math class without your books. Use a little common sense. Let eveything be done decently and in order. Confusion is not godly.

To a Christian, all things should become new. This is really being said in a spiritual sense. If your spiritual outlook becomes different, it will change everything about your life. A Christian ought to be able to do everything a sinner can do, better; if the Christian and the sinner have the same ability, the Christian ought to be able to outshine the sinner in any area of life. I would like to see every one of you amount to something for the Lord and go out and serve the Lord. But even Christ wasn't successful with all of his men, and we probably won't be successful with all of you. "Well," some of you might say, "I'm going to be one of the sinners." Now, that's kind of dumb. You are going to pay the price for that, not me.

Maybe you have never really claimed this verse as a Christian: Therefore, whoever is in Christ shall be a new creature. Old things will be passed away and behold all things shall become new. I hope you will. I think it will mean a great deal to you if you do. I want to have an invitation today and I want you to bow your heads right now. [Students bow their heads and close their eyes. It is totally quiet when Headmaster McGraw begins to speak again.] First of all some of you may say, "Mr. McGraw, that message wasn't really for me because you were saying, 'new creatures,' and I've never trusted Christ as my savior." Well, it doesn't take long. I know we don't have many who have never trusted Christ, but do we have a few? Don't be embarrassed. I'm not going to embarrass you. All I'm going to do is ask that you see Mr. Swanson or myself before this day is over. That's all.

Right now, I'm not going to ask you to come forward. I'm not going to ask you to do anything like that. Is there anyone who would at least acknowledge today, "Mr. McGraw, I have never trusted Christ as my savior; I am not a new creature in Christ." Is there anybody like that? [Seeing no hands, he concludes his chapel message.] All right, let's have a word of prayer.

Our Father, we are thankful for this time we've had. We had to perhaps cut it a little bit short because of the time, but, Father, we pray that you'll be with us today, seal these thoughts to our hearts, and guide and lead and direct now, that this year might be a great year in each of these young people's lives. In Jesus' name, we pray. Amen.

These extensive comments that Headmaster McGraw delivers to his high school students are indicative of several critical aspects of style and substance at BBA. The "preacher" style is evident in his adoption of a scriptural verse, 2 Corinthians 5:17, and using its message of the born-again Christian as a "new creature" to provide both form and content for his entire talk. The message, appropriate for a group composed largely of born-again students, provided entree to McGraw's clarification and elaboration of school purpose regarding big matters—serving the Lord—and small—wearing short hair and modest clothing. The explicitness of school purpose also typifies BBA procedure: students always are told, and told repeatedly, the nature of their school's mission, and the distinctiveness of their school's instructional program as contrasted with that of the public school. Bringing one's Bible to all classes except physical education symbolizes their profound departure from the often-evoked, much-excoriated public school. By the time McGraw reached his invitational call, he had set forth the themes the students would hear all year long: the Word of God as the school's consistent foundation, the teacher as authority, the twenty-four hour application of school rules, and the excelling of Christians because they are Christians. Finally, most chapel sessions end, as do most church services, with an invitation to those present to become saved, get right with the Lord, or in some other way to make their life congruent with the ideals of fundamentalist Christianity.

Inferences about pedagogy can be drawn from these and other observations of McGraw's. He and others also speak more directly to matters relating to the nature of young learners, instruction, the knowledge that is of most worth, and the like. It is to this general area—the pedagogical implications of doctrinal dictates—that I want to turn now.

Christian Pedagogy

Bethany educators use various images of the nature of children, depending on the point they wish to make. They are lambs, insofar as they are to submit to the authority of parents, teachers, and God. They are warriors, insofar as they are to relate to the world, forcefully resisting its allures and forcefully presenting the path of salvation to the unsaved. They are sinners and babes in Christ, insofar as they are not fully informed by the Word of God, and therefore must learn to give their problems to God and become strong to prevent the flesh from taking over. As "kids, but not dumb kids," they require adult teachers who reign supreme in their classrooms. Most of all, says McGraw, they need a judicious blend of love and discipline.

Because children love to be disciplined, Bethanyites believe, they will develop psychological problems if they rebel against authority. Moreover, "If a boy runs your classroom," McGraw tells his teachers, "this won't teach him submission to God. If a girl runs your classroom, this won't teach her submission to her husband. As humans, we have a problem in this area of authority."

Corollary to Bethany's view of youth is their view of the teacher as overseer. Given their scriptural commitments (for example, "Train up a child in the way he should go: and when he is old, he will not depart from it" [Proverbs 22:6]), teachers must operate according to what McGraw calls "our whole philosophy of supervision":

> We believe in teachers being right on top of things, to where somebody could easily misunderstand what we are doing and accuse us of looking over their [the students'] shoulders all the time. Well, I guess we do that, and we don't apologize for it. We realize that you can't leave kids alone, for instance, in unchaperoned situations, whether it's a youth activity, school activity, or whatever. It just doesn't work.

If many students are traveling to a game or taking a trip, boys and girls ride in separate buses; if few are going, boys sit in the back and girls in the front of the same bus. "We believe that those kinds of arrangements prevent problems; it's a realistic view of the nature of man."

And given the teachers' scriptural commitments, they and their fellow Christian teachers throughout America enjoy a unity of purpose that distinguishes them from most teachers anywhere in the world. They belong to the same church, share a virtually identical view of the Bible, and are directed by leaders who are persistently faithful adherents of the same doctrine. "I can't name a single policy of the school," says McGraw, "that doesn't somewhere fall into a doctrinal statement of the church." He acknowledges differences of opinion regarding nonessentials like the wearing of slacks, use of cosmetics, playing music in the church, etc.

> Most of these disagreements come from misunderstanding. There's a verse in Corinthians [actually, 1 Peter 3:3] dealing with plaiting the hair and wearing brass [gold] and so on. In those days, it was a mark of the harlot.

Regarding essentials, unity prevails. Headmaster McGraw considers BBA's unity of purpose the characteristic which most distinguishes it from the public school. Whereas a diversity of religious and nonreligious views characterize teachers in even the most homogeneous public school, Christian educators are of one mind on the central elements of belief. As true believers, they collectively endeavor to make true believers of their students—that is, persons who perceive the Bible as absolute truth and who believe and mean to live by these truths absolutely. True believers do not conceive of competing, alternative truths. Truth is singular; it is to be possessed, not sought after. To reject the true believer's way is to err and suffer the appropriate consequences. In mundane matters, truth may be pursued; in the critical matters of this life and of the hereafter, Truth is known, revealed by God in his scriptures, and must be acquired. To search for that which already is known, is to give credence to a vain intellectualism which vitiates the integrity of an inerrant Bible. Bethany's Christians reject Lessing's view that

> if God were to hold out enclosed in His right hand all Truth, and in His left hand just the active search for Truth . . . and should say to me: Choose! I should humbly take this left hand and say: Father! Give me this one; absolute truth belongs to Thee alone" (*Wolfenbüttfer Fragmente*).

Obviously, teachers at BBA fulfill both an academic and a religious role, intending to perform in ways that integrate the two. Leading students to the Lord, abetting their efforts to get right with the Lord, edifying them in regard to the Word of the Lord—all these functions merge with more conventional academic ones to shape the teacher's role. For teachers to be fitting agents of the Lord, as McGraw advises them, they must be strong Christians themselves.

Christians must learn how to resist the devil. He can attack in new areas. Pick friends who are stronger than yourself. Keep you life free from sin. Confess daily both sins of omission and commission. Thoughts are sins if they're wrong; don't let the devil take root. You can't prevent a bird from flying over you, but you can prevent it from building a nest in your hair.

In regard to having impact in their classroom, teachers' lives weigh more heavily than the subjects they teach. The latter, however, are of consequence and have varying priorities. To be sure, the compulsory Bible class, thrice-weekly chapel, and daily devotions are salient, but there remains a full day of experiences to be ordered in some way. Other subjects, whatever their content, are to be integrated with Scripture, not in a necessarily conscious, planned way, but naturally—in fact, quite literally—as the spirit moves them. Thus, when teachers are replete with the Word of God, they become aware of the occasions for integration as these occur in the course of a lesson. Fundamentalist Christian educators commonly use the term "integration" to designate their need to merge Scripture and subject matter in their daily classroom routine. Whatever the subject and activity, they are urged to integrate to the fullest extent possible, although I believe they would accept the warning of the Christian educator A. J. Jacquot that "It's a sin against God to let your class lead you to always discuss doctrine and neglect subject matter."

From Headmaster McGraw's perspective there is a clear order of subject-matter priorities at BBA. Religious instruction is most important, followed by English. McGraw's valuation of English is straightforward: Christianity is based on the Word of God, access to the Word of God is gained through mastery of language, and mastery of language is acquired through instruction in English. He observes that the priest interprets doctrine for the Catholic, but for the fundamentalist "every believer is a priest before God." Thus, to be an effective "priest" the Christian must be literate. Teachers add a vocational argument to the case for four years of compulsory English: the world's employers value workers accomplished in reading, writing, and speaking English.

A one-year required speech course is closely allied to the English program. In support of speech, McGraw quotes Romans 10:17: "So then faith cometh by hearing, and hearing by the word of God." Speech students concentrate on the mechanics of effective oral presentation, using both sacred and secular content. An optional two years of drama instruction, taught as a regular class, not as an extracurricular activity, bolsters the speech option and extends the work students do in speech. A school that values the identification of would-be preachers can easily justify emphasizing the development of verbal skills.

Music belongs in this cluster of core subjects but is not exactly a part of it. In McGraw's view, "music is a universal language. . . . It relates very definitely to the spiritual emphasis by preparing the heart for the overall spiritual impact." In fact, music is much esteemed, and both vocal and instrumental opportunities abound in regular classes offered during the school day. Yet, since no class in music is required of all students, its importance must be inferred from the way BBA treats it in regard to making time for its programs, releasing students from class for practice, and the like. The case for the importance of music at BBA is like the one that can be made for athletics at most public schools.

In considering the position of the rest of his school's curriculum, McGraw refers to Bob Jones University in South Carolina, his alma mater and former employer, and the most preferred school for BBA's graduates "because of their doctrinal position and their position on separation." Bob Jones has many departments and courses of study, but it stresses the training of preachers and teachers, the two notably Christian vocations. Accordingly, BBA stresses those parts of its curriculum which bear on a student's becoming a full-time Christian and entering full-time Christian service. It considers all other subjects—mathematics, social studies, science, etc.—as useful and interesting, though clearly of secondary importance. BBA divides its curriculum into two broad categories, the more valued one containing the core experiences of Bible, chapel, English, speech, drama, and music, and the less valued one containing all other subjects—the periphery.

McGraw's advice to his teachers suggests another way to think about the two categories of instruction. He tells the teachers that they should urge their students "to read the newspapers and watch the news. This won't change their lives—only changing their hearts will do that—but it's still important." In short, the core subjects have a greater capacity to affect the heart and thereby change lives.

McGraw and BBA hold an instrumental view of learning. Many BBA graduates will end up in secular jobs, but when funds and time are limited, and priorities lie elsewhere, instructional opportunities geared to such employment are foregone. In fact, BBA neither means to be geared to non-Christian vocations nor apologizes for their comparative neglect. BBA is most definitely a vocational school, designed to inculcate youth with the desire to become Christian professionals, at the same time that it provides a general education suitable for being a Christian person. "We don't let kids get excused at noon to go to work," says McGraw. "I don't see the sense of kids leaving school early to pump gas or work at K Mart." The view of instruction as instrumental in spiritual terms also applies to the development of Christian intellectuals. Intellectualism is often too much a matter of pride, McGraw believes, rather than of service of the sort which should provide the primary rationale for learning.

> You look at our library . . . we don't have the emphasis [number of books] there to turn out a high school kid who'd say he wants to be a university professor. What we don't want is to worship learning. To a Christian there has to be a goal that is something beyond. We think of scholarship as an avenue of service, as opposed to scholarship for its own sake.

Administrator and teacher commitment to Scripture do not dictate common classroom procedures. To be sure, McGraw and others offer guidelines to teachers for sound instruction, and some of these guidelines are traceable to scriptural views of values, children, and authority. Still, there is the type of diversity that one may find in any school, based on variations in teachers' experience and their personalities, and on the subject matter being taught. Nonetheless, BBA has a common view of ideal teaching practice, as heard in the words of Headmaster McGraw speaking either at preschool or during-the-semester in-service meetings with his teachers.

"Our job is teaching the truth." I don't believe there is a more essential premise for understanding the Christian approach to instruction that this statement which McGraw spoke without the least hint of hubris. BBA believes it can teach the truth, because it believes it possesses the truth, not regarding man's contemporary issues of how to reduce national debt, cure cancer, or prevent acid rain, but regarding his cosmic concerns about the origins of man and earth, life and death, man's ultimate fate, the nature of God, and proper conduct. Moreover, since Christian truth can explain why things are the way they are, Christian teachers can provide answers when public school teachers only shrug with uncertainty: "Why don't the parts of an atom fly apart? Because God holds all things together."

For identifying BBA priorities, it may be useful to note the school's core and peripheral experiences, but this delineation is not useful in characterizing teaching practice. No one advises teachers about how to teach in relationship to either of these two categories, but, rather, in relationship to their notions of truth and authority. If some matter falls within the scriptural domain of truth, it is incumbent upon teachers to present that matter as uncontestably, unequivocally true. Students can wonder why, seek explanations, raise questions on any topic, and, in the end, they can reserve judgment about what to accept as true. What is deemed to be true, however, will never be taught as though it might be open to question; above all, when teachers have pronounced what is true, students may not question the teachers' authority to do so. For the essence of the proper student response to authority is submission, total and unqualified, as long as the person in authority is not violating scriptural doctrine. Pedagogical variety exists in the context of an essentially teacher-centered classroom, wherein neither student idiosyncrasies nor the textbook should ever dominate, and where all teaching efforts must be directed to shape students' minds to Christ. In McGraw's words "Bethany is a closed system within the biblical framework. We would say that that opens it to everything. The world, of course, would disagree." Students are free to accept or reject this perspective, but it is the only one that BBA sanctions.

McGraw and Donna Reynolds, BBA's elementary school supervisor and a contributor to teacher in-service programs, provide observations on teacher practice. McGraw says:

> The more you do that is student-centered, the more you surrender control of the class. Teacher-directed activity is the key to learning. Lecturing is more important than discussion. We believe strongly in the prepared person and that comes from our preaching heritage. Don't apologize for telling the kids what is right. They should be taught not to question you. Tell them, "This is my classroom and this is what I expect. This classroom is not a democracy. It's a dictatorship. You don't vote on anything!" This is what I tell the kids.

Administrative guidance to teachers extends considerably beyond these points; it extends to the familiar homilies mined from the background of any experienced teacher—know your subject, have a plan, use audiovisual aids, practice reinforcement, avoid sarcasm, motivate—while never forgetting, as Donna Reynolds emphasizes, that

> as a Christian teacher you are concerned with a student's life. You must communicate the subject matter; you must also teach God's principles of right and wrong and show in

your life God's standard of Christian living. What do you see
when you look at your students? Individuals for whom
Christ died! Individual Christian leaders of tomorrow!

Bethany educators take great pride in their school's orderliness.
They are committed to firm discipline based on well-established policies
and regulations (see chap. 3). To this end, they have devised a demerit
system which communicates to students a general rank order of infractions, ranging from tardiness and gum-chewing to lying, attending
movies, and cheating on tests. Demerits extend to misdeeds committed
both in and out of school. Since BBA takes its students to be BBA
students at all times and places, there is no limit to the application of
school regulations: "Our testimony [as a school] wouldn't be worth five
cents if we didn't follow this policy. We're trying to teach these kid how
to live all the time—not just from Monday to Friday." Corporal punishment is scripturally sanctioned and may substitute for demerits, but the
older a student is the more sparingly it is used. Teachers are urged to
manage their classes without frequent recourse to demerits. At the
same time, they are urged to apply school rules strictly, and to understand that the world's rejection of authority makes it all the more
necessary for them to enforce a strict code of conduct.

About every school it can be asked, "What kind of person does it
strive to develop?" Seldom can the question be answered simply, and
seldom do schools take pains to articulate an answer which can serve as
a blueprint for the educative experiences they should organize. But if
pressed, answer they can, or answers can be inferred from classroom
practice. They want their students to be vocationally successful, socially
adept, good citizens in political terms, and the like. I will discuss
classroom practice and other school activities in later chapters, but here,
in connection with the general ideas that govern the entire school's
operations, it is possible to be definitive about the kind of person BBA
means to develop.

The school attends primarily to developing youth to live in God's will
and to serve Christ, but it also emphasizes right conduct, such as
punctuality, honesty, cleanliness, and forgivingness. The Bible is presented as the handbook for good conduct, so that what is scriptural is
allowable, what is unscriptural is shunned, and what is in doubt is best
avoided. Christian students are to learn to live separate from the world,
as full-time Christians in terms of spirituality and faithfulness, totally
submissive to God's will and to the vicars of his will.

All schools have behavioral norms to guide student conduct; they are
most often contained in student handbooks and are the subject of

occasional talks. Seldom, however, has any American school been as professedly, unabashedly, unremittingly absorbed by normative commitments as the Christian school. It bristles with established norms at both the center and the periphery of its corporate life (notwithstanding the tiny, transitory islands of student counterculture depicted in chapter 10). I infer from the exhortations and the behavior of BBA's adult arbiters and practitioners of Christian virtue that the norms are obligatory, absolute, beyond discussion, and good for all occasions. There is right conduct and wrong conduct, without qualification.

With its emphatic normative commitment, BBA can be relatively relaxed about its paucity of instructional technology, its slim curricular and extracurricular offerings, and its truly modest library holdings. The spare quality of its material resources may be remedied in time, but for now it is not a cause for critical comment from within the Bethany community. Laboratory materials and books are valued, as are a broader range of vocational subjects. In fact, however, the dominant goals of BBA can be attained without possessing more of the material things of education. Unsurprisingly, the school is not relaxed about establishing the means to attain those goals which abide at the heart of BBA's existence.

3

The King's Witnesses Called to Teach

> I don't love all the teachers there, but I know that everyone of them is born again and this makes me feel secure.
>
> BBA student

The Teachers' Backgrounds

Bethany Baptist Academy's twelve full- and part-time high school teachers are not all cut from the same cloth. They were born and raised in the North Central or Northeastern states, their fathers held a variety of mostly middle-class jobs (three of them were ministers), and, with one exception, they attended public elementary and secondary schools. All of them attended college, six going to Bob Jones University (the largest fundamentalist university in the country, with approximately seven thousand students), two to Maranatha Bible College, and four to state universities; of these four, however, three did graduate work at Christian colleges and universities. Of the five married female teachers, two are married to ministers. Two of the female teachers are unmarried, as is one of the seven male teachers. All the school-aged children of the nine married teachers attend BBA and pay full tuition to do so. Though enrollment of teachers' children at BBA is not mandatory, it is inconceivable that they would do otherwise.[1]

At the time of this study, the teachers had worked at BBA an average of about four years; the school itself was in its ninth year. Some had begun their post-secondary schooling thinking they wanted to be nurses, musicians, secretaries, or naturalists, but they all ended up as trained teachers and they remain committed to teaching, though only to teaching in Christian schools. Three male teachers thought that someday they might leave teaching, but the alternatives of two of the three were fully in the Christian domain—one to be a pastor and the other a performer of Christian music.

Going to a Christian college was not always in the plans of each of the eight who did, nor was becoming a teacher. Pastors and parents strongly influenced these decisions, most particularly in the case of one teacher whose experience also illustrates the role of the Lord in the life of a Christian teacher. She had graduated from high school with no intention of continuing her education; in fact, she was engaged and eager to be married. One day a singing group came to perform at her church and her mother begged her repeatedly to hear them. Finally, she relented.

> After I made up my mind to go, I was going to enjoy myself. I listened to the songs, and I looked at that group of young people, and I could not believe there was such a big group of happy, Christian young people. When they were done, Dr. Browne preached a little bit and told some about his college. Later I went to the display table where they had literature on the college. My mom was right behind me. I turned around and said, "Mom, I want to go to college. I really don't want to get married." It just came, like a ton of bricks. It was one of the biggest turning points in my life. It took the thing that was dearest to me, that was to be married, to break me to do the Lord's will. I really had no intentions to go to college, but then when I heard about Maranatha, it was just snap [she snaps her fingers], like that.

And parents also figured in the decision of another teacher who as a high school senior thought he would like to study at Illinois Wesleyan. Only Maranatha, Tennessee Temple, and Bob Jones University were the "good fundamental Christian colleges" that his parents would support. Wesleyan was not in this category.

Choosing to Be a Teacher

When Bethany's teachers reflect on the circumstances that led them to become teachers, they sound both like public school teachers and like the servants of the Lord they are expected to be. For example, as one teacher explained,

> After you've been here several years, you realize you're in the place the Lord wants you to be. You could go elsewhere and make more money but you probably wouldn't be happy. Then, when I think about leaving, I think about the three-month vacation. That keeps me here.

More specifically, they refer to selecting teaching because it is a practical major if one loves children; to turning away from a major in voice and to teaching because "I discovered I had a real talent with kids"; to being reminded by mother, when interest in the French horn flagged, "Why not phys ed? You used to want to do it"; to becoming a teacher because "I liked the coaching aspect"; to learning that drama was impractical for a Christian after taking an acting course in which "I was assigned to play a part in a play called 'The Nude in the Washing Machine'"; and to realizing that "I loved children and being my own boss and influencing lives."

For the most part, these explanations could have been voiced by teachers anywhere.[2] Each BBA teacher, however, has an additional story to tell which fits the special way that Christian educators view themselves, their work, and their institutions. It derives from the exceptional fact that all Bethany teachers have surrendered their lives to the Lord and declared their unqualified readiness to be guided by his plan for them. Indeed, all of BBA's teachers believe that God has called them to be Christian school teachers. Bethany's teachers identify with the prophet Isaiah, who "heard the voice of the Lord saying, Whom shall I send, and who will go for us? Then said I, Here am I; send me" (Isaiah 6:8).

Some teachers enter their profession and learn only after the fact that it was God's will for them that they teach. "You can be direct with the Lord and tell him," a teacher explained. You can tell him, "'This is what I think you want me to do. I'm going to set my course of action.' You know if that's not what he wants, he'll change it." One teacher speaks of the Lord pushing rather than calling her. She never wanted to be a preacher's wife, but once she became one, she knew it was the right thing to do; she never wanted to be a teacher, but once she was urged to teach, she knew she had made the right (that is, God's) decision. Another teacher, who felt strongly attracted to preaching and is trained to preach, thought he wanted to serve under Pastor Muller and the only way to do this was through "the back door" of teaching in his school. "If you were to ask me today if I'm in God's will, I'd say 'definitely.'"

Here are two final examples that illustrate the process of realizing that one has been called. Bethany's science teacher recalls that, first, he was led to attend college in a town where there was a good fundamentalist church and school; next, he felt led to study biology; and, finally, when he was ready for a job, the science post at BBA was open. The mathematics teacher recollects a process that is equally elaborate.

> I remember during my freshman year at college I was praying a lot about what I should do. I got up at one church and gave my testimony and said I felt the Lord was calling me to full-time service in Christian education. During the next summer I was visiting churches and giving my testimony and I received a peace about my decision to teach. I decided the Lord was showing me the way. And I definitely saw the need for male teachers in Christian schools because I'd traveled a lot and saw schools full of women teachers. I'm not against women, but I feel like the boys need to see men teachers, not just their pastors, who have given everything to the Lord.

The Weekly Round of Teacher Activities

Giving all to the Lord is evident in the ordinary round of a typical teacher's week, a week that begins on Sunday. From morning to evening, Sunday is replete with church-related activities, though midafternoons often are available for rest, and the period following the evening service, beginning about 9:00 P.M., is often devoted to socializing. By contract, but more importantly by personal conviction, teachers attend all ordinary and special services; also by contract, they make available their time and talents for at least one church need (such as bus driving or Sunday School teaching), usually on Sunday, and special efforts of teachers are also manifest throughout the week.

Sunday

The framework for everyone's Sunday is the same: 9:30 A.M.–Sunday school; 10:30 A.M.—morning service; and 7:00 P.M.—evening service. This is a teacher's minimum involvement. Frank begins his Sunday at 8:30 A.M., when he drives a bus to pick up older members of the congregation, and he drives them home at noon when the morning service is over. In addition, he helps out in one of the Sunday school primary grades and takes the roll for Sunday school classes. Several of the teachers teach these classes. Laura is a participant in Bethany's bus ministry, which is designed to attract unchurched children to Christian instruction and services. She drives out at 8:00 A.M. to pick up Sunday school children whose parents do not attend church, and arrives back in time to teach her own Sunday school class. Then, following her afternoon break, she joins the church choir at 5:00 or 5:30 P.M. for practice. Lee and his wife (who is not a teacher) offer morning instruction to a group of community college students. On Sunday evening, they direct a "singspiration," which involves singing and a snack at the house of some church member. About every other weekend they organize an outing for these college students. Donna is the superintendent of grades one to six in the Sunday school. Russ teaches thirty boys in the seventh and eighth grades. When the older children and adults are at the regular service, Art delivers a twenty- to twenty-five-minute sermon, first to the third- and fourth-graders and then to the fifth- and sixth- graders. Since baptism at Bethany is by complete immersion, Art helps the pastor put on his waders and he also helps the men who are about to be baptized.

This exceptionally full schedule of church activities knits the faithful together over a span of almost twelve hours in their celebration of the Lord's day, the most important day of the week.

Monday

Frank awakens by 6:00 or 6:15 A.M. so as to be ready to leave the school grounds by 6:50 for the morning bus pickups. While Frank is collecting children, most other teachers arrive at school at least by the expected 7:55 A.M., and they remain in their classrooms until 3:45 P.M., thirty minutes after the students have been dismissed. Lee, Frank's bus-driving counterpart, is ready by 3:20 P.M. to drive students home; he completes his trip just before 5:00. Otherwise, after-school activities on Monday usually involve only the coaches and the cheerleader sponsor; all other teachers are likely to go home to enjoy one of the few evenings on which there is seldom a school or church event. The single exception is the deacon's meeting on the first Monday of each month. Art Swanson is the only teacher who also is a deacon.

Tuesday

This school day is much like any other unless there is a scheduled interschool soccer competition. If the game is at home, teachers rotate as ticket sellers or crowd controllers, or they may attend the game just for the fun of it. If the game is out of town, the coach and the cheerleader sponsor may return home as late as 11:00 P.M..

Wednesday

The church's midweek service at 7:30 P.M. distinguishes this day; there is also an occasional meeting of BBA or Sunday school teachers scheduled for the thirty to forty-five minutes preceding the service. Teachers can expect to be home by 9:00 P.M. The one additional task on Wednesday evening involves the several teachers who work with the younger childrens' choir when the rest of the congregation, separated by sex and age, goes off for about thirty minutes of prayer. These relatively long prayer sessions have their much briefer counterpart in teachers' meetings and student homeroom devotions. The person in charge may lead off the prayer session by directing attention to several situations worthy of prayer (for example, a church member's sickness, job, financial problem, troubled children, or unsaved relatives); this lead is followed spontaneously by persons who cite other persons and situations in need of prayer. When it is clear that no more prayer requests are forthcoming, heads are bowed and eyes are closed as individuals, again spontaneously, begin to pray, weaving the specific problems mentioned into their vocal prayer for help, support, relief, or thanks, as well as bringing up problems of their own that no one else has mentioned. Before the prayers are finished, each problem aired by the group has been incorporated into someone's prayer. By means of these meetings the concerns and joys of church and school participants are made public and at least minimally woven into the fabric of each other's lives. On Wednesday evening, Russ Warren serves as usher and Frank Fortner as bus driver for the same persons he serves on Sunday.

Thursday

Frank Fortner also drives on this day, but not for the old folks. Thursday evening is devoted to what Bethany calls "soul-winning visitation." Though Scripture enjoins the Christian to witness his faith every chance he gets (Matthew 24:14—"And this gospel of the kingdom shall be presented in all the world for a witness unto all nations"), Thursdays throughout the year are specially designated for this purpose. Frank's extra duty, which lasts from about 6:45 to 8:00 or 8:30 P.M., involves driving students to their visitation sites so they can invite other teenagers to church on Sunday.

While Frank does this, his colleagues join other church members for the adults' visitation. A small minority of other church members do voluntarily what is obligatory for the teachers. When all the participants come to Thursday's pre-visitation meeting, they are given cards containing the name, address, and circumstance (newcomer in town, visitor last Sunday at church, etc.) of each person they will try to see. Bethany tries to match visitors (who go two by two) with the persons to be visited in terms of age, sex, and marital status. Bethany does not announce ahead of time its intention of scheduling a visit; consequently, the visitors often fail to find anyone at home. When this happens, a religious tract may be left or a card that says, in effect, "We have tried to visit you; come to church on Sunday." A serious effort is made to revisit persons not found at home.

Visitation is a profoundly serious affair because it entails bringing some people to the Lord for the first time and reclaiming others who have backslid. Knowing that it is "what God wants us to do" puts teachers more at ease when knocking uninvited on doors. Some teachers, nonetheless, evangelize reluctantly, if not with some dislike: "It would be awfully easy not to do because it takes something extra. It's not very acceptable to go around saying, 'Are you saved?'"

Visitation is used for a variety of purposes. Sunday school teachers try to visit the home of each of their students; they use the occasion to urge unchurched parents to come to church. If an opening to evangelize arises, the opportunity is seized. One teacher reports that she had three successes one year and thought she had done well: "It just depends, you know, on whether the Lord has them ready for you, because he has to do it. We can't do it."

Responses to visitation vary considerably. Teachers have come to expect unanswered knocks and partially opened doors, as well as invitations to enter. "Catholics are the toughest; they don't even want to talk to you when you say you're Baptist." Sometimes slammed doors and curses are the reaction to greetings from Bethany's visitors; once inside a home, they may be greeted by the sound of a television or stereo set that is never softened sufficiently to permit discussion of the certainty of one's future. It just does not do, a teacher said, to shout over the blare of electronic noise and ask, "If you were to die tonight, do you know for sure you'd enter heaven?"

Friday

A day much looked forward to by workers in factories, offices, and schools across the nation, Friday is the last day of teaching at BBA also, but it is far from the end of teacher involvement in church and school activities. Basketball games are scheduled for Friday nights; this means work for the coaches and for the teachers on duty. The evening may also have a scheduled youth activity. Several teachers assist Pastor Burt, who is in charge of both Friday and Saturday night youth activities.

Saturday

Female teachers may sleep later than usual on Saturday morning, but male teachers get up early to attend the men's prayer breakfast. Though Headmaster McGraw does not require his teachers to attend, he indicates his preference that they be there. Teachers appreciate the importance of this occasion. It begins with remarks from Pastor Muller about matters that merit prayer, continues with the spontaneous formation of small groups in different rooms within the church building for prayers similar to those on Wednesday nights, and concludes with a breakfast in the school cafeteria cooked and served by Bethany church women. This session begins at 7:00 A.M. and is over about 8:15. Bethany's female teachers help to prepare and serve the breakfast whenever their turn comes around. Teacher David Conroy says he would not miss these breakfasts:

> Coming to prayer breakfast helps me be more effective as a teacher because I get to see some of the parents of some of the kids that I teach. But I'd come no matter what because I enjoy the fellowship and praying together. You can't beat it.

Fellowship is the term Bethanyites most often use to describe a gathering of Christians. In this setting, it is more than being together, it is being with one's brothers. However different practicing born-again Christians may be in other ways, they are alike at the very center of their lives, and thereby linked to those with whom they eat, chat, and pray.

Their breakfast over, some teachers, like Frank Fortner, go home to watch basketball games and read the sports page, while others, like Russ Warren, drive the youth-activity bus or call up each student in his Sunday School class: "I like to give them a call and let their parents meet me 'cause they don't know who I am."

Saturday morning also is set aside for bus visitation. The participants personally go to the homes of Sunday school students to assure their attendance for the next day's pickup; to confirm bus arrangements, if there has been a change in schedules; and to visit new youngsters in nearby houses, every one of whom is seen as a potential candidate for Bethany's Sunday school. Bethany takes pride in its fleet of yellow buses that fan out through Hartney to gather up children for hearing God's word. BBA teachers join other church members in vigorous recruitment of these children; indeed, the bus captains and their fellow workers compete in this recruitment, their results recorded on a chart hung on a church corridor wall.

> I don't want to be a burden to these bus children, but I want them to come to church to have an opportunity to know the truth. If they don't want to hear it, I'm not going to shove it down their throat. I want them to have a good opinion of me and of my Lord—of my Lord first.

Bethany's teachers may vary considerably in their availability to participate in the events of church and school, but this variability is based more on the personal circumstances of their lives than on their relative commitment. Single teachers and married teachers either without children or with grown-up children are more readily available. Teachers engage quite willingly in an extensive round of activities that could be onerous, but they have a cause, and they accede to its imperatives. Indeed, cause and commitment are the logical concomitants of absolute truth. Given Truth, as at Bethany, imperatives inexorably follow.

The Teachers' Personal Activities

A price teachers pay for their extensive church and school involvement is a dearth of time for recreational reading, television and radio, and nonchurch organizational activity. Few teachers are serious readers. The taste of those who do read runs from light, misty romances to historical novels and biographies. On the nonfiction side, they favor character-building and spiritual books, altogether reading less nonfiction than fiction, even though with the latter there is always the risk of encountering objectionable subject matter. The avoidance of what is scripturally objectionable usually guides the selection of leisure-time activities. Consequently, on their radios they hear the news, sports, or easy-listening music; on their TVs they watch old movies (with John Wayne, Clark Gable, or Errol Flynn), sports, or "Little House on the Prairie." A few like "Hogan's Heroes," "Lou Grant," and "60 Minutes;" those few who tune in "M.A.S.H." and "Dallas" are reluctant to speak about it. Even the relatively heavy TV viewers do not really watch much—up to ten hours a week; four teachers do not own a television set.

Perhaps all teachers read the local *Hartney Herald*, and all read at least one magazine. *U.S. News and World Report* and *Reader's Digest* are most popular, followed by *Good Housekeeping, Better Homes and Gardens,* and *Ladies Home Journal.* Except for *Faith for the Family,* a Bob Jones University publication distributed free by BBA, teachers do not ordinarily read or subscribe to religious magazines. *Time* and *Newsweek* are unpopular because they are not conservative enough and they contain objectionable material.

Only one Bethany teacher belonged to any organization other than Bethany Baptist Church: the Christian Women's Club. She explained that though Bethany does not "look kindly on it," she sees nothing wrong with their activities and she attends their meetings. Several teachers explained their nonparticipation in organizations:

> We put the Lord first.
>
> Kiwanis, Lions, Elks—they're do-gooders, they're OK. But if I'm going to put my time and energy into something, it's going to be in the church.
>
> Church and church friends take all my time.

Though most teachers do not belong to organizations, a number of them are members of the Republican party and several have been elected as committeemen, following a meeting called by Associate Pastor Harry Lowe to encourage grassroots political participation by born-again Christians. This meeting, inspired by the American Association of Christian Schools (see appendix D for their political action outline), is the local counterpart of the Christian move toward politicization at the national and state levels.

Ordinary people might find the Bethany teachers' weekly round of mostly obligatory activities intolerably confining and excessively intrusive into their personal prerogatives on the use of time. In fact, Bethany teachers estimate that they give 65 percent of their waking time to the school and 15 percent to the church.[3] The remaining 20 percent is spent with family or friends, although very few of the teachers acknowledge any social life outside the Bethany church community. Those who do are local people who grew up in Hartney and have friends and relatives nearby.

If BBA's teachers feel strained by, or impatient with, the pressure of their densely crowded schedules, most did not acknowledge this feeling to me. Perhaps they would not even acknowledge it to themselves, because to do so would imply uncertainty about their dedication to the Lord's service. No teacher denied that he or she was very busy, and each one thought it would be nice to have more free time. Yet, except for preferring a shift of the Thursday night visitation activities to early Wednesday evening before the Wednesday mid-week service, all were content with their present schedule and had no other modifications to suggest. Contractually obligated though they may be to comply with the objectives of church and school, the teachers do not feel that a contract is necessary to insure the fulfillment of their spiritual duties. "First comes the Lord," says Sue Matthews, "then my husband, and then my family." Her priorities are not established by a piece of paper. She and her fellow teachers most definitely are the King's witnesses.

Of course, teachers experience some strain; it derives not only from being very busy, but also from living a fishbowl life. I am surprised that teachers do not feel more strain. It seems to vary in relation to marital status, to whether or not they have children living at home, and to the length of time they have served as Christian schoolteachers. For example, the unmarried teacher:

> You can't date a guy in the church without everybody having you engaged to him within a week. That's the thing that bothers me—not having any privacy in your dating life. But that's going to be true anyplace where everybody knows everybody else.

The married teacher without children:

> If you don't have anything to hide, you don't feel you live in a fishbowl. If I had a secret sin like I used to, like when I smoked cigars or had beer in the icebox, then I might feel that way. But the people here know me as I am. I don't do anything at home that I don't do here. I might lose my temper, but I don't cuss even then.

The married teacher with children:

> I feel exposed in relation to my kids. You're worried that they're going to pull something that looks really bad. They kind of expect more out of our kids than they do everybody else's kids. It's almost like they're preacher's kids.

The veteran teacher, long accustomed to being in the public eye:

> When you're doing what the Lord wants you to do, you're always very happy.

In truth, the veteran may feel as personally exposed and as sensitive about her children's behavior as do her colleagues; her focus, however, is on the satisfaction she feels from doing the right thing. To be sure, she has days of distress, moments when she is downcast, but she is utterly convinced, and glows as she articulates that true joy and serving the Lord are one and the same thing. Though her new, young colleague Claudia is equally convinced, Claudia speaks with restrained ambiguity about having social contacts outside the Bethany circle:

> Why would I want a friend outside? Just to say I had a friend? But it doesn't bother me because I'm happy with the friends I have here. I'm not desperate for friends. I'm free, I'm happy, I'm OK. But if I had a couple, I wouldn't mind. If I was home more and spent more time there . . . but I'm never home. I don't know them and they don't know me and that's just the way it is. But if I was home more, I'm sure I would.

Claudia would say "amen" to her fellow teacher's observation that, whatever else they may be, Christians are persons living in the world, enduring aches, pains, problems, and squabbles with their mates, somewhat, but not exactly, as non-Christians do. She would wholly endorse the benefits all Christians feel they have: most people want a purpose in life; Christians have one. Most people are worried about death; Christians are saved and anticipate eternal life at God's side. Most people gripe and get mad when authorities compel them to do something; Christians know that this is the behavior of the natural man and that they need not waste effort on such feelings. Most people wonder if they are doing the right thing; Christians in God's will know they are. Most people in distress don't know where to turn for certain solace; Christians always do.

Here are some teacher comments that reveal how different from the world's people BBA's Christians feel:

> I used to have a problem wondering why I couldn't do what other people did. I had that problem until I got my heart straightened out. I finally said, "OK, Lord, I'll do whatever you want me to do."

> I can't do some of the things I got a big kick out of before, because they really aren't a good testimony for the Lord. I loved to dance. Sometimes I feel really good and I hop around a while, but it couldn't be considered dancing.

The whole world is groping for peace. Men are disturbed. Yet for a Christian it's really thrilling to just be able to realize that the whole thing is part of God's plan. We are in warfare because the devil is a roaring lion seeking whom he may devour. Yes, it's warfare and it always will be until the Lord takes us home and we're done with Satan.

Claudia may quietly yearn for a friend outside of Bethany; her fellow teacher may wistfully recall when she used to dance. This is just the natural side of teachers who believe that God has called them to be "peculiar people, zealous of good works" (Titus 2:14).

What Bethany's Teachers Learn about Teaching

Throughout the year, BBA teachers receive in-service instruction from Headmaster McGraw, but also from Pastor Muller and the elementary and secondary school supervisors. The most common form of instruction is the lecture, as it is in the teacher's own classroom. Discussion, apart from the raising of questions, is uncommon. When teachers are instructed about pedagogy, character building, their role as teachers, etc., they listen attentively, their eyes usually on the speaker, exemplifying, thereby, a canon of good teaching much stressed at Bethany: "Be sure the eyes of your student are on you at all time. Control what comes through the eye gate." They often hear what they already know and believe and thus are committed to putting into practice. The idea seems to be that if one gets satiated with good words, either the Lord's or his vicars', then one is more inclined to act upon them.

To listen to what teachers hear on the job in the course of a year is to grasp the basic orientation of conservative Christian churches toward teachers, learners, and schooling, as advocated by the American Association of Christian Schools and its members. Teachers learn, for example, that in relation to students they function as substitute parents throughout the school day. "*In loco parentis*," Art Swanson explains to his students,

> means that while you're here I've got a tremendous responsibility. This comes from Proverbs 4:1–2 where it says, "Hear, ye children, the instruction of a father. . . . For I give you good doctrine." Because of what it says here I can stand here knowing I've brought you the truth!

Teachers are alert to their students' spiritual needs, especially to the needs of the unsaved for whom a special burden is borne. In preclass teachers' meetings, McGraw mentions unsaved students by name—"Rae Dunstan is an openly unsaved senior girl. She's definitely feeling the spiritual pressure. We'll just wait and see what happens"—and asks teachers to include Rae Dunstan in their morning prayers.

If teachers need counsel about how to handle any sort of problem, McGraw asks them where to go: "To your college textbooks or to the Word of God?" McGraw has no doubt about these two alternatives: "We are a Christian school and need to be different," he tells his teachers, just as he has told his students. "When you read the Word of God you'll find that many problems are not problems." Teachers learn that the world's answers are not acceptable. "I have doubts about psychology," says McGraw, "because it is man trying to understand man. I also reject anthropology and sociology because they are man-centered. How can man understand his own ways?"

To verify the applicability of the Bible, McGraw and others who take an instructional role with teachers frequently open their comments with a Bible verse, citing scriptural authority in much the same way that professors of education at one time would have quoted John Dewey. The difference is that McGraw knows his authority possesses un-equivocal, unchanging Truth. Thus he turns to the Bible, mining it for pedagogical principles, assured that it is full of gold. Deuteronomy 6:6–7 tells us, "And these words, which I command thee this day, shall be in thine heart: And thou shalt teach them diligently unto thy children, and shalt talk of them when thou sittest . . . walkest . . . liest down . . . risest up." McGraw interprets these words to mean that the Word of God should permeate every moment of the school: "That's why we use the term 'integrate.'"

Pedagogical principles are also presented without recourse to spiritual verification or any other specific source. Thus, BBA teachers learn about "preventive discipline:" keep things moving crisply, quickly learn the names of kids, call upon kids with wavering attention, and be businesslike and establish a routine. And they learn about grading and its relationship to attendance.

> I like grades [McGraw tells his teachers]. Society puts a great stock on grades. It's a means of measuring progress. We in the Christian school movement believe in failing, but our goal is to help kids to learn. It's hard to fail in the public schools.

Having been informed that their students are like clay, rather than like "hunks of metal," teachers are challenged to shape their character. On the occasion of BBA's annual candy sale, teachers get explicit instructions about the distribution of boxes of candy and the collection of money. They are not to view this candy venture in narrow pecuniary terms. McGraw, consistent in all his pronouncements, explains:

> The key is selling on Saturdays, and the weekend in general, if the Lord gives us good weather. You should ask students every day if anyone has the money for their *whole* case. This will encourage them to sell their whole case. Doing this is a good character trait.

McGraw uses an actual incident, as he might use a Bible verse, as a means both to instruct teachers about a matter that concerns the school, and to show how they ought to think and behave in regard to its particulars. On one occasion, a number of boys, including the son of a local pastor, voluntarily withdrew from school. Anticipating the interest their decision was likely to arouse, McGraw told his teachers:

> I received a letter from Pastor Cripps whose son is leaving school tomorrow. You know people will ask you about this. If you haven't been in the discussions, just say that you don't know the details. Or else tell them to see me and say, "Whatever the school does, I'm behind it." There's an important principle of loyalty involved here on your part.

If it is not principles of character that McGraw and others uphold before teachers, it may be principles of spiritual inspiration: "If the Lord does a job, it'll be done. Challenge seniors with these words. They need to let the Word of their Lord direct their lives now." Or it may be principles of community. More than being informed that Christians are brethren and that they are their brothers' keepers, they learn again and again of their charge to bring Christ to the world of unbelievers, and also of the need to maintain their community of believers. "If the foundations be destroyed, what can the righteous do?" is the question teachers are asked to consider one bright October morning, a day so fine one could almost believe that everyone's foundations were quite in order. The stimuli for this verse are the numerous free books BBA has received, some of them approved and shelved, others disapproved and discarded. These books, seen as typical of the public schools and therefore requiring careful scrutiny, lead McGraw to observe that "we can't depend on the public sector of our society. We need things that relate to our church and our school."

Teachers most often are instructed on matters relating directly to students and their classroom behavior. But in the same way that Bethany construes its umbrella policy to mean that when students enroll at Bethany, they must comply at all times with the pledge they sign, Bethany's leaders believe that there is no limit to the matters on which they can instruct their teachers. Accordingly, teachers are reminded of the proper relationship between husbands and wives, learning that while fulfilling their obligations to Bethany church and school, they should not forget their spouses.

Teachers often hear about humanism, a catch-all term that Bethany-ites use to characterize what the world believes. McGraw presents the "five basic tenets of humanism" as: (1) atheism; (2) immorality; (3) evolution; (4) the belief that man can do anything he wants to do; and (5) ecumenism.

Deep antagonism to humanism is a constant sentiment; other concerns are more topical. Thus, in the course of a year when Jimmy Carter was still in office and the presidential election was several months away, McGraw urged teachers to register: "We're putting on a push through the ministry to register. You can't cast that good, Christian, conservative vote if you don't." And once registered, they were directed, by reference to marked ballots for the local Reagan delegate, to vote in the primary election. A few days later teachers found a statement from Reagan headquarters pinned to the bulletin board in the teachers' room. It listed Reagan delegates and alternates for the state primary election; each name had an X in the box opposite it. No other candidate's campaign literature was ever put in the teachers' room.

When teachers came for their mail during this preelection period, they could learn how to boost Reagan's campaign for the nomination, and they could also sign a petition that McGraw placed on their work table, addressed to the "President of the United States from the National Born Again Task Force." Its text read: "As a Bible-believing Christian I vigorously oppose any effort from the White House or Congress to extend the provisions of the Civil Rights Act to homosexuals . . . "

In this springtime of their apprehension over the outcome of presidential politics, they were animated almost as much by the swirl of activities related to the Equal Rights Amendment. Bethany leaders saw the then-proposed drafting of women as of a piece with the ERA. Both would establish as law what they see as contrary to scriptural injunctions about the nature of women and their relationship to men. "Righteousness exalteth a nation: but sin is a reproach to any people" (Proverbs 14:34) was the text McGraw used in his talk to teachers on the eve of the high school students' trip to the state capital to participate in an anti-ERA rally. In the course of his talk, this exchange took place:

> *McGraw*: We'll get our anti-ERA pins and demonstrate our feelings.
> *Teacher*: A lady called me last night to say the other side will be there at 7:00 A.M. She says Carter's calling all the time to support it.
> *McGraw*: You might pray for this because it violates a Bible principle. It's not a matter of the status of women but of the authority structure.
> *Teacher*: If this goes through, it'll force women to support households and put children in child care.
> *McGraw*: This would be like a Communist country in which the state rears the kids.

These comments occurred midst a general nodding of heads and murmuring of affirmation. Indeed, on matters of consequence both inside and outside the classroom, Bethany's educators are of one mind.

What Bethany's Teachers Think about the Goals of Education

Since Christian schoolteachers deal quite naturally with exalted matters in their daily work, they speak without self-consciousness about spending eternity in heaven or hell and living Christlike lives. They acknowledge feeling special, as persons committed full-time to the Lord's work; they also look and sound like teachers anywhere. For all Christian students are not angelic, and all Christian teachers may not competently control their classes. In weeks when unsolved problems conspire to make Friday seem a month away from Tuesday, any given class can stand out as the school's "bad class." Here, at the end of a morning teachers' meeting, the teachers chatter about such a class:

> Do you have the eighth grade?
> Yes, ma'am.
> I really pray for you.
> Why?
> They're not a piece of cake.
> They're the pits.
> I nearly had a nervous breakdown from them.

Now, don't pick on my babies.
They really need to be prayed for.

In any event, BBA teachers agree that an important goal of their school is the salvation of each student. Accordingly, each August, when new students enter the academy, teachers look for signs that identify the unsaved: their inability to pray, their ignorance of devotions, or their use of inappropriate language (for example, saying "gee" or "gosh"). When they see the signs, they search for the chance to engage the student in conversation to verify their inference and to set forth the plan of salvation. "I have a burden that each student in my classroom be led to the Lord," one teacher says.

We see in the teachers' ruminations about school goals their fundamental accord, albeit expressed in somewhat different language. Salvation is indeed a primary goal for any unsaved students, but once saved, then they are to be induced "to put Christ first in their life." Teachers acknowledge that churches and schools can overemphasize salvation, to the neglect of edifying the saved; this is not the case at Bethany where less than 5 percent of the students are unsaved.

When teachers focus on the academy's major goals, they mention academic development only incidentally. This does not imply that academic success is unimportant, of no account to parents and neglected by teachers, but, undoubtedly, it is of secondary concern to all Bethany teachers. They are not instructed to believe otherwise. Most teachers agree that

> Even though our students may be Christians, they still have to know how to function in the world—to balance their checkbooks, talk to people, spend their money, vote, and drive a car. There's lots of things they have to know, but those are secondary goals.

Several teachers expanded their observations about spiritual goals to include the academic. "It's not separate, you know," explained a teacher. The spiritual dimension "is woven in with everything because all subjects are taught in the light of God's word." For those who teach literature, growing in the Lord and growing in literature are one and the same: "I like to teach all kinds of truths and philosophy and it all pretty much agrees with the Bible. If it doesn't, I just don't teach that part in literature," says an English teacher. BBA does not purge its school of everything that is non-Christian in order to insure that Christian growth

is unimpeded, but, a teacher explains, "if we can control the environment, then we should control it," short of absurdly eliminating everything that is not of Christian origin.

I asked all teachers what they try most to achieve in their classrooms.
Their responses are consistent with their views of BBA's major goals.

> *Bible.* Theoretically, to bring out the glory of God; practi-
> cally, to give kids a broad spectrum of the Word of
> God and to get them interested in studying and under-
> standing it.
>
> *Science.* To develop a Christian mind so that kids see ev-
> erything from God's viewpoint.
>
> *Social studies.* To make sure they are living closer to the
> Lord and to make sure I get my subject across to
> them. This doesn't mean that I preach more than I
> teach, of course.
>
> *Speech and drama.* It's not to put students on the stage
> but to get them to be more effective witnesses for the
> Lord.
>
> *Mathematics.* Spiritual growth, self-discipline, and then
> achievement in subject matter.
>
> *Physical education.* First off, to get their attitudes right
> toward Christ, and then, like my exact work, to get
> them physically fit.
>
> *Typing.* Of course, I want them to learn how to type, but
> above all I want them to be good Christians.
>
> *Band.* I want to instill in kids the character of Christ so
> that when they're playing their horns, it's for the
> Lord. The end result of my teaching should be that
> they give their music to the Lord and they learn to
> give their lives to the Lord.
>
> *English.* After the spiritual, to develop character and re-
> sponsibility and to teach students English.

Clearly, BBA's teachers are the "spiritually born-again people" Pastor
Muller said he looked for to instruct his Christian young people.

Teacher Ideals

In addition to wanting to know what teachers most emphasized in
their classrooms, I wanted to acquire their view of ideal teacher behavior in relationship to students, fellow teachers, administrators, parents, and prayer. Their views, which I solicited as advice to a new BBA
teacher, are expressed below in the form of paraphrased summaries of

what the teachers said. They should be read as the monologue of an experienced teacher talking to a newcomer.

Teacher Behavior with Students

Remember your bond with students: they are born again and so are you. This bond is the central fact governing all our relationship here. The Christian bond means caring and compassion for students beyond what is ordinarily true in public schools. It means wanting students to be the best for the Lord, rather than to be successes in the world's terms. We can address students with the authority of God: "Well, what do you think God would think of your behavior today?" you can ask them. This gets to them because they don't want to hurt his feelings.

Realize that students are still children and that no matter how they behave, they still have their original nature— underneath they are sinners. Treat students like they were your own children; love them that much. In fact, they want to be told that you love them. Love, in this instance, is the sum of being tough, kind, firm, consistent, and loving. If you are not consistent, students will exploit your inconsistencies. As close as you come, you must maintain distance from them to avoid a buddy-buddy relationship. Teachers must be friendly, expecting and getting student respect, but remember, in your classroom you establish a "loving dictatorship." To our role as leaders, students are disciples. So, take command the first day, eat nails for breakfast, learn their names at once, don't tolerate bad behavior. Set high standards and check and recheck to be sure they are operating. Be as willing to discuss spiritual matters as academic matters. Don't teach anything contrary to the Bible. And expect their total loyalty.

As a teacher in this school you have the option to lace your instruction with prayer, Scripture, and, when so moved, preaching. You just don't plain deal with your subject, you deal with student lives. Public schools teach kids how to make a living and we teach them how to live.

Teacher Behavior with Teachers

Be friendly with all teachers, respect all of them, but be careful who you chose as a friend. Seek their advice about teaching and take it. If you have a problem involving another teacher, take your problem to that teacher. Failing that, take your problem to the headmaster. Above all, do not discuss it with third parties, and do not join other teachers in complaints about any school affairs. We work hard. We expect everyone to carry their share of the load. So, do your duty. Because it is easiest to be acquainted with other teachers, teachers may congregate at church and elsewhere. This gives the impression of being cliquish. To avoid this, do not sit only with other teachers at church or have fellowship only with them.

The bond of Christ between us does not create instant friendship with everyone here, but you can say with certainty about any of our teachers who are still strangers to you, "We're aiming our students toward the same purposes." And when you enter this building, your personal life is not left out in the parking lot. You'll find yourself praying for Lee Kruger's father whom you will probably never meet.

Teacher Behavior with Parents

"Co-laborers"—that is how we see parents. While parents, at their best, are allies in the realization of our goals, they remain parents. This means that they may not be objective about their own children. Understand this. Appreciate their right to know what your concerns are; communicate with them as fully as possible. Avoid turning spur-of-the-moment encounters at church into nose-to-nose discussions of their children; such brief occasions are best used to praise the children. Otherwise, talk to parents with grade book in hand so the full picture of their youngster's work is before you. Be open, frank, and honest. Keep things positive, friendly, and to the point. Don't discuss other parents' children or listen to comments about them.

Teacher Behavior with Administrators

Guided by scriptural injunctions about authority, we are to be submissive to our administrators. When we work for somebody, we do things his way. All orders come from the top, administrators have the final authority, and, therefore, teacher obedience is appropriate and expected. Of course, you won't always agree with your leader's policies, but you must accept them with a good attitude. The relationship is reciprocal: if you are obedient, dependable, prompt in your work, and willing to go that extra mile, administrators should be supportive and responsive to your concerns. Don't be afraid to bring any problem to them; above all, don't take your problems with them or the academy outside the academy. They expect your loyalty and you should give it.

The most important thing to know about Mr. McGraw is that he is born again. This sums up a world of understanding that is the basis for a harmonious school. In a public school, teachers grate on each other as they work. Here the Holy Spirit adds the oil and things work smoother.

Griping, however, disrupts a school's harmony; it is strictly prohibited at Bethany. Unsaved persons and carnal Christians gripe. When you gripe, you complain about something nobody can change, or about something legitimately out of order, but to the wrong person. We view griping as a disease. It causes unhappiness, discouragement, and demoralization that spreads from person to person and destroys an organization. So, you should take seriously 1 Corinthians 1:10: "that ye all speak the same thing, and that there be no divisions among you; but that ye be perfectly joined together in the same mind and in the same judgment."

Teachers and Prayer

Energetically and frequently pray about your work: in the morning devotions; at school during the noon break, chapel, or class; while driving a bus; in the evening with your family or while conducting your own evening devotions; on Wednesday and Sunday nights; and before meetings with parents. Prayer always is appropriate. Indeed, by not seeking the Lord's help, you attribute undue power and wisdom to yourself.

If you have students with bad attitudes or who feel they are being persecuted, seek help through prayer. If you lose your temper and your students' attention, ask the Lord for control and creativity. If you feel pushed by a group of unruly students and feel unwanted emotions, pray for love: "Lord, just give me love for some of these students who are not cooperating because it's hard in my own human nature, my own nature of the old man, to love them. So, Lord, change my heart."

Under ideal circumstances, the spiritual man is in control, but it is a constant battle. Thus, pray for help to live consistent with scriptural standards so your testimony is a model for students. You will not be alone. Our coaches pray so their motives for teaching remain pure, undefiled by the attractions of plaques, trophies, and first-place honors that detract from glorifying God; and our music teachers pray so the music they select will glorify God.

Right in the midst of a lesson you can see furrowed student foreheads that indicate unclear teacher explanations and an occasion for prayer. You've explained something three times and the furrows still refuse to disappear. So you close your eyes and say, "OK, Lord, I've been doing it on my own strength and not getting anywhere. Now you've got to help me do this." And in the midst of a student fight, put the altercation in a spiritual context by means of prayer: "Boys," you can tell them, "we've got a problem. Let's just ask the Lord to be with us while we talk about it." If you pray first, it will help everybody tell the truth better.

Contrasts with Public Schools

BBA teachers are aware of public schools from their personal experience and their in-service instruction. They feel negatively toward them, believing they not only are different from Christian schools, but deficient and worse. Thus, when teachers characterize the public school they also depict a notion of the good school—their own.

Bethany's teachers, without exception, feel that it is easier to teach in a Christian school because they can maintain their normal social elations, uncomplicated by the type of joking and personal encounters found in a worldly setting. In support of his preference for Christian schools, a teacher recalls his own public school days: "In my health class we'd hear about the dangers of drugs, and then we'd turn around and go into a sociology class where there was a guy who talked about the wonderful experience he had on drugs."

The only advantages Bethany teachers attribute to the public schools result from the latter's greater size and financial resources, advantages which Bethany teachers refuse to accept as enduring. They concede their limitations regarding equipment, library books, instructional materials, and the number of courses and extracurricular activities they offer students. These limitations, they feel, do not make them inferior to any public school. The public school's material advantages are overshadowed by their comparatively poor discipline, social problems, undedicated teachers, and indifferent parents, and also by their inability to develop character and to teach the truth. Here is one teacher's summation of the Academy's advantageous position:

> The Bible says, "Love not the world, neither the things that are in the world. If any man love the world, the love of the Father is not in him" [1 John 2:15]. Public school kids love the world. They are allowed to drink, have sex, and take drugs, but here we teach kids to shun that. That's why there are so many activities on Friday and Saturday night. Pastor Burt gets them together, gets them in the Word, but having fun, you know. How could the Christian school not be superior when teachers are free to shout the Word of God and say, "This is Truth"?

By being able to teach the truth, teachers feel they have freedom, in the way that servants of God can and servants of humanism can not. In one way or another this point is expressed again and again: "I teach the Lord is the truth. If I could not give out the truth, I would not teach."

In contrast with the public school's heterogeneous environment, Bethany's students interact almost exclusively with students and adults who are born-again Christians. Mindful that conditions at BBA differ significantly from those in the world, teachers revel in the differences. Without exception, they agree that the academy shelters its students— educating them "in a hothouse" is the expression they use—and, as a result, believe that students will have an easier time when they are required to face the world.

The hothouse, they say, is essential for the proper nurturance of their still tender students; ideally this special nurturance will extend over sixteen years to include a Christian college experience. They offer a botanical analogy. Students are like young plants. If they are prematurely exposed to the natural elements of wind and rain and sun, they may perish. Better to bring them along slowly, in a carefully controlled environment, so they become strong enough to withstand the impact of the world's uncontrolled environment.

Bethanyites are certain that worldliness predominates in the public schools, and that peer pressure to forgo Christian standards is enormous. Thus, to place a Christian child in a public school is to dare him "to beat the odds," to leave him insufficiently armed with God's Word to fend off the unrighteous: "A kid is a kid. He's got to learn to be an adult. One way or another it's brainwashing, or call it brain cultivating. They [public schools] teach Communist values and we teach respectability." The public school is too uncontrolled; some teachers see a Christian boarding high school as too controlled. All believe the Christian day school is just right, because students are free to learn about the world from their contact through television, jobs, and shopping. At the same time, they are sufficiently divorced from the world to resist its temptations, at that stage in their lives when their resources to withstand temptations are not yet fully developed. "Sheltered" is a pejorative designation. What outsiders label as sheltered, Bethany calls being properly solicitous: "After all, you don't send unseasoned troops to fight in the front lines."

Costs and Benefits of Teaching in a Christian School

I never saw reason to doubt that Bethany's teachers believed the Lord called them to be teachers and that being a teacher at the academy was indeed a full-time undertaking. I thought they were strikingly uncomplaining about Bethany's extensive claims upon their time and energy, particularly in light of their low salaries. Teachers gave me this impression in the course of discussing their weekly round of activities. They responded more negatively, albeit always in muted terms, when I asked what they liked least about teaching and what, if anything, they think they lose by being Christian school teachers. Their displeasure centered on lesson preparations, grading papers and tests, and, in general, on the time involved in being a teacher. Other concerns referred to the job's energy drain and the disappointment felt when one invests so much effort and it takes so long to see the fruits of one's labor. Several concerns emerged from the school's Christian orientation. On occasion, they felt their work was weakened by parents who "didn't appreciate what Christian discipline means," and by students who did not appreciate the school's performance standards: "The thing I like least about teaching is when I sense in kids that they're not giving God their best." One teacher chafed at Bethany's expectation that teachers be perfect in behavior to an extent not demanded of other persons associated with the church.

Finally, most teachers feel that their major loss from teaching is "in material things." At the time teachers were interviewed (1980), the base salary was $5,900. Increments had been awarded over the previous four years at the rate of $200 per year, and the next year's across-the-board increase was 10 percent. Married men receive a special annual supplement of $1,000; married women receive none. Single teachers get a supplement of $600. Teachers, accordingly, refer to their financial sacrifice, to not making a living wage.[4] They speak of their summer jobs as the Lord's way of taking care of their needs. In a teaching family where both husband and wife held summer jobs, one of them remarked with a candor that exposed the ambiguity of his position:

Hey, this is fun to have money, to not go with your check from the school office to the bank and not having anything left over. I've given up things, but, in reality, they were nothing to give up. These things are going to decay. Being in God's will, I've got far better. I'd be scared not to be in God's will.

The closest a teacher came to unqualified complaint about money was one who said, "I don't live to make money, but a teacher has to live, too."

Overall, teachers spoke minimally about the costs or sacrifice their job entailed, perhaps because a calling is not really a job. They accepted their personal material disadvantages—trusting that their Lord never fails those who trust in him—and spoke much more effusively about the rewards of teaching, as if to say, "If you ask me what I lose by being a Christian teacher, I'll tell you, but I don't think it's a big deal. And you shouldn't think so either." They identified rewards primarily in the spiritual realm,[5] fully in keeping with what they wanted most to achieve as teachers. What pleased them most was seeing their students grow in their Christian life, taking an "interest in the right things," rather than wasting their time "by sacrificing the permanent on the altar of the immediate." (This quotation, cited as the words of Bob Jones, is indicative of the pervasive influence Bob Jones University has on BBA.) They described their joy when students decide they want to be saved, attend a Christian college, or surrender their lives for full-time service, and they expressed their special satisfaction at seeing a child who entered the academy in a rebellious spirit leave it intending to be a missionary.

Very few teachers referred without probing to rewards from their academic teaching. When they did speak of these rewards, it was in the language of teachers who care about their subject matter.

It really tickles me to death to see a kid get interested in science and want to learn more.

What a satisfaction to see the look on a child's face when you've been explaining something and suddenly it all fits into place and he goes, "Ohh."

In my gymnastics class I see them start out afraid even to jump up and grab the bars. Eventually I see them able to perform gracefully. I like to see them grow.

This sampling of observations should suffice to indicate that

Bethany's teachers, though fully devoted to their spiritual commitments, can still sound like schoolteachers anywhere in the United
States. Yet there is no doubt where their hearts are. Some teachers, even
when discussing the rewards of their academic endeavors, included the
spiritual in a way that further verifies its pervasiveness at Bethany.
Academic activities always are perceived in a spiritual context, as instrumental to the fulfillment of spiritual ends and never as ends in
themselves. Thus, when the history teacher reflects on his work, he
says that his students may not be able to grasp all that he teaches about
history, but "if something in my teaching changes students' lives for the
better spiritually, that's the reward." And when the band teacher
expands on the joy of seeing students master an instrument which
previously they had never even touched, his face glows, but for a reason
reflecting BBA's special mission: "I really enjoy seeing a kid learn to play
the flute and start to play hymns, and then want more and more hymns
to take home and play."

After months of interviewing BBA teachers and observing them at
work, I was persuaded that they were overwhelmingly content with
their choice of teaching in a Christian school, and that they felt special in
the way that one must who believes that God has called him to perform
a certain job. I was not persuaded to the contrary when I heard teachers
discuss their displeasure with teaching or when I gave them a magic
wand and invited them to change anything they wanted about the
academy. Their responses rang true with almost everything they had
said before. No teacher asked for more money or for less pressure on
their time. I believe they would accept more money and a less busy life.
However, since current financial constraints and time pressures emerge
out of the unavoidable realities of life at Bethany, remedying their
unwanted outcomes escaped inclusion on everyone's wish list. What
teachers did want was in the realm of professional materials—more
books, more equipment, more instructional materials,[6] the only things
they had mentioned as the points favoring the public school.

The teachers are at BBA and remain there because of their calling to
serve the Lord in a Christian educational institution, not because of
their inability to acquire work elsewhere. Three of the twelve high
school teachers had taught in public schools; they left for various
reasons, none of them related to their competency as teachers. I saw no
evidence that they could not have continued their employment in
public schools, and none to indicate that most of their colleagues could
not be competitive for jobs there either. Any doubt about the authenticity of their calling is dispelled by their acceptance of appalling salaries

and extraordinary demands on their time and energy. Parents rightfully feel secure about Bethany's teachers, whose correct behavior is built into the teachers' and the institution's definition of their role. For better or for worse, teachers are content with their jobs, their school, their church, and their lives. They immodestly perceive Christian schools as necessary for the survival of our country. In the words of one teacher, "To me, as a Christian, they're the hope of America."

4

The Structure of Control Until the Love of Christ Constraineth

> Of course, we believe in the inherent sinfulness of man. One of the reasons we are strong on discipline is because we feel it's needed.
>
> AACS Official

> We cannot always be there to tell students what to look at and what not to look at, or what to listen to. But we address values and principles, especially scriptural teachings that will affect them wherever they are and whatever they are doing.
>
> AACS Official

Introduction

Eighteen-year-old BBA senior Mike Dunlop awakes each weekday morning at 6:45 to shower, shave, and eat his breakfast after first reciting a silent prayer. Then he settles down for fifteen minutes of reading in his Bible; this morning he completes several chapters in Romans, part of his systematic progression through the New Testament. For company during his twenty-minute drive to school, he turns on the radio, changing stations until he finds one playing the more acceptable "easy listening" tunes that do not have the hard, hip-swinging beat of rock. When he reaches BBA's parking lot, he slows down to the required five miles per hour, parks his car, and walks directly to the lunchroom. He knows it is forbidden to go to his locker or to the restroom without a pass from the duty teacher. Mike has twenty-five minutes, from 8:00 to 8:25, to buy candy at the senior-run snack shack, to meet friends and make plans for the day or the weekend, and to talk to his girl friend during one of the few times of the day BBA allows boy-girl talk.

Teacher Norma Newhurst begins her day much like Mike Dunlop, but school rules require her to arrive at 7:55 a.m. Since she has lunchroom duty this morning, she misses the daily faculty meeting. As a duty monitor, she checks the hallway by the lunchroom entrance and outside the locker rooms to be sure students do not congregate in the hall, and she maintains decorum in the lunchroom even, if necessary, by handing out demerits. At 8:25, a bell rings to inform Mike that he can go to his locker and Mrs. Newhurst that she must proceed to her homeroom.

Thus we see that BBA's structure of control begins at the onset of each school day. Bible reading in the morning is recommended so that the Word of God is fresh in mind to direct the day's activities, but the academy does not mandate it. Mike and his fellow students know that what their school does mandate is their appropriate response to an elaborate structure of control. Such structures are not sinister; they are not unique to Christian schools. What may be unique are the particular means a group uses to establish its control and the particular behaviors the group intends to control. At BBA, the broad reach of its structure to well beyond school hours and school site is most assuredly unique.

BBA's structure of control is well-developed, perfectly congruent with its Christian foundation, and, unsurprisingly, taken very seriously. How could it be otherwise? If we are born with a burden of sin and inhabit a world replete with temptations, and if, moreover, we are still youths and therefore relative newcomers to Christ, then we must be controlled. As must our teachers and parents, for even mature Christians are apt to backslide. Though BBA emphatically directs its structure of control at students, students clearly are meant to join their seniors as allies in the promotion and perpetuation of their own control. Youths though they may be, Christian youths ideally join their elders in the enterprise of establishing order and thus moderate the we-they polarity that typically exists in American society between adolescents and adults. There is only one "game" going at BBA; no other is sanctioned. Everyone is asked to play; no one need be left out. It is the game of becoming and being Christian.

If the BBA collectivity unites many persons of different statuses, BBA makes clear that the status of Christian is preeminent. Indeed, it is the prefix to all other statuses—Christian son, Christian mother, Christian teacher, Christian wife—and thereby unites everyone in a shared enterprise. Distinctions that otherwise differentiate person from person, Bethany means to set aside in favor of the one that joins together all believers, at the same time that their beliefs (at once, both inclusive and exclusive) set them apart from all nonbelievers. Achieved and ascribed qualities are of consequence insofar as they have bearing on a person's conduct as a Christian. Thus, being of an old, established family has consequence only if the family's commitment to Christ is old and established, not its money or its lineage. This is the ideal. Though all Christians are brethren and can expect equally unhindered access to heaven, a hierarchy results from the scriptural injunction to respond correctly to those with authority over you. Obedience, consequently, governs relationships in a Christian social order; it is the key to establishing and maintaining BBA's structure of control.

Before continuing with the particulars of obedience and of the structure of control at BBA, I will consider the terms themselves, as well as several others which commonly are used to describe various aspects of organizations.

Structure refers to the arrangement of elements in a system. BBA's structure of control encompasses the behavior of parents, students, teachers, and other Bethany employees. Control implies regulations (the contents of control), regulators (the makers and exercisers of control), scope (who is controlled and to what extent), and order (the outcome of control). Regarding outcomes, a school can emphasize those aspects that relate to affect, character, and spirituality, or those aspects that relate to skills and knowledge. We may call these two aspects, respectively, the expressive order and the instrumental order (see Bernstein 1975:38).

Although no school ever confines itself either to expressive or to instrumental order, it may favor one over the other. At BBA, the expressive dimension prevails, and the order which results from its structure of control is designed primarily, albeit not exclusively, to promote Christian conduct and character. This is reflected in the operations of the regulators in their emphasis on normative, rather than coercive and remunerative means to effect control (see Etzioni 1961). "Normative power rests on the manipulation of symbolic rewards" (Shipman 1968:102), and BBA has powerful symbols to manipulate in the praise, prestige, and honor they can offer those who mean to have their life exemplify the life of Jesus Christ.

Reasonably clear evidence that the expressive and instrumental orders exist and that the former predominates at BBA is seen in table 1. (see Tables section following Notes). For each of the five activities selected I asked students to indicate the extent to which their school *does* emphasize it and the extent to which it *should* emphasize it.

From the more than 50 percent of BBA students who agree that their school prepares them for postschool jobs, everyday life, and intellectual development, we can verify that the school has an instrumental order. The prominence of its expressive order, however, is clear in the large gap between the 54 to 65 percent who say BBA emphasizes the three instrumental areas and the 84 to 93 percent who say BBA emphasizes character and spiritual development. It also is clear in the large difference between the 84 percent at BBA and the 39 percent at Hartney High who say their school emphasizes character development. The discrepancy between the "does" and the "should" percentages across the five activities demonstrates that students at each school prefer a different emphasis from that which now prevails. BBA students get as much as (or more than) they want of character development; their judgment of an excessive emphasis on the spiritual side perhaps reflects their sense of being overwhelmed by socializing efforts directed toward spiritual development. I doubt that it reflects any devaluing of spirituality.

McGraw's administrative decisions further verify the priority BBA gives to its expressive order. One year the school's basketball team was second in nationwide Christian school competition; the next year four returning players quit school. McGraw made no effort to keep them in school, and when one of the players returned he was put on probation for several weeks to be certain that his general conduct warranted his rejoining the team. BBA's basketball team lost every game the year its star players left school.

Pastor Gerald Carlson, an official of the American Association of Christian Schools, states concusively that in the association's member schools "teaching methods, teaching personnel, administrative personnel, and operating policies are all to be permeated by the person of Jesus Christ." Given this commitment, BBA logically extends its structure of control to teachers and parents. Since the primary target of control is the students, the structure determines what they study, the textbooks they use, and what books the library makes available. In addition, it manages the selection of student leaders, defines acceptable social relationships, and controls personal movement both during and after school. Because after-school conduct is not readily controlled, the school makes a concerted effort to inculcate principles that if internalized will lead to proper behavior in these domains.

A critical aspect of BBA's control structure is its scope, that is, McGraw's "umbrella policy" of twenty-four-hour concern for his students' behavior. He justifies the school's broad outreach in a straightforward way:

> I think the policing never stops. I have a definite obligation to try and prevent a problem. So if I get wind of a party, I call in the ring leaders and that squelches the party right there. On one occasion, Pastor Burt [Bethany's youth pastor] and I went over to a house; you know, just dropped in. And on another occasion, the party was out of town. Russ Warren and I drove up. We didn't make any big deal—just the fact that we were there, the party was over. I've done that a number of times. It's almost standard operating procedure. If the kids thought nobody cared what they did over the weekend, we'd lose all our credibility. It's the same thing during the summer. I've disciplined students for smoking at work and going to the movies. If the matter is ultra, ultra serious, like drinking and drugs, I won't take them back in the fall. Our policy is like a fence that keeps a poor cow from falling over a cliff. The fence has to be there. Paul said, "the love of Christ constraineth me." The rules at Bethany Baptist Academy have to be there until the love of Christ takes over.

Meanwhile, BBA's structure of control is designed to insure that students experience only desirable behavior, belief, and knowledge. It is God's plan that Christian parents and educators instruct and that students obey. Students do not have to like or to understand what they are instructed to do, but to receive God's blessings, they must obey. "A bad spirit, a critical spirit," Pastor Hill tells students at chapel, "that is pagan. If you want to live like a pagan, you should be at public school. But then you won't have the Lord on your side."

The Control of Parents

Even if each BBA parent was a faithful and spiritual born-again Christian, they would still need to know about the essential elements of the school's procedures and expectations. But since this is not the case, BBA makes emphatically explicit its structure of control. This process of communication begins when parents first meet Headmaster McGraw and he explains Bethany's philosophy and presents some details of student life in a Christian school. It continues as parents learn that they must sign a "Pledge of Acceptance" as a condition for their child's enrollment.

The parents' pledge contains twelve points, including support for the school's policy of student obedience; acceptance of the school's regulations, disciplinary procedures, and student dress code; and provision of moral and financial support (see appendix E). The *BBA Handbook* contains a reminder of their role as Christian school parents. Though meant primarily for students, the *Handbook*'s opening pages contain a letter addressed "Dear Parent" from Headmaster McGraw. He welcomes them to the BBA family and reminds them, through Deuteronomy 6:6–7, of their obligation to teach their children about the Lord and his commandments. In fact, however, this expectation is more wish than reality. When parents "pledge that our child will bring to the school a heritage of Christian culture," they often are promising more than they can or will deliver, and more than the school will hold them to. Otherwise, the *Handbook* contains scattered references to parents: that they "call the school office the day their child is absent," that they never make an out-of-school appointment that conflicts with chapel sessions, and that they enforce the use of "sir" and "ma'am" at home.

Unsurprisingly, McGraw does not consider parental signing of their pledge a pro forma act. When necessary, he reminds parents of what they have agreed to—corporal punishment for their child, no disparaging talk about the school, etc. The pledge provides him leverage, as he recalls in an incident with a father who believed his child's teacher lied both to him and to his child:

> I said, "George, you've signed a pledge to cooperate with us. Your choice is simple—either drop the matter or remove your son from school." Monday morning he came by and withdrew his kid. That's how it is. If parents can't persuade us otherwise, they either accept our view or remove their child. We understand that when parents send a check to us each month they feel that they're buying a service. This makes them think they can criticize us, just like they would poor service at Kroger's. In the parent pledge we're saying we're not just another service. There's a spiritual aspect to our work and we've got to have parental cooperation.

To the extent that parents, students, teachers, and BBA employees grasp the meaning and implications of the academy's "spiritual aspect," to that extent they are able to respond to the various demands of their status as Christians and contribute to the development and perpetuation of the school's structure of control. In addition to the admission interview, the pledge, and the BBA *Handbook*, parents are further informed of their role as Christian school parents during parent-teacher fellowship meetings at school, occasionally at church, in sermons Pastor Muller delivers, and from memos McGraw sends home. Whenever possible, McGraw arranges an evening visit with parents, especially with those who belong to no church, fundamentalist or otherwise. These visits serve several purposes: to get acquainted, to clarify BBA's mission, to reconnect persons who seem estranged from the school, and to win souls. If parents doubt their inclusion in BBA's expressive order, they are reassured by their invitation (when their children are seniors) to attend the junior-senior banquet, and most parents do in fact accept the invitation. "I guess it's part of our philosophy," McGraw explains, "that we think parents are an important part of the whole school thing. And we don't think our kids should have anything to hide from their parents." What is a purely social, adolescent-centered event at public schools is typically a social-spiritual occasion at Christian schools. When and where Bethany's Christians congregate, God is never absent.

Headmaster McGraw's view of the operation of his school is the decisive element in Bethany's structure of control as it pertains to parents. Supported by Pastor Muller, it is the prevailing view:

> Parents tend to look at things very parochially, from the standpoint of their family and their kids. And that's just not the way you should run a school. I wouldn't be in a board-run school or in a parent-controlled school. In our type of school, you have to have standards and you have to have direction to be effective. These things don't lend themselves to parent control. At Bob Jones, for example, one of their secrets is that the input of parents stops when they decide to send their child there. That's it.

Though McGraw and Muller readily concede the primacy of parent responsibility for their children's education, they see no place for parents in determining the nature and operation of their children's Christian school. Parents pay their money and take what they get—a matter of principle and policy at BBA.

The Control of Teachers

A school at which the expressive order predominates could not be unconcerned about its teachers' contribution to this domain. McGraw tries to insure this in his teacher selection procedure:

We hire for philosophy. The kids who come out of Christian
colleges—they understand authority and how it works.
They're not student protesters; they're not going to tell us
how to run the place. A Christian school is not geared to that
sort of structure.

McGraw hires no one who cannot attest to Christian status by signing the employee's contractual agreement, which reads:

I affirm that I am a born-again Christian believing the Bible
to be the inspired Word of God without contradiction or
error in its original languages. I believe that every Christian
should be separated from worldly habits.

This is the first item in the teacher's contract. It continues with items on
insurance, sick leave, personal leave, maternity, and vacation (see
appendix F).

If one becomes a born-again Christian one remains a fallible human
being, subject to lapses of behavior. Thus there is a structure of control
to facilitate and insure that teacher conduct approximates the Bethany
ideal. The elements of control briefly set forth in the teacher contract are
significantly elaborated in the teacher handbook. It discusses matters
which teachers everywhere must master, such as how to deal with
supplies, homework, reports, records, and fire-drill instructions. It
directs their attention to student regulations which teachers must enforce—for example, hall rules which forbid couples from loitering,
"young ladies" from standing outside locker rooms, and locker doors
from being banged. "Any disobedience or disrespect," the handbook
says, "should be reported on a demerit slip."

The teacher handbook begins with a letter Headmaster McGraw
addresses to his colleagues:

We are engaged together in an important ministry. God has
allowed us the privilege of snatching precious young people
from Satan's clutches. Let us make the most of each day by
being "prayed-up," "planned-up" and "practiced-up."

It continues with a five-point Code of Conduct which reiterates the
stipulations of the teacher contract and adds that a teacher is expected
"to be above reproach in the area of the use of the tongue," "to look on
his position as a calling of God," and "to be examples of the believer."
(See appendixes G and H for further elaboration of the teacher's role
and duties.)

McGraw reinforces the directives for teacher conduct during the daily 8:00 A.M. teacher meetings.

> Wisdom comes only from God, but you can obtain knowledge in many ways. Knowledge changes, for example, about computers and science, but wisdom does not change. Wisdom is higher than knowledge because it comes directly from God. Real principles are related to wisdom and that is why in our classes we must emphasize principles. Man's basic nature and needs never change and that is what wisdom and principles are all about.

Upon finishing he looked around the room to see if there was any other business. One teacher said that a parent asked her if we still insist on "yes, ma'am" and "yes, sir." McGraw responded, "If a child is not doing this, it shows a little bit of rebellion." Shortly after this meeting McGraw pinned this statement on the teachers' room bulletin board: "'Proverbs 2:6—For the Lord giveth wisdom: out of his mouth cometh knowledge and understanding!' Insist on Yes and No, sir, at all times."

In addition, Pastor Muller and Headmaster McGraw characterize proper teacher conduct at occasional teacher meetings, and most particularly at the preterm, in-service week BBA holds each fall. McGraw addresses his teachers on a hot late-August morning, reminding them of what they already know. He reads to them directly from their contract and concludes with a declaration that undoubtedly is routine to his teachers. "Church activities take precedence over all school and personal activities." To be sure, this unqualified dictum overstates the case—when a teacher's young child is ill, she will, with impunity, stay home from school. And when Pastor Muller asks for volunteers to complete the roof on the new bus shed, male teachers can, with impunity, refuse to volunteer. As an intent, however, it unequivocally establishes priorities for teacher behavior and creates the sense of their membership in a religious order, almost like that of monks and nuns who surrender their lives to the Lord and put themselves full-time in his service. This is an extraordinary commitment!

If, for whatever reason, a teacher's behavior is unsatisfactory, McGraw will try to improve it; Pastor Muller may join the effort. On failing to improve the teacher may be dismissed. This is a relatively simple matter because Christian school teachers do not have tenure. Due process is acknowledged, but since it is not stated in their contract, teachers have no recourse within the system other than reason.[1] Dismissal is the ultimate penalty to control teachers, as it is in the case of parents and their school children. Teacher dismissal is uncommon. The primary reward which operates in the control structure to reinforce proper conduct derives from doing what the Lord wants one to do. "We are here for Christ," says Bible teacher Art Swanson. At best, monetary rewards are modest, but BBA teachers may get the same intangible reinforcers as do their public school counterparts—the praise, gratitude, and respect of pleased students and parents.

The Control of Students

Like a mime pretending to be inside a bottle, BBA students can reach out in all directions and imagine that they are surrounded by their school's structure of control. With the priority given its role of developing Christian character and the assumptions it holds about man's sinful nature, BBA attends above all to managing student behavior.

The Student Pledge, etc.

The elements of control are embodied in several documents and in procedures that have become routine, though not yet written down. The Student Pledge is the basic document (see appendix I). In it BBA communicates its standards of conduct, particularly regarding its doctrine of separation. Indeed, six of the pledge's ten points refer to separation, the born-again Christians' way of saying that their lives must be both different and apart from that of worldly persons. Specifically, BBA's students are required to be separate in terms of (1) whom they count as friends, (2) how they dress, (3) where they go, (4) what they do, (5) what they see and hear, and (6) what they say. In learning to serve God, students are taught that nothing of consequence remains outside BBA's purview.

Two more of the pledge's ten points refer to obedience to parents and teachers, on the one hand, and to the school's rules, on the other. The remaining two points require students to respect school property and to "witness as a Christian by looking, acting and talking like a true Christian." This latter point runs afoul of the realities of some students who are not Christians in Bethany's terms. These few students graduate from BBA still members of a nonfundamentalist church. They manage to adjust to BBA's expectations without subscribing to the school's doctrine.

Being separate not only dominates most of the Student Pledge, it also runs as a theme through BBA's entire instructional effort. Students are enjoined to learn what elements and attributes assemble on either side of the gulf of separation. Lined up behind Christ and Satan, respectively, are Christian society and the world; brethren and outsiders; security and risk; light and darkness; goodness and evil; and purity and impurity. Polarities abound, ad infinitum. Specifically, students are directed not to drink, smoke, take drugs, gamble, dance, go to movie theaters, swear, listen to popular music, lie, or be immoral. If "shalt nots" dominate the pledge, students nonetheless have countless occasions on which to learn what they "shalt." BBA wants its students to be distinctive young persons attending a distinctive school.

Student dress and grooming get careful scrutiny in the Student Pledge, the *BBA Handbook*, and the dress code. Modesty and propriety are guiding principles. In practice this means no blue jeans, shorts, T-shirts, or sandals for either sex on any school occasion. Boys can wear trousers of corduroy or other materials; their shirts must have a collar and be tucked in. Their hair, a matter of continuous attention, must be off the forehead and above the ears and the collar. Male athletes must wear suits and ties on the day of an interschool athletic event. High school girls wear stockings or panty hose; their skirts or dresses must reach at least to the top of the knee. Long-slitted garments and low-cut necklines are strictly forbidden. Their physical education outfit is knee-length culottes and a blouse with short sleeves. "By God's grace," says the *BBA Handbook*, "may our appearance always be pleasing to Him." And what the consequences are if one is not "pleasing to Him" McGraw clarifies in a talk he gave in chapel one morning:

> You girls, we insist on modesty. We usually send a girl whose clothing is questionable up to one of our lady faculty members, and if the dress can be corrected, fine. If not, we'll say, "Sorry, you can't wear that outfit to school anymore." So when you buy clothes, girls, try to buy them to fit our Christian standards.

The *Handbook* is a catalog of school rules and regulations (see Appendix J). It mostly covers the same territory as any public school handbook (for example, absenteeism, detentions, field trips, parking, lost and found, insurance, and tardiness) and in much the same language. Here and there, however, BBA requires behavior that marks its distinction from "man-centered" institutions. Its sections on respect for authority, dress and grooming, restrictions on personal contact—"Couples (any boy and girl) are not allowed to walk together."—illustrate this distinction.

73609

Student Leaders

Student leadership at BBA deserves elaboration. The designation "leader" includes class officers—president, vice-president, secretary, and chaplain—and cheerleaders, but not athletes. Although the *Handbook* simply states that leaders should "exemplify Christ and the standards set forth in the Word of God" and sign a leadership pledge (see appendix K), they also must have the right skills for the office in question, at least a C average, with no Fs in major courses, and a reputation for spirituality and for faithfulness in attending church services and activities.

A final qualification for officer eligibility is participation in the annual summer youth trip Bethany Baptist Church sponsors and its youth pastor organizes. Church and school conceive this two-week trip as an occasion for spiritual growth. To McGraw, the burden of proof is upon a student to establish why, if he means to be a leader in a Christian school, he does not join the trip, in the same way he would have to explain why he does not participate regularly in Bethany's year-round organized youth activities.

A two-step system operates in selecting class officers. First, BBA staff identify a panel of "acceptable" students for each office, and then BBA students vote for the candidate of their choice from this panel. "This way," explains McGraw, "we have strong input and control. We nominate a kid and he is always a winner." Five persons help identify the nominees—McGraw, the assistant headmaster, the high school supervisor, the elementary school supervisor, and the youth pastor.[2] Only students who have attended BBA for at least one year can be nominated. The nominators scrutinize the list of eligible students several times before they pick a final slate. If they decide that suitable candidates are not available, they will make alternative arrangements. For example, one year grades ten and eleven combined to elect one set of officers because the nominators thought the eleventh grade had a dearth of leaders. Another year, they judged no twelfth-grade male student worthy of the office of chaplain;[3] the Bible teacher served as chaplain that year. The belief of Independent Baptist churches that Scripture precludes women from holding any position of leadership over men limits the number of class-officer candidates. Female students are eligible only for the positions of vice-president and secretary, never for president or chaplain.

As with all BBA policies, Headmaster McGraw feels his faculty-nomination policy rests firmly on scriptural ground. Having been a student and teacher in public schools, he knows at first hand our national custom of giving students the opportunity to nominate and to elect their own officers. Consistent with BBA's view of control, students are denied the opportunity "to make a mistake" in a matter as central to the life of the school as student leadership. If a school means to determine what students learn, believe, value, do, etc., it must control its students' peer leaders, who stand beside teachers as sound Christian models. "We want leaders who really are with the school philosophically," says McGraw. "From a testimony standpoint they are as consistent as teenage kids can be."

Once elected, officers must sign a leadership pledge and remain as good as they were perceived to be to get nominated in the first place. They must attest weekly to their faithfulness by submitting to high school supervisor Art Swanson a check-off form that indicates which of the following required activities they did or did not attend: Sunday morning, Sunday evening, and Wednesday evening services; Sunday school; Sunday evening youth chapel and youth sing; Thursday night visitation (calling on teenagers to encourage them to come to church, attend youth activities, get saved, etc.); and the Friday or Saturday night youth activities, which are combined spiritual and recreational occasions. The net result of leader participation in all these activities, as well as other school events, is that BBA effectively controls most of their after-school time.

Cheerleaders (but not athletes) are considered leaders because cheerleaders, like class officers, appear before the student body and the public all year long. Cheerleaders must meet all the requirements set for class officers, in addition to being proficient in the activities of cheerleading and having a pleasing physical appearance. BBA educators are ambivalent about the exclusion of athletes from the leadership category. Some are prepared to include them; others, including McGraw, feel the requirements of leadership are too stringent to apply now when the school is so small that there is not much of a selectivity factor operating in the choice of student athletes. Most boys participate in athletics; if they did not, BBA's athletic program could not exist. For the moment, athletes are required only to maintain a C average and attend Sunday morning service.

BBA's commitment to its expressive order is unequivocally clear in its cheerleader and class-officer selection procedures. Even in the Academic Tournament, a nationwide competition involving academic, musical, and oratorical events sponsored by the American Association of Christian Schools, participants must demonstrate more than the technical skill required by the event. Doris Lowe, the teacher who works most closely with students aspiring to compete in the Academic Tournament says:

> I think of one girl who wanted to sing a spiritual song for her solo. It would be very hypocritical to bestow this honor on somebody who did not live up to the rules of our school because first of all we are trying to promote spirituality.

With this attention to detail, the academy strives to insure that all students in the public eye are worthy Christian models. By controlling who becomes its student stars, BBA extends its control over all student behavior.

Student Peers

The peer group supporting school standards at BBA includes far more than the student stars. All BBA students are subject to strong scriptural motivation to Christian behavior, ranging from accepting the role of their brother's keeper to maintaining their testimony so they can reach non-Christians and avoid being a stumbling block to other young Christians. Girl friends influence boy friends; friends intervene in the lives of friends; classmates warn and shush wrongdoers; and anyone witnessing serious student misdeeds (cheating, for example) may report them to the authorities. What public school students call tattling, Christian school students are taught to construe otherwise. An AACS publication sent to all member schools clarified (citing Matthew, 1 Timothy, and Galatians) that "The Bible nowhere condemns the bringing of information about evil to one who is in a position of God-given authority" (Britt n.d.:1). Moreover, the Christian has a duty to "restore other believers who have fallen." It follows directly from these beliefs that if students know of student misdeeds, they should advise the wrongdoers to report themselves; if the offenders fail to do so, they should then expect to be reported by other students. Behavior scorned at other schools is upheld as the norm at BBA.

BBA believes that goodness is its own reward. Nonetheless, it rewards its virtuous students: deeming them fit to be leaders and eligible to compete in state and national tournaments; trusting and making allowances for them in the way teachers do for such students at any type of school; and bestowing awards upon them—Christian Example, School Spirit, School Citizenship—at a schoolwide assembly to which parents are invited.

Parents

Parents are more than passive recipients of missives from BBA, and more than members of the audience at school events. The approximately 70 percent of the parents who are members of Bethany Baptist Church do not need a pledge to know how a Christian should construe the school rules, obedience, and BBA's mission. These parents establish structures of control which are likely to be in harmony with Bethany's values, and they support Bethany's efforts to shape the lives of their children. Children have an easier time at school when there are no major discrepancies between home and school in matters of control. They can more readily observe the school's prohibition of rock music and salacious TV movies when their parents also accept the prohibition and, more than this, grasp its rationale.

Chapel

BBA has many parental allies to help maintain its structure of control, but parents seldom have a platform for expression comparable to that provided by the school's chapel meetings. The chapel message is usually given by Headmaster McGraw, Bible teacher Art Swanson, or Youth Pastor Burt Harrison, less frequently by the other pastors of Bethany Baptist Church. Though their outlines and verses vary from day to day, they typically return to the same central points—obey God, do not sin; depend on God, do not go your own way; consistently live the word of God, do not backslide—delivered in somber, passionate, beseeching, shouting, or quietly reasoned tones, and, often, delivered in all of these tones in the course of a forty-minute meeting. Below is a sampling of chapel comments, first of selections from McGraw and Swanson, and then from a visiting evangelist, one of the several who come to Bethany each year for a week-long visit and conduct daily chapel sessions for the students:

> As a Christian young person, you are to be above reproach. It starts right here with the rules of our school. You have to please and glorify God. Stop to think, "What does God want me to do?" That is what we must ask.

> Peter was put in prison for his convictions. He did not resist being arrested. Here is the mature Peter. He did not question authority. He went gladly for Christ's sake. The point: you had better get this idea out of your life that you can do it alone.

And you say, "What if my teacher is wrong?" Look at the verse, "And submit yourself as one who must give account." God is saying that it's your job to obey and submit. Get down on your knees and pray, "Lord, help me do what I'm supposed to do, and help my teacher." That's Christian. A bad attitude is pagan. Maybe you can start your own American Association of Pagan Schools someday. But you'll get no help from the Lord.

Guest speaker Brother Bill during Revival Week tells the students they are "God's people" and thus they must look right. "Outward appearance isn't as important as inside, but it is important. God's people ought to look right, not like slobs." Moreover, because they are God's people, they'll be going south all their lives, while "the world will be going north." Bethany's children learn at an early age that they are different. Brother Bill warns them:

> All your life you'll go against the grain of society. It won't hurt you. It's not hard to say no to the movies, to drugs, to disco, to rock and roll. You've got an entire society [the Christian brethren] within a society.

If there is a prototypical setting at BBA, it is the thrice-weekly chapel session. Each one lasts as long as Headmaster McGraw wants it to last, but never less than a full period and often longer. Though no exams and grades are associated with chapel, it is BBA's most consistently businesslike session. If McGraw is not the speaker, he is always present on the podium looking right at the students. He is notoriously anti-foot-shuffling and anti-diverted-gaze. Students' minds may wander but they know that their headmaster tolerates no visible sign that communicates this fact. Chapel talks contain an amalgam of every consequential point Bethany means to stress: students pledge allegiance to the flag for at least the second time that day; they sing some Christian songs to get them prepared for the session's message; they hear a message that simultaneously contains a lesson in Bible, guidelines for daily living, and commentary on current events; and they listen to McGraw's concluding announcements whose subject matter ranges broadly across all school affairs.

Teachers and Other Employees

Teachers seldom speak at chapel. They have occasion enough, however, to do their share to enforce and reinforce BBA's structure of control during the many interstitial moments of a school day when they happen to be in the halls or the gymnasium, but especially during their class periods. Four students withdrew themselves from school after a teacher, who heard them speaking in the lunch line about disliking BBA, reported them to McGraw. In the midst of any lesson, teachers routinely use language to exercise control, frequently but not invariably in Christian terms. Teachers are reminded to do this by McGraw—"I believe in Christian education permeating everything," he tells his teachers one morning. "We have a full-time obligation." Teachers need little reminding. In the midst of physical education the teacher says to a student, "That's baloney and it's not Christian, either. Are you gonna give of yourself? Are you gonna be a proper witness? Or are you gonna take, take, take?" In the midst of world history the teacher says to the class, "OK, the next person who does anything wrong gets written up. Folks, this is a spiritual problem. If you disobey me, it's a sin." And in the midst of Bible class the teacher admonishes, "You must give your all. Is there a part of you that you're keeping from God? Don't, young people. Give your all." One English teacher, a vigorous reinforcer, monitors student behavior during Bethany's church services and reports wrongdoers to the administration. Students get extra credit on her quizzes if they attend church on Sunday.

Joining teachers in their supervisory role are all other adults associated with the school. This includes the school secretary, who does not hesitate to advise, warn, or scold students; the female custodian, who will tell students sitting out in the hall preparing for a regional Bible competition to stick to their business; and especially the youth pastor, who, because of his role as head of youth activities and Sunday school teacher of high-school-aged students, gets to know the students very well. He serves as a counselor and, as noted earlier, shares in judging the spiritual eligibility of prospective student leaders. In addition, he speaks at chapel, teaches a regularly scheduled but optional class on soul winning, and conducts the summer youth trip.

The Demerit System

Bethany Christians believe that their Lord punishes. Salvation is not a shield against punishment for repeated transgressions of his Word. Students are informed about the Lord's retribution, but, since this is out of BBA's hands, they hear more about and are more immediately affected by BBA's own penalty system. This system involves a disciplinary committee composed of the headmaster or assistant headmaster, two student leaders (selected on a rotating basis from students in grades nine to twelve), and the school secretary. She maintains a permanent record of demerits each student earns. The students are present as observers, never as participants in the decision making; they occasionally contribute information, of the special sort that students are likely to possess about student life, useful to making a decision. The headmaster hears each student's case and awards an appropriate number of demerits.

Teachers are advised to use the demerit system sparingly, to control behavior by other means and to resort to demerits when the other means fail. "If a teacher turns in more than three or four demerit slips a week, other than for tardies, the teacher has a problem the demerit system won't cure," says McGraw. Their overuse of the system is a matter for discussion with him. When teachers see school rules broken, they are to "write up" a student by submitting the pertinent information to the school office. Each Wednesday, the list of all students who have been written up is posted on a bulletin board, reminding them to appear before the Disciplinary Committee, or DC, as it is called, on Thursday during their lunch period. Students earning five or fewer demerits in a semester are forgiven and their permanent record is wiped clean. Acumulation begins with the sixth demerit, until at twenty-five their parents get a letter; at fifty their parents get a second letter; at seventy-five they are automatically placed on "permanent restriction" (which entails exclusion from all teams, offices, and any competitive events); and at one hundred fifty accumulated in one semester they are automatically expelled. Demerits do not accumulate beyond the semester in which they are awarded.

Corporal punishment, in the form of swats with a paddle, may be used at various points along the demerit process according to the judgment of teachers and administrators. At a January chapel meeting McGraw tells the students: "When you walk across the parking lot to come to chapel, you must walk. If you run into somebody, it'll cost you a paddling. And no snowballs. We paddle for throwing one." Only administrators paddle and always in the presence of an adult witness. Although as a condition for admission parents must accept BBA's corporal-punishment policy, parents always are notified prior to a paddling. Should they or their child refuse to accept this punishment, the child is expelled. Generally, paddling is confined to younger students, from eighth grade down, but at least in one situation—being sent out of class for misbehavior—paddling is part of the sequence of penalties. The sequence includes a warning the first time, twenty-five demerits the second, fifty demerits and a paddling the third, and automatic expulsion the fourth. Students have been expelled for various reasons, but never in McGraw's administration by this route.

> We take the biblical approach that spanking is correct [McGraw informs his teachers during their preterm in-service week]. The Bible says correction drives out wickedness, especially spanking. It should never be done with joy and always with an explanation. We'd close down before we gave up the paddling policy.

For Headmaster McGraw, the demerit system operates with flexibility based on judgment. He does hold to absolutes—always give demerits for any instance of disrespect or disobedience and always give one hundred demerits for major offenses like lying, stealing, smoking, and cheating, because in such cases a "student has broken beyond the instruction boundary into the punishment area." But judgment is an essential part of the system, as we see in these actual cases: Did a student actually go to the movies and then lie that he did not? This is two major offenses, and expulsion follows—as it did with a senior boy who was ready to graduate. Was there a drinking party involving several students where one was the ringleader? The ringleader gets more demerits. Has a steady couple been caught talking and touching while standing at their lockers? Don't embarrass them further by bringing them before the Disciplinary Committee. Place them right on social restriction for two weeks, which involves no talking, touching, or dating for this span of time. Has a senior student stayed away from church all summer and shown no evidence of spirituality? Require him to join the summer youth trip as a condition for entry in fall.

McGraw uses judgment. And a light touch. Listen to him conduct a session of the Disciplinary Committee. He opens the meeting with prayer. "Lord, be with us. Give us wisdom. In Jesus' name, amen." A student member ushers each waiting student one at a time into the library. The "written-up" student stands before the seated committee.

> How are you, Jon? I like your belt buckle. "Talking after being warned," [he reads from the demerit slip]. "I didn't say a word." OK, you're forgiven.

> Hi, Rita. "Moved your seat to talk to Perry." "Yes, but I didn't talk. Just moved my hands." That's communicating and it disrupts the study hall. Five demerits.

Jenny, come right in and join the fellowship. "Talking with Sue after being warned." "The second time Sue and I just looked at each other." No talking at all? "No, sir." OK.

Hello, Dick. What a mass of these [demerit slips] you have. It's a good thing I don't have arthritis or I couldn't lift the pile. "Not paying attention during lecture." [Dick explains.] OK, we'll forget that one, but it leaves seven others for a total of ten demerits. More than you've had all semester. There'll be a letter to your parents.

Ron, you've just set a new national record. My policy is if a student gets seven demerits, he gets an automatic paddling. [Dick's seven earned him no paddling or mention of it.] You've got four tardies. I assume you're guilty of these. [Ron's explanation excuses him of one and he is saved from a paddling.]

Dick's father is a deacon. His "home situation" is forthrightly supportive of Bethany standards and no one seems to doubt that once past his adolescence he will settle into the good, BBA-citizen role. Ron's parents are not Bethany church members. He is a new student and has been recalcitrant since his admission. Optimism for Ron's future is hard to find.

McGraw makes judgments within the framework of an extensive structure designed to control students' time, thought, movement, and social relations. He and his fellow educators hope students will develop self-discipline that is securely rooted in the Word, so that their love of Christ, not a signed pledge or a demerit system, will constrain their behavior. Structures of control, however, do not seem to wither away. The presence of such a structure in the few colleges Bethany approves for its graduates and in the provisions BBA sets forth for teachers in their contract and handbook suggest its desirability for persons well past the time when they are babes in Christ.

Anticipating the world's criticism of the Christian school's structure of control, Pastor Carter Hill takes pains to explain that what they do is not sinister, that it is, in fact, much like what transpires in the non-Christian world:

> People who criticize us for controlling our students are dishonest because they do the same thing. The type of influence [he prefers this word to control] we do would be somewhat of the type every advertiser on television does.

The people who complain about us have television sets in their house that manipulate their minds and their children's minds. I think we're being rather honest about it. From a Christian perspective, parents do not see themselves or the school as an absolute authority, but they have confidence that the school wants their child to do what God wants him to do.

Doing "what God wants him to do" is the Christian's first and last principle. As Bethany's leaders see it, they establish a school, select teachers, admit students, and devise a structure of control as God wants them to. When they speak of what they do, they refer often to a scriptural verse for authentication. Nonetheless, it is understood—with or without a verse made explicit—that God's sanction supports whatever they do.

5

Bethany's Didactic Milieu
A Match for the Devil's Darts

> The average Christian hears only one or two sermons a week. His private devotional life is often pathetic and erratic. He is just too weak to be any match for the Devil's darts.
>
> Bob Jones III

> If you want your child to grow up to be an outstanding servant of the Lord, it is absolutely necessary that you guard his mind so that it will be exposed only to those things which would be pleasing to Him.
>
> Charles Walker

When Would a Visitor Know?

In my early months at Bethany, during quiet moments when the teacher had assigned desk work or students were taking a test, I would play a game. I called it When Would a Visitor Know? That is, how long would it take a visitor to know with certainty not only that he was in a Christian school, but in a very Christian Christian school? I had the occasional need to amuse myself when left without something to observe, but, more than this, I carried over from the time before I began the actual fieldwork a concern to be sure the Christian school I located was thoroughly committed to implementing its doctrinal ideals. Thus, in the early days of my fieldwork, I wondered if I had made a wise choice; I hoped that my Christian school was not a public school in Christian clothing.

Just to get started with my game I had to set aside some obvious, give-away facts, because BBA and its host church share the same grounds, and a sign set adjacent to the school's front door reads: Education from a Christian Point of View. I concede the set-asides, pass through the front door, and enter a short corridor whose walls are decorated with pictures of American presidents. Immediately to the left of the entrance is the school office. Looking inside for indicators of a Christian school, I spot a large wall calendar with a religious inscription across its top. I dismiss this as the sort of thing found in schools whose patrons do not press their children's school administrators to eliminate fastidiously all signs of religious identification. Similarly, I try to dismiss the corridor's bulletin boards, which include references to the Lord and to Bible verses. Yet it is not the Christmas season, when public schools in some places honor Christmas as a Christian occasion. Unable to account for the bulletin boards with their Christian themes, I concede I'm probably in a religious school.

For a moment, I try considering that the school is a private secular school with a Christian veneer. The appearance of its students persuades me that I am not in a public school. A strict dress code is evident: blue jeans are nowhere in sight, boys have short hair, and girls wear stockings and nice dresses. Perhaps I am seeing students on a dress-up day for taking yearbook pictures. Perhaps, but this is America, and blue jeans are ubiquitous, if only one pair worn by one rebellious student; the boys' neatly trimmed short hair could be a fad. So, I'm not in a public school, I'm in a strict private school, possibly on a dress-up day. I temporarily set aside the bulletin boards and follow a group of students into their classroom. It's a math class. As the bell rings, the clamor of the students ends abruptly. Yes, I know discipline is supposed to be good in Christian schools, but it also is good in other schools and, I reason, the math teacher is the school's champion bear, the biter of all heads whose mouths are still moving once the bell has rung. In a moment, however, my non-Christian private school hypothesis is in trouble again when Mr. Bear first invites students to mention their prayer requests and then calls on Dan to "lead us in prayer."

After math, the students cross the parking lot and enter the large church building where they assemble for chapel. It is not Sunday, a holiday, or any other known occasion warranting meeting in a church building for a session called "chapel." In a sense, the game is over. I concede that I'm in a religiously oriented private school, but, I argue, everything I've seen and heard so far is easily mandated. It requires no great effort to put up the bulletin boards, hold a ten-minute devotion during each morning's homeroom meeting, start off each class with prayers, and require three chapel meetings a week. But it takes more than a list of school goals and decrees from a school's administrators to establish a school that is permeated with a Christian point of view, as Bethany's welcoming sign announces. If this commitment was evident as a daily fact of life at BBA, then I would have to conclude that BBA was a Christian school both in name and in fact. Accordingly, let us take note of what students typically hear in the academy's various settings.

Spiritual Words

A school, any school, is awash with words. If the golden silence of bygone days still enjoys some respect today, it is nowhere more revered than in Christian schools. Silence there is applauded not merely for its own sake, but to enable words to be apprehended as they are written, spoken, sung, recited, prayed, and preached. Schools are known by their words: read their bulletin boards, yearbooks, and newspapers; study their tests and homework assignments; listen to their students and teachers talk; and note their textbooks and lectures. See where the meanings of the words from these many sources converge in intent, where the messages join to inculcate and reinforce the same point. Given an abundance of these points, we have a school whose instructional elements are working together to attain the school's purposes.

At Bethany it is more than the modest dress of the girls and the short hair of the boys, and more than order in the corridors and the absence of graffiti on bathroom walls, that sets it apart from public schools and non-Christian private schools. It is the words. They roll about, pouring forth anywhere at any time, shalts and shalt nots piling up, a scriptural pearl never more than a breath away. No public school ever has been so charged with such an explicit, accepted mission, or packaged a set of means so calculated to fulfill its mission. The educators exhort, plead, and warn their young Christians; they edify, cajole, and threaten them to be immersed in the Word, and to obey and to promulgate what they have heard.

For students there is no escaping the words: feigned interest is soon detected; disregard invites gloved and ungloved rebuke; repeated scorn is the road to dismissal. While the Word is hardy, its immature student listeners are not. As tender shoots, easily bent toward the world's ways, their school must be no place for skeptics, no market for the sifting and winnowing of ideas, no garden in which a thousand flowers may bloom. BBA excludes the sort of education which, because it is "of man, by man, for man—based on the autonomy of man's reason . . . honors and serves the dominion of Satan" (Kranendonk 1978:53). It favors, instead, instruction based on "the immutable facts of God's Word" (Carlson 1982:1).

The Integration of Scripture and Subject Matter

Salvation and instruction in the Word of God preoccupy but do not usurp the time and occasion for all educative experiences under Bethany's tutelage. Notwithstanding my When Would a Visitor Know? game, most moments are not laced with fundamentalist dogma, and the visitor would see and hear much that could occur in any public school.

When Bethany's students describe how their school differs from a public school, they immediately think of the strict dress code and the standards of conduct embodied in their pledge. If reminded, they recall religious content in their classes; references to God and the Bible are so commonplace that they do not stand out in the students' minds. In fact, students are accustomed both to spiritually thin and to spiritually dense classes, taking no special note of either. The ideal is that "God and the Bible are first and foremost in every class" (Carlson 1982:1). I spent many hours attempting to learn to what extent this ideal was Bethany's norm, whether the fine words of their publicity brochure were in fact everyday reality at this Christian school.

In the course of eighteen months, I observed the teachers' involvement with this ideal. By the time they begin to teach their first-hour class, most have already received spiritual nourishment at home from their own devotions. ("A soldier puts his armor on in the morning. A Christian puts on the Word," says Mrs. Reynolds, the elementary school supervisor.) Then at school there is their daily 8:00 A.M. meeting with Headmaster McGraw. If a spiritual warm-up is necessary and useful, Bethany's teachers certainly have one.

Though mindful of their obligation to integrate the Word of God with their subject matter, teachers acknowledge that the different subjects provide different types of opportunities to integrate. For example, since they conceive of the body as the Lord's temple, physical education has a general association with spirituality. Its concern is not just with physical fitness: "Christian men ought to be men; they ought not to be prissy or out of shape so they can't compete." It also involves sportsmanship, attitudes toward winning, playing by the rules, helping someone who is hurt, and not quitting when things get tough. These are considered spiritual principles. In typing, general principles also apply. Becoming a good typist, wanting to do one's best, punctuality—these are the sort of ideas that may be developed.

Driver training and functional math are among the subjects that do not readily provide occasions for integration, but like typing and physical education, they do involve behavior that is important to one's testimony. How one drives affects one's testimony. If one drives poorly, one is not just a poor driver, but, from Bethany's perspective, a poor *Christian* driver whose behavior affects the fundamentalist Christian establishment. Similarly, in functional math students learn about handling finances and paying bills. Paying one's bills on time contributes positively to one's Christian testimony; not paying one's bills is stealing and discredits one's testimony. This course has other integrative experiences. For example, students learn that as the stewards of God's money, they should manage it with care. If they allot their pretax 10 percent to tithing, they will be rewarded by "God helping the remaining 90 percent to go further than the original 100 percent." All teachers, including the math teacher, appreciate the difficulty of integration in this area. After observing that mathematics "works" because it is within God's order and that some word problems can incorporate biblical examples, the math teacher concludes there are few natural chances to integrate. Feeling the same way about his industrial arts class, he had his boys memorize verses: "I told them, 'Every time you read the Bible and learn Scripture, it will strengthen your faith. We're going to strengthen your faith for 10 percent of your grade.'"

The science teacher and the Bible study teacher use textbooks published by Bob Jones University Press. For the most part, all other teachers use the least offensive instructional materials available from non-Christian publishers, selecting items which, while not promoting spirituality, do not hinder it. In time, Bob Jones University Press is likely to offer textbooks covering the full range of high school subjects. Meanwhile, the publisher's advertising clarifies that Christian schools necessarily fall short of the ideal to the extent that "education is drawn from secular documentation," since "secular textbooks are written to promulgate the secular humanist world view . . . the 'official religion' of the American public school system." In those Christian-published textbooks that are available students see a persistent juxtaposition of Scripture and content. In science this means a predictably creationist, antievolutionary perspective, continual exclamations about phenomena as God's creations, and descriptions of their complexity as exemplary of God's wisdom.

In history Frank Fortner often asks students to ponder the propriety of some historical decision from a Christian perspective. For example, was it proper for the American colonists to rebel against their king? Did the king's policies violate scriptural principles, and if not, should he not have been honored for his Caesarean prerogatives? The Reformation is a particularly important period in world history to Protestants of any designation, and Fortner gives this period due emphasis.

No teachers integrate more consistently than the English and Bible-study teachers, the former using Scripture and spiritual matters to teach English and the latter using the Bible to teach about life. Mrs. Reynolds consummately communicates to her students the Scripture–subject matter connection in the first class session of the new school year. At a time of the year more typically devoted to vacationing than to learning, she starts off her sixth-period senior English class with a biblical bang. Her greeting to her class is an order to open Bibles to Romans 12:1–2 ("I beseech you therefore, brethren, by the mercies of God, that ye present your bodies a living sacrifice, holy, acceptable unto God, which is your reasonable service.") and take out a half sheet of paper. Then she calls the roll, has a volunteer lead the class in prayer, and begins her quiz with the following questions:

> Paraphrase the word "beseech."
> What do we call a word like "brethren" when it is separated by two commas? I don't mean what part of speech but how it is used in the sentence.
> What group of people is Paul speaking to when he uses the word "brethren"?
> "By the mercies of God"—what does this mean? What word could you substitute for "by"?
> In this passage your body is supposed to be holy by whose standards?
> What does "conformed" mean?
> What does "transformed" mean?
> What does "renewing" mean?
> What does "prove" mean?
> If you do all that the verse requests, what would you find in your life?
> Here's a bonus. Pick out the prepositional phrase and write it out.

For Mrs. Reynolds, being a good Christian and being competent in language are inseparable: "One cannot be a good Christian if one does not know how to use English well. How do you expect to write sermons or letters or communicate the Word of the Lord if you can't use good English?" Her composition assignments frequently include topics that invite reflection on spiritual matters: "Scared Christians," "One Prayer of Mine God Has Specifically Answered," "My Salvation," and "Jesus Paid It All." While students believe that when given a choice they are better off choosing a religious topic, their pious sentiments do not divert her red pencil from misplaced commas, misspellings, and incorrect capitalization.

Bible teacher Art Swanson switches effortlessly from lesson plan to down-to-earth commentary.

> OK, point number two, "Deathlessness." Are you fearful of death, Robbie? David? Beth? [They each say no.] The natural instinct is to fear death. Deathlessness—the body dies, but the spirit moves on. That's nice to know, isn't it? Number three, "To reveal Christ. Philippians 1:21." [He reads the verse.] Is that your attitude today? Do you say, "I don't want to die, I want to get married first? I want my driver's license first?" The sophomores can't wait for that. Are you torn between wanting to stay here on earth and wanting to be with Christ in heaven?

Swanson knows this point evokes ambivalence even in mature Christians; he understands the pull of the flesh that makes his fully healthy fellows, young and old, equivocal about forgoing worldly pleasures for eternal joys. Few can say and mean it, as does Pastor Muller, "I'm ready now. Let him come."

Only a new student might remark on the frequency of spiritual discourse throughout the day. Otherwise, students and teachers know that the content of their classes is to be recognizably differentiated from Bible study and chapel, however much a teacher is given to integration. In driver training, mathematics, and typing they expect very little; in English, social studies, and history they expect more. A student says:

> In history Mr. Fortner is always for the guy with the Christian stand and good moral standards. In English, Mrs. Reynolds, she's always telling us it's a sin to do less than our best, and like last week we had this theme to write on, "Christian Love." Or she'll say, "OK, turn to such and such verse in the Bible. I want you to find adjectives, pronouns, and verbs." I look at the verse, you know, and I think about the verse, and sometimes something comes to me that really, you know, the Lord sent and used that class to send to me.

No Bethany teachers said they prepared in advance to integrate; it happens when the Holy Spirit moves them. While the history and the band teachers might be equally moved, the inclinations of the former lead him to seize more opportunities, especially of an unintegrated type. For example, students said that when Mr. Fortner is "feeling burdened" for his class, he may devote most of the period to expressing his burden without reference to history. "He'd come and say to us, 'Look, I've been thinking about this, and I've been reading and praying about it,' and there'd go the period." In this and other instances, teachers are not trying to integrate Scripture and subject matter, they are communicating some spiritual matter at a timely moment. Mrs. Matthews and her class discuss a short story that leads her to observe that people get exactly what they need. After requiring the class to recite in unison, "I'm in a state where I'm totally content because I have what I need," she recounts the story of her brother who is rich but does not know the Lord. She begins to cry, saying, sadly, "I see his children being raised without proper guidance. Some day they'll come to judgment." The lesson then continues; no child, however, has looked askance at her story. If not an everyday occurrence, such stories are sufficiently common, and perceived as appropriate, to elicit no wondering looks. Students are, after all, in the world of Bethany, a setting which precludes snickers about matters that elsewhere might evoke scorn. When Mr. Cline asked his seventh-graders for prayer requests, one boy said, "My goldfish is still sick," followed by a girl who said, "My dog still has fleas." The prayer that resulted from these and other requests encompassed the goldfish, two dogs, four "unspokens" (mentioned as such by students, and never described), and one sick aunt. There were no suppressed smiles, no laughter. Prayer is not funny business in BBA's seventh grade.

The Religious Message

The formal school experience at Bethany covers a vast range of content, as it does at any school, but in few places do the teachers who present it vary so little in their beliefs and values. By the time youngsters have been at Bethany for a few years, they are seldom surprised. Pastor Burt, the youth pastor, concludes his chapel sermon with a prayer to "Help us be thankful about the freedom we have as Christians and Americans." Students can expect to hear the other educator-adults in their lives speak in a basically comparable vein about the nature of freedom and about being Christian and American. When visitors come to speak to students, they may vary in their appeal as speakers, but not in the thrust of their content. Being a fundamentalist Christian assures the speaker's orthodoxy.

Jesus—Suffering—Sin—Salvation

Though there is no coordination among the various teachers and preachers (quoted below as they address Bethany's students), their messages return repeatedly to a number of themes in a continuous process of illumination, beginning always with the life and death of Christ:

> Let's read Philippians 2:5–8, first. We'll talk about the death on the cross today. What is this death? What does it mean to you? Death on the cross was the most miserable, painful death there was. [Mr. McGraw graphically describes the details of a crucifixion before he concludes.] A person died of suffocation on the cross; they soon drowned in their own body fluids. [Student sighs are audible.] Christ went through such a death for you and me. Whose sins put Jesus Christ on the cross? We can go through a whole year and not think it was our sin that nailed Christ to the cross. He gave his life because we are sinners and offers us the gift of salvation.

Jesus—suffering—sin—salvation: these notions surround the students from the moment they enter Bethany; they embody Bethany's way. They are the superstructure that gives form and substance to the entire Bethany experience. They are the premise of the invitation proffered Bethany's young people to get with the Lord in the first instance, or to get right with him, in the second. These invitations typically are extended at the end of each chapel sermon.

Students learn of the single path to salvation—by accepting Jesus as their personal savior. Neither their parents piety nor their own good works, not their baptism or perfectly faithful attendance at any church advances them one inch down this path. Such mistaken belief leads to "fire, brimstone, pain, and wailing, together with murderers, gamblers, drunkards, and liars," as well as with nominal Christians who ignore the Bible's true course to a heavenly eternity.

God's Will and God's Wrath

As I have written earlier, however, the concern for most Bethany students relates not to salvation—most are saved—but to how they conduct themselves as Christians. For there never is a guarantee that the born-again Christian, albeit permanently saved, will abide by scriptural prescriptions. Straight and clear though the prescriptions may be, man is free to go his own way, preferring, if he so wills, Satan to Jesus. The challenge for Christians is to learn what God wills for them and then to prepare themselves to fulfill God's plan; they cannot do this by sitting in their front-porch rocker.

> I have the responsibility to work as God wants me to work. He called me here to teach. But I can't come in unprepared. I can't just walk in and say, "God, fill my mouth." He will, of course, with hot air. I need to do my own work to come prepared.

While prepare he must, Mr. Swanson knows full well, and strives to inform his students, that he is not on his own and, moreover, that he must avoid the vanity of so believing. The Christian is free to choose, but he must not think that he is perfectly free to follow his own will, that is, without potentially paying a price at the hand of a God both loving and wrathful. A Christian's destiny is in the Lord's plan. There is no turning away from it with impunity, as evangelist Ron Comfort informs BBA students.

> I'm afraid to get out of the will of the Lord because I'm afraid he'll put his hand on my two daughters or on my wife. Of course, do things because you love God, but you know God punishes those who get out of his will.

He tells about Clarence Loner, whose refusal to heed God's call to the mission field led to his young wife's death, his girlfriend's rape, and his own brains being blown out. Whether or not this horrendous tale terrorizes the students probably depends on many factors. In fact, only the stories of revivalists and preachers change, the vehicles of the Word; their message about the terror of God's wrath and his love do not, although some students may be unable to sort out Pastor Comfort's tale of a wrathful God from Mr. Swanson's, told on another occasion, about a long-suffering God who forgives sinners "seventy times seven" (Matthew 18:22).

Church Membership

Ron Comfort, his words and voice emphasizing the imperative nature of his observations, tells Bethany's high schoolers:

> You can't be a duck and not like to swim. You can't be a pig
> and not want to be in the slop. And you can't be a Christian
> and not want to go to church. If you don't want to go to
> church, you're not a Christian. I'm happiest right here in the
> house of the Lord.

It is insufficient just to go to church, he said; you must *want* to go, or you
must doubt your Christianness. The doubting, already saved Christian
may feel compelled to raise his hand during the invitation part of a
sermon and ask to be prayed for; he may even come forward to renew
his commitment in a symbolic act that communicates to himself and to
others that he intends to reaffirm his acceptance of Jesus as his personal
savior and to accept the consequences of this commitment.

Ron Comfort's reference to Christians attending church derives from
much more than a concern that fledgling Christians develop a church-
going habit so collection plates are filled and those who earn their living
from the church can stay solvent. Bethany denigrates the popular
television ministries for making Christian commitment too easy, for
deluding people into thinking that their spiritual life is in order by virtue
of regular TV watching and regular financial support of their favorite
Christian TV personality. Since Bethany rejects this view, the students
know that the 700 Club and the PTL Club, for example, are unacceptable
substitutes for faithful church attendance. They have listened to Mr.
Swanson:

> Hebrews 13:17—you've heard this: "Obey them that have
> the rule over you and submit yourselves: for they watch for
> your souls. "See, young people, Pastor Muller has a
> tremendous responsibility for our lives. You ought to be
> fearful when you get out from under that authority. All the
> proof you need to decide if you should join up with a local
> church is right there. If you worship on your own, you have
> nobody to protect you. If you are not attending a church
> faithfully, you are living in rebellion. You are wide open to
> Satan.

Soul Winning

While keeping their spiritual life untouched by the world, students
are expected to reach out by witnessing to the unsaved in the world. At
a chapel session they hear:

> There are young people in this school who haven't been

saved. Are you living right for their sake? Have you witnessed to them for their sake? Or are you just concerned
about yourself? If so, that's a sorry Christianity, and I wonder, then, if you're really saved. When the rapture comes to
place us at God's side, he'll have many tears to wipe away
for our friends and dads who we failed to witness to.

At their 8:00 A.M. sessions, teachers exclaim over the latest lamb to
join the flock. Young and old alike rejoice in their victories for the Lord.
Outside of Bethany, such victories are hard won, and students must
learn not only what to say but what sort of reactions their well-meant
efforts might elicit.

Pastor Burt tries to get his soul winners to understand how their
personal limitations may affect their soul-winning activities. He informs them, for example, that if they overvalue peer approval they may
not want to risk a friendship by inviting an unsaved friend to become
born again. Pastor Burt reminds them that they are not supposed to be
best friends with non-Christians, anyway, and that they certainly
would want to avoid the Judgment Day accusation, "You said you were
my friend, but you never told me about Jesus Christ." Knowing that
fear may restrain their witnessing, he tells the students: Memorize your
approach questions, pray about your fears, admit that you have them,
and realize that the Lord is with you. And he offers concrete suggestions for their soul-winning procedure: Don't carry a big Bible in your
hand; carry a New Testament that fits in your pocket. Don't spend time
praying in your car in a prospect's driveway. He'll wonder what you're
doing there. Don't give references for the verses you quote; too many
numbers are confusing. "Watch your grooming and your manner of
dress. Be friendly and smile. Ask a friend to check your breath before
you visit the prospect." This is the easy part. Students want to know
what to do once they enter the house. "OK," Pastor Burt says, "let's
role-play this." One student, somewhat diffident to perform before his
classmates, begins and Pastor Burt comments on each of the student's
lines:

—What's your name?

Well, what would be a little more direct?

—Do you believe the Bible?

OK, good.

—Do you think much about spiritual things?

Now that's a good thing. Just about everyone thinks about spiritual things.

—Do you want to plan for the future?

Do you want *a* plan for the future? Well, something about the future. There's a more direct way. You could ask, "If you should die tonight, would you be sure you'd go to heaven?" Tracts are another way to begin. At Christmas time, there's lots of opportunities to leave tracts. Always carry them with you. If you're in a restaurant, leave a tip and a tract. When you go to a grocery store or a garage, leave a tract. Another way is to give your testimony and tell how Christ came into your life and gave you a reason to live.

Christians Persecuted

These budding soul winners and all their fellow students are led to expect rebuffs, not only for trying to reach the unsaved, but also just for being a Christian. Persecution, they are taught, is their expected lot at the hands of the Satan-led populace. They are reminded of the courage needed by Jesus' disciples:

Where did Peter and John get such courage? The same place we can get it—from the power of the Holy Spirit. We need disciples today, soldiers who are willing to take the sword of God's word. The Bible likens Christians to soldiers many times. The Lord will bring victories if you are faithful to him.

They are assured that persecution and the need for courage are not passé: "Kids, the day will come, maybe soon, that the world will treat us like animals. Psychiatrists will call us nuts." Lest they think that only in young Christians do sin and righteousness engage in mortal combat, students are told repeatedly that every Christian wages this battle. Thus, while it is relatively easy to become a born-again Christian and go to heaven, it is exceedingly difficult to live like a Christian in this world.

Prayer

As the Christian struggles against his own flesh, he requires prayer. Prayers punctuate a student's day. Everyone is expected to pray before eating; all school activities begin with prayer. For an out-of-town bas-ketball game, the bus-driver-coach prays before the bus begins its journey; before the game begins, someone will pray that both teams be safe and play for the glory of Jesus Christ. Mrs. Reynolds requires her students to pray each day, during the in-class prayer, for a different missionary of the many Bethany Baptist Church supports; they know she does the same in her own prayers. Mr. Kruger advises his students to think of others when they pray, to recall those of their troubled classmates who would benefit from prayer. He even advises them to pray for new teachers like himself: "The more you pray for us, the more you'll get out of your classes." Mr. Swanson, recalling 2 Timothy 1:3—"without ceasing I have remembrance of thee [Paul remembering Timothy] in my prayers night and day"—sets forth for the high school students assembled in chapel a list of those for whom they ought to pray: themselves, parents, siblings, pastor, teachers, lost friends, missionaries, and specific things as needed. Prayer is not a routine posturing at meal times and before other ceremonial occasions; it is a communication with a God who never tires of hearing the prayers of those directed to him through his son Jesus. "See if God doesn't answer your prayers," encourages Mr. Swanson.

Prayer is the occasion for students to address God in their own words, as it is the occasion, one of so many, for hearing the words of their mentors. Enjoined to seek God's guidance when making the major decisions of their lives, students also seek support through prayer to keep their testimony intact.

Testimony

At every turn, Bethany students are reminded of their testimony—the bright face of goodness they can beam forth to the world, or the burdened countenance, heavy with sin, that places a stumbling block before others. In her English class, Mrs. Reynolds simultaneously teaches independent and dependent clauses and challenges her students with a poem:

> When you think, or speak, or read, or write,
> When you sing or walk, or seek for delight,
> To be kept from all wrong when at home or abroad
> Live always as under the eyes of the Lord.

The poem continues with the idea that one should never do or say anything he would be ashamed of were Jesus suddenly to appear at his side. It is a negative poem, mentioning only what not to do that displeases Jesus, but it serves the purpose of establishing Jesus as a

Jiminy Cricket conscience to young Christians for whom spurning the world's ways is hard.

Material Possessions

The good Christian testimony is not sustained by a life of asceticism; at no time does Bethany advocate renunciation and hardship as virtues. Yet, given the temporality of this life, one must have the right perspective on material acquisitions, balancing the understandable concern to live in comfort now with due regard to the requirements of eternity. "It's a tragedy," Pastor Muller informs the students in chapel, "when things of this life appeal to you more than the things of the Lord." Like all of Bethany's critical lessons, this one is not easy to incorporate in one's life. The moral is straightforward, the words readily learned: "Money itself is not bad. The *love* of money is bad. Worldliness begins to set in with possessions. We live in a pleasure-mad world. We need pleasure, but it should be in the right proportion and not draw us away from God." I never heard anyone refer to Matthew 19:24—"It is easier for a camel to go through the eye of a needle, than for a rich man to enter into the kingdom of God." In chapel, students are more likely to hear 1 John 2:15: "Love not the world, neither the things that are in the world. If any man love the world, the love of the Father is not in him." As they are more likely to hear Mr. Swanson dictate for their notetaking: "Treasures in heaven: avoid things that moths can destroy; avoid that which corrodes."

The Last Things

Reference to the Kingdom of God is common. Indeed, the Christian school experience is marked by its commitment to students understanding the last things. A clear socialization for jobs and living in this world is part of their school experience, but an awareness of the end of the world, eternity, and Christ's Second Coming frames Bethany's entire educative effort. Visiting evangelists, chapel speakers, and teachers address when the end of the world will come, what the period of tribulation entails, how wonderful will be "rapture" when those who are saved and still living at the last day will be carried up into heaven without first dying, who will be seen when all Christians are united in heaven, how the body must be transformed before it can enter heaven, etc. They discuss the return of Jesus with the palpable reality of last Sunday's football game. Students are urged to think of the imminence of his return and to welcome it.

> Every day I think today may be the day Jesus will return. Are
> you ready? Are you looking forward to that day? No proph-
> ecy [from Revelation] is unfulfilled to stand between the
> return of Jesus Christ and being raptured to heaven.

Evangelist Bill Hall speaks these words during a week of revival
meetings that are organized during the day for students and at night for
both students and adults. He describes the precursors of Christ's return. His list of events is indicative of the fundamentalist's political,
economic, and social orientation that also is an integral part of schooling
at Bethany. While the specifics Hall selects differ from those identified
by other speakers, the diversity is more a matter of personal choice from
a world of unfortunate events than of principle. For they all believe that
the end is near, and Jesus will come soon. Hall's choice reflects the time
of his revival session—December 1979.

> All the signs are prevalent. Internationally we're in a mess;
> Khomeini is a religious fanatic who is leading the world to
> war. The stage is set for Antichrist. Nationally we're in a
> mess; our leadership is bankrupt. Educationally we're in a
> mess; the NEA [National Education Association] is
> hopelessly communistic, humanistic, and liberal. Theologi-
> cally we're in a mess; people deny that Jesus was born of a
> virgin. The U.S. is becoming more and more pagan.

Character Development

This, then, is a picture of the religious doctrine that Bethany communicates to its youth. Accompanying this picture is one that includes the
particulars of behavior in everyday circumstances. However less grand,
and less implicated with eschatological considerations, these particulars receive serious attention on every imaginable occasion, for they
relate to character, to Christian character, to the front that is seen by
Christian and nonChristian alike.

> Mr. McGraw, oh, yes, he is strong on character in every-
> thing he says and does [observes a teacher]. When I first
> came here, it was academics with me more than anything
> else, but that isn't the right perspective.

Headmaster McGraw most decisively instructs and reinforces character traits, whether it is one more reminder that teachers unfailingly

require "yes, sirs" and "no, ma'ams," or that students risk the permanent removal of salt, pepper, and mustard from lunchroom tables if
they are misused. In the cause of character development the voices are
many, as are the targets. Respect your parents, urges Pastor Muller in
chapel. "Think, gang. Think about tomorrow. Most of the time you
think mom and dad are old fogies. Give them a chance. Think of how
they work to keep you in a Christian school." Disrespect of adults,
explains Assistant Headmaster Russ Warren to the participants in the
statewide Academic Tournament, will earn fouls for one's team: "Fouls
are earned for unchristian behavior, like quarreling or showing a bad
attitude toward the judges."

Sex Roles

Quite understandably, Bethany carefully defines sex roles and the
nature of the male-female relationship. The student newspaper prints a
letter from "Concerned," who is troubled by boys who make "nasty
side remarks" in the presence of girls. "The young ladies don't like it."
Mr. Swanson reads from Ephesians 5 and comments to his twelfth-
grade Bible class:

> Relationship of man to wife—I'm the head of my wife and
> my kids come under her. That's God's order. If a wife
> doesn't submit, the doors are wide open to Satan. Wives
> learn to submit, husbands learn to love. If there's a problem,
> we talk it out. I allow her her say. If I make a wrong decision,
> then she's not responsible.

What are the special needs of male and female children? Bruce
Jackson, Educational Director of the AACS, answers the question and
makes explicit the Christian view of sex roles. Sons need to learn craft
skills, work habits, gardening, manners, economics, leadership, music,
and rhetoric. Daughters need to learn cooking, housekeeping, house-
hold management, manners, sewing, growing and arranging flowers,
interior decoration, literary skills, and child care (1982:1). These are not
mutually exclusive lists. For example, women are expected to become
leaders in women's organizations, but leadership, otherwise, is a clear
male prerogative. This ideal is not always attainable.

> I would not say that I'd never vote for a woman [says Mr.
> McGraw], because long ago I accepted secular politics as a

gray area. I don't think it's a proper role for a woman. Jane
Byrne [then mayor of Chicago] is a good example. I don't
think God ever intended to have a woman in city hall in
Chicago lording it over who knows how many men.

Pastor Muller also recognizes the grayness of women's participation in
politics when, at a mid-week service, he encourages the women to go to
the state capital and protest the Equal Rights Amendment:

If there are some ladies who want to go, I think we can
arrange a little transport. Some of you may think we're
heading down a doubtful pass in doing this, but don't say
this. They're saying this about us outside the church. I'm not
saying it's something you must do. I'm just making the
opportunity available.

Of more immediate concern to the academy are boy-girl relationships.
The hormones of Christian students have not been modified by virtue of
being born again. Hand holding and moonstruck gazes are constrained
by school regulations, but there are more serious concerns.

The sin of Abraham—he is afraid and so he lies about Sarah.
Why did he lie?. I could interject here to be careful, guys. If
she [their girl] is too beautiful, you may lie about her. Girls,
what lessons can you learn? [Mr. Swanson listens to
answers.] Yes, be careful who you marry. Until then, be
faithful.

Pastor Muller tackles dating in a chapel message. Limited though
student chances are to meet non-Christians, they hear few scriptural
verses more often than 2 Corinthians 6:14, which directs them to "Be ye
not unequally yoked with unbelievers." This means that dating non-
Christians is taboo. Pastor Muller reassures his students that their
interest in the "opposite sex" is perfectly natural and "absolutely necessary according to God's program, unless he gives you the gift of
celibacy."

What sort of person ought a Christian young person marry
according to that Scripture [2 Corinthians 6:14]? Right, a
Christian. You may think it's OK to date anybody, but if
you're not going to marry them, why date them? I'm not
trying to say that once you start dating that that's the person
you're going to marry. But according to the Word of God

you ought not date someone you *couldn't* marry. If you date
somebody who is a bum, with no spiritual convictions,
thinking you'll reform them, forget it. It's just like with
apples—the rotten one spoils the good ones; the good ones
don't make the bad apple good.

Bible Class Worksheet

The range of injunctions Bethany means to impress upon its charges
exceeds what can be presented here. Some idea of its extent is illustrated
in the following discussion of a Bible class worksheet, cheerleader
tryouts, and the summer youth trip.

The dittoed Bible class worksheet is a page of notebook-sized paper
divided in half vertically. On the left, inside a darkened, ominous-
looking heart, are the words "My will," surrounded by appropriate
accompaniments—"born of the flesh," "received from Adam," and
"old nature." On the right, inside a glistening heart, are the words
"God's will." Its accompaniments are "born of the spirit," "received in
Christ," and "new nature." Listed under the dark heart are sentences
that express attitudes of the flesh: "But I've seen other Christians doing
it . . . so WHY CAN'T I?" "Just this once won't hurt. No one will know."
"It's my life! I'll live it anyway I please." "I just CAN'T break that habit."
"I'll get even if it's the last thing I do." Of course, these are attitudes to
shun. Students are instructed to learn the correct "spiritual antidote" to
these objectionable attitudes by selecting from the scriptural verses
listed under the bright heart the one that reveals God's opposing truth.
For example, students should counter the old-nature sentiment, "But
Mom . . . ALL the girls are wearing them," with the new-nature
antidote of Ephesians 6:1,2, paraphrased on the worksheet as, "Even
when I can't understand their reasons, Lord, help me obey my parents
to honor your command."

Cheerleader Tryouts

Cheerleader tryouts are a long way from the classroom, but no
distance at all in doctrinal terms. American high schools have athletic
teams and cheerleaders; Christian high schools are as committed to
winning and cheering as any public school. The process of cheerleader
selection at Bethany, however, differs from its crosstown, public school
counterparts.

On Wednesday of the week before school begins, when teachers
have been attending day-long, in-service sessions, BBA's high school

girls fill the gym. They are alive with nervous excitement as they anticipate their trial before peers, two teacher sponsors, and Assistant Headmaster Russ Warren. He sets the stage for the several days of tryouts and decision making. Thirty-two girls sit on the gym floor listening to him explain the selection procedure. Earlier, each girl has received a copy of the cheerleader guidelines, which she and her parents had to sign. Mr. Warren elaborates these guidelines, beginning with the observation that no girl can be chosen unless she is "an example of the believers, in word, in conversation, in charity, in spirit, in faith, in purity" (1 Timothy 4:12). Since fulfilling this criterion is a matter of reputation, there is nothing a candidate can do in this regard at the time of the tryout: either she has or has not been "an example of the believer" to a degree sufficient to satisfy the guardians of Bethany's standards. The test of a girl's spiritual reputation is made by McGraw, Russ Warren, the youth pastor, and Pastor Muller. One of the sponsors recalls a girl about whom there was indecision:

> Sarah went on the youth trip, so that part was OK, but we weren't really sure she had made the decision to be 100 percent. It seemed like she was going to do just enough [spiritually] to get by, but not follow the Lord all the way. She was going to go her own way and the Lord wasn't going to have ahold of her. In your Christian life you have to decide to follow the Lord 100 percent.

The remaining criteria are like those found in any school—dependability, appearance, facial expression, pep, gracefulness, and rhythm.

As Mr. Warren discusses the guidelines, his tone is serious and the culotte-clad girls are perfectly quiet and attentive. The two cheerleader sponsors, still dressed as they have been for the day's in-service meeting, lean against the stage listening to him say:

> If these ladies [the two sponsors] don't see the joy of the Lord on your face right now in the tryout, it won't be there afterwards. You know you'll have to submit to leadership baptism [sign the leadership pledge] if you make it. Do your best. Give your best. But realize that the Lord might have something else for you to do this year than be a cheerleader.

Warren stresses the importance of dependability and having the right attitude; teachers frequently refer to attitude, not explaining what the specific behaviors of "right attitude" are. As a conventional expression it refers to virtues that everyone understands.

Learning how to lose is an invariable part of the cheerleading experience. Losing at Bethany is not simply a matter of limited talent or not having an "in" with the judges; it also is a matter of God's will. At the decision point of the two-day trials, the gym now quiet after hours of leaping, arm-waving, rhythmic foot stomping, and interminable yells ("This is Bethany country, you beware . . ."), one of the sponsoring "ladies" prepares her sweating charges for the prospects of disappointment that will follow the forthcoming announcement of the "winners."

> I hope you prayed before you came today to learn what God's will was for you. You need to ask, "What are his goals for me?" It's hard to know. Sometimes you find a closed door. There's lots to be said for being a gracious loser and a sympathetic winner. God may not explain to you a thousand things about his dealings with you. I'm not saying, "blessed are the losers," but God is trying to work out something in your life if you lose. Cheerleading is a giving ministry. If God hasn't called you to this ministry, OK.

Summer Youth Trip

For the losers, there always is next year, when both they and the winners must go—as they must each year—on the two-week summer youth trip if they wish to be eligible for selection as a cheerleader. Youth Pastor Burt, assisted by several BBA teachers, leads this intense experience in the mountains of Wyoming or Montana. A typical day contains an early morning service, a break, a prelunch service, afternoon classes, an evangelistic service in the evening, and, finally, bedtime devotions. Students are expected to benefit from the cumulative effect of overwhelming contact with the Word of the Lord undiminished by any competing alternatives. For Bethany students, this is their most total spiritual experience; for Bethany educators, it is their chance to ready student leaders for the year ahead and to motivate all students to dedicate themselves to full-time Christian service.

> By the third day [recalls a participating teacher] the ball got rolling. We'd gone this long without a decision [for example, to become a preacher] so we started praying for the Holy Spirit to move that night. Pastor preached on the home that night and a lot of decisions were made.

Aside from the clearly recreational and spiritual aspects of this trip, it is also an occasion to reinforce desirable character traits. From a sheet titled "Laws to Live By" tripgoers learn that tobacco, liquor, and questionable literature are forbidden. They are expected to be smiling, cheerful, and willing; "rebellious spirits" are not allowed. Finally, romantic expression is controlled much as it is at school: girls sit in the front and boys in the back of the bus; no physical contact is allowed; and no couples can go off by themselves.

The spiritual sojourn in mountain isolation culminates on a Sunday, when the trippers return to Hartney. At that day's evening service all youth who wish to speak their testimony stand before the Bethany congregation and reveal their tales of spiritual victory to thrilled parents and parishioners. The mountains well behind them, students begin classes a week later; with their return comes their reintroduction to life in the unpristine world of Hartney and environs.

In Caesar's Domain

The academy's focus is not restricted to lofty matters of spirituality and character development; it is directed, as well, toward what to believe about the ordinary matters that touch their lives—economics and politics, for example—and about non-Christians and misguided Christians who abound in the world and are prospects for proselytizing.

Religious Conservatism

In fact, notwithstanding the administrators' acknowledgment of respect for cultural and ideological diversity, Bethany's students learn about nonfundamentalists as candidates for conversion, on the one hand, and in ways that reconfirm the correctness of their own doctrinal stance, on the other. Bethany's leadership is fully aware of the special qualities of American society that relate to freedom of religious practice, political choice, etc. The church's annual report to its fifteen hundred members expresses gratitude to the "Lord once again for the freedoms that have we have here . . . to go out knocking on doors as we do." Carter Hill, AACS official, elaborates the organization's stand on the principal of absoluteness:

> Christian educators have never assumed that our Christian view of absolute standards of morality and truth is to be foisted on the entire public. Partly we feel it's impractical, and partly we perceive that's not the spirit of the Constitution. America allows for people who believe in absolutes

and people who believe in relatives. People do think there's something sinister going on in Christian schools, that we are removing kids from the mainstream of life. But the point I'm belaboring is that we realize we are absolute about our point of view, yet a person convinced against his will will have the same opinion still.

Headmaster McGraw agrees with Carter Hill that if there is a problem with uniformity, it is in public schools. Like Hill, he endorses diversity, seeing it as a basis for the country's greatness, and he criticizes Nazi Germany for its elimination of Jews and the resulting loss to the richness of German society. The paradox of Bethany's professed regard for diversity and its commitment to absolute truth is manifest in McGraw's chapel message to high schoolers one April morning. Anticipating the next week's arrival of Bill Rice III for revival meetings, he tells the students to have their hearts ready for Rice's blessings:

> Turn to John 14:6. "I am *the* way, *the* truth, and *the* life" [he emphasizes]: "no man cometh unto the Father, but by me." If you have the truth, you need to do something about it. That billboard advertisement you see, "Attend the church of your choice," is the philosophy of the world. It's a message from the National Council of Churches and it's wicked, satanic, and wrong because of John 14:6. You are custodians of the truth. We are the way. Mormons don't have it.

Indeed, Mormons and everyone else do not "have it," as students learn in various settings. Carter Hill hopes that Christian "young people will learn that the doctrine of the Mormon is wrong," but that rejection of their doctrine will be accompanied by "compassion for the person." (In this regard, Pastor Muller remarked to his church members one evening about writing their congressmen to oppose ERA. "There are biblical reasons to do so," he explained, but, more than this, "just looking at the crowd that supports ERA is enough to make you oppose it.") Conceding Bethany's relative failure to promote "compassion for the person," Hill concludes that public schools, with all their diversity, have not kept the people of America "real open and understanding and loving." He is persuaded that Christian-educated youth have more respect for diversity because of their school's emphasis on character training.

Homosexuals, Hill also feels, provide a case of Christian regard for diversity:

> Homosexuality is a sin. We hate the sin, but we love the
> sinner. That's from the theological standpoint, which leads
> then to the practical standpoint—that the person is not
> wrong, but his thinking or method or doctrine is.

Bethany excoriates more than Mormons. They are on the soul-winning
class's list of cults, which includes astrology, Jesus People, "Moonies,"
Hare Krishna, Jehovah's Witnesses, Baha'i, Christian Scientists, and
Seventh-Day Adventists. Pastor Burt defines a cult as a "system of
religious worship . . . that doesn't look to God for its final authority." He
suggests different sources the students can use for their research, one of
them a book on Jehovah's Witnesses, which he marked "Caution:
heresy," in case any one picks it off his shelf to read. As far as he is
concerned, he informs his class, "this is a bunch of hogwash," referring
specifically to the book's reference to hell merely as part of a parable.
"They don't believe there is a literal hell. They worship Jehovah rather
than God. It's sad when you read through this book. It's interesting but
it's not God's final word to man."

Pastor Burt helps the students to select one of his designated cults for
their oral reports, informs them that they cannot attend any of their
chosen group's services, and sets forth the report's major points: the
cult's "history, financial structure, organizational structure, false doctrine, weird practices," and "what positive things we can learn from
them, like the Jehovah's Witnesses who knock on your door with such
diligence." In their reports I heard students say:

> I've been studying Christian Science. Satan is leading all
> those people astray from the truth. You know, some of them
> say they believe in the Bible, but their doctrine is twisted.

> Catholics, they worship the mother Mary. They go to mass
> and everything. That's their religion, but it's weird to me.
> And the Quakers, they're *really* weird.

"Hogwash," "heresy," "false doctrine," "weird practices"—these
strongly disparaging terms are designed to put right and wrong groups
in perspective for the students with the clarity of an old-fashioned,
Saturday afternoon movie about cowboys and Indians.

In chapel and in regular church services Pastor Muller often refers to
other religious groups. When introducing a missionary who was trying
to raise money to "fish for souls" in Japan, Muller elaborated on the
need to bring Jesus Christ "to the millions who know no God or who
know the false gods of Shintoism and Buddhism." He was angry about

President Carter's handling of the hostage crisis in Iran, and angry with Iran. One day, while speaking of Jonah and his example to Christians, he inserted a comment (more as an aside than an integral part of his sermon message) about the Ayatollah Khomeini's religion and various others: "They're dead. Their gods are dead. Ours is alive."

Bethany's strongest negative reactions are to the Roman Catholic Church. Social studies teacher Frank Fortner says, "A lot of Catholics think they're going to heaven, but I don't think they really are because they're basing it on [doing good] works." Evangelist Bill Hall, using Revelation for his text, tells students that Babylon is the mother of whores:

> Some people believe the Roman Catholic Church is this great harlot. I believe it's just one of the daughters, like the charismatic movement. We don't need the gift of tongues anymore, but today on Notre Dame's campus is one of the largest tongues group anywhere. What brings all the tongues people together isn't doctrine. It's music, feelings—"I feel so good." The National Council of Churches and the World Council of Churches was about to run out of steam until this charismatic thing came along.

A similar perspective is reported in the Bob Jones University family magazine *Faith*, which is provided free to all teachers. The Bob Jones imprimatur is a powerful one in the Bethany community. One *Faith* article, unsigned, takes issue with the charge of bigotry that the Roman Catholic Bishop of Charleston leveled against Dr. Bob Jones for identifying the pope as Antichrist. The writer notes the "subterfuge and deceit of the Roman Catholic Church":

> When Baptists believe that Romanism is nothing but another Protestant denomination, they have fallen victim to one of Satan's most vicious lies. . . . The Catholic Church is trying many new things to deceive. . . . One thing that has not changed is Rome's habit of describing as a "bigot" any one who cries out against her doctrinal atrocities, Scriptural errors, and the vain deceit and idolatry of her Mass. [1980:13].

The lip-service that Bethany leaders give to pluralism is exceptionally difficult to translate into practice at school. Bethany Christians are not the least bit diffident about the absoluteness and universality of their doctrine, but rather than tussle with the dilemmas produced by the acceptance of both pluralism and absolute, universal truth, they leave the principle of pluralism as an abstraction, one that is literally overwhelmed by their Truth and its ramifications: "Are fundamental, Bible-believing churches right and others wrong?" I asked Frank Fortner. "Yes," he answered, "because we're not based on our own viewpoint, we're based on the Bible." "The whole world, everybody on the globe, should be a Christian?" Pastor Muller was asked on a television show. "We believe so," he answered. "And your mission is to lend your own energy to that?" "That's true. That is why we send missionaries out there and spend thousands of dollars to do so. I mean, our faith means something to us."

Steeped in absolutist convictions, Bethany's educators and pastoral leaders have no tradition, nor do they feel any need, to give sympathetic attention to the beliefs and opinions of any group outside the fundamentalist fold.

Political and Social Conservatism

Nor are these educators and leaders any less resolute about societal issues that they perceive to be covered by scriptural principles. If the application of such principles does not have reasonably close bearing on the issue in question, then and only then will they take a qualified position. Unsurprisingly, the fundamentalist Christian is a self-styled conservative. No teacher doubts that Christians should vote conservative. Most think that the conservative position on contemporary issues corresponds with the Word of God, and that it is a characteristic of Christians "to be conservative, to not necessarily be quick to change." "Like Mr. McGraw has mentioned several times," a teacher recalls, "Reagan is the only definitely pro-life candidate. I absolutely believe abortion is murder and totally against anything the Bible has to say about life."

In this way, a political position is established—if liberals support abortion and conservatives oppose it, and if the case for opposition is drawn from Scripture, then Christians are conservative. In fact, opposition to the Equal Rights Amendment and to equal rights for homosexuals joins abortion as a trio of issues that form the core of current conservatism and the basis for selecting political candidates. Christians invariably link the issues together on the grounds that ERA supporters also advocate abortion and homosexual rights, which to Christians are the unwritten, implicit aspects of the amendment. Teachers do not dispute the justice of equal pay for both sexes, but they see ERA as contrary to the biblical view of sex roles and therefore as undermining

God's truth. They believe that sexual equality denies God's word; abortion is murder; and homosexuality is a sin.

Bethany's teachers are equally forthright on the subject of welfare: The Bible says if you don't work, you don't eat. Most recognize that there are genuinely needy persons, but they believe that the welfare system in America caters to the undeserving. Ideally, welfare should be organized through the church—"The Bible says we are to bear one another's burdens." If welfare is warranted sometimes, the welfare system nonetheless "is wrong, very wrong; it is socialistic for me to pay some lady in Chicago for having illegitimate babies."

Teachers are basically of one mind on the subject of race relations. In God's sight, everyone is equal. Mr. Swanson tells his class:

> When I was in high school, there was a black guy on a Chicago basketball team who could scratch his knees without bending over. I really envied him. Blacks have long arms and fingers, but the black man is not a missing link. They are not inferior to whites. We are all one.

Integration of races in school and work is perfectly acceptable, but not if it is forced. Busing, for example, forces integration. Interracial dating and marriage are objectionable. "I love blacks," says teacher Sue Matthews, "but I don't like intermarriages. I've made my daughter promise she wouldn't marry a black." No one cited scriptural authority for this common conclusion, though some thought it violated the principal of not being unequally yoked. Mostly, the teachers reasoned: "If God had wanted the races to be together, he would not have put them in different parts of the earth"; "I think God created us the way that he did with a purpose"; and "I can defend this on a logical, common sense basis, but not on Scripture." Bethany joins Bob Jones University and other Christian schools in the strict prohibition of interracial dating.

In the 1980 season of presidential campaigning, Bethany students hear talk of politics to a degree that is uncommon at any other time. Students know their teachers perceive the choice of president as a critical matter and understand the reasons why. English teacher Donna Reynolds states the case succinctly: "It's important to the academy that Reagan become president; it's for the future of our Christians, I think." Headmaster McGraw, who prides himself on his knowledge of history and is a political activist, elaborates Bethany's perspective:

> Jimmy Carter claims to be born again. Well, the Bible says, "By their fruits, ye shall know them." I can't question his

personal salvation, but I question his biblical understanding. Look at his key appointments—not one of them even
claims to be born again.

For the world of Bethany, this is an incredible omission. To be born
again is to possess the badge of respectability in the fullest sense and in
the *only* way that counts. It is a necessary yardstick for measuring
essential virtue, a password to acceptance by the brethren. Therefore, if
a supposedly born-again president can fully ignore the fact of being
born again as a criterion for making appointments, then the president's
integrity and intelligence must be subject to doubt. McGraw continues
on the same point when he speaks to students during a chapel session:

> We've never been at a lower state in this country because
> Carter does not have a single Christian in his cabinet. He
> doesn't seek advice from godly men. Recently, I was in
> Washington talking to Senator Percy's aide; he was scornful
> of anything godly. [Now he turns directly to the students
> with his message.] You have a free will, so you have the
> choice to act upon either good or bad advice. I'm begging
> and pleading with you to check your sources of advice. The
> number one problem with our nation today is that for the
> last fifteen years our presidents have not had spiritual
> advice.

Social studies teacher Frank Fortner understandably devotes more
time to discussing the election than any other teacher. Throughout the
hostage crisis in Iran he was openly distressed at Carter's seeming
unwillingness to do anything; he is sure Reagan would have done
something had he been president. On the eve of election day, Fortner
tells his students he wants to discuss a few things before the voting
begins. He wears a Reagan-Bush button on the lapel of his sport jacket.

> Things look good for Reagan, now. If he loses, the American
> people will have to realize they put Carter in. I don't respect
> President Carter. When it gets down to it, Carter's anti-
> American. He gave away the Panama Canal, stabbed
> Taiwan in the back, allowed a third-rate country like Iran to
> control us, and then let the IRS interfere in our school.
> Carter is not a Communist, but anyone with a biddy brain
> wouldn't have given away Taiwan. Our biggest threat is
> Communism. Carter's philosophy supports the SALT II
> treaty. How many of you believe Russia will comply with a

treaty? They're liars and atheists. Russia is anti-God, anti-capitalism, antidemocracy, and anti-anything we do."

Fortner identifies several major, enduring concerns of Christians: the Panama Canal, Taiwan, and Communism and the Soviet Union. His positions are those students will hear repeatedly before they graduate. Fortner's comments in class end with an unexpected exchange. A student raises his hand to speak: "I don't think it's right for you to call my president anti-American."

> I have a right [Fortner replies]. I have a right as an American citizen to say what I want. The Panama Canal will eventually be controlled by Communists, and Taiwan's been stabbed in the back.

"I'm with Reagan on all issues," the student continues, backing down somewhat from the boldness of his original statement. "What I'm saying is that I don't think a man can be in the presidential office and be anti-American."

> Folks, don't get me wrong. I'm pro-America and that's why I'm for Reagan. Carter's *actions* have been anti-America; maybe *he* hasn't been anti-America. Are you satisfied, Billy? [he asks the protesting student]. The American people tolerate everybody—Gus Hall, Angela Davis, the Communist party. That makes me stinkin' mad. I'm hoping the right man gets in. I'm not trying to cut down Carter; I'm trying to teach you about Americanism.

Economic Conservatism

If Frank Fortner instructs the students on political Americanism, Mr. McGraw instructs them in his compulsory, one-semester economics course on economic Americanism, abetted by teachings from the Bible class. The thrust is free-enterprise capitalism. His pedagogical orientation to the classroom, as it is to chapel messages and teacher meetings, is advocacy. He knows what the Bible supports and he knows, accordingly, the kind of America he favors. When he reaches what he labels a gray area—one to which he believes the Word of God does not speak directly—he may note that his remarks are outside the realm of scriptural authority, but his advocacy is no less forthright. At various times he made the following statements in his economics class.

On free enterprise:
I hope you come out of this class with a solid free-enterprise ideology, believing that profits are not evil. Free enterprise means a person can go as far as possible, given only the restraints of law. There are, of course, additional laws for Christians, a higher law, such as not lying or misrepresenting.

On government support:
It interferes with survival of the fittest. The government saves inefficient businesses. I think it was a mistake to help Chrysler, Lockheed, and Penn Central.

On competition:
It helps us get the best price. Advertising is my friend; it's one of the key elements that keeps us on our toes. Increased competition is my friend.

On money:
What does it mean to call someone worldly? It means they have goals of the world, such as money. That's why I counsel young people about making pro athletes their heroes. I read about two Swedes who got several million dollars to come here to play hockey. Sweden is one of the most ungodly countries in the world today. . . . Girls, I hope you never look at a guy because of his money. It ruins a guy's spiritual goals.

On unions:
I'm not antiunion but I think much of the blame [for our economic problems] does lie with unions.

On debts:
Don't be a servant to man. How does this happen? Monetarily is one way. If I've got debts and God calls me to the mission field, I won't be able to go.

McGraw's economic orientation gets support from other teachers, perhaps most regularly from Art Swanson. For example, Swanson gives his students dittoed material called Bible Action Truths, which contain a list of thirty-seven "specific goals for their actions and attitudes." Embedded in these "truths" is the hard-work aspect of the Protestant work ethic, not so designated, but nonetheless clearly articulated. With specific scriptural verses provided, these actions are encouraged: goal setting for work that is to be performed with commitment, honesty, enthusiasm, and faithfulness, in the knowledge that God rewards faithful work.

Immersed in the Word

BBA teachers heed Charles Walker's advice about a Christian child's upbringing—that is, to "guard his mind." Guarding minds is a hallmark of BBA's didactic milieu. Teachers make sure that religiosity permeates the academy. Though not a practice marking only fundamentalist schools, it is Bethany's common, intended practice. The permeation, moreover, is as complete as Bethany educators can manage. Unlike public schools and, perhaps many private schools, BBA has strikingly little divisiveness of belief and behavior among persons charged with conducting its curricular and extracurricular activities. The teachers' doctrinal orthodoxy assures that divisiveness does not exist on any matters of consequence.

More than most schools, Bethany emphasizes doing and being, rather than knowing about, but this is a relative matter. BBA, after all, instructs its children about the linguistic, numerical, and environmental aspects of their life. Thus, the study of verb tenses, logarithms, climate, and the constitution composes the nonspiritual, cognitive experience at Bethany. In these moments, obviously, I did best at my When Would a Visitor Know? game. While teachers value and seldom ignore this aspect of their work, it is perhaps the least of what they do, not in terms of time but of commitment: most of what they do is directed toward becoming and *being* Christian. They operate in the active mode, leaving no doubt that the proof of their Christian pudding is in the action of living always as a Christian. Informed that there is but one standard, one outlook, one code of conduct, students are expected to see all of life as one, with no warrant for situational adjustments: right behavior does not vary with time and place.

BBA rejects the notion that students benefit by dealing with alternative perspectives of ideology, interpretation, and policy. Choice, doubt, suspended judgment, evidence—these are excluded from its pedagogical arsenal. On principle, they are strangers to the Christian classroom, alien presences where Truth reigns. Also on principle, students are taught the beliefs and behavior of spirituality and right conduct; they are shown the application of Scripture to mundane affairs like choosing a president and competing in a capitalist economy.

Students do not learn to respect non-Christian others in their own right, but, rather to love them with that peculiar sort of love fundamentalist Christians reserve for the lost, the inhabitants of the world of unrighteousness and darkness with whom they must avoid being unequally yoked. At assemblies they hear recited:

> We're free to witness, visit, teach
> The same dear truths we heard Dad preach!
> And now we vow to God above
> To pass it on to those we love.

"Those we love" are free to reject their offering of truth, but they are condemned should they decide to do so.

Bethany's students are pressed to listen to what their Lord is telling them. They pass their days immersed in an environment replete with their teachers' recital of the Lord's Word and their perceptions of the implications of this Word. Not one school hour passes without reference to the Word or its implications. Bob Jones III can be assured that Bethany goes all out to guard its young Christians from the Devil's darts.

6

Bethany's Deviance
Schooling for Spirituality

Introduction

To this point I have described Bethany Baptist Academy in terms of its doctrinal outlook, its teachers, its structure of control, and its socializing regimen. In this and the next three chapters I want to examine its students, beginning with the ubiquity of "spirituality" in their beliefs and behavior. Of course, I expected youngsters who come to and remain in a school like BBA to differ from their public school peers. And differ they do, but never completely.

They delight in a class session that is intended for English but sidetracks into something else:

> When we don't want to do literature, we'll get Mrs. Reynolds talking about the junior-senior banquet 'cause, see, she's our banquet leader. Like the other day before class kids came up to me and said, "The plan in English today is to talk about the banquet. Everybody has to start asking her questions." That's what we did and the exam ended up being postponed.

They have their share of athletes whose interest in academic performance is dictated by their desire to remain eligible to compete:

> Now that wrestling is over I got two progress reports, meaning I'm failing in Bible and English. When I'm wrestling, they check your grades every two weeks. So I always have a

reminder I've got to study for a test, 'cause if I don't do it, I won't get to wrestle.

BBA students test their first-year teachers, carefully noting and exploiting their vulnerability. Their discriminating reaction to teachers extends just that measure of responsiveness each teacher's disciplinary control merits. Thus, the same set of students pass from first-period teacher A, in whose class the loudest sound heard when the teacher stops talking is a wall clock's advancing minute hand or ballpoint pens rolling across notebook paper, to second-period teacher B, in whose class the students' discordant voices penetrate the walls, the disorder interrupted only briefly when the teacher's even more strident voice penetrates the noise. Student self-entertainment, in those precious moments when the bell has rung but the teacher has not yet arrived, is the fun of all students, not just Christian students. After all, they are not desperately constrained by a straitjacket of rules and regulations. They are spirited, fun-loving youngsters, albeit different from public school peers in ways I will describe later.

The students' self-entertainment in class with teachers present is relatively decorous; it becomes more boisterous when teachers are gone. Waiting for their Bible teacher to arrive, ninth-grade students discuss "Saturday Night Live," the TV show, and how much they enjoy Rosanne Rosannadana. Before the homeroom teacher arrives to begin the morning devotions, several twelfth-grade boys turn upside down all the pictures on the bulletin boards and the room walls. After devotions, when the teacher momentarily leaves her tenth-grade class, students begin to talk: "What have you got in your purse, Carla, dope?" "Yeah, want some?" Others discuss the forthcoming basketball game: "Are you coming tonight?" "Yeah, I'm coming." "Are you bringing your woman?" "Naw."

Before U.S. history begins, Roy reads *Pleasure Seller*; he holds the book up so fellow students can see the sexy cover and he can elicit their "wows." Before drama class begins, one student spoofs Mr. McGraw and, before the class is done laughing, another spoofs a teacher who just the day before had told the students that she demanded so much because she loved them so much. The moment the drama teacher enters the room class begins. Students perform at the front of the room, while peers and teacher assess them: "Organization: Did the introduction capture attention? Was the development orderly? Was the conclusion effective?" It could have been drama class anywhere. Or world history anywhere, as students learn about Louis XVI, the nobility and peasants, the Estates General, and Napoleon. Or English anywhere, as the teacher says, "OK, class, look at the third example. What is the subject and what is the verb? Hmm. For some of you I can see this is as clear as mud. How many think they understand it? At least let me go home with a little encouragement over the weekend." Or testing anywhere, as teachers verify student mastery of content with objective tests: fill in the blanks, matching, multiple choice, list, as in "list six rules for capitalization," and true-false. Or graduation anywhere, as twelfth-graders, who may or may not have mastered the intricacies of verb forms, see their mates being recognized for meritorious citizenship and school spirit, and with John Philip Sousa, National Choir, and Bausch and Lomb Science Awards.

In response to my question, "What do students do at school that is most fun?" students describe their bathroom mischief:

> We may sucker the teachers to get out of class so we can roam around. We'll give an excuse like going to the bathroom. If you go to the bathroom, you can write things on the walls in those little pews, little things, nothing cool. Acting wild—it gets you through the day.

Some of the worst "little things" students write on the bathroom walls are: "Bo Derek is a fox and a half." "I love Bo, '10.'" "Let it rip." And, "Roses are red. Toilets are white. If you eat beans. You'll be here all night."

Though "acting wild" is too extreme to describe student misbehavior in class, they do indeed amuse themselves, both when their teachers are present and when they are absent. As the science teacher asks rhetorically, "What is a carbohydrate?" and begins a lecture in response to this question, his students embark upon a variety of self-amusements. A girl hums, causing the boy next to her to smile when he hears her. She rocks her foot, notices that her stocking is not perfectly taut, and pulls it until all the wrinkles are gone. The teacher talks about enzymes and then nucleic acid. She taps her pen on the seat of her chair; it drops on the floor and the girl in front of her picks it up. Three boys read music books they will use for their ensemble performance. One boy sings and accompanies himself with drumming fingers and tapping toes. A student distracts the teacher with the pupa of a moth he has brought to class. Mr. Kruger picks up on this at once.

> From nature, as Christians, we can learn something here. Scientists have found if you cut it open at this stage, so the moth can get out easier, it won't develop to full capacity. It's

not as strong. That's the way it is with Christians: if you go through a struggle, you'll fight against the devil. God is testing your strength."

He returns to his prepared lecture, and students return to their amusements. They doodle in the midst of taking lecture notes. One boy writes, "The specific heat is the heat of one gram of any substance when its temperature goes up one degree centigrade." Around these words he writes, "Honda, Kawasaki, Yamaha, let the good times roll." And, "Anyway you want it, that's the way you need it." A girl puts on perfume and waves away the fumes she created. The boy at the next desk passes her a tightly wadded note. She throws it back at him. Other note passing connections are more successful. On a piece of notebook paper two students scribble:

> Kiss me, I want mono.
> Who said I had mono?
> Bert has it. You want him to kiss you?
> Ha! Ha! Fairy funny!

Another contains an exchange between a pair of students sitting several rows apart.

> Cassie, I just don't want you thinking I'm mad at you. So just clear your mind of it. (RIGHT NOW) Do you understand? You had better. Ha! Ha! I'm not mad. Friend Forever, Sissy.

> Sissy, Hi! I'm bored. Remember and write me this hour. 'Cause we aren't together next hour. I'll write you next hour as well as this hour. Please write soon! Very Best Friends Forever (I hope) Cassie.

The girl who earlier had tightened her hose raises her hand. "Do we need to know that?" she asks. "What?" "What you just got through explaining." "Yes, it'll be good for you to know this."

These incidents occur in school. They are what students do to amuse themselves and thereby add elements of their own creation to the special environment Bethany's educators establish. In this way, students shape, at least in part, the circumstances at school that impinge upon them. Some students, uneasy with their school's norms, need to do this much more than others. In a sense, they reclaim space, time, and activity so that they are better able to accept the school's legitimated order. These moments of playfulness provide relief, functioning as safety valves for those to whom playing by the book becomes wearying, if not overwhelming.

Finally, Bethany's Christian-Americans exhibit the marvelous contradictions of adolescence. Here is Clara Tilton, freshman student, who has attended BBA since her first day of school.

> Cheerleading is about the funnest thing in school. I just got kicked out of class and that's one of the reasons I'm not going to try out this year. Too many demerits. They said I had terrific cheerleading ability, terrific personality, good spiritual background, everything. I just keep getting more demerits. Like in band today. This package came with stuff that you could make a popping sound with your fingers. Julie and I had a piece behind our backs and were popping 'em when we weren't playing. Mr. Conroy said he heard us popping when we were playing, so I folded my hands right in front of me. Then the piece fell on the floor and Mr. Conroy goes, "What are you doing?" I go, "I wasn't doing anything." And he goes, "You're lying. Go to the office." I went there and came back and apologized and explained everything.

In short, within the framework of the special school Christian educators have established, there is an ordinary school, as ordinary as acne and McDonald's yellow arches.

Notwithstanding their recognizable similarity to other American youth, Bethany's students are meant to deviate from national norms. Indeed, Bethany's educators would feel they had failed if the product of their considerable labor was not a deviant who fit a counterculture to the right of the American mainstream, and yet, by their own lights, was prototypically American in behavior and belief, in manners and morals. As adolescents, like other adolescents, the students must deal with the requirements of classes and peers. So they learn to get by in their academic life and in their social life, but within the narrow boundaries of scriptural tolerance. Their deviance, in keeping with Bethany's ideals, begins at the simple level of appearance and reaches to the complex level of deep, genuine separation from many of the prevailing norms and behavior of American society.

The reality of the Christian student's deviant behavior is, however, not immediately, continuously, or uniformly apparent. After all, both public and Christian schools have similar structures. For example, BBA is a small school, with about 350 students in grades K-12, and about 125 in the junior-senior high school section that is the focus of this study. Thus the dynamics of smallness operate: a need for high rates of student participation in order for extracurricular activities to flourish, extensive face-to-face interactions, and the difficulty students have in finding isolation or invisibility. And it has a number of extracurricular activities that require considerable student and teacher time, talent, and leadership for the product or performance of each activity to be competitive in its appropriate setting. Within its regular class schedule, BBA offers journalism (which produces the school yearbook and newspaper), drama (which produces plays and other performances presented at school and at state and national competitions), and choir and band (both of which, like drama, have school, state, and national arenas). After-school activities include cheerleading and volleyball for girls, and soccer, wrestling, basketball, cross-country running, and baseball for boys. Boys' and girls' teams play other Christian schools, striving for victories that lead to state and national championships. There is not a special subtype of athletics called "Christian athletics." As in public schools, Christian schools observe the standard rules of the game, depend on their coaches to develop student talent, use yellow school buses for interschool transport, and employ referees who wear black-and-white vertical-striped shirts. I noted a few distinctive features of sports at a Christian school, including the pregame prayer and the infrequency of student profanity. Otherwise, wrestling is wrestling, and baseball is baseball, but these events and the others that engage Bethany's students are almost invariably framed by their several distinguishing differences.

Why Students Like Their Schools

Indeed, the differences observed form only a small part of Bethany's deviance; for the rest, one must ask questions to get at the unseen and dimly seen dimensions. I asked Bethany's students and, for comparative purposes, a group of 104 high school students from Hartney's public schools why they liked their schools. Their answers reveal Bethany's idiosyncratic orientation. Students indicated on a four-point scale the importance of each of six reasons for liking their school; then they indicated which of the six was the single most important reason. The percentages shown in table 2 combine the students who chose "important" and those who chose "very important" as their rating of each response. Clearly, public school students do not prize their school for spiritual reasons; equally clearly, Bethany students do. The public–Christian school discrepancy is not nearly so great for any other reason.

The lower ratings Bethany students attach to the conventional gradu-ate-and-get-a-job outcome is consistent with their school's orientation.

The discrepant rating of spirituality persists when students identify the single most important reason they like their school (table 3). From these data we readily see several major distinctions between public and Christian schools: public school students rank highest their school's vocational potential. Although both groups value academic opportuni-ties and friends, BBA students overwhelmingly single out the spiritual factor as most important. None of the other reasons—including the school's academic experience, which BBA students rated highest when they did not have to make a single choice—offers spirituality much competition.

Advice to a Hypothetical New Student

Manifestations of a spiritual factor turned up almost everywhere we looked; it is a ubiquitous element in student life. For example, to obtain one perspective of student culture, we asked Bethany educators to provide advice to a hypothetical new high school student who wants to be a success at BBA. The advice that McGraw and his teachers offer is contained in the following amalgam of quotations and paraphrased statements.

> Get saved—that's the first thing to do if you wish to feel a part of the school, because so much goes on that the un-saved student does not understand. If you're not saved, you're likely to buck the system, and if you do this, then you're always on the outside feeling miserable.

> Beyond being saved, be in church every time the door is open. Have your devotions every day and listen to what speakers in chapel say. Then apply what you hear to your everyday life. Prayer, of course, is very important. Seek the Lord's guidance *before* you act. "The problem with some students is they want to do everything themselves. They want to think for themselves. I know that's the way I was when I was a kid."

> When you do act, be a consistent Christian. Let your friends know that you are not wishy-washy, against rock music at one moment and willing at the next to listen to it on someone's car radio. Or against attending movie theaters, but willing to tolerate talk about some recent movie.

> With regard to school work, get it done and handed in on

time; with regard to the rules, obey them to the letter and
you won't get demerits. And don't be a griper. Dress well,
because you represent the Lord: "Christians ought to be the
sharpest people."

As your authorities, teachers deserve proper respect. Do
not smart-mouth them. Cooperate with them and be submissive. Show them that you really want to learn and
there'll be no limit to their willingness to help you. They like
students to be friendly with them.

For girls to get along with the guys, remember—don't
take the initiative. Smile, be friendly, but let them make the
first move. And set your sights high: "Make sure the guy
you're interested in is on a higher spiritual plain than you
are, that he's someone you can look up to as a spiritual
leader, who loves the Lord and puts him first."

For guys to get along with the girls, don't be rough,
tough, and loud. Avoid the girls, until you get to know
them. Girls often chase any new boy that comes along. No
matter who cares, stand up for what you believe. Be a
leader. Girls respect that: "They need leaders; they need to
be led. God didn't put them in a position to lead. He put
them in a position to follow."

Choose your friends of either sex very carefully. Friends
can be an influence for good or bad. Nine times out of ten, a
bad one will bring the good one down. That's just the way it
is. Like in a public school, there's kids here who'll mock
what we stand for. They're here because of their parents.
Find out who they are and avoid them.

Public school teachers would find sense for their students in much of
the advice Bethany's educators offer. This is equally true in the advice
and information Bethany's students volunteered. Here are BBA girls
informing a hypothetical new girl:

Remember, this is a Christian school. There are all kinds
of kids here, from the super spiritual to the rowdy. Some put
on a front, some are really good Christians, some don't care.
Overall, most are about in between. Wherever you fit, don't
act pious; that's the fastest way to lose friends. If you are
really rebellious, don't ever let it show or you won't last long
here.

The school has many rules and regulations. Obey the
major ones. If you ignore them, be ready for trouble. Don't
worry if you get a few demerits; they won't hurt you. In

general, have a good attitude toward the rules and regulations. They're enforced and nobody gets special treatment.

Do the work the teachers assign. Try hard and take good notes. Apply yourself and the work won't be hard to finish. You can get most of it done in class. Some teachers collect homework, others don't; you'll soon learn who wants what. In math, always do it. In Engish, sometimes it matters, sometimes not. In history, don't bother. It's the same with being strict. All the teachers are strict, but some are new and almost anything goes. Others really mean what they say, but you can still have fun with them.

"You have to sort of be flexible as you go from class to class. Just sit back and watch for a while until you figure out the teachers' personalities." Say yes and no, ma'am, and don't be snotty. Don't smart off, but if you ever do, apologize at once. If you get in trouble, don't show any sign that you intended to do the wrong thing. If you get in trouble and it's obvious, don't try to wiggle out of it. That'll just make it worse. You can get along with all the teachers. All you have to do is obey them and be friendly. They care about us. Like if you're doing bad in a course or something, the teacher will take a special time and explain it to you. They'll talk to you whenever you want. It makes you feel like you're wanted.

For getting along with the girls, be friendly, don't push, and don't be shy. Bragging is out. Just be yourself. Keep a secret and don't ever break a confidence. Don't be a loudmouth about your opinions. For getting along with the guys, be friendly, say hi. Don't be giggly. Talk to them, but not in a loud voice. Don't flirt and scheme or ask a guy out. They'll be offended. That kind of stuff may be accepted some places, but not here. Don't brag about yourself. A guy's got to like you just the way you are. "I like the guys here. It's the first school I've been to when you go out with a guy he's not just out for one thing. Here you can go out and have fun and not have to be anybody's girlfriend."

On the weekends we have youth activities and play games, frisbee, American eagle, stuff like that. Then we have testimonies and a little sermon and singing. Sometimes the fun part and sometimes the religious part gets to you. It just depends on what mood you are in.

And here are BBA boys informing a hypothetical new boy:

The rules and regulations are made for your own good; there's a reason for all of them. Obey them, but don't get upset if you break them sometimes. Everybody does. When you do, expect consequences. After a while, they're not really too hard to follow. There'll be rules you don't like. OK, just be quiet and go along with them. If you like rock music and movies, don't talk about this in public because the word will eventually get back to the teachers and Mr. McGraw. Remember, Bethany's not like a public school. You've got to watch what you do both in and out of school. "There are so many things that are natural for kids our age to do, like going to the movies and dances and things like that. It's hard to keep away from it unless you've never been exposed to it."

This school is serious about Christianity. Act like a Christian even if you're not one; you can still have good morals. If you need spiritual help, there's always someone to help you. Don't think it's funny when you see someone praying. If you're called on to pray, don't make your prayer too short. Go to church, have a good attitude in chapel, and have your devotions every day.

Teachers here really want to help you. "I mean, if you don't understand something, you should ask them. I tend to think that makes a teacher feel good because then they know whether they're getting across to you." There's a number of things to know, however, if you want to get along with them. They are friendly and easy to get along with, but you've got to show respect. Yes, sir, yes, ma'am, that sort of thing. And no sass, no talking out of turn. Look them in the eye when they speak to you, speak in a right tone of voice, and do what they say. The work's not too hard if you pay attention in class, take good notes, and try your best. "It's more of a school that teaches you more about the Bible than any other course. They make it kind of Bible." You'll stay out of trouble if you do your assignments as soon as possible and don't talk where you're not supposed to. You can get away with it with some teachers but not with others.

The guys here are friendly. Just be yourself. Don't be shy or act like a hotshot. If you're OK, they'll talk to you. Talk about what they're interested in—cars, girls, what's doing on the weekend. It helps if you have a sense of humor. Don't be a backbiter or cut down people. If you hear a secret, keep it.

This school is like any other. It's easy to find a wrong crowd and it's easy to find a better one that's living for God. There's guys who party on Friday and Saturday nights, or at least say they do, who sneak around to movies, things like

that. Good guys are right with God. They'll talk about Scripture and they don't laugh at dirty jokes told by the other
crowd.

Mostly, the girls are about like the guys: don't act phony,
be yourself, because people want to know who you are. It
helps to smile a lot and say hi. Be polite; don't hurt their
feelings. If you tease them, don't be hateful. Open the door
for them. They usually like that. Remember that most are
Christians, so you better watch what you say or they'll tell
on you. And remember the school's personal contact rules—
no talking to girls in the halls, and no touching either. It's
OK to date if you're ready for it. "There's certain things they
don't like here about girls. You gotta be careful where you
take 'em—no movies or dark-lit restaurants. And no petting
or different things like that. If you start kissing and you're
not careful, you'll go on to the next thing and the next thing.
Pretty soon you'll be going all the way. You've got to control
your emotions, and stuff like that."

Romance

Romance is very much a part of student life, but it is romance in
Bethany's style. Though strictly enforced prohibitions against public
displays of affection minimize the more usual manifestations of boy-girl
attachments, there are ample indications that love is at home at
Bethany. In the senior homeroom, during the ten minutes before devotions are held, two couples sit side by side, as close as is legally allowed.
They talk, they huddle, they gaze, appearing in striking contrast to their
classmates who casually go about their business of getting ready for
another day. If few students drop out because of pregnancy or get
engaged before graduation, some serious couples plan futures that
extend beyond next weekend's date.

It took us a long time to put it together and a lot of thought
and prayer until we decided that we'll get Karen through
Tennessee Temple real fast—she'll study nursing—and
then I'll start my studies in accounting while she works.

Such cases are the exception, however. More time is spent talking
and anguishing over love interests in the different ways characteristic of
American youth. The school newspaper's gossip column is laden with
over-the-shoulder whisperings understood only by insiders. In early
September, students receive their first newspaper of the year and turn

immediately to page 5 to learn what the pseudonymous "Gladys & Gertie" have to say:

> I guess those Montana [summer youth trip] relationships really do last. Right, Bill and Sara?
>
> Competition with Janie is getting rough, but Hal is in the lead.
>
> Can't Hank make up his mind?
>
> Which two of the junior girls get Bob this week?

The risqué, the salacious style, Bethany rejects. Sex is not a taboo subject; sex is not presented to students as "dirty." The innocence of romantic interests at BBA is a world away from that of their relatively more sophisticated and liberated crosstown counterparts. It is one of those differences calculated to bring cheer to Bethany educators and parents. For example, though they might frown on sophomore Leila Lee's choice of subject matter to exemplify her grasp of proper comma usage, they could not find fault with its innocence. Here is her English class doodling:

> Direct object—Matt, would you help me with my Algebra?
> Closing—Dear Matt, . . . Love, Leila
> Indirect quotation—Yes, I will see Matt at church.
> Appositive—Matt Tomkins, my boyfriend, is a hunk of a guy.
> Quotation—Matt, "Please help me with my Algebra."
> Clauses—Shall I wait for you in church, in front of the church, or at your car?

The passing of notes between students is the bane of teachers everywhere. Yet who at Bethany could take issue with the message of the following notes, the first two passed between freshman girls and the other between a sophomore boy and girl?

> Dear Connie
>   The bus was really good last night. Ray and I talked a lot. On the way home Me and Ray sat in the back. He was looking at my pictures and he saw Beth's. He really likes her but I don't care at least we're friends. Don't tell anyone about my retainer. I don't want anyone to know. OK.
>   Rose

Dear Rose
   I won't tell anyone about your retainer. That's the way I
feel about Ken. I know he has a girlfriend. I'm just glad we're
friends. That's all that matters.
                                                            Connie

   Retainers and unrequited love are typical concerns of adolescents.
Rachel's message to Joe is another matter. But innocence prevails:

Joe
   I'm not the kind of girl who lets a guy boss me around. I
don't like any guy doing that to any girl. I'm not committing
myself to any one guy right now.
   If you save me a seat at lunch I'll sit with you, but I don't
want to sit with Timmy and those guys.
   I'm not going to meet you anywhere on my bike 'cause
Mom will somehow find out and I'd be in big trouble. Plus,
I'd feel very bad 'cause I'd have to lie about where I was
going and what I was doing.
   If you walk home after practice and want to walk together
that's fine, just so we don't lie about it. Talk to ya later.
                                                            Rachel

Academics

However much students and teachers may value other things, they
must reckon with their school's academic side. If academic achievement
at BBA takes a back seat to salvation, the development of Christian
character, and serving the Lord, its educators are pleased that their
students regularly exceed national norms on standardized achievement
tests. This success is the proud claim of many Christian schools across
the nation. Lacking labs, workshops, and other costly features of
schools, they nonetheless feel they can answer would-be critics on
grounds that concern many parents—satisfactory student performance
in the basics as revealed by test scores.
   In their actual responses to classroom demands, students run the
gamut from serious, intense effort to careful indifference. Very few
ignore their work outright, because most of their parents have the
heightened concern that comes with paying tuition costs, and because
their teachers persistently monitor student performance. Most students
agree that BBA is neither very easy nor very hard. While As are hard to
get—marks must be 94 percent or higher to score an A—getting Cs is

not. English usually is deemed the toughest subject and Bible the easiest, instruction here taking the form of dictated notes and tests requiring only memorization for top scores. Reasonably attentive listening in class and then pretest boning up suffice for passing tests. Homework is commonly given, but with both in-class and study hall time available, it does not necessarily require work at home. High achievers are found in every class, some of them among the faithful homework doers and serious test preparers, whereas others do equally well with no apparent effort. Serious academic competition probably exists only in the twelfth grade, when the choice of valedictorian and salutatorian is made, and even then it is limited to very few students. There is no clique of academically oriented students, nor is the realm of academics usually the high point of a student's day at Bethany. One bright junior girl described with pleasure her exceptional experience in history one day when the class debated whether General Sherman's burning of Atlanta could be justified. The search for facts and the openness of the discussion, she said, and "that the teacher actually let us argue about it in class and present our side" were firsts for her at BBA (which she had attended for nine years). Top students are not unduly teased or singled out by fellow students in any way; they need not hide their success or feel uneasy about it.

Being Spiritual in the Right and Wrong Ways

Academic competition joins a moderate level of vying in the areas of dress, sports, and spirituality that seldom reaches a point of engendering hard feelings. Each of these competitions is an element of peer group formation at Bethany Baptist Academy, but none of them is more salient than that which involves spirituality, the pervasive quality that establishes BBA as an institution promoting deviance.

Although students disagree somewhat on the extent to which their school should emphasize the development of spirituality and on the number of students who are spiritual (their estimates ranged from about 50 to 75 percent), they do agree that it is an extremely important school goal. They all do not use the very same expressions to describe the behavior of a spiritual person, but they are not far apart on what constitutes its major attributes.

At the heart of spirituality students place several core behaviors —putting God first in one's life, reading the Bible, praying, wanting to and trying to do right, faithfully attending church, and witnessing one's faith to others. Beyond this core, there is not so much disagreement as there is a personalized expression of this prime attribute that each Bethany student must come to terms with in one way or another.

For John, a longtime BBA student, spirituality has become the norm. He sums it up with ease: "Spiritual people stay out of trouble, read their Bible, have a concern for others, witness, have a good attitude—just an all-round good kid, I guess." Harry, in still more informal terms, unhesitatingly answers the question, "How does a person act spiritually?"

> OK, let's say we were on a bus riding down to Bob Jones and you got this spiritual kid and this unspiritual kid. Let's say each of 'em rolls up some socks and starts throwing them around. Later that night the unspiritual kid might start telling dirty stories. But the spiritual one would move his seat because he doesn't like to hear such stories, or he might ask you not to tell those stories. See, throwing socks wouldn't be wrong, but telling dirty stories would.

Sally adds a point about the spiritual person that many of her classmates share: though spirituality is a good thing, it can be phony, put on to manage impressions, and it can be expressed in unacceptable ways. The spiritual person, Sally says, should act like a "real good Christian" whether or not other people are around.

Students sometimes put on a false Christian front, motivated by the desire to gain acceptance from fellow students and teachers in a setting that endorses a single standard of acceptability. Adolescents in a Christian school like BBA may wear spiritual garb in order to be at home in the best company at school and, indeed, in most of the settings they frequent.

Wendy describes a "make-believe spirituality" that has the effect of making other, less imbued classmates act more spiritual than they really are. "It just kind of goes through the school," says Wendy, "like when everyone comes back from Winter Weekend [two days of fun in the snow combined with experiences to promote salvation, rededication, commitment to full-time Christian service, etc.] and everybody's really spiritual. After a while it'll kind of leave, and, you know, you get back to normal." In addition, she says that when you are at school and you want teachers to think more highly of you, you act more spiritual than you are, but "when you're out with your friends, you're your regular self."

Sally also wants her "real good Christian" to be good without being a "real pious-type person," someone whose behavior is motivated by the need to appear better than acceptable. Students have appropriate labels for the too-pious classmates they identify as undesirably spiritual. They do not abound at BBA; the consensus is that there is at least one unacceptably spiritual student in every class. Students do not scorn or reject their zealous fellows so much as regret them, even feeling sorry for them when, if they are both too pious and socially incompetent, they have become isolates. Here is how they characterize them.

A Holy Joe is a person "who refuses to participate when everyone else in class has just chalked the erasers and is hiding under the desk waiting for the teacher to return. If you come down too heavy with your religion, they'll call you a Holy Joe." It is not usually a complimentary term, but there are negative and positive types. "The positive type is the one who is trying to take a stand when you are backsliding." The negative type is "the hypocrite who is good just to impress people at school." When they are out of sight of school, they are out of goodness. There is a Mr. Righteous, a Mr. Goodie Goodie trying to be good but for the wrong reasons. He is "trying to be better than anyone else" as if he were competing in a goodness sweepstakes. And there is a Miss Pious—"that's a person who seems never to get in trouble; if you do wrong, she'll completely ignore you"; and a Joe Bible, also a snob, whose behavior tells you that you are less holy than he is (when you already believe that your own behavior—though this side of angelic—is up to standard).

> We had a Miss God here last year. She'd tell everybody she saw what she got out of her morning devotions and then ask you what you got out of yours. If you hadn't had your devotions she'd say, "Well, I'll pray for you." She was a real nice girl but she had this problem. It just turned everybody off.

Spiritual Talk

The excesses of Miss Pious, Miss God, and the Holy Joes must be seen within a context where students, other than the newest of newcomers or the few who remain at BBA only because of parental insistence, manifest their spirituality quite naturally. Spirituality is the norm at BBA. It follows, therefore, that good and bad examples will develop. It is the abiding condition of school life, compelling action and reaction. Thus, while topics like last night's basketball game and this weekend's skating party claim more of their time, the spiritual-oriented talk of Bethany's students is one more marker of their school's distinctiveness.

Concerns and questions generated by Bethany's doctrinal commitments are points of discussion before school in the lunchroom, in class before lessons begin, during lunch and study hall, after church, and on long bus trips. For example, what are the limits of propriety on a date? Is it acceptable to date a non-Christian? Is all country-western and rock music objectionable? Is the academy's absolute prohibition of such music justified? Is a student's testimony impaired in any way if he owns and drives a hotrod? Is speaking in tongues an acceptable Christian practice or are the pentecostal churches off base? Is long hair un-Christian? These questions are not about abstractions. They relate to the actual behavior of Bethany students; the answers affect what they will do today, whether they will feel guilty about what they do, and how they will judge the behavior of others.

Other matters, often more profound, also stimulate student discussion. Is Bethany right to criticize the TV ministries ("PTL" and "700 Club")? "I don't think this is right," says Phil, "because they probably lead a lot more students to the Lord than we would ever do." What is eternity and the Second Coming of Christ? "I can't understand eternal things. I can't picture in my mind being in heaven or hell for eternity," says Brad, yet his school life is replete with references to this concept. "Revelation is kind of hard to understand," he adds, "and we talk about that." As do many of his classmates:

> We talk about the millennium, when it's coming and what we think it's going to be like then. And different things like if the earth is going to be made over and if we would have a choice of where we wanted to live and what kind of house we wanted to have.

Predestination is another puzzler that generates student talk as they struggle to grasp both that they have free will and that everything that happens to them is in accordance with God's plan.

More on the light side is the occasion one day in junior English class when the teacher was gone for a long time and a student, for some reason, quoted a Bible verse. Someone said, "Well, aren't you Mr. Bible?" Other students began to quote Bible verses, one right after the other. "I guess maybe it looked like a game of 'I can quote more verses than you,' but it wasn't like that. It was great fun. Really neat. It brought us back to Bible verses we'd learned at home."

An abiding concern among those students who cannot unquestioningly accept Bethany's proscriptions is how to reconcile their own strong sense of being in God's will, with the realization that they are

violating a known school standard. For many students, Bethany's doctrinal thrust exists side by side with countervailing behavioral possibilities generated by their family, the media, and other sources. Accordingly, there are and always will be students (some will be described in
chapter 9) who depart from established strictures but reject neither the
designation of, nor the basis for being, a born-again Christian. In this
regard, sophomore Jill Bourne describes a conversation she had with
classmate Tom Fisher:

> Every day we discuss religious matters among ourselves.
> It's just a natural thing. Just last hour Tom and I were talking
> about—how do I say it?—we have to live under our own
> convictions, because someone else shouldn't make their
> convictions sins to us. We should do what *we* think God
> wants us to do. And when we're in the right relationship
> with God, he'll show us what is right and wrong. Those
> other people don't have to live with us; we have to live with
> ourselves.

While far short of rebellion, this mixture of orthodoxy and independence is not Bethany's ideal.

Our Brother's Keeper

Bethany's educators would be pleased to learn how fully considerations
of spirituality enter their students' lives. Student commitment to being
their brother's keeper is an illustration. Helping one's friends is not
newsworthy. Typically, people anywhere assist those dear to them,
preventing them from getting hurt or going overboard with ill-fated
plans. At Bethany, students learn that the proper compass of their
concern is all Christians; they also see peer models who have internalized this ideal. In short, peer involvement in the socialization of their
peers for spiritual ends is BBA's norm, albeit not one that all students
uniformly accept or even that its adherents invariably practice. The
picture I mean to convey is one in which students intrude quite naturally in the lives of their classmates. They do so not as vigilantes or as
agents of adult authority, but, rather, in the name of standards that by
high school years are an ingrained dimension of their lives. That
Bethany students strive to influence their peers to get right with the
Lord is one of the school's most distinctive qualities.

Peer influences range from efforts to control classmates who have
become rowdy in the absence of their teacher to witnessing to friends

known never to have been saved. Indeed, there appears to be no major infraction of the school's pledge and no spiritual shortcoming that fails to attract peer attention. Is a group of senior boys "getting out of hand?"

> Well [said Danny], my classmates had heard us talking about different things we'd done and they started writing these things down and went to Mr. McGraw with a list of the stuff. He talked about putting us on disciplinary probation and even making us start coming here to church. If it'd come to that, I'd have left school.

One of the "good" seniors recalls that he and some of his friends were getting tired of their reputation as a "bad" class. When he got a chance to serve as chaplain, he "preached" and "laid it right on the line" to the "bad" ones. Danny, a basketball player, also heard frequent admonitions about swearing in the locker room, his response to the frustration of a winless season.

> One guy said to me, "Danny, I know you're saved, but get right with God." That's all he said and then he left. I hated his timing. It was right after the last home game and we'd been beat again and I hadn't scored. I'd fouled out and I was mad. I guess I don't mind if they do this sort of thing in a nice way, not like they're better than you and you should be like they are."

Phil Bestor, Danny's fellow basketball player and also a target of reform, heard the same admonitions during the season, but unlike Danny he responded positively after his close friend Guy had changed his own ways and then persuaded Phil "to get right."

> See, Guy knew the way I was living was wrong and if he hung around me, I could drag him down. Him and his girlfriend and two other girls at school had been praying for me until one Friday night after a game it happened: I got saved. When it happened, we prayed and cried and hugged each other.

Danny never fully conformed when he thought he was beyond the hearing of authority.

> Danny was in the shop room humming rock songs [says Brad]. I asked him to stop and he did but he started to heckle

me a bit. Like, "We don't want to corrupt Brad's brain, do we?" That was just his way of getting back at me. I don't mind. I was just standing up for what the school stands for. I'd classify myself as a coward if I hadn't said anything to him.

Rock music is a troublesome area for students. Though they know the academy strictly forbids it, some students put listening to rock in the category of personal discretion. In the case of cheating on a test, Rae says that if she is sure the student cheated, she will tell a teacher. In the case of listening to rock, she knows the school forbids it, but since it is "in your private life," she would not report a student who listened to it regularly. Her classmate strongly disagrees.

> During homeroom the teacher had been talking about what's wrong with rock and a lot of the kids disagreed. We were still talking about it at lunch. One girl said, "There's nothing wrong with it. I don't have any convictions about it!" Well, I talked to her for a long time and told her verses [from Scripture]. Usually we tell each other verses because your friends won't listen to you if you just say they're wrong. People take it pretty well if they know you are really trying to help them.

Advice backstopped by verses is the form in which students receive advice from the adults in their lives. Teachers daily hear Headmaster McGraw draw upon one of his many favorites in Proverbs. They, in turn, underpin their commands with scriptural authority. Thus, students have a clear model regarding how to address a peer perceived to be in need of correction. Sophomore Tracy Quinn recalls a recent occasion when she helped a classmate:

> This girl, she's always mad over dumb little things. Miss Bennett, our PE teacher, was always yelling at her for not getting her clothes on on time. So I took God's word and I showed how she shouldn't get mad, but she should try harder to please God and Miss Bennett.

Brad, opposed to Danny's humming, was himself the object of a friend's spiritual intervention, for he had stopped having his devotions until his friend Sally reached him. Long-time friends, they usually spent some time each school night on the phone. One day she asked him if he had had his devotions. When he said no, Sally said, "I'll be praying for you because you need them." While Brad's friends and teachers would never classify him as one of the school's spiritual leaders, he has accepted the school's standards in a distinctive way. He is unusually stalwart.

> If somebody is doing something wrong, Brad'll say, "Why don't you guys straighten up?" Not too long ago I was on the ball field and two of the guys were arguing on the mound. Brad was in the outfield and there were some spectators in the stands. Brad came up to these guys and told them to knock it off because arguing wouldn't look right to people watching us. The next day a couple of teachers told him he'd done the right thing.

In this instance Brad was responding to the much-repeated advice students hear to be sensitive to how their behavior will reflect on the school. If Bethany students look and sound like the world, how can they communicate Bethany's Truth to the world? Yet, Brad will go to the movies during the summer when, he reasons, his time is his own and he is beyond the reach of his school's pledge.

Clearly, students intervene in the life of their peers. They discourage the telling of dirty jokes, the dating of non-Christians, the "wrong" weekend plans, and the smoking habits of their friends. The discouragement may be generated by various motives, it may be done deftly or clumsily, and it may involve considerable social risk, as in the case of a new Bethany student who saw her friends (among them the brightest, most popular students in the class) cheating and told the teacher. The cheating students, understandably annoyed at being caught and reported, did not reject their exposer.

Freshman Jackie Wright was less fortunate. Her good friend smoked, told Jackie about her habit, and tried to get her to promise she would not tell anyone about it. When Jackie failed to convince her friend to stop smoking, she told a teacher.

> The girl ended up getting real mad, her sister got mad, and everybody got mad. I lost a friend, but I'd do the same thing again. Number one, she shouldn't have been doing it. She was hurting herself. Number two, it hurts our school, you know, if people find out. And three, she could be influencing others.

This fourteen-year-old had learned her lessons well—she knows that smoking is prohibited, but, more than this, she knows all the reasons that any Bethany adult would have offered to substantiate the prohibition. To be sure, public schools also have their Jackies, but would they ever be more than an exceptionally small minority, one that their peers would scorn? If Jackies are not the majority at Bethany, they are nonetheless fully acceptable—not merely tolerated—within the school's adolescent culture.

Spirituality in Student Social Life

The spirituality that establishes Bethany's students as deviant is an integral part of the school's landscape.

> You hear it, you know, in chapel on Monday, Wednesday, and Friday, you hear it in homeroom Monday through Friday. And then I hear it on Saturday mornings when I go bus calling, Thursday nights at visitation, and Wednesday night, Sunday morning, and Sunday night at services, besides my own devotions and those every day with my parents.

Little wonder, then, that in addition to the typical bases for student social groupings—personality traits or shared interest in sports, dating, or music—degree of spirituality also is a major factor. It is not farfetched to conclude that, other things being approximately equal, birds of a spiritual feather flock together.

Senior Phil Ramsey's recollections serve as an introduction to the part that the individual's degree of spirituality plays in social relations at Bethany, a topic I explored through both interviews and questionnaires.

> Everybody in my class knew I had a wild nature. A lot of kids here at school ignore you sometimes, and then they kind of talk to you, try to witness to you, at other times. The only time they'd ever talk to me was when they tried to witness. Otherwise, forget it. I felt bad but there's a lot of students that had been saved and backslid and we just kind of hung around together.

Billy, a more conforming young man, confirms Phil's observations:

> Every school has, like, its good kids and bad kids. I think that if you are not quite living up to the standards of certain

kids around here, then you can be with the not-so-good kids. Or if you act good enough, you can be with the good kids.

And Phil Ramsey's classmate, Gary, from the other side of the spiritual tracks, further elaborates:

Some of the group, it's kind of hard to hang out with them because you can get in trouble. So, you just have to be friendly, show love and concern. But you really can't hang out with them because you can't do some of the things they do, like skip church, or something.

To ascertain the place of spirituality among a set of personal qualities that could affect a student's popularity, I asked Bethany and Hartney students to rank these attributes in order of importance: athletic, comes from the right family, fun-loving, intelligent, good-looking, spiritual, cares about others. The results are shown in table 4. They confirm the impressions derived from interview and observation data about the primacy of spirituality at Bethany compared to six other likely factors that contribute to popularity; good looks are a distant second, even more so for boys at both schools, though it is the single most important factor among Hartney students. "Cares about others" is important at BBA and moderately important at Hartney until we consider its combined ranking. Then it rivals spirituality at BBA for both sexes and good looks for boys at Hartney. "Fun-loving," "intelligent," "right family," and "athletic" assume greater importance in the combined rank percentages of both sets of students, with "fun-loving" and "intelligent" given lesser salience by BBA students. Coming from the "right family" ranks higher than "spiritual" at Hartney, but students at neither school give it much prominence. Being athletic is surprisingly important for BBA girls compared to BBA boys and Hartney boys and girls.

In reality, degree of spirituality interacts with other characteristics in the formation of student groups. For example, students who actively participate in the church's youth programs and religious services have little time and inclination to be with students less committed than they are. Students who are more or less equally committed will sort themselves out in terms of other factors affecting social choices. Moreover, in season, boys from the wrestling team may hang out together at lunch time and at postmeet festivities. Girls in the same class who are equally "boy crazy" may congregate. In these and other instances, however, spirituality tends to be the other-things-being-equal factor that acts as a necessary condition for students to assemble in a group who otherwise are alike in terms of personality and interests.

Students are taught to conform to the academy's code of conduct. The more conforming students are uneasy being close to the less conforming ones; differential standards of speech, conduct, and social contacts generate tension in a setting wherein all are taught that the less spiritual, like rotten apples, always spoil their more spiritual companions. There is no reason to believe that student groups at Bethany should enjoy a greater or lesser extent of stability than those at public schools, but when a Bethany student shifts from one group to another, the factor of spiritual congruence is likely to remain relatively constant. One's pals need not agree on the propriety of strewing toilet paper in the trees around a teacher's home (to which conduct Scripture has no particular connection), but they probably must be of one mind about listening to rock music, and most definitely about smoking, drinking, and using profanity, because Bethany's educators proscribe these behaviors.

Spirituality also functions as a necessary condition in the identification of elite individuals and groups. As discussed earlier, students cannot serve as class officers or cheerleaders unless they have demonstrated their spiritual acceptability to Headmaster McGraw and others with administrative responsibility. There is no route to being a school hero that circumvents the school's standards. Students seldom identify an in group in their own class or in the school, but when they do, the group always combines manifest talent in music, sports, or drama, for example, with manifest high spirituality; being only very bright, beautiful, or athletic does not suffice to attain elite status.

Notwithstanding the presence of individuals and groups who vary along a spiritual continuum, BBA tolerates variance in student behavior within fairly clear limits. A student may get caught attending a movie theater once a semester without being expelled; yet, if he shows a pattern of movie-going, Headmaster McGraw will expel him, as he would any student who, though falling short of the set number of demerits requisite for expulsion, regularly violates a major Bethany standard (e.g., smoking, drinking, lying). Students who are known to reject Bethany's core doctrinal beliefs are not only uncomfortable at this school, they are not permitted to stay. In fact, as we will see, if Bethany's students vary in degree of spirituality and rowdiness, they still are strikingly consistent in accepting their school's central tenets.

7

By Their Fruits
The Impact of Orthodoxy

A good tree cannot bring forth evil fruit, neither can a corrupt tree bring forth good fruit. Every tree that bringeth not forth good fruit is hewn down, and cast into fire. Wherefore by their fruits ye shall know them.

Matthew 7:18–20

I'm proud of my school because I've been here all my life. . . . And I'd have to say that if anybody tried to pick a fight with me about the school, I'm the type of kid who would probably fight back.

Bethany junior

Introduction

Bethany Baptist Academy strives to be "a good tree" that will triumph over the corrupt trees of the world. That religious day schools can, in their own terms, bear "good fruit" is clear from studies conducted in a variety of denominational schools.[1]

Since the academy had graduated only three classes of seniors at the time of my study, I thought it untimely to do a full-scale study of the impact of Christian schooling on its graduates. Indeed, only Greeley and Rossi (1966) have conducted such research. I intended, rather, to characterize the fundamentalist schooling experience by portraying Bethany's socializing means and by describing its students and some of the factors that contribute to why they are the way they are.

I found the students' public behavior—their closed eyes, bowed heads, prelunch prayers, their classroom responses, and their essays—

indicative of religious commitment, but this behavior occurs in an institution that powerfully encourages and rewards it. I did not discount their conforming behavior in public, such as in the following pre-Thanksgiving chapel scene, when the speaker asks students to say what they are thankful for:

> *Student*: A good Christian school.
> *Student*: Jesus dying on the cross.
> *Student*: Food.
> *Speaker*: Let me ask you, "What's the most important food?"
> *Student*: The Bible.
> *Speaker*: Do you try to eat the Bible? [Students laugh.] We shall not live by bread alone. We eat the Bible with our ears. Anything else?
> *Student*: Freedom.
> *Speaker*: Freedom for what?
> *Student*: To read God's Word.

But I needed to obtain a more comprehensive measure of their behavior. For these students knew what answers the chapel speaker wanted and they provided them, as did the student who, in the school newspaper, reported the results of an opinion poll of student television watching and concluded:

> Another question that should have been asked can be answered by everyone inside his own mind. It is between you and God. If you fully realized that Christ is with you all of the time, would you stop watching some TV shows? Would you watch any shows at all?

Teachers cheer this public behavior, but for the purpose of this chapter and the next, I turn to students' reports of their own behavior and feelings in questionnaires and multiple-session interviews, and to the results of parent and teacher questionnaires. We interviewed students after five months of daily contact with them and we administered the questionnaires eighteen months after the study began. Honesty is a much-prized virtue in Bethany's school and church and I am persuaded on the basis of their responses that the students are either excellent actors or the most forthright students I ever met.

I will present the positive picture—the good fruit—in this and the next chapter and the negative picture thereafter, although reporting the one dimension often reveals the other. In scriptural terms, students rarely are perfectly consistent and perfectly correct in thought and deed;

however, save for those few who detest BBA and reject its doctrine, both the students who cheer and those who distress their teachers do so from within its doctrinal fold. All mix obedience and independence; if Bethany measured success only by constant goodness, it would have to declare itself a failure.

Orthodoxy of Contact[2]

A prime measure of Bethany's success is the extent to which its students are encapsulated in a social network that essentially endorses its doctrinal standards. "Bethany's success" does not refer to results that are necessarily attributable to BBA's efforts, but to outcomes that please the school's teachers and administrators. Though Bethanyites know they possess Truth, they know also that their Truth is not instantly grasped and accepted by either their young or old adherents, nor, once grasped and accepted, that constancy can be expected. The unsaved world thwarts God's way and thus the more fully BBA students associate only with their brethren and are immersed in the Word of God, the more certainly, Bethany believes, do they tread the right path.

And associate with their brethren they do! Of the 115 students who took my questionnaire, 69 percent said that their church or school sponsors all or most of their nonhome activities. Furthermore, I asked students to indicate if the persons they associated with in various places and circumstances usually accepted Bethany's doctrine, or in McGraw's words, their biblical standards. This was true of the persons they associated with at school—87 percent chose the "always" or "most of the time" responses; after school—79 percent; on weekends—84 percent; and during vacation times—75 percent. Similarly, of the 5 persons whom each of the 115 students identified as being most influential in their lives, 80 percent (of 575) are in Bethany's doctrinal camp. To corroborate further the orthodoxy of student contacts, I asked students to indicate on a five-point scale the degree of spirituality of several key persons, with average being the middle point. Eighty-nine percent rated their mothers average to high in spirituality; their fathers—80 percent; their siblings—79 percent; their best school friend—76 percent; their best nonschool friend—44 percent; their relatives—49 percent; and themselves—82 percent.

Faithfulness in attending church services, activities, and programs is one important indicator of the degree of contact one has with a formal, organized source of the Word of God. On this dimension, students also rated significant persons in their lives: 79 percent rate their mothers average to high in faithfulness; their fathers—77 percent; their siblings—83 percent; their best school friend—89 percent; their best non-school friend—54 percent; their relatives—54 percent; and themselves—91 percent.

Students consistently rate themselves more spiritual and more faithful than most persons they regularly see. Their faithfulness is borne out by the data they provided about their own *usual* behavior, defined as what they do always or most of the time: 90 percent attend Sunday school; 92 percent attend Sunday morning services; 80 percent attend Sunday evening services; 67 percent attend Wednesday evening services; and 72 percent participate in their church's youth activities. Their participation in these several church activities can be a matter of parental, peer, or school pressure. Consequently, I asked them to indicate their willingness to participate. They least willingly go to visitation—67 percent, and to Sunday youth chapel—72 percent; otherwise, the extent of their willingness is not less than 85 percent. Their willingness to be faithful church members exceeds the actual extent of their participation.

A student's home influence is important to consider when evaluating orthodoxy of contact. Accordingly, I administered a questionnaire to 120 parents and got back 47.[3] These 47 seem to be a highly religious group, judging from their extensive participation in church services and activities, and from the fact that (1) 98 percent say they are happiest when living in the Lord's will; (2) 98 percent ask God to help them when they are making an important decision; and (3) 89 percent feel that their fellow church members are just like members of their family. Of the 47, 37 have been saved for ten or more years; 35 belong to Bethany Baptist Church; 12 belong to different Baptist and fundamentalist churches. In terms of spirituality, most rank themselves and their spouses above average.

I asked several questions designed to ascertain the orthodoxy of the persons with whom parents were most involved. Orthodoxy is defined as acceptance ("agree" or "strongly agree") of the academy's biblical standards. The results are as follows for the five most influential persons in their lives: 87 percent of those they identify as their first most influential person accept BBA standards; 89 percent—their second most influential person; 81 percent—their third most influential person; 85 percent—their fourth most influential person; and 72 percent—their fifth most influential person. I asked parents to provide similar information about their closest friends: 85 percent of those they identify as their closest friend accepts BBA standards; 74 percent—second closest friend; and 59 percent—their third closest friend. Finally, 85 percent of the 47 parents estimated that at least half of the regular visitors to their homes were born-again Christians.

Students spend a major portion of their time with their teachers. Though BBA hires teachers on the basis of their reputed faithfulness and spirituality, to what extent do they live up to expectations? The questionnaire data provide an answer. In regard to faithfulness, their participation approximates 100 percent or they do not remain employees of Bethany Baptist Academy. That they willingly participate in Bethany's services and activities is evident from the orthodoxy of their own regular social contacts. Bethany's church or school sponsors their usual (defined as what occurs always or most of the time) nonhome activities 100 percent of the time. Of the people they usually see away from school, 100 percent accept the academy's doctrinal standards. Of the five different persons each of the 16 teachers identify as most influential in their lives,[4] 98 percent accept the academy's doctrinal standards; of the 16 teachers' three closest friends, 98 percent are born-again Christians (the one exception is a Protestant but not born again); of all their friends, 13 of the 16 teachers said at least 85 percent are born-again Christians. Finally, their spouses, and their own and their spouse's parents, grandparents, and siblings are overwhelmingly born-again Christians.

In their personal conduct, many teachers, like their students, are inconsistently orthodox. I asked them to indicate the extent to which several of their free-time activities were congruent with BBA doctrinal standards. In their responses we see the other side of the uniform front they present while on the job. Of the 16 teachers, 62 percent said that at least some of the time they watch movies that their doctrinal standards do not encourage; 50 percent said this about the books they read; 50 percent about the television shows they watch; and 25 percent about the music they listen to.

Also in regard to free-time activities, I asked teachers to report on the frequency of three behaviors that BBA instructs its students to accept as the obligations of born-again Christians. "When you get a chance, do you witness to persons you know are not saved?" Sixty-nine percent said "usually." "If a close friend of yours is not right with the Lord, do you make an effort to set him straight?" Sixty-two percent said "usually." "When you have an important decision to make, do you ask the Lord for help?" One-hundred percent said "usually." In none of these three instances did any of the teachers answer "never." Asking the Lord for help is the easiest of the three acts of devotion, as the teacher responses indicate.

The data above convey a sense of the orthodoxy of the teachers Bethany employs to socialize its students. In the case of the teachers' spouses and close relatives, and in their choice of friends and significant others, they could not be much more orthodox. But no teacher or administrator is uniformly, consistently orthodox in behavior. Since their doctrinal standards are many and demanding, they, too, fall short of perfection, though closer to it than their students and close enough to act as role models for them.

Commitment to Community

Bethany Baptist Academy, as an agent of Bethany Baptist Church, contributes to that sense of belonging that is a hallmark of religious groups. Though BBA devotes considerable attention to developing an attachment to one's born-again brethren, whoever and wherever they are, the school's and the church's reinforcement of faithfulness means that there is substantial contact among the faithful and, accordingly, the possibility of attachment to one's local church as the most palpable institutional manifestation of one's faith and spirit. Students appear to have developed such an attachment. "Are you more interested in news of your church than of your town?" I asked; 62 percent answered "usually," and only 11 percent said "never." "Do you feel more loyal to your church than to your country?" This is a tough question for students whose school steeps them in patriotism second only to fundamentalist doctrine. Only 2 of 115 students failed to answer. Of the remaining 113, 42 percent said "usually" and 27 percent said "never." "Are church members almost like your family members?" To this, my last question exploring the student's sense of their church as their community, 66 percent said "usually" and only 10 percent said "never."

At every turn, BBA students are taught that they are their brother's keeper and, moreover, that they live in a hostile, humanist world. By virtue of their faithfulness at church activities, students and adults have frequent contacts that facilitate knowing a great deal about their affiliated others. This process is enhanced by the occasional act of giving one's testimony, a public statement that usually contains confessions of sins and renewed spiritual commitments; and also by the common practice of public prayer of the type that precedes each BBA class and is part of the Wednesday church service and the Saturday men's prayer group. Thus, by means of both testimony and prayer, Bethany's young and old acquire a great deal of personal knowledge about each other.

French sociologist Emile Durkheim wrote, "In vain do we sever—or attempt to sever—the bonds that connect us to each other. . . . We cling necessarily to the milieu surrounding us. It pervades us, it blends with us" (1915:71). Bethany's fond hope is to create such a milieu so that students will find it unthinkable to sever their bonds with each other, their brethren, and God's binding Word.

Religious Commitment

In many different ways I have been trying to establish a central fact about Bethany Baptist Academy—that its students are basically committed Christians in Bethany's terms. What BBA has laid down as its norms, the students accept as theirs. Here I shall present further data that characterize the students' religious orientation. It is essentially a positive picture drawn primarily from our interviews with approximately sixty students.

Public documents, such as articles in the student newspaper and essays written for English assignments, are likely to reveal a socialized response, one tuned in to what teachers want to hear. Here is one written for the school newspaper:

> Love is what every Christian needs in his life. He needs not the love that two sweethearts share in the back of a car seat, but the love of God. This is the love that makes people go to the most backward tribes to teach them about the Word of God.

And here is another prepared for tenth-grade English:

> The things that I'm afraid of spiritually are forgetting about God and His will for my life, or falling into a deep sin. I never want to quit thanking God for all he has done for me. I sometimes get afraid if I ever quit having my devotions what God would do to me. I'm just thankful He's a merciful God.

I do not know how genuine these sentiments are; both statements indicate that the students at least learned their lessons well. I am more convinced of the authenticity of student expressions in the private letters they write to their friends, although here, too, they could be putting forward their best spiritual foot. Here are two examples:

> Hello little sister! How ya doing? Hey, I'm really sorry to hear that your dad's in the hospital! I will pray for him. Aren't these [revival] meetings just great? [Evangelist] Bill Rice is my favorite speaker. He always has been.

How is baseball season? Don't be discouraged about not playing so much. We all know your good at it. The coach will get his head on straight some day!! Maybe I shouldn't have said that. God has a purpose in everything!!! I really enjoyed the Bill Rice meetings—they helped me alot!! It's gonna be hard to give up country western music but I know God will help me!

I am most persuaded of the authenticity of student responses obtained during our interviews. They knew that we were not Christians, that we were trustworthy, and that they did not have to put on the spiritual dog for us. "You are OK as you are," was the message we communicated after assuring them of absolute anonymity and confidentiality. We addressed each of the following questions to a different student.

Is everything that happens God's will?

I imagine it is, because like if you have done something bad, he'll let something happen to you to cause you to get ahold of yourself and see what it is you're doing wrong.

Have you ever been a class officer?

The year I was chosen chaplain I didn't really want it. I thought it was too much responsibility thrown on me. If you do one wrong thing the whole class looks down on you. So I talked to our youth pastor and he said, "Bob, God won't let you have it if you're not the one he wants for it." I said, "OK."

Do you feel it's your duty to witness to other students?

More or less just to my closer friends because, you know, I want them to go to heaven and not to hell. They always ask me, you know, like, "Do you gotta go?" And I tell them "yeah."

When you're away from Bethany, say in a mall, do you ever feel like you're different from the other people you see?

Yeah, like in a way I feel sorry for them because they're missing out on what a person should really be.

Do you give some time each day to prayer?

The Bible someplace talks about having a prayerful spirit. So, a lot of times, I'm just walking and talking and praying to the Lord when I'm doing my chores and stuff.

Do you ever pray during basketball games?

We'll pray that we do the best we can. You shouldn't pray to win. You pray that if it be his will you'll win, but not just that we win, win, win.

Do you feel rebellious sometimes?

Sometimes. Not lately. About a month ago I didn't feel like going to church. If you're used to reading your Bible like every night, and, say, you read a couple of chapters and then one night you don't, and you also forget to pray—there's an open door for the devil to come in and start you to thinking, you know, dirty thoughts or something like that. If that's a Saturday night, you won't get much sleep and the next morning you won't want to go to church.

What does it mean to live separate from the world?

It means not get into the worldly ways. I've been called a chicken, but I don't want to get in with them. You're supposed to live separately and not go along with the world because the world is a crook now.

Is it hard to knock on doors when you're out on visitation?

Not really. If you pray about it and you ask the Lord to help you not to have fears, I think he'll help you. It's not you that speaks [during visitation], it's the Lord that speaks through you.

After school do you visit with anybody?

No, I don't really hang around with people I used to go to school with. I've lost all contact 'cause they're all totally different. The girls have reputations and I don't want to get my reputation the same as theirs.

Are saved and unsaved friends any different?

Yes, with saved friends you can talk about God and stuff without being real embarrassed.

Male-female relationships constitute another area that Bethany believes Scripture covers with unequivocal completeness. Neither male nor female students contest the subordinate role of women. They believe it is God-ordained, even when they would uphold a female in a leadership position; when it is not God-ordained, it is just the way things feel best. The world believes it is sexism.

What do you think of ERA?

It's kind of stupid, really. I'm not saying women belong in the home, or anything; they can get out and work. I don't think they should have equal rights [sophomore boy].

I don't think women really want equal rights because they wouldn't be able to live up to it. I'm not for ERA because it just says women are exactly equal to men. I don't think they are equal because they are made differently. They aren't inferior, they are different from men [junior girl].

Do you think your wife will work?

I don't mind if my wife got a job; I wouldn't really like her being paid as much as me 'cause that sort of cuts me down [freshman boy].

What's the best way that a girl can fulfill her calling in life?

Just being a good wife, a preacher's wife, or something. Raising a family. A career's OK as long as it doesn't take up so much of their time that they don't have time for the kids or anything [senior boy].

Would you vote for a girl for class president?

If I thought she was good and everything. I'd probably vote for a guy first, though. I'm a little chauvinist, I guess. I'm sure they're capable as guys, but I think as long as we've got guys who are capable of doing it, give it to them. Give it to the guys [junior boy].

Yes, if I looked up to her and if I knew she was a real honest and sincere person. And able to lead. I think boys should be leaders. That was stressed because it says in the Bible the woman is the weaker vessel. It usually talks about the home, but I think you could apply it to other things, too [junior girl].

No, because it says in the Bible the man's supposed to be the leader and the woman is supposed to submit [senior girl].

If she was the only one, I would. I mean if there weren't any guys anywhere near for the job. Women are a lot more emotional than men. I don't think a woman leader would have as much authority [sophomore girl].

Internal Conformity

The generalizability of the interview findings is corroborated by the responses of the 115 students who took my questionnaire. As part of a large questionnaire we prepared a set of questions designed to explore the students' internal conformity, that is, their acceptance of the beliefs developed from BBA's doctrinal standards. The specific beliefs used in the questionnaire were drawn from our experiences listening to teachers, administrators, and pastors address students in class, chapel, church, and assembly. In short, each item incorporates a belief that is typically taught in Bethany's socializing settings. The results are summarized in table 5.

For each of the seven beliefs covered in table 5 at least 63 percent of the students usually accept their school's stance; on most of the seven, more than 70 percent do. The two responses that fall below 70 percent are tough cases for adolescents. One asks students if they would report a cheater who will not report himself (63 percent say they would), and the other asks if they should be friends only with born-again Christians (66 percent say they should).

BBA students differ significantly in their responses to each of the three items for which there are comparative data from Hartney students. Bethany's leaders might hope and expect that a larger proportion of their students would "do the right thing" towards cheaters, but if they look at other youngsters, much like their own in terms of age, sex, place of residence, and similar socializing experiences in the Hartney community, then they can see just how far removed their own students are from non-Christian school peers. Only 26 percent of the public school students would urge cheaters to report themselves (compared to BBA's 73 percent), and only 22 percent would report cheaters who did not report themselves (compared to BBA's 63 percent). On the third point of comparison, relating to whether learning to question authority is important, 25 percent of BBA's and 56 percent of Hartney's students responded affirmatively.

The final documentation of the students' commitment to scriptural standards relates to projective behavior, that is, to what they believe they will do in their post–high school lives, particularly when they are adults, married, and have their own children. Table 6 summarizes the results. To the extent that they know themselves, most of Bethany's adolescents expect their futures to be foursquare, in keeping with the most their mentors could expect of them. They have not mindlessly circled numbers on a page; rather, when they felt most deeply about the behavior in question—as in the case of marrying a born-again Christian (71 percent strongly agreed) or sending their own children to a Christian school (63 percent strongly agreed)—they so indicated. When their sentiments were less intense—as in the case of the Bible being the center of their lives (only 43 percent strongly agreed) or whether their best friends will be born-again Christians (50 percent strongly agreed)—they also indicated accordingly. By these comments I mean to demonstrate that the academy's students have not responded either to interview or questionnaire queries from the uniform perspective of loyalists defending their faith or of critics rapping their school and church. This does not suggest that they definitely will be in the future what they project they will be, but that they are trustworthy reporters of what they think they will be like in the future.

Of the five projected situations, the most proximate point is their college attendance. The data from the three classes that had graduated by the time I completed my study establish the BBA graduate's clear preference for attending a Christian college. Of the 38 students from the classes of 1978, 1979, and 1980 who went to college, 35 attended a Christian college and 3 a non-Christian college. Of these 35, 23 attended Bob Jones University and 8 attended Maranatha Baptist Bible College, the only two Christian colleges the academy openly endorses; the remaining 4 attended Tennessee Temple or Pensacola Christian College.

Although most academy students plan to attend a Christian college, most do not plan to enter full-time Christian service. In fact, 36 of 115 reported a preference for such service as their ideal adult job and 36 of 115 reported they actually expected to get such jobs. The students were not particularly attracted to any other occupational area. Only 18 expressed an interest in non-Christian professional careers, such as accountant, architect, lawyer, scientist, or dentist.

From their job interests alone it is not easy to infer how important they feel it is to earn a lot of money, but I asked them and Hartney's public school students about money. Their replies are summarized in table 7. A 1980 national survey of high school seniors found that 31 percent believed that "having lots of money" is very important (Wagenaar 1981: 31), many more than Bethany's 10 percent and many fewer than Hartney's 59 percent. Whatever a lot of money signifies to these students, the fact that 58 percent of BBA's students note it as fairly or very important suggests that financial gain is not alien to their outlook. That 41 percent, however (compared to the public schools' 6 percent), say it is fairly or very unimportant testifies again to how different Bethany's students are from their public school peers.

Student Explanation of Conformity

Unlike the schools most American youth attend, BBA is not a pluralistic institution (see Oliver 1976:8–9). Whatever diversity exists among its students—of nationality, race, social class, sex, or personal interests—it does not significantly affect decisions regarding curricular or extracurricular activities. The imperatives of Scripture override all personal distinctions, and the cornerstone for proper student behavior is obedience. From all indications, Bethany's students are obedient. I asked them if it is important to learn to question authority—75 percent said no.

Church officials and academy educators leave no doubt about why authority is to be unquestioned and why, as in the song students sing in chapel, "obedience is the very best thing." Students both understand and accept the explanations for this much-stressed behavior. Most commonly, students cited their immaturity as a basis for obedience—teachers and parents are more experienced and knowing, and it is proper and wise to defer to age. They also cited the functionality of obedience, that is, living as we all do in a world of authorities—"you're always under somebody, aren't you?"—it is useful to learn how to be subject to them. More than being useful on the job, obedience prepares one to accept the realities of life: "There's going to be so many things in life that you have to do whether you want to or not; it's really important to learn to do them without complaining." We interviewed almost half of the students and no more than a handful presented an unqualified case for questioning rather than obeying authority. One questions, they explained, to clarify and thus to grasp what is taught as truth. Questioning, otherwise, is backtalk, a bad habit, behavior to outgrow.

I also asked students if they obey the student pledge during the school year; 86 percent of 115 students said yes. A surprisingly high 67 percent said they usually obey the pledge during the summer. Moreover, 70 percent obey the pledge "for the right reasons." They had several reasons to account for their obedience, but their most important reason was "to please the Lord"—56 percent; other reasons were "it's the right thing to do"—8 percent; "to keep my testimony strong"—3 percent; "I fear the consequences of sinning—2 percent; and "it has become a habit to do so"—1 percent.

Perhaps one of Bethany's signal achievements is the students' acceptance of the school's mission to make them better persons. I am impressed by a school whose fourteen-year-olds can exclaim: "Everybody I know knows I go to this school. If they see me doing something wrong, they'll think, 'Well, why pay so much to go to a school when it doesn't make you any better a person.'" And whose eighteen-year-olds can say, "In a pure, right relationship with Christ you're naturally going to watch how you're acting because you want to glorify Christ. If you're doing those things that aren't Christ-honoring, then you're going to drag Christ's name down."

The pledge's stipulations, plus the faculty's persistent reminders, impress students that they must be selective in their choice of aural and visual experiences. I met only one student who admitted no remorse or felt no restrictions about anything he saw or heard. By virtue of their internalized principles, the fear of getting caught, and the brother's-keeper network that places many eyes and ears upon their actions, students usually are careful about what they read and listen to. And they usually rationalize their "transgressions" in an effort to square them with the known injunction to abstain. Nonetheless, even their rationalizations testify to the impact of Bethany's doctrinal standards on the students' thinking and behavior:

> I don't think I ought to go to the movies; Mom never lets any of us go. I always keep a scrapbook of all the movies that come out and I always think it would be nice to go to that movie, and that one and that one. Then I'll say, "No, I really wouldn't want to go!" It's probably a rebellious spirit in me. But I look at it this way. When they come on TV, I'll watch them then, 'cause on TV they'll only put a few of the R-rated ones, and they'll cut out some of the [bad] parts.

Sex and profanity—these are the elements to beware in television programs, movies, books, and music. Students "suppose" violence also is unacceptable. They are uncertain, possibly because violence is not regularly part of Bethany's litany of rejectionist principles:

> Well, sexy stuff I should not watch. But violence doesn't really bother me that much. I like war pictures; I don't know why. I've always liked anything that has to do with World War II. Gore never has really bothered me.

> There's all kinds of violence and that doesn't bother me. It's happening every day in the world. But you shouldn't watch movies that have sex and violence in them, but how can you help that, you know? Violence is all over.

> I really see nothing wrong with violence. Shows with violence in them, they're OK. Some books, different maga-

zines, paperbacks that deal with a lot of sex, you know, *they* are bad.

In public media, sex is unredeemably bad. One should not "look at people making love. Some of it is filth. You shouldn't look." Avoiding X- and R-rated movies does not seem to be a serious problem—they are "just something that you don't really even want to see." "*Fear of Flying*—I mean warped minds, you know. I just do not like sleazy love stories, like those of Barbara Cartland." "'Soap,' I couldn't believe it when I watched it. I'd never watch it again," says a senior girl, but she watches "'Saturday Night Live,' except when it gets too bad."

Bethany's students do not like the demerit system that operates to control their lives; nonetheless they do not reject it because they believe it contributes to the well-being of their school. All have some reason to account for its rationality, and they all amount to the same thing: Students need to be controlled so they will not get out of line. If, they say, you are not scared by the prospect of punishment, you will not behave, and they cited expulsion as the punishment that matters most. Short of expulsion, the restrictions that one earns after seventy-five demerits also are instructive. "We usually straighten out pretty good around seventy-five" because then students cannot talk to the opposite sex or drive to school, and officers, athletes, and cheerleaders lose their positions.

> When Ben was caught cheating and got a hundred demerits I thought, "Oh, man, at least they could let him play the last game." But if they did that, if you bend the rules once, it's going to happen over and over again. They [the school authorities] have to stand up for what they think.

This student was Ben's teammate and could well have resented Ben's loss to the team. He was not pleased by the strict enforcement of the demerit system, but he understood and accepted its process, as do, I believe, the majority of BBA students.

The academy's dress code is rigorously enforced, but do students chafe at the sartorial restrictions their dress code imposes upon them? No, not even the otherwise most rebellious of students. Without a dress code, students say, they would dress somewhat differently—girls would wear slacks, especially on cold days, and boys would wear "good" blue jeans and keep their hair a little longer. As things stand, dress code infractions are uncommon and students seem to grasp one or another rationale to explain their acceptance of the dress code.

For example, a Christian motive is prominent in the students' accounts of why there is and should be a dress code: "That's one thing you're supposed to live up to in a Christian school, how God and Jesus would have us to be dressed. If God were here on earth, he'd like us to be dressed in our best." More specifically, students know that they are to be separate from the world and that looking different is an important way to be separate, especially from public school students.

> They want us to look . . . they want it so that when visitors come in here they can tell we are Christians from our dress, from our hair length.

> People are supposed to be able to look at us and tell that we're different from the world. We're supposed to be different. We're supposed to be changed. We're supposed to be a new man.

Students accept the admonitions of their elders that the sexes should most definitely not look like each other; this is a frequent chapel warning, and one that hits home with most students. And, finally, they accept the obligation to maintain the reputation of the school; for reputation, they know, is a correlate of testimony. Bethany stresses—and its students understand—this relationship.

> If we go out on a field trip or anything, people will be able to tell us apart as a Christian school. We dress neat and everything and don't look sloppy or nothing 'cause that would put a bad name on the school.

> If we didn't have a dress code some kids would probably try to look like slobs and everything and just ruin the testimony of the school.

Bethany's attention to even relatively small elements of control is reflected in the aforementioned discussion of the staff-nominated slate of student class officers. Bethany does not repeatedly reinforce the rationale for this election procedure. Still, students readily account for it with reference once again to testimony and authority.

> Well, you can't have somebody in office who's not really a

> good testimony as far as coming to church and being spiritual.

> I think it's good, you know, because they [Bethany administrators] know how the students are and if they'd be good, be leaders and stuff.

Moreover, a system that insures the election of a class's most qualified students is congruent with the students' basic disposition to have the right thing done. In the past, when students nominated their candidates, each class experienced the election of a "goof off" who would not do the right thing. Though students express some regret at the loss of their prerogative, they know that the procedure is fully congruent with the ethos of their school. As a senior student pointed out, students still have a choice; if they do not like the change in procedure, well, it is a settled fact and, therefore, obedience is in order.

> The kids do have their choice of who gets in [from among the candidates nominated for them] but, you know, it's a limited choice. That's the best way, I think. When we first did it this way there might have been grumbling, but no real big scandal or uprising. Of course, around here nothing like that is allowed, anyway.

External Conformity

To obtain a picture of the extent of the students' external conformity with Bethany's doctrinal standards, I developed several scales. The results are reported in tables 8, 9, and 10. Obviously, students discriminate. They know what behavior Scripture dictates in regard to each circumstance noted in the three tables, and they respond differentially to the dictates.

As we see in table 8, well over 80 percent of the students claim that school standards usually guide their behavior at school and with their parents; about 70 percent state this is the case with strangers, with friends, and where they are not known. The number of students applying biblical standards drops a bit at weekend parties (63 percent) and when shopping (64 percent), and plummets while on dates (29 percent). It could be a matter of concern to BBA educators that 16 percent of the students say that they never apply biblical standards when shopping, 19 percent never do when they are where nobody knows them, and 23 percent never do at weekend parties.

Free-time activities (see table 9) are those which church and school officials typically do not supervise. In many families, however, parents and older siblings do supervise them. Still, students may engage in these activities on their own—in their bedrooms behind closed doors and when parents are out. In the best of circumstances, students may often be left alone with nothing but their biblical standards to judge the worthiness of the sounds and images their ears and eyes bring to them. They are most conforming in regard to what they read—54 percent never break with the standard; they are least conforming in regard to music—41 percent usually break with the standard. A fair number "some of the time" watch "unacceptable" movies (46 percent) and television shows (56 percent), and a much smaller number usually do so (29 and 24 percent, respectively).

The extent of student conformity is further seen in table 10. They are most up to the mark of biblical standards when it is easiest to be—doing the best they can and asking for the Lord's help, and farthest from the mark when it involves the public confrontation of proselytizing and the always difficult break with friends who do not meet BBA standards. We see the countervailing societal norm of loyalty to friends in the 30 percent who profess never to reject such friends.

Overall, the results shown in these three tables attest to most students' high, albeit somewhat variable, degree of external conformity.

Political Conformity

Chapter 5 set forth the intent of Bethany's political socialization; here I want to consider the extent to which the students conform with the contents of this socialization, particularly in regard to the area of pluralism.

Bethany's educators' support of Ronald Reagan in the 1980 presidential election is indicated by their conduct at school and their actual voting. All 16 teachers in my sample voted for Reagan; 11 of the 16 said they were Republicans and 5 said they were independents. Students closely followed their teachers—93 percent said Reagan was their presidential choice, compared to 67 percent of Hartney's public school students.

One day, shortly before the 1980 election, Bethany's elementary-grade youngsters were playing outside during the noon hour. One fourth-grade boy spontaneously called out, "Who votes for Carter?" Following a moment of silence, the ten or so children around him stuck out their tongues and gave Carter the raspberry. "Who votes for Reagan?" the same boy asked. All hands went up, along with cheers.

"Do you think a person's religious views should affect how he or she votes in local, state, and national elections?" we asked students during our interviews. "Absolutely," was their response. When they explain their answers, we see that it is unthinkable they would believe otherwise: "If you vote for somebody who doesn't hold your stand, that would be kind of dumb 'cause you want the world to be better and not worse. You want the government to believe the things that you do, keep your standards."

No, they would not invariably vote for a Christian, because merely being a Christian does not insure that a candidate lives by a born-again philosophy. What students say they must do is verify the degree of congruence between their own positions—for example, hard on Communism and opposed to ERA, abortion, and gun control—and those of the candidate, and vote accordingly, knowing that in the political realm one must take what one can get, unless *informed* born-again candidates are available. Reagan, not considered a born-again Christian, proved closer to Bethany's political preferences than the born-again Carter, whom they scorned for his violation of doctrinal positions.

> As far as politics go [said a senior boy], it would be toward the Republican party. I don't know, we are always pointed to the good side of the conservatives, the Republicans. It seems like the good points of the other side rarely get pointed out. They don't say you have to be Republican, but sometimes that's the feeling you get.

> Mr. McGraw [recalled another senior boy] said he talked to Mr. Reagan in Chicago and asked him about Christian schools. Mr. Reagan said he thinks they are about the only hope that the country has.

Bethany's students endorse the political positions that their church perceives Scripture as defining in a clear-cut way. National policy toward the Soviet Union is one of these. The connection is clear: the Soviet Union's Communist doctrine opposes religion and thus threatens the work of Christians. Consequently, the doctrine and the country are a menace and we must be prepared to defend ourselves against their aggressive intentions. Student views reflect the sense of a Red scare:

> Take ERA, gay rights, and Communism [says a sophomore boy in speech class]. If I was president, I wouldn't let them give demonstrations because they are rowdy and tear down

America. We have Communists in government [in 1979], in the White House, and stuff. If people want Communism, we should deport them to Russia for a year.

Another position students take relates to the ideal form of government. This topic is not given major attention at BBA, but it turns up occasionally. The following excerpt from a student theme captures BBA thinking:

As Americans we think that democracy is the best form of government—but it is not. The most perfect form of government is total monarchy. Look to the end of time. Who and what type of government will there be in heaven? The only king will be God. The only problem that the United States would have is to get a good monarch that would rule for the people, not for himself.

I do not quote this student's essay to imply that Bethany's leaders favor a monarchy and therefore wish to alter the political form of American society. I do suggest, however, that the essay verifies the logic that operates among fundamentalists: the Kingdom of God is just that— a kingdom. It is perfect. Given a ruler with the right qualities, a monarchy would be the best form of government on earth. The essay shows Scripture as the measure of all things, the indispensable measure from whose standard one departs only when compelled by mankind's frailties; in addition, it shows that students learn what they are taught.

Support for Pluralism

Disposed by their view of Truth to believe that there is one right way to be and believe, Bethany students may hold a restricted view of who is acceptable. In order to find out, I developed a pluralism scale that, through factor analysis, was broken down into three scales—racial attitudes, civil rights, and religious pluralism. Tables 11, 12, and 13 present the results, including the responses, whenever available, from BBA teachers and parents, Hartney public school students, students in a small, rural public school located about ninety miles from Hartney, and from Roman Catholics (as reported in Greeley and Rossi's 1966 study of the impact of parochial schools).

Taking the data one segment at a time, we see that the Bethany students' racial attitudes (table 11) are equally or more positive than those of all other persons reported here on all items except two.[5] First,

Catholic adults felt more strongly about the obligation of whites to end racial discrimination. I include the Catholic data for comparative purposes, but I am reluctant to speculate about the results of comparison because the data were collected so long ago (1963–64), and from adults. Second, the strongest point of exception in table 11 is the disparity between Bethany's 30 percent approval of interracial marriage and Hartney's 61 percent. In fact, the academy is a multiracial school; its teachers, when they do make racial references, speak in terms of equality—"We're all the same in the eyes of God." While Bethany's words and deeds incline toward promoting positive racial attitudes, their record over the course of my three-semester observations suggests that they are most determined to communicate only one point—that interracial marriage violates the word of God. (The rural students, most of whom are not born-again Christians, responded similarly, albeit, I believe, for racist reasons).

In regard to civil rights (table 12), students in the three schools support the rights of the godless, the undemocratic, and the radical. Bethany's students are only a little less supportive than the others until the rights of Communists and homosexuals are in question.[6] Since "Communist" carries profoundly negative meanings for them, they strikingly part company with Hartney and rural students, only 29 percent believing libraries should contain books written by Communists, compared to 73 percent in Hartney and 70 percent in the rural school. Catholic adults are much closer in belief to Bethany's youth than they are to the public school students. BBA parents, while more liberal than their children in each case except those involving the radical political groups, vary substantially (47 percent) from the BBA teachers' 81 percent support for Communist books in public libraries. They are more liberal than their children regarding both Communists and homosexuals, while BBA teachers are more liberal or as liberal as their students in each instance, most notably regarding Communists.

Of the five groups covered in table 12, two—communists and homosexuals—are a regular part of Bethany's socialization effort. As previously noted, Bethany students learn that Communism is antithetical to Scripture, but no more so than homosexuality, which sin they are to reject, while loving the sinner.

Finally, in this general portrait of pluralism, I consider the matter of religious diversity. Most persons in the six groups that responded to the items in table 13 agree that belief in God is not a condition for being a good American. After this, they no longer agree. Is it good we have so many different churches and religions in America? Strongly yes, say the public school students; decidedly not, say Bethany's students and teachers. Is there one absolute, true religion? To this question, public school students respond less pluralistically but still much more so than do BBA students and teachers.[7]

Bethany educators do not directly teach that there is only one true religion—theirs—but the invariable, constant communication that there is only one right way appears to produce this effect. Indeed, what other effect could teachers produce when 94 percent agree or strongly agree that there is only one true religion? Accordingly, students readily conclude that a religion, by whatever name, that accepts Bethany's doctrinal standards is an absolutely true one. And that others are not.

On the last item in table 13, we see that BBA students attribute far more seriousness (64 percent) to Catholic religious endeavors than do their teachers (31 percent) or their parents (17 percent), but this particular point is not one that Bethany sources ordinarily mention, let alone stress. In regard to religious pluralism, however, as with civil rights and racial attitudes, if Bethany articulates a certain belief (whether there is one true religion or whether it is good to have many churches and religions), the message reaches a large majority of the students.

General Attributes: A Bethany–Public School Comparison

In one final set of areas, I compare Bethany's and Hartney's students. One of these areas is "machiavellianism" taken as pertaining to how calculating (as opposed to straightforward) one is with regard to the letter and spirit of the law, morality, human relations, etc. (table 14). The other three areas are (1) alienation;[8] (2) locus of control, seen as a measure of a person's sense of his fate being in his own hands (internal control) or at the mercy of others (external control); and (3) certainty, or the possession of behavioral norms, as opposed to normlessness (table 15).[9]

Compared to their fellow students across the city, BBA students choose the less machiavellian response on each item except the one that states, "It's smart to be nice to important people even if you don't really like them." I believe they read this statement to mean that it is good to be nice to everyone, regardless of whether they are important, or unimportant, missing the cynicism signaled by "smart." Otherwise, they consistently choose the nice-person answer, most particularly on the necessity of cutting corners to get ahead (only 33 percent of BBA students say they need to, compared to 72 percent of Hartney students). I do not know whether in fact they would cut corners any more or any less than Hartney students. There is no doubt that on my questionnaire they reject the necessity of cutting corners to an extent that sharply differentiates them from other students, a position that is consistent with Bethany's character-building efforts.[10]

The responses shown in table 15 indicate that BBA's students compared to Hartney's are significantly less alienated, are similar in regard to locus of control, and are significantly more certain.[11] On the alienation scale, the one major difference is the lesser extent to which BBA's students (20 percent compared to Hartney's 39 percent) wondered if anything is worthwhile anymore.

As their responses to the locus-of-control items indicate, BBA and Hartney students differ primarily in their attitudes toward not trying hard (13 and 23 percent, respectively). BBA's greater acceptance of trying hard fits their school's prevailing ethic. Thus, I am surprised to see the students' relatively high agreement (23 percent) with the item, "Usually, when something is wrong, there is little I can do to make it right." Trying hard and righting wrongs seem to be tapping the same behavioral domain, but I believe God enters the latter item. Students always hear that they are expected to do their best, at the risk of sinning if they do otherwise. In addition, however, since they also learn that they should do nothing without the Lord's help, they could interpret the statement about righting wrongs to mean "when something is wrong there's little I alone, without the Lord's help, can do to make it right."

By this interpretation I do not mean to be seeking ways to demonstrate that BBA students are other than they really are. I believe there is a plausible explanation for their response. More so than at most American schools of any type, the Christian school is notable for its special language, concepts, terms and values. Students are steeped in this language and values from the moment they enter BBA. Since they always learn that they are nothing without God, that they can do nothing of any consequence without his help, to believe that they can act alone is to err in favor of the rejected individualist's perspective. Thus, this item on righting of wrongs was interpreted, I would argue, to favor the individualism which they reject, in contrast to the dependence on the Lord, which they accept.

In regard to the certainty scale, the first two items relate to the pressure of expectations and of choosing what to believe, matters that are prone to trouble American adolescents. The extent to which BBA students agree with the first two statements indicates that they, too, are troubled, but to a lesser degree than Hartney students. Otherwise, the exceptionally normative, doctrine-bound nature of their school and social network appears to diminish greatly the extent to which they—compared to public schools students—are troubled by uncertainty. As for the third statement, relating to knowing how to behave with people one does not know well, I cannot readily account for BBA's greater agreement with Hartney. While BBA does not coach its students to develop social skills, its emphatic concern for right conduct based on explicit standards may serve students in the particular social circumstances they ordinarily encounter (witnessing and visitation, for example), and therefore in other, novel circumstances, also.

Conclusions

Bethany Baptist Church and Academy endeavor to promote a social order of born-again Christians within the social order of American society. Although they are ardent supporters of the America of their conception—aren't we all?—they primarily invest their energy and thought in socializing their Christian young people for life in a community of Christian brethren which can survive and flourish in a world of non-Christians. Their major means to accomplish this purpose is intensive instruction in the Word of God, their Truth that undergirds what they ought to believe and how they ought to behave, and an elaborate structure of control designed to preclude or minimize contact with competing truths. Bethany fosters no Jeffersonian marketplace of contending ideas; none is intended. On the contrary, church and school consciously, unapologetically work to restrict their students' cognitive associations "in order to avoid contact with people, books and ideas, and social, religious, and political events that would threaten the validity of one's belief system" (Rokeach 1960:48).

I interpret my data to read that the efforts of Bethany and its allied churches and parents are largely successful. Students are obedient, they do what they are urged to do, and, moreover, they do so for the "right" reasons. Their external conformity is not a "sheer formalism carried out merely because of duty . . . or a diffuse respect for tradition" (O'Dea 1967:79). Bethany students indicate, both through their questionnaire and interview responses, that they have internalized the norms of their institutions. More than this, they seem basically to accept the "positive image of self" (Wrong 1961:85) that church and school define. They communicate this by their frequent recourse to the need to maintain their testimony, by responses such as the one that 56 percent of the students gave as to why they obey the student pledge—"to please the Lord," and by other uninvited explanations they provided. In the course of presenting the weekly round of their activities, students frequently felt constrained to explain what they were not asked to explain, that is, why they did not witness, participate in the Thursday evening visitation program, hold their devotions, or attend the weekend youth activities. These events are an integral part of the expectations Bethany fully subsumes within its normative structure. Since most students view themselves as members of Bethany's social order, they feel obliged to account for their departure from what they take to be normal, even though we did not urge them to do so.

Bethany's elders never suggest to their wards that it is easy to be a faithful and spiritual Christian. Temptations of the flesh abound. The Christian's path is beset with temptations. Bethany's successes, by which I mean those of the combined impact of church, school, family, and student peers, must be seen in the perspective of how challenging it is to sustain the Christian walk. One remarkably conforming, loyal Bethany adult described how easy it is "to slip." She recalled that she missed two consecutive Sunday night services because of illness and discovered that not going was easier than going, despite the fact that prior to her illness she had not missed this service for a year.

The gap between knowing and doing the right thing is not easily bridged. For the most part, Bethany students know the right thing; to a lesser extent, they do the right thing. The discrepancy between the two can be inferred, for example, by comparing the extent of the "always" and "most of the time" with the "some of the time" and "never" responses they give to questionnaire items. Doing the right thing results from an amalgam of motivations, no one of which alone would likely suffice. In this regard, several young men, former BBA students, related a conversation they had one weekend when they were away at school. They were Bob Jones University students at the time, had plans to eat in a restaurant, and were subject to a regulation that requires male students to wear a tie whenever they dine out. To fail to do so is to risk getting the demerits that may eventually result in expulsion. "Who will see us?" they asked themselves. "Someone will see us," they responded. So they wore ties. These students loved their school, knew and approved of its rules, fully endorsed its doctrine, but still had to work out their conformity to the simple but bothersome requirement of wearing a tie under certain circumstances. In the multitude of such situations, one's behavior becomes molded—not necessarily programmed, but at least predictably disposed.

8

By Their Fruits
Four Student Portraits

The four students presented here in first-person accounts are faithful, "spiritual" Christians. They "take a stand" for what they believe, and what they believe is basically congruent with Bethany's doctrinal standards. When they differ, it is in relatively minor matters. They are attractive and popular, models for their classmates to emulate; yet none of them is perfectly compliant. Indeed, several combine a striking degree of independence with their orthodoxy, knowing full well when they have struck off on their own, and doing so unapologetically.

Mary Becker, Senior: "Always Preaching"

A newcomer to BBA but not to fundamentalism, Mary soon finds a niche for herself at school, but never feels comfortable at Bethany Baptist Church. She takes pride in helping a new boyfriend to get right with the Lord and other students to get saved. As her first year at BBA progressed, she removed Elvis Presley paraphernalia from her bedroom walls. But not all of it. Foursquare in fundamentalism, she still finds his music comforting. Like most of the students we interviewed, Mary feels more independent than she acts at school. She is delighted to be a student at BBA, horrified at the thought of public schooling, and bound by the academy's rules and regulations. She joins the student majority in giving obedience its due, while giving personal choice its due, as well. Unable to accept fully Bethany's definition of orthodoxy, she joins her fellow students in marking off ground for self-definition, areas in which her sense of right does not coincide with Bethany's. Thus she simultaneously experiences the necessity of conforming to an established orthodoxy and of reinterpreting orthodoxy where she finds that it violates the realm of her personally defined values. In this behavior she is not alone. It is a rare student who does not have a private world. In Mary's case, and those of the other three students presented here, she does not denigrate basic doctrinal prerogatives; in relatively minor ways, she notes where the academy has overextended its authority and where it has gone wrong. It is premature to speculate on the possible consequences of her personal acts of definition.

> The school encourages us to go to a Christian college. They don't want you to go to a public school because they're afraid that the worldly people are going to come around us and, it's just, the worldly forces are just going to pull us away. I'm planning to go to Bob Jones when I graduate. You know, I kind of have second thoughts about it. I want to be a missionary, but I don't know if I want to go to a different school or not. I wonder about B.J., sometimes, because I don't know if it's what I want to do. It might be what the Lord wants me to do, but I want to have a part in it, too. I want to be happy there. I might be happy if God wants me to do that, but I think I would like to do it myself. I'm really mixed up and have to take the first step. Everybody says if it's not what God wants you to do, he'll close the door. So I just might as well take a step. For seven years I've wanted to marry a preacher and become a missionary. It excites me because there are so many people in the world that don't know Jesus and I just want to go out and tell them, especially out in the jungle. Mr. Swanson was reading to us in the Bible class and it's about this missionary and he was in the woods and he gets killed. They risk their lives to tell about Jesus. That just keeps you going a little bit farther.
>
> I went eleven years to public school. To put it bluntly, you could do anything you wanted. You could make out in the halls and wouldn't get in trouble either. Here you can't even talk to a guy in the hall. It's a big change. I decided that I wanted to go to Christian school. So Mom took away all my jeans and got me dresses. I never had a dress in my life, maybe two at the most. Before, I cussed a little bit, and I never did obey my parents. I would sneak out of the house and Mom would say do this and I wouldn't do it and I was constantly backtalking her. Now I don't do that. My mom

thinks I changed a lot. I went back to my public school on our day off here. Everybody says I'm quieter than I was. I talked to a lot of kids and they think I've changed. I don't backtalk my mom or anything anymore.

In the morning, I talk to Lorry for a few minutes, work in the snack shack, and then we go to class. Some days I work in the snack shack a little bit and then, when Bill comes, we go back in the lunchroom and sit and talk. We have our devotions together. Bill usually does it. The guy's supposed to be the spiritual leader in your house, so I just thought, well, if he is, he might as well. It's giving him a good start now, so he does it, and usually he can just open his Bible and explain anything.

Bill, when I started off witnessing to him, he was saved and everything, but he just couldn't give his whole life over. I just showed him the things. I was glad that God had given me that so I could share it with other people. He gets down mentally and he can't pick himself up and it takes me to drag him up. Sometimes I'll open the Bible and just show him some verses. Jackie King, I was witnessing to her, but she left and went to another school. She wasn't ready for this school's standards. Everybody tried to push them on her. Mr. McGraw told her if she didn't accept them, she was going to get kicked out. They thought that if they could get her saved, that she'd be different than she was. She got mad at me once because I wouldn't go out drinking with her. She asked me and I told her no. Paul Tuttle—I witnessed to him but it was only once and he came to me.

I started going back to my old church because the people out here I just don't like. It's not a loving church. You know, you want people to come up and say "Hi" to you, "How are you?" you know. Somebody that's going to be open, not, "Oh, I'm better than you. Get away." They are the kind of people that look at your dress and appearance and they look down on you. I don't think that they should do that. I think that any way that you come, God is going to accept you any way you are. And so I went back there and I got my aunt and those guys going back to church. We tried last night to get my mom, too. I go, "Mom, why don't you go to church with me tomorrow?" And she goes, "No, I just don't want to. I'm not a Baptist." She's a Christian [member of the Disciples of Christ] and Christians are the same belief as us, but they think that to be baptized means to be saved. I just don't think she is saved 'cause if she was, you could see it by her actions.

Since I started going with Bill he has changed from wanting to go to a state university to B.J. He took his exam last Saturday, and I wonder if it's me because he always tells me that God put me in his life to show him and direct him through. He said that God called him three years ago to be a preacher and he ignored the call.

You know, Jack Arnold got saved the other day. Well, he started crying when it happened; it made me so happy to hear that—especially out of Jack Arnold. He came to talk to me first about it, but I told him to talk to Bill, because it is easier for a guy to talk to a guy. I thought it was neat that he came to talk to me first. He came to me because his girlfriend and I are super good friends and he wanted to know a way that he wouldn't lose her, and I go, "Being saved is not a way that you won't lose her, but you will have better goals and a better respect for life." He goes, "Well, will you help me with it?" I go, "I can't do anything at all; it's you that's got to do it." He goes, "What do you mean?" And I go, "Why don't you just go talk to Bill before the game," and so he did. He made a lot more points in that game; he did a lot better. A lot of boys took it different in the locker room. Like Danny came up to Jack Arnold and said, "Did Bill talk to you?" And Jack says, "Sure, and I just got saved before the game, too." and Danny says, "Oh," and they haven't talked since that much. They used to go to parties all the time, Jack and Danny did, but they don't any more.

I'm one of those students who are always preaching. Some of the students are for it and some of them just think, "Oh, man, here comes Miss Holy again." It's really bad. Some day they are going to pay for it, because God knows what they're thinking and he is going to punish them. Hank apologized to me after I'd been telling him he was doing wrong. Before, he kept saying, "Miss Becker's [gym] pants are always below her knees." And he said, "Oh, Miss Holy, she doesn't wear any revealing tops or anything" and I don't think the girls should 'cause it makes the guys just lust after them. It just makes me sick to think about it, but he just didn't understand. I told him, I was kind of hateful, but I just showed him what I thought and what I believed in because I just was tired of his smart mouth. Every time he called me Miss Holy or Mr. Preacher I would stand up for what I believed, and not too many people around here do. The ones that do stand firm. Some of the girls unbutton their shirts way down and I tell them. Like there is Lilly Sawyer, she's a cheerleader and she is very well respected and she had her shirt unbuttoned all the way down to here and I told her. All the girls looked down on her that time and I don't see why she would go to that extreme.

There was seven or eight kids that got caught cheating the other day. I think tattling is just as much of a sin as cheating. The kid that tattled got out of it and the people that were caught cheating got one hundred demerits. In the Bible it says that you aren't supposed to tell on your brothers. There's a lot of tattling here because everybody wants to get on top of the totem pole, and the way they do it, they knock down everybody else. Like if they are kids who want to be brownies with the teachers, they'll knock the people down from the top to get up there.

I read this magazine called *Campus Life*; it's Christian people writing for high schools and colleges. There's this one guy in there I like. If kids have troubles relating to sex and stuff like that . . . it's like a Dear Abby. I want to learn how to do this, to cope with people's problems through missionary work. Bill got me a book for Christmas and it's really good. It's a Christian love story. He reads it more than I do. I love books, especially the ones about people who get into trouble, 'cause I feel like I could, well, if I was them, I'd do this or that to get out of trouble. Generally I read Christian love stories, but there's been some I've read that haven't been.

Sometimes when I want to go see some movies—but I don't want to, you know—I go and buy the book. And that's the end of my wanting to go see the movie. I picked up *The Rose* and started reading it and it had so many foul words in it, so I put it down, but then I'd skip over them because I wanted to see what happened. I like Elvis Presley movies. They [BBA] don't like him, but, you know, I like him.

Some movies I think we should be able to see because not all of them are bad. But they prohibit us from going to any of them and I think it's your own business what you do out of school. 'Cause the school rules you during the day and you're supposed to listen to them. But when you are out of school, you're not supposed to. I'd like to go see some movies but I won't. That's about it. These rules—I know the reason why you should follow them, and once you know the reason why it's so much easier. It's mostly to live up to Christian standards. I would live differently if I wasn't coming to this school because I would not be living the right life. I would be completely out of God's will. You know, the school kind of holds me together.

If you can abide the rules, this is the best place for you to learn to have a backbone. It gives you the backbone, helps you for years to come. Still, not talking in the halls to guys is hard. I don't see nothing wrong with talking to guys. If I thought it was a real drastic stand, I wouldn't do it, you know. I don't think touching a guy accidentally or hitting him is offending. Some people might think it is, but it doesn't say anywhere in the Bible that you can't. If you get caught doing that you get demerits. I guess if you talk to a guy in the hall, it'll lead to more things in the hall, and they don't want that to happen. 'Cause you can't do it at college, and they are getting us prepared for a Christian college. What are we going to do if we can't even hold hands with a guy on campus for four or five months at a time until we get breaks to go home? If we can't do it for three or five minutes in the hall, we'll not be able to do it for four months.

They like spiritual relationships here, no physical contact. If they drove by your house and saw you kissing your boyfriend they'd give you demerits for it. I think that is so dumb because what you do outside of school shouldn't be any of their business. I don't see nothing wrong with holding hands or him putting his arm around you or kissing you, but anything else I think you should save until you are married, you know, because it gives you something to look forward to. I would never take that away from anybody. That's mine. Miss Bennett is my example of what I do. She's a coach and that's what I want to be, so I look to her more, I think. She's just got the standards and she is just like a big sister to me.

It's really dragging these days because we don't talk to the guys. They're in basketball conferences, and they're real good games, and they're not supposed to talk to girls because it'll take their mind off of basketball. But to me, if you take something away from them, they're going to want to do it twice as much. And every time I look at Bill, he's looking the other way. And if he is looking at me, I'm looking the other way because we don't want to talk and it is hard. I get to see him Friday night after the game. We're going bowling, so I can talk to him then. But if they win Friday night I can't see him because they go to state then.

I pray every day before classes, every morning, and at lunch, supper, and breakfast. If I need help, it might be more. After I take a test, I'll pray that I did good. Sometimes I could pray all day if I wanted to. I could never run out of things to pray about. And last night, I bet you I sat down and prayed after devotions about fifteen minutes and then I still had things to say afterwards. 'Cause I don't want to leave anything or anybody out. I feel if you leave anyone out, then that could be blowing their salvation. A lot of girls will come up and ask me to pray for them. Dora was having troubles with her mom and dad and she asked me to pray for her for that. Heather wanted me to pray for her that Jack would overcome his jealousy of other boys. And then Ann Norton wanted me to pray for her and Bob because she wanted to keep the lust out of her mind. And then I pray for Danny and those guys because I think they are lost and they need help. And I pray for Richard and I pray for you [my research assistants], and I pray for . . . we call him Doc, I pray for him.

Sometimes I wish that the Lord would just hurry up and come. Then I'll see all the people in the Bible that I admire so much. I would just like to sit down and talk to Mary. It would be so neat, just to ask her the feeling that she had when, you know, she knew that it wasn't really Joseph's baby. She knew that it was God's baby and he conceived her with it from heaven. Bill can't wait to go, but there's so many things that he wants to accomplish here on earth before he goes. There's so many things I want. I want to finish school. I want to be a PE major. I want to have a volleyball team. I want to have six kids. And I want to be married to a preacher. Those are my goals and I want to accomplish them before I have to go, at least have one kid, you know, to see what it's like, or be married. Our teacher Mrs. Summers told all of us girls that she prayed that the rapture wouldn't come until after she was married, and then she prayed and prayed again that she'd have a baby before the rapture.

What a picture Mary Becker presents! Like an Old Testament prophet, she lashes out at Lilly Sawyer's unbuttoned blouses; declares biblical authority for keeping quiet about your brother's misdeeds, contrary to school standards; and hopes for rapture, when Christ returns to earth and he takes born-again Christians to heaven, but not before she has at least one of her hoped-for six children. Though she rails against the restrictions of the student's pledge, she praises BBA for holding her together and giving kids backbone. I believe she had backbone before entering the academy.

Ted Rogers, Senior: "A Privilege to Be Here"

"You should have seen him as a freshman and sophomore," said his teachers and classmates of senior class president Ted Rogers. No longer the cut-up of his early days in BBA, he easily, confidently presides over his class and occupies a central position in his school. He would be a leader in any school: he is intelligent, works well with people, and enjoys the tasks of leadership. Though less vocally spiritual than Mary Becker and others who will be depicted here, he nonetheless operates as a supporter of Bethany's doctrinal order, combining in a winning way great popularity with his peers and an unstuffy spirituality. Ted Rogers is not likely to preach to classmates about being good, but being attractively good himself, he reinforces Bethany's ideals, though not the cherished one of entering full-time Christian service. He plans to go to Bob Jones University, but the path of the preacher, teacher, or missionary is not for him.

To be a class officer you need leadership. You can't pick somebody that doesn't have any leadership or the kids don't respect them. If you didn't go on the summer youth trip, with not necessarily our church, but with some church, you couldn't be a officer at all. I guess they're judging your spirituality. I don't think that's right, because they don't know what the conditions are. I know one person who didn't get to go because he couldn't get off work, and so therefore he couldn't be a class officer, and I don't think that's right. And some parents don't let their kids go because they can't afford it. I have never spoken to anybody about this point, 'cause once they've decided on something, you can't change their mind.

The duties of the president of the senior class mean that usually I'm in charge of class meetings, organize them, what we're doing, the challenge, get drinks, or whatever we're going to do. That's basically all that a senior class officer does. Senior class officers are not near as busy as junior class officers. I was president of our class last year, too. It's more relaxed the senior year because Mr. McGraw takes care of the senior trip. My junior year I spent two or three hours a night putting together the banquet. It's worth it. When you see the end result, it's well worth it.

Sometimes I help with the Saturday evening youth activities. What we do is play games and stuff like that. Usually around a hundred kids come to a Saturday night activity. The kids who come to Sunday morning services are usually there on Saturday night, too. A lot of kids won't come if it doesn't sound like fun. Kids that would rather go out and party and get rowdy wouldn't come to Saturday night. For me, going is a matter of principle, you know. It's there for us to do; if the church is going to do it, we should go and have

the best time we can. 'Cause it's definitely not convenient
for Pastor Burt to leave his family every Saturday night, and
on Friday night for the junior high.

The youth activity starts at 6:30. First of all, they have like
a news broadcast and they say corny things that happened
to different people. When the skits are all over, we have a
break and go to the snack shack; everyone buys their candy
and stuff. Then, after fifteen or twenty minutes for that, we
come back out to the gym. One time a group got up on the
stage and the others tried to name a song that they didn't
know. And once all our adult leaders were up there and we
tried to name Christian songs that we knew and that they
didn't. The last thing we do is go back in the cafeteria and
have the service. We sing songs, give testimonies, and then
Pastor Burt goes into his sermon and ends with the invitation.

It's not hard to live up to the expectations they hold for us
here. Not necessarily. Once you learn them, it's not hard.
But it's kind of hard sometimes to get in your mind why they
sometimes have some of them. I can pretty well accept
everything without too much trouble. There are things I'd
like to do but I don't do—like go to the movies.

If you go to the movies, you're in trouble. They give one
hundred demerits. It's not the movies that are necessarily
wrong. I think they look at it like you are giving your money
to the moviemakers. Like if I went to see *The Wilderness
Family*, I would be giving money to not necessarily just that
movie, but to that company to produce other kinds of films
that might not be G-rated. I think I would enjoy Walt Disney
movies, but I guess if you're going to take a stand you are
just going to have to take the breaks at wherever that line is
drawn. The line is drawn at none. I went to three when I was
in Canada because the group I was with went and I didn't
feel comfortable saying no. It didn't cost that much, so I
don't think my money was paying for other films.

The school policy on music—well, you can listen to anything you want to, but they prefer that you not listen to rock
and roll music. Personally I think rock and roll is just repul-
sive. I wouldn't want to listen to it. I've heard it and don't
like it. I've heard stories about what it makes you do. If you
listen to rock music, then you get rowdy and go out and
vandalize and stuff. And the rock music goes along with the
drug parties; it gets you in the mood. I don't think you get
demerits for listening to rock and roll. That's just like watching TV. They won't give you demerits for watching it because that's something you're doing in your private life;

that's controlling your private life. Controlling your movie behavior isn't controlling your private life, because at a movie you're in public. It's your reputation, because if somebody knew that you went to a movie, and somebody asked you where you went to school, you'd say, "Bethany Baptist Academy." They would say, "Well, that's kind of funny that students who go there go to movies." They know the stand that we take about movies and it would harm the school's reputation. You are a public figure.

Right now I'm reading a book about the Trapp Family Singers. I enjoy novels and things like that; a lot of the modern stuff I don't care for. What turns me off is the attitudes of a lot of the people in the books, you know, about life and what they do with their time. The way they spend their time, I wouldn't spend my time, so I don't really want to read about them. The way they look on life, if it feels good, do it, and if I want to do it, I'll do it. No church would let people come in and go running around nude all over the place. Nor would they allow cussing. So I don't think I should be letting them [bad things] come into my eyes and ears.

I should not read pornography and books that are like *Rosemary's Baby*. I've never seen the movie or read the book. I do know what it's about; I hear that it's bad and I don't want to see it or read it. And *The Exorcist* and all those things, I just don't think Christians should . . . it's showing you what demons are like. I don't think that the demons shown there are really the way that demons are.

There have been a fair number of kids who have dropped out of school. I think it's probably due to a bad attitude. They don't like the rules; maybe some of them are people who just can't afford it. Most of them that left this year from my class, I would say, are ones that left because they didn't want to be here, who had a bad attitude about the rules. I guess they were more independent. They think they are grown up and the rules are stupid. I don't have any trouble with the rules, because I know that eventually I'm not going to be under them. In two months I'm going to be out from under the rules, but I'll still use the same morals and everything. I guess I consider it a privilege to be here. It's not that I feel that I'm pushed to obey all the rules. It's nothing that goes against my will. A lot of them are just common-sense rules. I'm not scared to do things, you know, 'cause if I do something, I must think it's right. If I'm living my life the way I should, then I don't have to worry about anything anybody else said.

If I could change the rules and regulations of the school, I'd change a few maybe. First of all, the one about not talking in the hall. Unless it's going to be a couple that consistently talk—they should be given social restriction. I don't see how it's going to hurt anybody if I talk to a girl in the hall. It doesn't make any sense; it may after a while after I graduate. Another is sitting in the first seven rows in church. Before, students could sit anywhere they wanted to in church, and now you have to sit in the first seven rows. If it was the kids sitting in the back goofing off, they could have taken care of it individually.

Anyway, we still goof off and have fun at school even though we have the pledge and so many rules. Dirty jokes are out but there are OK academy jokes. Here's some. What's the difference between an academy girl and a garbage can? A garbage can gets taken out once a week. What's the difference between an academy girl and an elephant? About five hundred pounds, and the girl is gaining. And then there's one about the guys. What's the difference between a mouse and an academy boy? A mouse has hair on his chest. Jokes like that, they come from Bob Jones and Maranatha. We make jokes about certain teachers. Like one about Mrs. Reynolds. As soon as she sings, she takes a big breath. Everybody imitates her singing. And the way Mr. Fortner talks with a southern drawl. Everybody goes around imitating him, and Mrs. Lowe's big eyeballs, and Mr. McGraw's chubby cheeks. At the banquet last year they did a satire on the teachers and whoever was imitating Mr. McGraw had a T-shirt on that had a "C.C." on it that stood for "chubby cheeks."

I've heard some people say that the academy kids don't keep up the standards during the summer that they do during school. Like myself, I don't see anything wrong when I go to downtown if I've got a pair of tennis shorts on. You know, summer is a more relaxed time of the year. I know a person saw me in downtown Hartney last year with a pair of tennis shorts on and he jumped on me. I think it was somebody who works with the youth group from the church. I said, "Well, if I want to ruin my reputation . . ." I guess I told him that it was my business. I know I shouldn't say this, but they are so old-fashioned.

Anyway, it'll all be over for me here soon. I'm planning on going to Bob Jones University and majoring in business. No full-time Christian service for me. In a sense, we do get, not pushed, but encouraged to do that. It's one of the major goals.

My major consideration for picking B.J. is how good their qualifications are under that major, what kind of courses they offer, what kind of reputation they have, how many of their students go on to be successful in whatever they've prepared in, and what kind of businesses would accept a person that has gone there to that school. But the business qualifications of the school was not the first consideration. The fact that it was a Christian school, that was first. I think it's important to get some Bible education and then if you feel that another school has better qualifications, after, say, at least two years of Bible training, then go on, after you got a good solid foundation in Bible. You don't get really the deeper meaning here at our school because it has to be kept on sort of equal plane for all of the students to understand. You learn the basics, but then I think at a Christian college you get more than the basics.

Judy King, Junior: "Not Supposed to Be Leading a Regular Life"

Pert Judy King exudes energy and verve. She is charming to young and old alike. For this lover of people words come pouring out, many of them in the service of her Lord. She enjoys doing the right thing with her friends, her boy friend Larry, and the Lord. She can muster as much enthusiasm about her Saturday morning ministry as she can about eating ice cream and cake in the park with Larry. Her engaging, enthusiastic demeanor seems almost prototypically American, although the focuses of her energy usually separate her from a world whose activities she sometimes finds appealing in ways that make her a paradox. Unhesitatingly, she describes a cheating incident that reveals the clay feet of Bethany's youth. It also reveals the strength of BBA's control structure, first, in the behavior of her friend, Sally Lathrop (the subject of the next first-person account), and, second, by her reactions and those of others to Sally Lathrop's behavior.

From kindergarten to ninth grade I went to a public school, and then my dad didn't want me to go to a public high school anymore. He suggested Bethany. I have to admit my first year here was so hard. I just felt like everybody was on my case. I was all ready to throw in the white flag. It was just all the preaching, so many rules and regulations, and dresses all the time.

Me and Beth were known as the rebels. We have just grown in the Lord a whole bunch in the last three years. Just the fact of wearing a dress every day, and just watching what you say. Like before I wasn't, "Yes, ma'am," "Yes, sir," where now it just comes naturally. The boys, they treat you so respectfully and open the doors for you. I think that's so neat. I'm used to it now. I love this school; I wouldn't trade it for anything.

After school the other day I had a job interview. I went to this office in a dress and everybody else there was wearing nice pants. This lady from the office said she noticed I was wearing a dress and I said that I'd just got out of school. She asked what school I was from. I said Bethany Baptist. A big grin came on her face. She said we've had a couple of other girls come in here from BBA that always looked real nice. You can tell that they know. It reflects to the public when you say, "I go to Bethany Baptist Academy" and you're in a nice dress and you're groomed well. I always thought of it that you take one of our girls that is dressed real nice and a public school girl in jeans, hair all greasy—I think that there is a big difference. There's just the testimony. We are supposed to be separated and I think we are. I think we set a good example for the public.

Just a few weeks ago I felt like leaving. Me and Tracy and Martha and Ben and Carla, all of us got caught cheating on a history test and we all got one hundred demerits and social, which means you can't talk to no boys. I was chairman for the invitation committee for the junior-senior banquet, and I got taken off that. Tracy was in charge of the whole banquet, and she got taken off that. And so did Ben, he was another one. And we got taken off all of our offices and driving privileges. They are making an exception for me because I drive in a car pool and so I have to take kids back and forth to school. I was thinking of quitting then. I was thinking, oh, what school is it that you can't talk to boys and you can't do all this. Then I prayed about it and the Lord gave me . . . well, my whole attitude changed about it. I had thought God just didn't care. If you get caught cheating on an examination, you usually get kicked out automatically, even if it's just one answer. Ben showed me one answer. We were just . . . you know how you do [she whispers], "Hey, do you have number five?" That's just how we did it, and Sally seen us, and . . . She didn't tell on us to get us in trouble. She told on us to teach us a lesson. And I was the first one to go up and say, "Hey, Sally, I really appreciate it."

Sally taught me a valuable lesson. Like if I'd have studied, I would have been prepared for that test and I wouldn't have had to cheat and I wouldn't have got into trouble, but since I did it, I have to pay the price for what I've done. My mom and dad always told me, and Sally said her mom and dad always told her this, too, that if you ever see anybody doing something wrong, and you don't tell on them, it's just as bad as if you did it. So, I'm paying the consequences for what I did. It taught me a valuable lesson.

Sometimes I come home and say, "Well, dad, I'm home from the sanitarium." I always joke around like that. It just depends on what kind of day it's been. Like maybe I had a bad attitude and I got yelled at once or twice and had tests all day. But then I think the school does as much as possible. I think the school tries its best to help us enjoy ourselves.

People say the school forces religion down kids' throats and stuff like that. I used to think that when I first went here to school that they have teachers hanging over you saying, "You are going to do this and that." But like Connie Long, she is a Pentecostal and she likes Christian rock and I'm against Christian rock myself, because you don't mix the spiritual with the nonspiritual. OK, all Christian rock is, is getting the world's music in with Christian words. The teachers don't look down upon Connie. And also Connie doesn't agree about long hair; she likes long hair on guys. She believes a lot different than Baptists do, but the teachers don't look down upon her for it.

Mrs. Conroy is A Number One. She's my favorite teacher. We always have devotions before class and she always simplifies the Bible. It just turns me off when somebody tries to impress their audience with using these big, profound words. The Bible is simple, it should really be taught simply, you know. She's just a newlywed; they have only been married, I think, five or six months. I can relate to her because I have sisters that just got married. She always has a way of cheering somebody up. She can be a crab like she was in study hall, but, on the whole, she is super. Mr. Swanson, my first year here, he really welcomed me, and so naturally I have just a natural liking for him, and I like Bible. It's easy to me. And I always get good grades in it. Chapel, it's OK. It really is. If Mr. McGraw gets up there . . . He can be interesting, don't get me wrong, but sometimes he can spend a whole hour on like gum wrappers. I've never met a person in my life who can talk a whole hour on gum wrappers on the floor. Mr. Swanson, he's always preaching from 2 Timothy, always. You know, when he gets up there, everyone just turns to 2 Timothy.

I don't think the school puts enough trust in us kids. I

really don't. I mean they sort of make our decisions. In a public school, you can sort of make your own decisions. In this school sometimes you are obligated to do things. I'm sure it builds character in you because some of the things they make you do are good for you. There are some times when I think the choice to be made should be left up to you. We went on a picnic and all the teachers went. It's just, I think it would be neater, like in the public school, if the seniors just had a picnic of their own. But every time they have a party here, or something, a teacher always has to be there. With teachers there, it isn't the same; you feel like the teacher is just eyeing you. Beth had a party and she invited just her friends. Mr. McGraw showed up, just to be checking. He just went up and said, "Hello there, little Miss Horton, I heard you guys were having a party here."

We have some couples here—they're supposed to be leaders—I just recently heard some things that they have done and I thought it was shocking. Boy- and-girl-type things. It's not like sex or that but it could lead to it. Jill and Corky, that was the couple that I was talking about. All the teachers think that Jill is just it. She's smart and she tries her best in classes. I have nothing against her. It's just that people like that turn me off. They're wishy-washy. You don't know if they mean what they're saying or not, because I know that Jill says some things that she doesn't even mean. She plays her cards right. I just look at her and there is a verse in the Bible that says whatsoever you sow that shall you also reap.

I know a lot of people who are petting. I don't know nobody who takes drugs. Or smoking. I don't know nobody that smokes. Alcohol, I know a lot of alkys. Steve is really getting into it. I told him he's going to be an alcoholic. He says, "No, I'm not." That bothers me when they find out that a student is doing something like that, they don't sit down with him and try to find out why he does that. Like most alcohol and drug problems come from somebody having problems in their life. They give them demerits and they kick them out of school. I don't think that solves the kid's problem at all. Obscene language—we don't hardly have that problem. Some people say "God" and stuff like that. That's just something they say like "gosh." I have a habit of saying "gosh." Then they go, "What?" What are you supposed to say, "Oh, spaghetti"?

Sitting in class one day somehow we got on the subject of dating and if we'd ever been kissed. I didn't say anything. This was last year in tenth grade. I was sitting by Donna, and me and Donna, we knew we'd both been kissed. I think it's natural. The other girls, we knew they'd been kissed, but they automatically started going, "Not us, no way." We heard these comments all around the room, "Oh, gross" and everything, and so I raised my hand and I said, "Well, I have been kissed and I like frenching." Mrs. Lowe just cracked up, and the whole class, you wouldn't believe it. And then I don't even remember the people that was there, but they raised their hand and said, "Wait, I remember a time when . . .", and they just went on and on and on. I bet you five bucks if I hadn't said anything Mrs. Lowe would think everybody was a total angel, sweet sixteen and never been kissed. I would never go to that extreme to let a guy give me hickies all over my neck and then go to school, but I see nothing wrong with kissing. Let me say, kissing can lead to other things, you know. You start out by holding hands and then . . . there has to be a limit. Like when you're left in the house all alone and you've got a nice album on, hmm . . . but there is a limit. There are some teachers here that think holding hands is wrong.

Everybody is concerned about their reputation, right? Kids say that they do certain things, which they don't, just so they can keep their reputation up and get along with the teachers throughout the year. Like if some of the teachers here found out that I like to dance, they would relate that dancing to going to discotheques and going to other dances. But I don't. I used to do it, I used to go dancing. Before I came to this school, I used to go dancing at this club on teen night. Also in my first year here. It was my bad year. Now I do it when nobody's around. I usually do it when my mom and dad's gone. I turn on a record or something and, you know, it's exercise to me. I love to exercise and I find toe touches, like twenty-five toe touches, quite boring. I don't hide it. I tell people, I say, "Well, I do it on my free time when nobody's home." I do it all the time, because I love doing it. I'm not hurting nobody, I'm not hurting myself, I don't think.

My intentions are not to use my body to turn a guy on or anything; I just use it for exercising because it's great for your whole body. Half of the girls in our class like to dance and I've taught them many dance steps. We've never had dancing or even loud music at any of the parties that we've ever had. If the teachers did find out that I like to dance, you can just imagine Ferris wheels spinning in their heads relating it to other things.

I don't like hard rock; I never could stand that. I don't

know why, but like mellow music, it just makes me feel the drum beat. I like that. It makes me feel peppy and stuff. Any song that deals with going to bed or getting drunk or running with your best friend's wife, I turn that right off. I don't like it, I turn it off. But if it's a mellow song with a good beat and talks about two people in love or something, I listen because I love love stories and love songs and stuff like that.

I like books about love, too. Some I've read are real suggestive, I mean detail and detail. Like the cover will look real nice, a simple little love story, and then they really get into detail about things. I don't know if this is true, but what I feel, OK, if no one has ever fallen in love, you know, then they probably wouldn't be too interested in that love sort of thing. But, like, if you *have* fallen in love and you *haven't* experienced anything like . . . I'm saving everything I've got for marriage; I just always believed that. You like to read and see, you know, what these things mean and everything. But I'm no longer at an age where I'm easily influenced. I have read books like that, I confess that, but I find it would be different like if I read them and then I passed them on to somebody else. I know I couldn't give it as a book report, but if I'm reading it just in my free time, and think things out . . .

A lot of kids in our class are right close to the Lord, trying to make themselves into a better person. I think the devotions, lately it has been speaking to me. Me and Sue—it's neat when friends can challenge each other. Like yesterday in chapel Pastor Burt was talking about why we were supposed to be here, our purpose, are we witnessing, and all these things. Like this Saturday, Sue and I are going to go door-to-door. I have to be at work by 5:00 so we figure an hour and a half. We're not supposed to be leading a regular life. We're supposed to be telling others. It was Sue's idea. But I was telling her that I was thinking that, too.

A few years ago, in fact, this is what got me saved. I'd seen a movie called *Burning Hell*. If anything ever opened my eyes to hell, it was that movie. The movie was trying to make hell as realistic as they can. When I think of hell, I think of total darkness. I think in the Bible it says it's a place where the worm dies not. Usually, if you burn a worm, it just shrivels up. In hell, the worm doesn't die, and it's going to be on your face. In the movie, it showed the worms were just all over and the people were just all screaming, like if you heard a rock concert and you feel like your eardrums are going to blow up. It is a lake of fire and they say it's going to be super hot. I think you're going to have a feeling like you're drowning. You know how you feel after you've been under water for a while and you can't get your breath. That same feeling is going to be there all the time, except that you're not going to die, you're going to keep living.

I'm sure you've heard the illustration where you take a bird and a big beach of sand and if the bird takes just one of those little specks of sand and he flies to the moon and then comes back, and then takes another one and flies to the moon and comes back. Well, after all, that's going to take a long time to take every teeny weeny speck of sand. Anyway, after doing millions and millions of tiny specks of sand on the beach, well, that's where eternity has just begun. And I can't see myself being in hell even for a short time. I can't stand pain. If I get a headache I think I'm dying. Like take me to a hospital. I can't picture myself in hell. And bugs—I cannot stand cockroaches, I can't stand grasshoppers, I can't imagine me and the worms. There is going to be gnashing of teeth and screaming. I can explain it, but I really can't picture it; you can't really picture the Lord putting someone in that much pain. But he is going to because they neglected his Son and nobody knows what God's wrath is going to be like until the end of time. God is mightier than anybody. I mean mightier than the Communist. The Communist can torture until the death and it won't even touch what God's wrath is.

You know, any Christian, the devil's going to try to get in your thoughts, and he has been trying to do it to me. He tries to put thoughts into your mind that you're not saved when you know you've asked the Lord into your heart. Like it was just about a month ago I thought I wasn't saved. I really don't know why. I was scared, and after church I was talking to Larry. I just told him, "I don't think I'm saved." And he said, "Judy, you better do something about getting something settled here." He said, "Don't even drive to work without knowing that." He said, "If you ever got into a wreck . . ." So I went to Dad and I said, "Dad, does the devil ever put thoughts into your mind that you're not saved?" He goes, "Oh, Judy." He said that I'm mature now and I've grown in the Lord and, like any Christian, we all have a backslidden nature to us. We still want to live for the Lord, but we still want to mix in with the world. And I go, "Dad, you remember when I was saved, don't you?" And he goes, "Yeah, I remember that night of the *Burning Hell* movie." "Good," I go; "I know I'm saved." And so we just prayed and just asked the Lord to take that thought away from me. And now, I know I'm saved. But that's the way the devil works—in mysterious ways.

Once I had a real, real close friend and I don't even know

if she is saved. We were best friends in eighth grade, and in eighth grade I was sort of away from the Lord until I started coming to this school. We got along fine because she swore, and once in a while I'd swear. Now all that has changed and when I see her, it's just not the same.

I have friends now that live in my town that are not Christians and I used to be best friends with them. Come weekends I usually go on church activities, and sometimes, most of the time, me and Larry go out. And if my old friends found out what me and Larry did on a date, they'd think, "God, that must be a boring time." Like last night, it was after choir practice and, OK, we had some pineapple upside-down cake and I bought a little thing of strawberry ice cream with the real strawberries in it. We decided we'd just eat it in this old park. Nobody uses it anymore, but they still keep it mowed and nice and they have picnic tables. It was 9:30 last night and we drove there and we sat for an hour and a half and talked and we ate; he ate all the ice cream. Just sitting there eating cake and ice cream would be boring to me, but if you sit there and you talk about things, you know . . . Once me and Larry start talking together, time just . . . I've got a bad case of flapjaw, in the immortal words of Mr. McGraw. It's so much more fun than with my old friends.

Larry and I have been talking about marriage plans lately, but I'm too young. I think a junior should have her mind on school. Some girls I know in this school are thinking about getting married. They always think the last year of high school, that's the thing to do, get married. I just hope I don't, myself. I mean, I don't really know what I'm trying to say, but the Lord is really dear to me and I just hope I don't let marriage interfere with what he has planned for me. I really don't know what his plans for me are. Like he might want me to go to Pensacola, Florida, to go to college. And if he called me there, I'd just know that marriage wouldn't work. I wish God could come down here and talk to us and tell us what we are to do, instead of having to find it sort of the hard way. We always talk about stuff like that. What we wish.

Sally Lathrop, Junior: "I Have a Lord Who Makes Me Happy"

Students speak admiringly of classmates who are "on fire for the Lord." These are not your Holy Joe or Miss Pious types, but, rather, several of the most popular BBA students. Having outgrown some of the awkwardness of adolescence, they are free to address their school's serious spiritual concerns. To them, being faithful and spiritual is more than just a habit; they readily articulate the underlying rationale for such behavior. Indeed, the joy they find in being "on fire" must be deeply satisfying to their BBA mentors. Teachers spot their wards who glow with scriptural convictions and welcome their participation as witnesses to the faith. Sally Lathrop is such a person.

I think the most important thing that any school should do for you, is . . . you know, I think learning is number two. Personality, beliefs, standards is what number one should be, and that's in any school. You can be a rotten kid and have A's, that's not really going to be getting you anywhere. Some kids, you know, their parents make them get A's, but that's all their parents make them do. That's unreasonable because if you don't want to learn to do good in your schooling, you're not going to do good in your life either. Some people do push too hard and I think kids rebel against it. I can see that in a lot of kids' attitudes. Sometimes too many rules can make a kid immature.

The pledge is all of my convictions. Everything on there I agree with 100 percent, you know, like something I would write if I was a school administrator. It gets the kids to really look at what they are really getting into before they get into it; it's just . . . it makes them aware of everything. With the Lord's help, I can live up to it completely. We are supposed to be so much like God. The world should be able to look at you and just say, "Hey, there goes a Christian guy."

I don't question any of their beliefs around here; I just obey what they say. I think a person who starts questioning has a bad attitude and is trying to make the authority look funny. Like, "Hey, why should I?" or "What's behind it?" They're just trying to cause a problem. Some kids'll try to do it in front of the class to look important and get themselves attention. If you never learn to obey, like, let's say you don't want to obey your parents, then it comes at school you don't want to obey your teachers. And from then on you probably won't obey the law, and then you won't obey God. And I believe the Lord only takes so much of that, and then—bye bye.

You know, you have to stand up in a Christian school 'cause good Christian kids are even made fun of in a Christian school. Like I told on some kids. I caught them cheating on a test and I told on them. I got made fun of and called names like "narc." I really don't care. Boys in my class made fun of me. So, like I'm saying, if you're going to stand up, you're going to get made fun of. There's jealousy, like they think, "Oh, we're a good Christian," you know. They watch each other to see if they sin, you know. The other kids that I told on, they thanked me. I didn't go to them before I was going to tell; I guess I should have. Some of them that cheated were smart anyway. They told me they loved me and thanks, you know, for caring. Then there were some who said thanks but you know they didn't mean it.

Everyone's capable of sinning. I'm not trying to lift myself up or anything, but Mom always said, "If you see someone do something wrong, and you don't tell, you are just as guilty as they are." And that's in the Bible; I've read that. I can't give you the exact verses. But I saw them doing it and they do it all the time, these girls that I caught. It's a character flaw, but it's something I don't want to see them out of school for, and so I said, "Hey, I saw you guys cheating on the test," and left it at that. And I really thought about it and I was talking to the teacher about the scores and I just said, "You know, some of the kids cheated on this test." "Are you serious?" he goes. And I go, "Whoops," and I figure I might as well tell him. "Yeah, I'm serious, they cheated." And I told him who.

The teacher went to Mr. Warren. I had to go in his office and testify, and then it went to Mr. McGraw and the youth pastor. I felt like maybe that I had gotten into something heavier than I meant to get into. At that point I did, because I love them. I really do. And it hurt me to see them do that. I just felt so terrible, I just said, "Oh, they're in so much trouble." Now everything has blown over and I'm glad I did it. If it happened again, I would go to them individually this time and say, "The Lord saw you and I saw you. This time you go to the teacher." That's what I would do. Then they'd have that option. I'm sure if they didn't go to the teacher, their conscience would just eat them up.

Here is a characterization of the cheating incident by Sally's friend Tracy, one of the cheaters:

About three weeks ago, six of us in Mr. Fortner's room, we were taking a test and I gave Martha one answer, Ben gave me one answer, and I gave him an anwer. That was our little group. We did our little thing and Sally told on us. It was for our own good, though, and we each got one hundred demerits and social restrictions. I was never angry at Sally. I think some of them were. Like Ben, he got put off the basketball team and I don't think he got to play in the last

game. He was claiming that he never got an answer from
me, but I know he did. Ben just came and said, "I didn't get
no answer." I was sitting there, but I didn't say, "Well, yes,
you did." I knew he did. We were all so mad, 'cause, like, I
would have made an A on that test. I asked one question,
you know, and now I've got a zero on it. It was so stupid.
The Lord convicted me and Judy about it all day. We were
going to go see Mr. Fortner, but he was gone on a field trip
and we didn't get in there on time to see him or we would
have been off the hook. But then Mr. Warren got called in.
As long as I know in my heart that I was convicted and I was
going to tell them, that was OK. 'Cause we told them, I go,
"I know it's too late now, but I did it, and I just want you to
know that I was going to come to you." It's drawn me and
Sally closer.

A lot of Christians believe that you have to be in everything in church in order to be a good Christian. I mean if you
miss, boom, you know, purgatory for a month. I don't
believe that. And then we're supposed to believe that Baptists are the only good ones. Sure Baptists, we—what can I
say?—I think we go along with the Bible the most, and I
think we try the hardest, and I think we do look upon
ourselves as better than anybody else. You know, "We
know so much more about the Bible; we are such sophisticated Christians." I'm urged to believe that, and I don't
believe that either. Baptists get in this mold. They try to put
everyone in the same mold, which is a good mold, but some
just think there is a certain mold for everybody.

My parents have this belief: If you take your kids and
make them go to everything at church, when they get out of
the house and they have their own thing, they're going to go
haywire. My parents make me go to church Sunday morning, Sunday night, and Wednesday. I have the choice to go
on visitation; I have the choice to go to activities. I have the
choice to be what, I mean, not what I want to be, but what
they want. They discipline me when I do wrong and they
want me to do what's right, but I have the choice of things.

Everyone is always pushing B.J. [Bob Jones University].
My parents don't push it; they don't push any college. But
the teachers say, "B.J. is the best school academically, it's
going to help you, you can go there and be something," and
stuff like that, you know. "Well, hey, I want to go to Maranatha and be something there." "Well, that's fine, but you
know B.J. is the best school." Therefore, it makes me want to
say, "Take your B.J., I don't want to go there." But I would

have gone and, you know, it's the Lord's school, too. By all means I want to give it a chance and I'll pray about it, but sometimes you just feel like rebelling because everyone tells you to go there. They don't realize that God might not want you there. They seem to think that B.J. is for everybody. I've heard a teacher say that.

I remember when I was real, real little, like about four, and I walked the aisle to be saved. I can remember sitting in there with all the deacons and stuff. When I was only like seven I remember our preacher preached on knowing Jesus by your head knowledge but never meaning it in your heart. So I walked down and I talked to Mrs. Lewis and she took me to the Romans Road. That is some verses, you know, like Romans 3:10, 3:23, 5:8, 5:12, 6:23, and 10:9. After I was saved, it gave me a whole new reason to live. Because if you're not saved, you really don't have a reason to live. You are living for yourself and you are just a devil's tool. No one can help you or nothing; you are on your own. I don't really know how it feels because I was too young, but I've always had the Lord to talk to and I just can't imagine what it would be like without him.

When I was seven years old, I started soul winning. I went to school on a bus and I witnessed to everybody. Even this Monday, I was playing basketball with Connie Long. We were playing with these little boys, one was nine and the other one maybe past twelve. And we were talking afterwards and I asked them, "Do you guys go to church anywhere?" and they said, "No," I invited them to church and then I asked them if I could ask them another question and I said, "This may sound funny, kids, but think about it." And I just said, "Do you know if you died if you would go to heaven?" And one started laughing and I go, "I think I'd laugh too if somebody came up and said that to me. But I'm doing this because God put me on the earth and he put you on the earth to serve him." I went through how he died on Calvary and then I took them through the Romans Road and they both got saved. They're both coming to church this Sunday. I cheer up when I go soul winning because I like to think about it myself. I try not to sound like a phony; I really try to sound sincere in, like, what I say. After you talk to somebody, it's like the Holy Spirit comes down in you and you get such a sweetness out of it. It's such a thrill. I guess it is just about the happiest that I am.

I want to be ready to face Jesus. Oh, that scares me. When you have to look at him and to see the holes in his hands and his side and stuff and you know that he more or less got tortured for us. You have to look in his eyes and, you know, you want him to say, "Well done, my good and faithful servant." I *am* excited. I'm excited to see Jesus, I am. It's so weird to get to see somebody that made you and you've talked to them all your life, but you've never got to see them. It's so weird, it's like "Charlie's Angels." You always hear their boss talking to them, but you never get to see him. I'm not comparing it to "Charlie's Angels." I think about it a lot; that's all I can say. I think about it a lot because I think a Christian should first get yourself and then other people to heaven.

Getting people to heaven makes me think about hell and about my relatives, most of all, my grandpa. That's terrible to say, "When you think about hell, you think about your grandpa." I started witnessing to him when I was twelve. Every Sunday I would write him letters. Out of all the kids, I was his favorite. All the time I'd cry as I witnessed to him. I prayed, every day I'd pray for him. When I was fourteen, I went to visit my friend in Georgia. I was gone for a week and my dad called and I got on the phone and all I remember is he said, "Sally," and I said, "What?" and he said, "Grandpa is dead." And I just fell apart, 'cause I can remember before I left grandpa kept staring at me and saying "Goodbye," and it was just weird. The Lord really had to comfort me then. Grandpa had known about salvation, and he had time to pray before he died, but he lived a terrible life. I mean, he was what you would call an evil man. He drank, smoked; he'd go to nasty places, see girls; and he just did everything, really. Everybody considered him an evil man, but still I loved him.

I think that the time for Jesus to come is coming pretty soon. The Russians are in Iran now, and I think that when they get through there, they'll move into Israel. Now, in Revelations it talks about the Father Country, or something pertaining to Russia, will move into Israel and try and take it over. We are going to have witchcraft and Satan will be really popular. That is getting ready for the Antichrist. The devil's working extra hard right now, because the Lord is coming and he wants to get everybody he can. The Lord, I don't think it will be but a couple of years till he comes. It scares me because every girl wants to get married, and stuff like that, but in a way I feel bad because I know a lot of people are going to miss heaven and a lot of kids aren't going to grow up and be privileged to do things for the Lord.

To a considerable extent, these four students exemplify the academy's norms. Not one of them goes straight down the fundamentalist Christian path, but when they stray, it is not too far and not for too long. Moreover, even though they are on the same path, much like each other because of what they share, they remain distinguishably different, both in the expression of their shared faith and in the manifestation of their personalities.

Sally, the most narrowly orthodox of the four, says she cheers up when she goes soul winning. With no trace of boasting she recalls her basketball game with some small boys and her victory in bringing them to Christ. She never won this victory for her much beloved, unsaved, "evil" grandfather. "If you're a Christian," she states, "you don't want to compromise." And she doesn't. For her, Christ is first and learning is second at BBA.

Ted joins her in the ease with which he accepts BBA's regulated status quo. He takes the regulator's side. By this time, he is so accustomed to his school's ways that they strike him as common sense. His objections to this rule or that policy do not alter his conclusions about the academy: It is "a privilege to be here," he says.

As it is to Mary and Judy, too. Yet each in her own way does not, and may never fully, comply with the right way, as Bethany defines it. Mary is a pillar to her friends and classmates, a Christian mother hen who advises them and prays for them (and me), available in the way that the strong are to the needy. The Bible teacher's tales of missionary deeds in the jungle thrill her. She is not thrilled, however, by BBA's boy-girl restrictions, its tattling students, or its unloving church. In this she joins other newcomers to Bethany who, having grown used to the less formal ways of other churches, feel a certain starchiness there.

The ebullient Judy probably feels no starchiness anywhere that she is. She loves to dance, she loves frenching, and she loves love songs, love stories, and Larry. Headmaster McGraw would probably laugh if he heard her describe his singular ability to discuss the evils of gum wrappers for an hour. He would probably laugh because she is so infectiously joyful, and he would be pleased that she shivers at the vivid images of *Burning Hell,* that she takes pride in looking different, the way Christian young people are supposed to, and that she gets alarmed when she thinks she is not really saved.

Mary, Ted, Judy, and Sally are not cast as Holy Joes by their peers. Respected by teachers and peers alike, they are a world away from their non-Christian, public school counterparts, yet notable for both their commitment and, to a much lesser extent, their autonomy. Academy students differ in the degree they claim the right to interpret and conform to their school's structure of control. Nonetheless, each has a domain of autonomy. Save for those instances about which a student would state flatly, "I know this is wrong, but I do it anyway," they find a justification for the exceptions to the rule they place in this domain.

9

In Satan's Clutches
Bethany's Scorners

A wise son heareth his father's instruction: but a scorner heareth not rebuke.

Proverbs 13:1

You know, they always want you thinking about spiritual things, all the time. And you can't, all the time.

Senior boy

Deviating from BBA's Norms

While most BBA students seem to be free of "Satan's clutches," some of them have not proved to be "A Match for the Devil's Darts" (Jones 1980:31). These are the scorners. They depart from Bethany's norms more than their mentors usually know, but so much less than their worldly peers as to hardly merit the name. Nonetheless, they stand apart from their more conforming peers. Not only do they reject this or that pledge requirement, they manifest a pattern of principled rejection. That is, they deviate, and usually they know why they do so.

BBA's conglomerate of students contains school-spirited ones who actively promote and enforce the academy's standards among their mates; quiet ones who never get a demerit; energetic ones who amass demerits but bring honor to their school because of their talent in athletics, music, or Bible knowledge; run-of-the-mill ones, undistinguished in terms of BBA's unique qualities of spirituality and faithfulness or even those ordinary qualities that any American school prizes; and rowdy ones, including those who remain within Bethany's doctrinal fold and those very few who mean to leave BBA as soon as possible. These and other configurations of behavior and belief characterize the students. Scorners can be found in each configuration, though they are more visible when associated with a rowdy group.

The primary story of BBA is about success—as Bethany views success. The point of indicating that the student group is a conglomerate is to suggest that its success is not measured by the production of unidimensional youngsters. To be sure, its socializing thrust is uniform, but its students are not. Only in regard to student responses to the orthodoxy-of-belief index is the range of responses so negligible as to conclude that the students are homogeneous. No fewer than 93 percent of all 115 students accepted the academy's position on the Bible as the Word of God and on Jesus as the son of God, born of a virgin, and physically resurrected after his crucifixion. Success is manifest in the sum total of the data noted in previous chapters which verify that as students these young people usually apply Bethany's scriptural standards to their conduct both inside and outside the school; as graduates, they mainly attend Christian colleges; and, as adults, they expect to live in accordance with BBA's standards.

Note, however, the discrepancy in belief and conduct that is the basis for this chapter on BBA's scorners. I will list three statements from the questionnaire that provide the context within which they should be viewed, including the percentage and number of the 115 students who strongly reject the school's preferred response to each item.

1. My school and I do not agree about biblical doctrine —seven students (6 percent of total).
2. The way I am urged to act and think in school is different from the way I really feel —thirty-one students (27 percent).
3. What I do after school is my business, not my school's — thirty-four students (30 percent).

Whereas only about 6 percent of Bethany's 115 students in grades 8 through 12 indicated that they reject their school's doctrinal orientation, 27 percent felt that Bethany pressed them in a direction that ran contrary to their feelings. Here we see the basis for the "false front" that some students assume at school and also for the sort of schizoid feeling that students often described. Somewhat more students (30 percent) express independence about their choice of after-school activities. Given this 30 percent, we would expect to see at least this many students indicate that they depart from pledge prohibitions when they leave Bethany's physical premises. Clearly, however, the number of students who in different ways profess independence is less than the number who usually act independently. For example, 69 percent said that most or all of their after-school activities are sponsored by their church or school, 75 percent disagreed that it is important for them to learn to question authority, and 84 percent said that the books and magazines they read seldom conflict with Bethany's doctrinal standards.

In recent years the media have devoted considerable attention to Christian schools, as well as to born-again Christians and fundamentalist preachers. The selective focus of the media has combined with both misinformation and some degree of hostility toward fundamentalist Christians and their institutions to engender stereotypes. Stereotypes illustrate a verifiable attribute that has been magnified and distorted, so that if Christian schools stress obedience, the stereotype pictures students as robotized conformers; and if they stress separation from the world, students are ascetic puritans.

Bethany neither desires nor has automatons for students. Early one day in May I watched their elementary children at play on the parking lot that becomes their playground during the lunch hour. They played with joy, looking like children anywhere. A mixed-sex group chases after a ball, kicking it, bumping each other. Little girls in a circle on the sidewalk play with dolls. Some kids play keep away. Others just walk through this hubbub of energy, pleased to be out of school. There's no sign that a stiff-necked, isolating educational machine has made them fearful and timid before the two onlooking adults whose whistle will soon send them away from the sun and the joy. They look like children anywhere, even if they are not.

And they are not, as is evidenced by the school's selective admission process, as well as by the fact that some students leave the school on their own and BBA expels others. Of the approximately 50 who left in the most recent three-year period, 9 moved away and 13 were experiencing hardship due to lack of money or distance from the school, but 5 were expelled and 22 quit (some of them to avoid expulsion) because they were unhappy with some aspect of BBA's rules or its academic or athletic program.

By vastly extending the scope of time and place within which they control student behavior, Bethany creates many occasions for student deviance. To what extent and in what ways do BBA students deviate from their school's norms? Table 16 provides a shorthand answer. It contains the most extreme negative response—from Bethany's perspective—to twenty-six items, most of which are reported more fully elsewhere in this book. All items relate to students' personal behavior and belief, their choices being indicated on a four-point or a five-point scale except where otherwise noted.

We learn from table 16 that the extent of student departure from school norms ranges from a low of 1 percent ("I strongly disagree that I will marry a born-again Christian.") to a high of 39 percent ("My best out-of-school friends are low in spirituality").

It is not easy to draw appropriate conclusions from this table. The average number of students who chose an extreme response by Bethany standards is 8, or 7 percent of the 115 students in my sample. But simply from the data in this table we cannot conclude that 7 percent of all students at BBA should be classified as scorners. In fact I estimate that close to all 115 students deviate from BBA norms in one or another respect. Recall that the students in the previously described cheating incident included the junior class's very best scholars and leaders. BBA has a great many demanding expectations which provide students many occasions for transgressing the boundaries of orthodoxy. Yet while actively seeking hard-core scorners, I could locate no more than a handful.

I composed eight statements of belief or intention that I thought would most strongly indicate rejection of BBA standards:

1. I would go to a public school if I could.
2. I do not obey the student pledge.
3. I consider myself to be low in spirituality.
4. BBA standards never guide my behavior with friends.
5. I feel strongly that what I do after school is none of my school's business.
6. I feel strongly that BBA urges me to act differently from the way I feel.
7. I strongly reject BBA's doctrine.
8. The most influential person in my life rejects BBA standards.

Forty students selected at least one of the above extreme responses, but not 1 of the 40 selected more than six of them. Only 7 of the 40 students chose the deviant responses on more than half of the eight. Thus, I conclude that 7 students (6 percent of the total 115) comprise the hard-core scorners.

However, they have a lot of company among groups of students who join them in some activities and in some feelings that may depart from Bethany's best hopes. Of the 40 students selected on the basis of the eight statements, 33 felt that their after-school activities were none of BBA's business, 16 said they do not obey the pledge, and 12 thought that BBA pushes them in a direction contrary to their own preferences. None of these eight statements, and none of a larger group that I used, provided any useful predictive capability. That is, if I knew, for example, that a student strongly rejected BBA doctrine, I could not count on that student also choosing the rejectionist position on any other logically related items.

Recall that I base the preceding observations on the students' extreme responses—strongly agree or strongly disagree. When I add the agree or disagree responses to the extreme ones, thereby providing what I consider a student's usual behavior, the quantitative picture changes. On almost every one of the twenty-six statements in table 16 the number of deviant responses more than doubles.

In any event, BBA's student scorners place themselves beyond the pale of their school's expectations in ways that are singular to Bethany, as well as in ways that are common to all schools. For example, students steal—at one time they stole expensive Bibles; at another, lunch tickets. At one 8:00 A.M. teachers' meeting, Headmaster McGraw discussed the latter theft:

> Lunch tickets have been stolen from the rooms of Mr. Kruger and Mr. Fortner. We will very quietly change the color of the tickets in the hope of catching the thieves. Don't give students any explanations why we are changing tickets. I want to know who trades in more than an expected amount.

BBA students do get pregnant while still students and unmarried, though very seldom. And they vandalize. One day as I walked out of the library with the librarian, she locked the door and said that nowadays she had to do this. Students not only had stolen fifty-eight cents in library fines, they also had written profanity in books. The books had to be thrown out. On another occasion, the headmaster, distressed by some recent incidents, made this announcement in chapel:

> Someone has been putting rolls of toilet paper in the toilet. If we catch the person who's doing this, he'll get demerits and paddled. It's vandalism. We've had a little trouble with people writing on desks and school walls. That's wicked. A person who does vandalism is a sick person. If we catch you doing these things, wasting God's money, you'll be severely dealt with.

Following these words, the chapel speaker of the day spoke from 2 Timothy 2:22, which begins, "Flee also youthful lusts: but follow righteousness . . ."

Some events the student pledge defines as violations occur outside the school but are discussed at lunch time. This is a risky thing to do given the propensity of students to be their brother's keepers. A student describes the talk at one of the lunch period's "bad tables."

> The bad tables are the ones, like, they don't pray before they eat and they talk about what movie they went to see, what's playing at the drive-ins, new songs. They talk just about stuff that is against the rules.

Scorners typically gather at these tables. The core group consists of senior boys; younger boys and girls from different classes occasionally join them. Roger Nordhoff, whose autobiographical portrait is the first of four I present in this chapter, is a core member. These four exemplify the variety of ways students may depart from Bethany's norms. Just as the four students presented in the preceding chapter show the complexity of the exemplary individuals, the following four accounts (with the possible exception of Doris's) show the complexity of the deviants: Bethany's rulebreakers vary in what they disavow, but they remain within the general framework of scriptural orthodoxy.

Four Portraits

Roger Nordhoff, Senior: "I Know What's Right, but . . ."

Roger must be listed among Bethany's most appealing scorners. He is a paradigm of the scorner's paradox: few speak more emphatically of their spiritual convictions, and few more frankly proclaim their unresisting participation in the things of this world.

All members of his immediate family belong to Bethany Baptist Church, and all of his siblings attend the academy. Now a senior, he has attended BBA since the ninth grade. Friends and habits from his public school days remain important in his life. Other students, Mary Becker, for example, are like Roger in having attended public school for many years. They differ from Roger in having left behind their public school life, happily free of past temptations and pleased with the chance Bethany offers to start over with new friends and new rules. Roger, however, both accepts and rejects his public school past in a way that does not particularly trouble him but that at times maddens his teachers. They do not understand or approve the contradictory behavior of one who enthusiastically joins them in all their most precious beliefs and comfortably belongs to the student subculture called "the rowdies." The contradiction does not disturb Roger. He knows his own mind and does not bother to rationalize the several Rogers he seems to be. With fine logic, he manages to compartmentalize the Roger who likes dancing from the one who rejects *Playboy's* use of sexual motivation; and the Roger who sees movie-going as bad for his testimony from the one who goes to the movies during summer vacation. He also manages to believe that he may have the best of both worlds: he is saved in Bethany's terms, and he has fun in his own.

I went from kindergarten through eighth grade in public school. I really liked it because all my friends were there. And then we started going to this church and I started getting a lot of friends here from coming on Friday and Saturday nights. They asked us if we wanted to try the school, you know, for one year, and if you don't like it you don't have to go. I know all my old friends thought I was a Jesus Freak, going to Christian school. But I told Mom and Dad I'd come one year, freshman year. It was OK, but I didn't espcially like it. And then my sophomore year I decided to come again. Mom talked me into it. After that, I had all my friends here so I stayed. This year I just decided to finish up here. I didn't really want to come my first year because I wasn't saved and I knew I wasn't. I didn't want to come because I didn't fit in with anybody else. Also, me and my old friends, we still got along after I was saved. We still do.

I should say I am *not* a religious student; I am *really* bad. I like to do things. Every once in a while I get in a mood to . . . I just like to go out with my friends and do something against the rules here. Like, I drink in the summertime and stuff like that. I mean, you've got to try it. Some kids, you know, never try things. I believe in the rules, like no drinking or smoking. I can understand the principle behind them. After school, I think a person should be able to do what he wants to. I signed the pledge and everything, because I don't believe in smoking at school and I don't do it during the school year, but during the summer I like to relax. I like to drink, not get bombed or anything. It's just . . .

You go swimming in the summer, you know, with a bunch of girls. We have parties with these girls and like, yeah, I don't think there's anything wrong with it. They think some things are wrong that I don't think are wrong. I go along with them anyway because I want to finish out the year here. And I believe the basic beliefs that they believe and as long as you are going to their school you should mind their rules, like keep your hair cut and all that stuff. I like to do my own thing, you know, when I have a chance and when it's OK to do it. I don't agree with all the rules here, but if you want to go here, you should obey them. Like they say, you don't have to go here if you don't want to.

I've got a lot of respect for the teachers down here. Like Mrs. Reynolds, I don't agree with all that she does and what a lot of the teachers do. A lot of people call her "bear." Mrs. Reynolds is a bear, but, really, if you get to know her, she wants you to learn. I mean, that's the reason she yells at you and the reason she wants you to mind.

In a public school you can learn, but you have to do it on your own. The students almost run the public school, any more. At least that's the way it was when I went to seventh and eighth grade. You are going to get punished in some way here and it don't seem like it works over in the public school. I think the public knows that. I think that's why a lot of people who are unsaved send their kids here. They know that there's some authority, and kids are going to get some punishment. Even the rules I disagree with sometimes, I know they're right. I just don't want to do them. Like everybody has their off days. I know what's right but sometimes I want to do it wrong. I guess that's in everybody's human nature.

I remember last year, somehow we got into a discussion of mixed marriages. The teacher [who soon left Bethany's employment], he asked us what we thought of them. And I go, "It's wrong, it's wrong." And he goes, "I don't think I would marry a black girl or anything but there ain't a verse in the Bible that says . . ." And I go, "Naw, that can't be right. Mixed marriages, you know, black and white, that ain't right." And he goes, "Well, show me a verse in the Bible where it's not." Well, we went around and around for two or three days. We'd go to a library and read about mixed marriages and then we'd look all through the Bible. I went over and asked Pastor Muller, and we asked Pastor Burt about it; guess they couldn't find a verse against it, but, let's see, I can't remember. It was just like they were against it, but they couldn't back it up with proof.

Then one time we had a discussion on dancing. Me and a couple of other guys, you know, we just wanted to get everybody rowdy and just off the subject. This was in study hall. The teacher said that we couldn't talk to each other and so we started talking to her, and then everybody started talking. I said, "Well, look at all the verses in the Bible where it says, 'They like danced with joy.'" She goes, "Well, that's a different kind of dancing." Well, of course, everybody has their different generation. Just like there's different things in music like back in the forties, swing or pop, whatever they called it, or jazz or whatever, and they danced different. And I go, "Now we dance different because we have a different kind of music." And she goes, "Oh, no." I just like to throw them things up and get them teachers thinking, you know. And let 'em know you got the brains.

Some people, I guess, think *Playboy* is an "art". People say those paintings and stuff in France is art, you know, nude models and stuff like that, but that's the same thing that *Playboy* is. They may have painted it back then, but now you have a camera so you don't have to do that. Yeah, it's wrong; I think it is. It's against the Bible and I believe in the Bible. *Playboy* deals with just one thing—they are trying to get across sex, you know, and I think it's wrong because they just have that motive behind it. I think that it's about like the movies. I think there's good movies and bad movies, but, anyway, I don't go see them because, you know, if you walk into a movie theater, you're going to ruin your testimony. The people driving by aren't looking at what's playing, they're seeing you go into the movie theater and the first thing that runs through their mind is, "I wonder what's playing there; it's probably something dirty." They'll tell somebody, maybe even that night, "Hey, you know, I seen Joe Religious walk in the movie theater and it was probably one of those X-rated movies." So, I just don't go to movies at all, now, until it's like summertime. I don't go and see movies until school is out and then I'm off the pledge.

You should try and get your friends saved, but if they won't, you should still be friends with them because they are a sinner, and you are a sinner even though you may be saved. You're supposed to be like an irritant to him. I got old girlfriends like Michelle; she's Catholic. I used to witness to her. Her religion, they teach that the Baptist religion is only a little white country church, you know, and they have Negro preachers and people run up and down the aisles going "Amen." And I go, "We ain't like that." And she goes, "Well, tell me how it is then." And I said, "Well, why don't you come with me sometime?" Well, her church don't agree with that and so she couldn't go. So she said, "Explain your religion to me." And so I told her and she said, "That sounds a lot better than our religion." I've brought her to basketball games and everything. She wanted to come and see like what my school was about and what we did and everything.

We talk about it constantly. I mean, you can't help it. I like it here so you just . . . I think I brought her to an activity. Activities, see, if kids have fun, then they want to come back and so they get the religion while they're doing it. That's a good way. It's nothing like a bribe. Some people call it a bribe, but it ain't. They don't have to come again if they don't like it.

Sometimes I'll lay in bed at night after I get done praying and, you know, having devotions, I'll just lay there and think for a while 'cause I can't get to sleep. First, I'll start thinking about God and then I'll start thinking of how great he is to create the earth and everything, how big heaven is going to be and how great God is. It blows your mind, really, to think that anybody could create man and everything. Or like on a stormy night, like last night, I went outside 'cause TV was bad, you know, no good shows on. I went outside and sat in the car and it was pouring down rain. Then it got real quiet and everything; for about a half hour it stopped raining and the thunder stopped. You just look around and think how great he is. You start to realize that somebody had to make you. I mean, I ain't ever going to believe that I come from a monkey.

I ain't got to the point where I want to settle down or anything yet. I like to do all kinds of stuff. I like to try everything and see what I like and what I don't. I don't know what you'd call it. I guess most people would call it immature, but I do a lot of crazy things. I just think I'm not the ideal student, but I am saved. I knew some students weren't and we were talking about it one day. This person goes, "I don't understand why they care so much here, and all that." I go, "Well, they don't want to see us go to hell." She goes, "Well, I don't care right now about any of that." And I go, "Well, it ain't so bad. Look at me. I have a lot of fun."

Sara Longman, Sophomore:
"I Have the Right to Make My Own Choices"

Bright, bubbling Sara, in her third year at BBA, has learned the language of orthodoxy, but is possibly more interested in social acceptance than in the Lord. For the past two years she has skirted the edge of expulsion, a consequence of demerits accumulated in the pleasure and company of wayward friends who, having gone beyond the edge, no longer attend BBA.

She does not long for her past with these friends. On the contrary, she rejoices in her newfound friends as she dwells on her acceptance by Bethany's more spiritual teens. She feels good being good, but not all the time. She has found a home at BBA, but the good times of her public school days, like Roger's, have left their mark. She would be happy if she could manage, by Bethany's standards, to be either perfectly good or perfectly deviant. Meanwhile, more than most students, who are able to locate themselves primarily in one camp or the other, she is mercurial. Unlike Roger, she has not reconciled her two sides. Her frequent use of "but" exposes the reigning ambiguity in her life.

Sara is a "nouvelle spirituelle," a johnny-come-lately to spiritual belief and practice. Like the nouveau riche in regard to money, her newcomer reaction to spirituality is unpolished, awkward, obtrusive. Her current degree of willing conformity seems inspired mostly by a yearning for mainstream social acceptability, which at BBA includes meeting spiritual criteria. Still the child of her recent wayward past, Sara hesitantly pursues her spiritual upward mobility and social acceptance.

Because she has been present as an outsider at BBA, her comments expose the school's social structure, most particularly when she talks about Sally and Rose. Sara recognizes what Mr. McGraw makes emphatic: talent does not suffice to attain recognition and achievement at BBA. The school discriminates in favor of those who demonstrate both talent and spirituality. Students seemingly accept the same criteria. "In this school," Sara tells us, "the most popular crowd is the goody ones."

I came to school here at the academy because Mom and Dad pretty much liked the idea of having, you know, Christian surroundings and all. I didn't want to come here at all. Not really. I've always obeyed my parents. If Mom and Dad says that I have to go, then I will.

I used to smoke and drink. At the time I thought it was, you know, cool. I was doing all right at my public school, but, really, you could goof off all day and not do anything and get by. I really changed the last three years just because I've gone to this school.

A couple of weeks ago, Jill came out with her friend Cathy. They were the two girls that I used to hang around with. They came out to my house and they brought a couple of guys which I didn't even know about. My parents tell me, "Sara, don't hang around with those kind of people." And then, in a way, I kind of feel like it. 'Cause occasionally, I wish I could go and drink, but I don't know. In a way I do and in a way I don't.

'Cause at times I wish that I could drink I know I'm definitely not right with God. In a way I am, and yet I've kind of got some problems. But, then, everybody has problems. Still, I'm getting more up to being with the right kind of people and getting my life right. I'm kind of in the process of making my life right. Still, there's something holding me back. It's like Satan is here pulling my one arm and God's almost letting me float up there, but he's still over there on the other side. You know, it's like that.

I used to get a bunch of demerits and I'd always be late to class and be messing around and cussing or something or being too close to the guys at the lunch table. I guess I kind of wished that I went to Hartney High. Then about the middle of the year it occurred to me that this is a better place to be. I can't get in trouble. Less people are going to hurt me here.

When I came here I wasn't saved. I guess that God just has to talk to you. He comes and talks to you and then he gives you your first step. I was saved in chapel. I used to just sit there and goof around and write notes. I still sometimes do that, like if I'm bored. That's one of my poor things, really. Finally, the Lord just, he just, I guess I just accepted the fact that I did believe in him.

At first my life wasn't different except for that I was saved and I could tell people that I was saved. I still had the wrong kind of friends. I liked rock music; I still do. That's why I'm not right with God. Because I don't have a devotional life, and I don't read my Bible every single day. I read it when it's required for me to read it. And I still like to dance sometimes, I guess 'cause I feel like it's kind of exercising, really. I'm enjoying myself so why should I give it up? But I feel sometimes, some time God is going to convict me. I don't know when, but some time. As of right now, I don't think I could give it up.

Last year we were ornery, always getting in trouble in the halls. You know, talk all the time. We'd always be tardy for all our classes. We would always just go in the bathroom and congregate, like we'd just sit there and talk, you know, like what we were going to wear tomorrow. We'd talk about guys and stuff, you know like normal people do.

Last year some of the kids thought we were OK, but like the ones that *are* OK, well, they didn't think we were. They liked us, but it wasn't like they were real good friends with us, 'cause they knew we were rowdy and we always liked to cause trouble. We didn't really care if we got in trouble or not. We'd just go ahead and get in trouble and see how many demerits we could get. The guys in my class, they are rowdy, but not like normal boys, you know. They can be rowdy at times, too, but I mean we were just troublemakers. Those guys were nice to us, but they weren't our best friends. Now, I feel closer to the guys, and even the other girls in our class. Last year we just kind of left the girls in our class out and we'd just hang around guys, senior guys that were here last year. Now they're gone, and Jill is gone, so I'm not in trouble.

Other kids would try to straighten me out. Sally, she's pretty spiritual and everything, she said that I should get my life right with God. And I kind of feel that I have. My friends that I have now in my class, they tried last year to get me to hang around with them, but I was too stubborn to figure it out.

The teachers want kids like Sally to get involved in everything 'cause they've got the grades. Like if I was more artistic at drawing something, they'd still want her to draw because she has the grades. The same way with cheerleading. I tried out but I didn't make it because I think it was my attitude. Last year they didn't like my attitude and I didn't have the grades. I thought I was much more peppy and had much more spirit than some of them do. Like Sally, she's a very bubbling person and everything, but she's not cut out to be a cheerleader. She made it because of her grades and everything and everybody likes her and she hangs around with the right kind of kids, you know. It's always coming around to the right crowd you hang around with.

Things are going better now. Rose, like she is one of the top people that are really popular in our school and she asked me to go to her house. She took me to the mall and we went out to eat. Then I had her over to spend the night. Rose and her friends, they are more—how can I put it—they are more Christian, you know. They are goody . . . well, not goody-goody. She thinks that I've changed from the people that I used to know. My attitude's changed and she can accept me. I like it better than last year with Jill because it seemed like all the time I'd be in trouble. With Rose I can be myself and she can kind of accept me. I was amazed when she told me that a bunch of the goody-goody kids, they've been out smoking and drinking and they listen to rock music. When we were in Montana she made a decision that she wasn't going to listen to it anymore. But like then she told me there's just no way that you can't.

Rose and her friend Sue, well, they have been real nice to

me. We all kind of get along together. But I never really had any problems with friends, though. I mean, everybody accepts me. But it's like they want to do more things with me now that I'm with the right crowd. That's it. I've been popular before, but I've been popular with the wrong crowd. In this school the most popular crowd is the goody ones. The rowdies, most of them, their parents send them here.

Last summer I went to that youth trip. I wanted to go. I thought it would help me get along with the kids and maybe, you know, have a better attitude towards the others, see what's going on and kind of find out who I'd want to hang around with this year. I was excited about it, the mountains and water and everything. At first, I thought, I'm never going to be able to live through this: no radio for two weeks, no TV for two weeks, you know. But, really, it was worth it. I could've stayed there for another two weeks. One day we rappelled and two days we climbed mountains.

It helped me a lot, helped me to really get started for this year. I thought I would try to be a better person, just be more kind and talk to people. It's just like, it's like the Holy Spirit comes—I don't know how the trip does it, but it just does— and then it just makes you feel like you've got another chance. First, when you hear a message, it goes in one ear and out the other. When they get to an area that you feel comfortable in, like the area of parents, I felt good in my heart that I had the right relationship with my parents. Then I could feel that the Holy Spirit was, how would you say, not congratulating me, but you know, that the Holy Spirit was glad 'cause I was getting along with them right, and I had my heart right with them. It's not like, "Oh, I can feel the Holy Spirit, there it is." No, it's not like that. It's just like a gradual thing that slowly comes, you know.

It's a joyful feeling that God's with you all the time. He's going to be watching over you and he is going to take care of you. And if you are not doing wrong, then he is going to help you. And he is going to make sure that you're taken care of and nothing's going to happen to you. If you do something wrong, then God's going to hurt you, either by hurting someone, like killing someone that you are real close to, or something like that. I found that out because not too long ago John Briggs, he used to go to our school, he got killed. We were really close friends. It just occurred to me, it's like the way I was before . . . I feel that the Lord was punishing John and teaching others through that. I've heard things about him and his girlfriend and I thought, "Well, if I'm not careful, then that is probably what could happen to me."

They are just so picky here on little things, like, "Oh, the slit in your dress is too high!" You know, that kind of thing, and it just bugs you. I feel that I have the right to make my own choices. I listen to rock music and I read dirty books (whatever you want to call them), not necessarily dirty books, but books that aren't necessarily on Christian topics. I don't have my heart right. I don't know. Right now, I'm not for sure. I just want to be happy, that's all. It feels like I'm split 'cause, sometimes, like you will get around some friends and they won't like you because of certain things that you do because they are more spiritual. You want them to be your friends because they are nice and you get along with them. But just because of those little things . . . It's definitely painful because you have to try to do things right, and then, you go and you do things wrong. If you do things wrong, you're always going to pay for it. But, maybe, like those things that I do wrong, I enjoy doing. If I didn't, I wouldn't do 'em and then I wouldn't be in a mess.

Doris Turner, Freshman: "I'm Supposed to Be an Individual"

Parents use Christian schools to achieve various purposes of their own, including some that are not congruent with the school's. Troubled by their child's academic failings and, possibly, their reckless behavior, they turn to a Christian school. Desperation rather than religion motivates their decision. In their search for a solution, parents may not reckon the price to be paid.

As soon as such children enter a Christian school, they and their parents learn about the price. Not one day passes before the errant children grasp that they have been placed in an environment that will strain their emotional and cognitive resources. If, literally, they do not see the light, they will suffer. The more they resist, the more their behavior becomes a topic for home-school discussion. For the Christian school regimen is no solution to their problems: unwillingly they came and unwillingly they stay. Doris Turner is such a child. Her frustrated, nonfundamentalist parents enrolled her at BBA hoping for the best. Though they may have got the school's best, and I believe they did, it was not the solution to problems Doris would acknowledge existed, problems that troubled her parents, not her. BBA's students, teachers, and administrators saw the challenge Doris presented to them and responded in their usual way. Doris took as affront what others meant as kindness. Getting right with Bethany's Lord is not her cup of tea.

Doris did not enter BBA seeking a new life. Consequently, teachers antagonize her when they ask, "Are you saved?" She perceives rejection of her beliefs in their efforts to reach her, and rejection of her behavior in teacher criticism of the way she walks. There is individuality at BBA, and Doris tests its limits. She is too young and too much an outsider at BBA to understand why her rulebreaking brings censure, while the rulebreaking of others seems not to. Because the Doris Turners threaten the order of Bethany, they suffer from an abundance of unwanted attention.

> I didn't decide to come here. My parents did. They sent me 'cause I was getting in trouble back in public school. And my grades—I was getting Fs in PE. I didn't like coming here, but there wasn't anything I could do. They just all of a sudden said, "You're going to this school." I hadn't even heard of this school before. I don't like to wear dresses and they make you wear dresses all the time. I'm not Baptist. It doesn't go hardly along with anything, you know, that our church believes in. I just think that it's too much religion for a school. You know, I'd rather just go to church and then go to school, separate. See, we never hardly went to church before. We did every once in a while, but not usually on a regular basis. I mean, I don't mind going to church. Church is pretty OK. But I don't like going every night, or something. We used to never go to church hardly, so I never got into it.
>
> They don't believe in drinking or anything here and we have wine at church and there's nothing wrong with it. My parents drink and my dad smokes, so I've grown up that that's OK, you know. I had never really thought it was wrong until I came here and they started telling me it's wrong. So, I don't really know.
>
> Teachers don't like you unless you are sort of like super religious. Mrs. Reynolds, the English teacher, has written on my papers, "Do you believe in God?" "Are you saved?" All these things. Teachers have asked me and, I don't know, I'll answer them and they'll kind of look at me strange. They just go, "Oh, really." I don't know, they kind of reject me, sort of. Mr. Swanson sort of does. He is nice, though. I like him. And Mrs. Reynolds does not like me at all. She has threatened to kick me out of her class twice, you know, for reasons I can't believe.

Everybody's got their own beliefs and I got my own. I'm not going to go believing everybody else's. I told my dad I thought it was sort of that way and he went and talked to Mr. McGraw. And they haven't been like kind of pushing me so much. They were kind of for a while, you know, asking me questions and stuff. I didn't like those things written on my papers.

Mrs. Conroy, she's the study hall teacher. Hal and I were sitting in the study hall and we were writing down the groups we like to listen to their music. I was writing down some groups and she saw it and she gave me a little conference afterwards and asked, "Are you saved? Do you believe in God?" And all that stuff. I told her, "I believe in God, but I don't think there is anything wrong with this [writing down the groups], you know." "Oh, you shouldn't do this," she said. "I'm going to have to report you."

They criticize a lot here. I didn't have a teacher last year at public school who called me a dummy or something. They do here. They say that you are not supposed to criticize other people and that it's wrong, yet when I was in the office yesterday, Mrs. Conroy was saying how fat this one girl was that had just walked out of the office. They all say that you're not supposed to criticize, that's what the Bible says, and all. It seems like they are not living up to what they say. I try to live up to what I say, but they don't seem to.

Mrs. Reynolds got me real mad once when she imitated how I walk in front of the class. She imitated my walking—and it looked like a really stupid walk—which wasn't very nice in front of everybody. And Mr. McGraw has told me that I walk wrong. I have no idea what he means; he says I show my bad attitude through my walk. I told him that I'm supposed to be an individual and walk different from everybody else, not like we're all robots that can walk the same. He said, "Why don't you have Miss Bennett or somebody teach you how to walk?" I just said, "No, thank you." And my mom hasn't said anything about my walk.

I don't know who but somebody told Mr. McGraw that he heard me talking about drugs. I talk to a lot of people in school about drugs and stuff if they ask me and if they talk about it. I'll talk about it and I don't think there's anything wrong with it. I wouldn't use them and then come to school. He just seems to blame it all on me and nobody else. I guess somebody overheard me talking and went in and narked on me, you know. I could tell them, I could go in and tell Mr. McGraw, that there were other people talking, but I wouldn't want to tell on any other people 'cause it would only get them in more trouble and wouldn't get me out of any trouble. There's a lot of that stuff, you know, snitching on other people. Mr. McGraw said I might be expelled. I might be able to finish till the end of the year. I don't know. In my class, about 90 percent breaks the rules and a couple that I know of smoke and stuff. There's not really too many, but there's more than you'd think in this school.

Jill and I were in the bathroom once and it was during sixth hour and I was supposed to be in speech. We weren't in there five minutes and when we walked out Mrs. Reynolds and Mr. Warren were standing there. She just said, "Now, this is what I'm talking about with you two girls." I just said, "We had something very important to discuss." And she said, "OK, you can come and talk to Mr. McGraw." Then I yelled at Mr. McGraw 'cause he is always picking on Jill. And I just said, "Why don't you leave her alone? You upset her a lot." I said, "I wouldn't have to go in there and calm her down if you wouldn't upset her." He said, "Well, I shouldn't have to do that." I said, "I like my friends, and I care if something's bothering them." He yelled at me and told me to leave his office.

When I'm riding home on the bus I have to sit with this little brat fourth-grader, and she tells me what to do and I get a little mad. She tells me that I'm not sitting right and stuff. Then she said she's smarter than me. She said, "I get As in Bible, I'm smarter than you." And I don't get very good grades. I get an F in Bible. I don't really think about it. I can't understand his tests. I study for them and then I mix everything all up. I memorize it and then, you know, I get the sentences mixed up. But I have mainly the right stuff written down.

Otherwise, I'm doing OK, except algebra. It's hard. I got an A in PE; that was real easy, though. And Mr. Kruger in biology is really easy. Mr. Kruger, he'll get in a mood and he'll start preaching, preaching, preaching, and one time he started crying. He was preaching, telling us some things and I don't know what it was, but all of a sudden he started crying and everybody in class thought it was so funny. I mean, men aren't suppose to cry over something like that. Every time he talks about an organ, he goes, "God made this for you. God made this this way." He talks about this creation/evolution thing. I've been taught evolution, and my dad believes in it, so I believe in it, too. They're having this creation/evolution controversy, they're talking about it, and they say, "Well, creation is a superior alternative." You know, "Creation is right and evolution is wrong." That's all they say and it's supposed to be giving both sides. But then it just cuts out evolution totally. I don't really care how it happened.

In my own religion I guess I'm saved, but I guess in the Baptist religion I'm not. I think everybody that goes to church is spiritual enough, you know. I go to my own church's dinners. I consider my mom pretty religious. I couldn't imagine her being like some of the kids here. It would be horrible to live with her. I know it would be 'cause she would never be home, she would be at church, and I would have to do all the laundry and everything. I don't know, maybe she's afraid she's gonna die or something. I think all of a sudden she feels she has to be religious. I personally think it's because we go to this school.

Brad Clawson, Sophomore: "If I Felt Guilty, I Wouldn't Do It."

Brad and his parents are members of Bethany Baptist Church. His parents accept BBA's doctrinal standards, but they permit behavior that Bethany prohibits. Brad chooses quite consciously to depart from Bethany's norms, though not because he wants to be disruptive for disruption's sake. He does not mean to subvert BBA's control structure, yet he clearly does not wish to see it operate so successfully that it precludes his personal pleasure. Unlike students who remain at BBA under great duress and are angry at both the school and their parents for what they must endure, Brad is a contented scorner. He goes along when and where he needs to, having learned, as Doris never does, how to stay in the system and, at the same time, to have fun.

Teachers prevail upon him to change his ways. Doris was a raw newcomer to Bethany's world, and she remained one. Brad belongs. With sorrow and regret, teachers endeavor to return him to the ranks of the conformer. But he knowingly persists in his backsliding, unmoved by the doctrinal norms he has internalized. They do not roar at him with a resounding, "No!" "Stop!" "Don't!" Instead they whisper—and he hears the whispers, but they are easily shrugged off as he continues his transgressing ways, admitting, heretically, that he can have a good life out of God's will.

> A bunch of times I have wanted to leave. The first couple of times I had that feeling I talked to my parents about it and they said, "No." So, anymore, whether I want to or not, I

don't. It's not that there's anything really wrong with the
school. One of the reasons I didn't like the school was
because of a type of favoritism which really shows out in
sports. It's not that bad now. It's a favoritism toward the
kind of kid that maybe had a parent who worked at school or
was known very well by everybody at the church. I know
that it's that way in every school, but things got kind of bad
when maybe the coach's boy wasn't that good in a sport and
he was still starting.

If you like to get in trouble, you can get in an awful lot of
trouble here. They don't let you do anything. I mean, they
regulate what you do. It's like water behind a dam. They'll
let you do things, but they keep you caged in. If I'm wanting
to go to a movie or something, I have to go to the late one
because, like out at the mall, if you go to the nine o'clock
one, there's nothing open out at the mall anyway. And if
anyone else is out there, you're sure they're out there for the
same reason you are. Some movies my parents don't mind,
as long as it's G or PG.

Teachers can get on your case an awfully lot and get mad
at you an awfully lot if you aren't spiritual. If you were
spiritual at one time and then you changed, they'll get mad
at you for changing. They might like say, "Brad, you're
backsliding; you know that's not right." That's happened to
me this year with more than one teacher. Mainly, they just
say to me, "Oh, Brad, you know I love you and I love your
family." They go through all this. "Now, the school cannot
be the most important thing in your life or else you'd be
doing things different." Which is true. They just tried to tell
me that I needed to change my habits towards school. I said
that I'd think about it. I had one teacher take me out of
last-hour study hall and talk to me about who I date. It had to
do with a girl that I was going with who had gotten in a little
bit of trouble once. She was hanging around some other girls
that weren't what they call very religious. And they took me
out and talked to me. They said that I should be careful of
who I dated. The teacher was going to give me a Christian
dating book that tells how you should date a Christian. I
didn't stop taking this girl out—not for a while, I didn't.
Well, it's all right if they want to tell you that you should be
more spiritual. But when they make it sound like they have
the right to make a person that way, then I draw the line
there. They shouldn't act like they have the right just because they are the authority or someting.

I believe one way and I act another. It's not that what I do is totally against what I believe, it just doesn't line up with what I do. Every once in a while one side of me says, "Don't do those things." I think about it and think about what is the best way. I think if what I'm doing is going to hurt me or not and I decide off that. Like, say, I want to go to a movie and one part of me says, "No, don't go." And I think, "Well, am I going to die if I do it?" Well, not like that, but just if I think "no," then I'll go. If I felt guilty, I wouldn't do it.

There was a girl just the other day at lunch who said she believes that there's nothing wrong with what they call "Christian rock." The words are no different than what the songs are that we sing here. It's just the beat. She says, "If I get the same thing out of that as I do out of some song here, then what is wrong?" "Well," I said, "there was nothing wrong with it. Except, what does the beat do?" I said, "It might cause you to do things you might not normally do. Maybe it causes you to get excited." She said, "Well, I suppose so," 'cause she said she was listening to it one day while she was driving the car and she said it made her start going a little bit faster. But still if you get the same thing out of it as out of the other music, there's really nothing wrong with it in that way.

They say you'll have a much, much more happier life if you're in the will of God. I don't know. I think you can have just as good of a life if you're not, as if you are. I think it just depends on what you do, how you run your life, whether it's in the will or out of the will of God. I just don't think that it's going to make that much difference—drinking, if you are of age, dancing, going to theaters, how you talk, who you're friends with. You can do some of those things and that's not going to make you unhappy. You probably wouldn't be making God happy by doing those things. That's what the main thing is, whether to be happy now or later. Right now, I'm just, I'd rather be happy here. It's probably better to not be happy here and be happy up there, but . . . I think about that an awful lot, but it doesn't bother me.

Whatever I do, I don't want to deny God. Whatever I do, I wouldn't ever do that. I fear him, to an extent. I believe in him. I wouldn't go around and say there was no God, because I know there is. It's hard to live up to what's expected of you at the school. Yes, I just couldn't do all that, be that good every day. I just couldn't. If they told me I had to, I'd say that I couldn't. They are saying you have to, but the thing is that you don't, because you can get away with it and not have to do it. I just feel that I'm in a school that is trying to do good, but if you want to, you can make it the same as a public school. It's up to you. Besides, I couldn't leave even if I wanted to.

The Bases for Scorning

Man is not fully malleable and in his recalcitrance toward complete sociability he possesses the potential for causing trouble.

Robert B. Edgerton

Deviant phenomena are common and natural. They are a normal and inevitable part of social life, as is their denunciation, regulation, and prohibition.

David Matza

No one needs convincing that "man is not fully malleable"; our own lives and that of everyone we know points inexorably to this fact. Nor need we be persuaded that "complete sociability" is an impossible ideal (Edgerton 1976:110). Fundamentalists explain this by man's basically sinful nature; "denunciation, regulation, and prohibition" are indeed their lot (Matza 1969:13). They denounce Satan and the world; they regulate their students' conduct; and they prohibit behavior thought inimical to living a scripturally based life. When Bethany's students show "recalcitrance" by doing what is "common and natural" for them to do, we are surprised only in relation to Bethany's enormous expenditure of effort to achieve "complete sociability."

Here I want to present student explanations of their scorning or, from Bethany's perspective, their deviant behavior. This is not an account of deviants. I surmise, however, that many of the particulars stated here would apply with equal force to those whose consistent, unmitigated, widespread deviations establish them as deviants from fundamentalism, as opposed to those who deviate intermittently with regard to a limited number of school norms, while holding fast to Bethany's core beliefs.

Opposing Views from Home, Church, and School

Of the 115 students who answered my questionnaire, about fifteen to twenty are members of nonfundamentalist churches. These children bring home stories of what Bethany teachers say about nonfundamentalist believers; they may not only take offense at what they hear, they may also continue to endorse their own contrary beliefs and practices.

> I get kind of upset in church [says a student] when Pastor
> Muller puts down Mormons. And then he says Presby-
> terians don't know that much about the Bible, that they just
> preach about you can go to heaven by works and stuff like
> that. It gets me mad 'cause my parents go to a Presbyterian
> church.

Parents feel "put down" by Bethany's views of other religious groups
and communicate their antagonism to children who thereby experience
a wedge between home and school that may not be resolved in favor of
the school. "Mom and Dad, they got really mad. They don't like
Bethany church; they think they're prejudiced. Baptists think being a
Baptist is everything, even though they say they don't."

Students whose parents belong to different churches, one Baptist
and one not, suffer the obvious problem of seeing their parents support
opposing belief systems. This type of conflict can preclude a student's
wholehearted involvement in Bethany's spiritual life. We see this in the
reflections of a girl with one Baptist and one Roman Catholic parent.

> Well, since I was saved, I'll always be a Christian, but it just
> kind of depends. If I do get married, and if I would marry
> into a Catholic family, then I'd go to a Catholic church with
> my husband. I think you should be together in your religion.
> I don't think, like my family, one should go one way and the
> other to go another.

Again, a wedge between home and school may exist when an otherwise believing and respected parent does something that Bethany rejects. Such is the case with divorce, which Bethany countenances only
when the grounds are adultery. Strict about divorce, Bethany does not
permit divorced persons to hold responsible positions either in the
church or in the school. On the one hand, students receive doctrinal
instruction in black-and-white terms. On the other, they may be
attached to a parent who, strictly speaking, has violated Bethany doctrine, but whose "violation" seems perfectly reasonable to the student.

> It says in the Bible [recalls one male student whose mother is
> a Bethany church member] that you're not supposed to get
> divorced except for like adultery. Like, see, my mom got
> divorced and I don't think she had an alternative. Her hus-
> band was an alcoholic, he ate up money, and he threatened
> to hurt us. She had no alternative, so I don't think we should
> be so fast to condemn people who are divorced.

And by coming to understand that one should not "be so fast to condemn," one finds a basis for taking exception to Bethany's teachings.

Parents, even those who most faithfully attend church, are not directly subject to the academy's control structure. Though pledged as a condition of their child's admission not to undermine the academy's purposes, parents nonetheless persist in behavior that communicates alternatives to Bethany's preferred way:

> On my mom's last birthday we went to a movie. We saw the Muppets.

> My parents listen to rock and roll; my dad smokes a pipe.

> My parents like rock and roll. When your parents do it, you kind of have to go along with it. They want me here because they think we learn more—we have smaller classes, and we get more attention from the teachers. They don't go along with everything the school says.

Persuaded by Bethany's standards, students may reject some of their parents' standards; Bethany does not directly encourage such behavior, particularly in light of the church's respect for parental authority. However, students always are taught that since the Word of God is supreme, it takes precedence over any mundane authority: one never renders unto man that which is the Lord's. Yet, if a student wants to locate an opening to escape the school's guidelines, parental behavior often can provide one. When two standards are extant—that of Bethany and that of parents—students may feel they have a choice, in spite of having been taught that right conduct is not a negotiable matter.

Some students are members of fundamentalist churches other than Bethany; their own pastors accept Bethany's major doctrinal beliefs but may part company on the meaning of this or that passage of Scripture. The discrepancy between Bethany's strict constructions and their own pastor's views may provide occasion for students' divergence from Bethany's views. Here is a student who exemplifies this possibility.

> I don't see where a group that allows drums and cymbals and stuff in their church service is wrong. The Bible distinctly says, you know, take trumpets and cymbals and stuff and praise the Lord with that. Over here in Bethany, if you don't have just a piano or organ, you are not going by the formal way the Baptists have always believed. Then, you know, then it's wrong, it's a sin, whatever. And if a guy has a

mustache and long hair—isn't clean-cut, you know—A
Number One Joe Christian, then he's not OK. When we get
to heaven God is going to bring judgment on a bunch of
people for sitting here nitpicking with all these formalities
when there was a world out there going to hell. You know,
that just gets to me.

The Perception of Double Standards and Inconsistencies

What also gets this student is what he calls a "double standard," one
that arises from his understanding of Scripture. He expands on an event
of the past year involving an "unacceptable" gift from his girlfriend.
The appearance of a double standard provides students another basis
for questioning Bethany's instruction.

She gave me a bracelet with my name on it for Christmas.
Had my name engraved on it, the whole deal. I wore it to a
Bethany church activity and the kids said, "You know, he's
turning queer. He's a fag." And all this stuff. I don't see
anything wrong with that bracelet because what's different
in me wearing my bracelet and Pastor Muller over here
puttting on hair spray? That used to be a lady's fashion. In
my eyes, that's a double standard. I don't buy that one bit.

The idea of double standards arises from impressions of the behavior
of role models like teachers and parents. Students perceive a discrepancy between their school's known, right standard and the supposedly
inconsistent behavior of those who are supposed to be exemplars of this
standard. Teacher favoritism is one instance. Students do not generally
feel that school rules are applied differentially, or that favoritism is
rampant, but about one-third of our sixty interviewees believe that
some students are more likely to "get away with murder," namely the
children of Bethany's pastors, teachers, and administrative staff. Such
inconsistency—if Jesus loves us all, why do teachers love some students
more than others—whether real or imagined, casts doubt on the absoluteness of the rules and their doctrinal underpinning.

Inconsistency is the bane of organizational efforts that focus on
socialization. "Do as I say and not as I do" does not wash. As adults, we
may claim that it is human to be inconsistent; as adolescents, we may
use adult inconsistencies as an excuse to free ourselves from the burden
of consistency. The astute scorner can find grounds to scorn both
doctrine and authority.

> I don't agree that seeing movies is wrong, no more than
> . . . OK, Pastor Burt and his wife and kids go sit in Pizza
> Hut. The rock music's always blazing there. It's a smoke-
> filled room and there's beer drinkers. Why is it right for
> them to go there to eat? That's as worldly as anybody going
> to a movie.

The student's point is that if it is wrong to see a G-rated movie in
theaters which also show forbidden R- and X-rated movies, why is it not
wrong to eat at restaurants which also allow forbidden music, drinking,
and smoking?

Another inconsistency arises between not laying up treasures this
side of heaven (that is, not being well-off on earth) and the supposed
affluence of church members, particularly the pastors.

> You look at the Lowes, Mr. McGraw, Pastor Muller—
> they've got all these wonderful houses, two cars, the whole
> bit [as ascertained by the criteria of the obviously less
> affluent student]. Man, they're in the preaching business for
> the money. I see Pastor Muller and it seems like he's wearing
> a new suit at least once a week. I know our family struggles
> to make the car payments.

Moreover, students see in teacher behavior the basis for finding open-
ings in Bethany's doctrinal fabric. Here are two examples.

> In class the other day there was a girl who had a book, one of
> those girls' books, not an overall dirty one. The teacher said,
> "Oh, can I read that after you're done?" And the girl said,
> "Yeah, but there's a few unnecessary words in it." The
> teacher said, "Well, I think I can let that pass." Now, if she
> can let that pass, why can't I go to a movie and let it pass?

> At the beginning of the day if you're standing at your locker
> talking to a girl and Miss Bennett should see you, she'll say
> you're not supposed to talk, but she won't write you up. She
> could if she wanted to. She won't, I think, because some
> teachers think that the rules are as dumb as we think they
> are. Not talking to girls—that's about the worst rule I think
> they've got here.

By ascribing a motive to Miss Bennett's nonenforcement of a rule, the
student sees her as joining him in recognizing the dumbness of some

rules. When Miss Bennett's nonenforcement is juxtaposed with a colleague's enforcement, the perceptive student locates ground for his own selective obedience of the rules: If they make judgments, why not me? If a rule is not absolute, why obey it absolutely?

Compelling, Forbidding, and Conforming

Another set of circumstances that encourages student deviance is the unwitting result of teachers' and parents' desire to have children conform. The intensity of their efforts can prove to be counterproductive. We do not always serve our own best interests when we become zealous, and Bethany certainly has an abundance of educators who zealously serve their school's ends. In so doing, they make attractive that which they pray will be avoided. The comments of students indicate these unintended reactions:

> Every time we don't have school and public schools do [says a junior girl] I always want to go visit just to see what I'm really missing, or if I'm missing anything. I've never been in a public high school, not even for one day. I want to see if it's like what I hear it's like. My folks will never let me because they're always afraid that I'll like it.

> A lot of times it's fun to read those [prohibited] things, just because it's something different, you know. And the TV shows that they stress not to watch, I go ahead and watch. I just like them. I don't know why. It's exciting, I guess.

The abundance of parental and teacher "shalt nots" creates pitfalls for the youthful would-be conformer: when what is disallowed is what elsewhere is demonstrably attractive, students may desire the forbidden.

Forbidding, particularly to the extent that is routine at Bethany, can set off reactions to authority. What is denied assumes an aura of desirability; in addition, one may want to resist the denier. Looking at the student pledge, one senior boy observes, "After a while you can kind of get in a habit, I suppose, of seeing how much you can get away with." His tone was casual, undefiant, containing no hint of principled disobedience. Listen to another boy reflect on his experience in chapel, a setting that reverberates with scripturally inspired injunctions:

> I don't know, I don't think anybody should be forced to do something they don't want to do. I hate taking away free-

dom. Like when I get older and have kids I'll have to ground them and I'll hate that. I just don't like to make people do what they don't want to do.

Clearly, he places much of what he hears in chapel in the category of being "forced to do." Being compelled or pressured to do even what one values can generate resistance and deviance. The element of "force" enters most in the case of injunctions that one neither wants to nor would normally follow.

> The toughest part of being a Christian teenager is, well, you are always thinking I'm supposed to do right. It's always trying to keep yourself from doing what the church and school consider wrong. It would be easier if *you* think the thing is wrong, but when it's just the church and school's conviction, then it's pretty hard to keep from not doing wrong.

In the name of doing good, teachers create defiance, even cynicism, toward themselves among students who already may be disposed to bend rules. Reacting to the pledge guideline that requires giving "honor, respect, and cooperation" to teachers, a senior boy says, "that's stupid." He rails against the inequity of teachers having a prerogative that students do not have.

> I don't think you should have to sit back and let a teacher call you a name. Last year a teacher called some of us guys a jackass and said we weren't saved. Right out in front of the class she went around mentioning students she didn't think was saved. Because we had written a composition about something, and she didn't like what we had wrote, she said, "I can tell by this composition that you are not saved."

That you should "be what God wants you to be" is set at the core of the school's socializing commitment. God, teachers, parents—together they constitute a "somebody else" to the students' "I": "What do *I* want to be?" students ask. "What will *I* make of *my* future?"

> It's trying to be what, you know, somebody else wants you to be, not what you are yourself. Some kids act like what they think the church wants them to be or what the teachers want them to be. It is just like a big front. They don't act like themselves; they want their teachers to think good of them.

Being what somebody else wants them to be places students under tremendous pressure if their self-perceptions are not reasonably congruent with those of the significant others in their life. The students' sense of seeking their own way, of accepting but not yet fully internalizing their fundamentalist order, places them at odds with Bethany's abundant injunctions and expectations. Accordingly, they may struggle to find themselves in the images that Bethany projects for them, painfully trying to reconcile what they are told—and probably even know is right—with the fact that it is told by insistent authorities. Thus, the known right choice may not feel like a free choice. The attribution of "imposition" to the choice provides grounds for student opposition to it.

> Right now Mother says it's a stage—I am just trying to find
> out who I really am. I have to be a certain way for my parents
> and my grandparents and my teachers. It's really weird. I
> should be one person in front of everybody. I just don't
> know which one I'm going to pick. I want to please my
> parents but I want to be happy. I talk to my friends a lot
> about this. We're all the same age, fourteen or fifteen, and
> we're trying to figure out what we're going to be, what we're
> going to be like. It's hard to talk to an adult. They say they've
> been through this, but it's hard to accept that they have.

The Christian life is not part-time; Bethany's twenty-four-hour, year-round pledge encompasses all that a student does. Bethany recognizes no cracks in its total commitment. The Christian way is demanding, and Bethany's teachers, as well as many parents, demand the fullest possible conformity. As a result, a student wearily describes her activities during a typical week.

> If I've been at a Saturday night activity and gone out for
> pizza afterwards and then have to get up at 6:30 for the
> Sunday morning bus ministry, I think, "Oh, why can't I just
> be like regular people and stay home [on Sunday morning]
> and go fishing, or something like that?"

"Oh, why can't I just be like regular people . . . ?" What a telling, poignant expression! She is not a "regular" person. Her church, school, and home have so modified her life that she knows—from the moment each school morning when she dons dress, hose, and high-heeled shoes to the time each night when she prays—she is different. As is the junior boy who wonders why he can't "be just a regular kid," an "ordinary guy" who runs around with the crowd like everyone else, and who, when he is older like his dad, will settle down and quit running because, "Then, nobody is looking down on you." Student yearning to be "regular" may be temporary, a transient moment soon to be supplanted by the sense of satisfaction derived from being different in a Christian way. Or it may be a moment, joined to many more, in a process of mounting resentments and antagonisms that lead to increasing deviation from Bethany's norms.

The antagonism can be enhanced by the intensity of Bethany's socializing process and by the often compulsory nature of its efforts, that is, by students being required rather than allowed or enabled to do the right thing. To be sure, Bethany unapologetically compels those things within its purview, for example, that all student leaders sign a pledge committing them to faithful attendance at church activities. But athletes are held to a lesser degree of required faithfulness:

> I looked at the basketball team [said one of its players], and I saw them coming just on Sunday, because they had to, you know. You could tell that was why they came because I saw they weren't coming on Wednesday nights. Now that the season's over, those guys who were coming just on Sunday aren't coming at all. Same with the wrestlers once the season was over.

Compulsion may lead to cynicism. It may also lead to feeling a loss of autonomy. "About signing the pledge, well, I guess it doesn't really bother me but I don't really like it. You know, I don't like for anyone to say what I have to do. I like doing my own thing." This statement was made by one of the school's leaders. During her many years at Bethany teachers urged her to believe that the world's way of "doing one's own thing" is anathema to a Christian walk. Doing her own thing, however, is what she wants to do.

Bethany's leaders firmly believe that its Christian youth need definite, enforced guidelines, that if left on their own, they would be susceptible to Satan's lures. Thus, those in authority compel. And thus they pay a price in the form of student negativism:

> In order to come back to school this year I had to go on the summer youth trip because they thought it would be a spiritual uplift for me. It was fun. It would have been funner if I'd gone of my own choice. I was forced to go and so I didn't like it that well.

The element of compulsion continued to work once the trip was underway:

> They started with that you had to learn the first five verses of this chapter. If you didn't learn them, you didn't get any supper. And then the next day you had to memorize five more and say those ten until you reach the end of the week when you had to recite the whole chapter. I didn't eat a couple of times. They think that you're going to learn Scripture and it's going to make you better. What good is it if it's going to make you rebellious, too? You're going to hate learning it and you'll learn it just to eat. No kid likes anything to be forced on him.

Feeling rebellious may be the most natural reaction of many students who intermittently, if not regularly, interpret Bethany's socializing practices not as benign and beneficial but as negative and burdensome:

> You know, they are always preaching on "stay out of the world," and "don't, don't, don't, don't, don't." If you throw that at people, you get the wrong thing because they hear these don'ts and wonder, "Well, what in the world *can* you do?" It kind of turns a lot of people off.

When negativism is seen as the pervasive sentiment, then reactions like the following occur: "Sometimes, like, you go out and you're worse than you would be otherwise because you can't do anything at school. You got to let it all out. That's about it."

Bethany's abundance of "don'ts" are matched by their dos, but the sense of being constrained, boxed in, exists in students who are located across the spiritual spectrum.

> I always feel all the time that I would like to back off completely [says an eighth-grader who has spent all of her school days at BBA]. I'll just sit there in chapel, you know, and I'll just sit back thinking, "Aw, I get this all the time." I think, "Oh, man, I just want to get away from here." I've felt that a lot lately.

In possibly the strongest statement about feeling pressured a student says:

> You feel like a dog that they put out in the yard. They tell you

that you've got the whole yard, but actually you've got a
chain around your neck. If you let them know that you know
you are caught . . . you realize all the pressure, all the rules.
I'm sure if you take advantage of the situation, you have a lot
of fun, but inside you feel there's something there holding
you back.

Another student says that when students have erred, teachers should
go to the Bible and "try to straighten us out," but they should not keep
taking out their Bible and nitpicking. "Don't be picking on us all the
time," is the way she summarizes her impression of the teacher's style
of reproof and correction. The student perceives a teacher's well-meant
corrections as overkill.

Finally, in regard to this point of teacher actions producing unintended resentment, human beings, young and old alike, differ in their
capacity to be consistent even with regard to ideals they accept. There is
no time off for Christians. In public, students learn, they always must be
examples of right behavior; in private, the Lord knows what they do
and think. This unmoderated demand for consistency is a strain. BBA
students never hear the temporizing language of "however," "but,"
and "on the other hand." BBA is not that kind of place.

Intellectual Independence of Students

The strong impression of student independence emerges in many of
the foregoing statements. In these, we hear students reacting to some
person, event, or situation: If Pastor Muller can wear hair spray, then
why can't I wear a bracelet? If Pastor Burt can take his kids to eat where
beer is sold, then why can't I go to the movies? In what follows the case
differs. We see students on their own examine, rather than be bound
by, the Word, taking an intellectual stance when obedience should be in
order. Indeed, such students may analyze Scripture because they are
prone to analyze everything, impelled by a disposition to wonder and
doubt, which Bethany educators may both fear and respect.

Students may become incredulous about the Bible for a variety of
reasons. They may find some aspects impossible to believe, transcend-
ing the limits of their faith, and they may even question the Bible's
authoritativeness, preferring personal judgment instead:

I believe the Bible, but just parts of it. Like they say all this
stuff about how God is so old. I just don't see how anybody
could live that long and create the world in six days. Just to

> believe in God . . . I don't really believe that. I do believe
> there's someone watching over us, but I don't know who
> it is.
>
> They do say that people who don't get the gospel, a lot of
> them are going to hell and everything. I don't see how that's
> possible. Those tribes who have never heard of Christ or
> anything, they are going to hell? I don't see how it's really
> possible, but I don't say anything in class. I just go with what
> they say.

Of course, BBA teachers would prefer that she express her disbelief in
class, because then they could deal with it. Unexamined, it remains
unresolved and a potential canker. More serious grounds for deviance
are seen in the student who knows the academy's position "that the
truth is always found in Scripture" but is not satisfied with it. She stands
apart from her peers by possessing an intellectual orientation that
challenges orthodoxy. She recognizes no personal limits to what she
should be able to read or hear.

> If you're going to do anything, you should reason it out,
> think for yourself. Don't just be a robot that walks around.
> You have to know and understand why something is true,
> instead of just learning that it is. With me, I try to find out
> whether it's the right thing to do, look at all angles, instead
> of just one specific place [Scripture].

Judging from student reactions to BBA's constraints and admonitions, I conclude that more than adolescent ardor motivates the scorners
to go their own way. In the following words I hear determination and
independence, not rebellion.

> I think the academy and its leaders are totally dedicated to
> the Lord. I feel, from a young person's point of view, I just
> haven't decided that I'm going to be that way yet. There are
> certain things . . . I have definitely decided I'm going to be
> saved and go to heaven, and yet I haven't decided I'm going
> to be totally like them. Maybe some day I will. I feel I've got
> to see a little more. It's not quite proven to me that it's worth
> it to give up a career somewhere else [outside Christian
> service]. Or to give up living for the things I want to do and
> that the church wouldn't agree with.

Students' Rationales for Deviation

Attracted to do what they are expressly forbidden to do—regarding choice of music, movies, close friends, and reading, for example—students identify a number of rationales by which they can justify their partaking of these forbidden fruits. Bethany's norms exist; students know and understand them. They artfully learn to liberate themselves from the bond of norms they wish to ignore.

1. *There's no escaping "bad" music* means that because such music is everywhere, one may unwittingly hear it and excusably learn to like it. Freed from the guilt of intentionality, students can simply shrug their shoulders and say, "It just happened—and I'm innocent."
2. *We are youths, and this is the way we are*: "I think, you know, at this point people don't want to dedicate their lives to the Lord. They just want to get through high school and have all the fun they can."
3. *Everyone's doing it, therefore . . .*: "A lot of times it's easier to turn around and say, 'Look, God, the world is doing it this way, you know. Everybody else is doing it, so . . . ,'" "I don't feel bad about watching something on TV. I come to school and somebody else will be talking about it. So, if they've watched it, why should I feel guilty?"
4. *What they say happens, doesn't happen*: In this view, students deny those consequences that Bethany claims follow from certain actions. "They say rock music gets you in a rowdy spirit and then you'll go out and do things you shouldn't do. I've never got through listening to the radio and gone out and robbed a bank. They say rock music tears the Lord down. They might have a point there, but I don't see where all rock music is tearing you down."
5. *We've been dragged down by out-of-school friends*: Students say this to explain their helpless, though not necessarily guiltless, behavior. Students learn that unsaved friends will drag them down, but "it's hard, like if they are your best friends, to cut them off, you know, after you went a long ways with them. Sometimes, it's either them or no one."
6. *I draw the line where I want*: This declaration of independence is, perhaps, the most common and the most powerful position students assert to defend their nonnormative behavior. It is the reaction of students who feel that "a lot of times I kind of get the feeling they are trying to run my whole life." What surprises me is not that he expresses this feeling, but how seldom BBA students do, for the academy does try to control the whole of its students' lives.

Variously expressed, the drawing of one's own line is at the heart of much scorning behavior. One student declared his independence as a matter of interpretation, leaving it implicit that he had the right to interpret. After referring to the verse (2 Corinthians 6:14) that supposedly precludes a close relationship with non-Christians, he said,

> Some people say that it's talking about just in marriage and others believe it's talking about non-Christian friends. I feel if you're not going to be friends with them, it's the same thing as being stuck up. I don't feel it's right to snub them because they are unsaved. So I just treat them like I would anybody else.

However, unsaved friends are not like anybody else. His justificatory interpretation frees him from the constraints of Bethany's standards. In this act of independence, he has much company, and in areas other than friendship. Moreover, the act involves related claims, for example, to the right to express personal taste and convictions, to have a "private area," to see gray where BBA proclaims black and white.

One senior girl's response to our question "Do you think there are TV shows you shouldn't watch?" illuminates a range of justifications for the right of independent student judgment. Her doctrinal orthodoxy rests within a heterodox context, as her comments reveal; she both acknowledges and qualifies the meaning Bethany places upon biblical authority.

> Well, I know there are shows that they say you shouldn't watch, but I think a lot of it is up to the person, because it's your own personal conviction. Some things, if you're not bothered by them, I don't think somebody else should condemn you for watching. Unless it's obviously bad, you know, like "Saturday Night Live." Some of it is funny, but the whole of it is just crude. Shows like that . . . that's just common sense.
>
> There's things, you know, the Bible says are right and wrong; they say it in black and white. And although they [Bethany] say there's no gray area, there's a lot of things, like TV, it's what you think is right. If it offends you, then you shouldn't do it. But you shouldn't put somebody else down for not being convicted of the same thing.
>
> There's things that if you think are wrong, then it is a sin for you. It's not necessarily sin for somebody else because

they're not convicted by it. They wouldn't say that here [at Bethany church and school].

I've come to the conclusion that I'll listen to their side objectively. If it changes me, then it changes me. But I won't feel bad about not agreeing with some things. I believe the plan of salvation the same as here. Things like that are black and white. I don't think you should fight over little things that don't have much bearing on whether you're going to heaven or not.

This young woman is a prototypical deviating conformer. She scorns some of Bethany's norms, though she does not mock, deride, or reject contemptuously. Rather, she clears a way through Bethany's doctrinal thicket, leaving intact those elements she designates indisputable, while permitting others to stand or fall insofar as they square with her convictions.

In whatever language the case is stated, the point remains that students arrogate to themselves prerogatives that, if they exist at all, Bethany assigns only to mature Christians. High school students Bethany does not consider mature.

Conclusion

When I completed my first week at BBA, a week spent entirely with teachers in a preterm, in-service session, I was prepared thereafter to see a school of teachers who worked as warriors for their Lord, discharging his will for them in full-time Christian service. I expected to see students who, for the most part, were miniature warriors, adolescent counterparts of their adult mentors. My expectations were fulfilled. That such students exist is more of an achievement than I appreciated at the end of that hot August week, for I was not yet aware of the magnitude of what it means to be a born-again Christian, in Bethany's terms, and thus what an accomplishment it is for home, church, and school when youngsters prove to be as spiritual as Bethany's students are (and as I have tried to portray them throughout this book).

As a group, BBA's students seem never to be mindless youth, frozen into routines, beliefs, and behavior patterns that control them as though they were machines. If their spirituality differentiates them from most nonfundamentalist Christian public school children, they are still recognizably spirited, fun-loving, enthusiastic, warm, and friendly. They behave and believe in ways that bring them closer to the world than their doctrinal standards permit them to be. In short, they deviate. The wonder is that they do not deviate more. For the constraints BBA's standards impose on them place them at odds with much that our society celebrates: the ideal of Christian adolescence they are meant to exemplify gets severely tested by the models of American adolescence that surround them.

In its socializing efforts, Bethany tries to make normal for its people, both young and old, what is abnormal outside Bethany. To say the least, this is a profound challenge, demanding even for adults; it is easiest, perhaps, for those children who attended no school other than Bethany Baptist Academy, whose parents are fully and comfortably conforming believers. For other students, including both the best-behaved and the rowdiest, departing from some of Bethany's norms has itself become normal. Could it be otherwise? I think not. Asked to believe and behave without exception, compromise, or adaptation, they nonetheless live in a world that honors moderation, compromise, and adaptiveness to changing times and circumstances.

Complicating the situation for young students, beseeched as born-again Christians to throw off the self of the worldly "old man," is the fact that the bad guys of the world, unlike those in Western movies, do not have black hats, stubby beards, and snarling speech. Thus they see seemingly attractive, if not much-admired, persons behaving and be-lieving in ways contrary to Bethany's standards. Will such people burn in hell? Will God punish them for their misdeeds? Can such otherwise intelligent people be so blind to scriptural Truth that they ignore it? These questions open the doorway to doubt, creating chinks of uncer-tainty that may lead to the personal redefinition of acceptable and unacceptable behavior and belief. To retreat from the uncompromising dogma of the pledge is to insert personal judgment in matters which, students are instructed, have the sanction of God's Word.

Absolute acceptance, unquestioning obedience—these are the appropriate responses to sacred standards, the underpinnings of Bethany's norms. BBA struggles to invest its pledge with an aura of sacredness, so that violations are not mere misbehavior, they are sins. However, students act as though their school's prescriptions and pro-scriptions are not sacred. By so doing, they begin a process of stripping away one tenet after another, and of ascribing to themselves the pre-rogative of defining the boundaries of the sacred. Thus freed from adopting the full panoply of doctrinal belief, they are left with a per-sonally crafted patchwork of doctrinally acceptable and unacceptable behavior. The whole cloth of belief risks unraveling, as in the case of the Roman Catholic John Robben, who relinquished a lifetime of orthodoxy when, in sequence, he practiced birth control, abandoned the confessional, and then left the communion. "If you remove one brick from the structure of belief," Robben writes, "other bricks begin to fall" (1972:39).

There are easier types of Christian to be than a fundamentalist one. Having been taught this, students are forewarned. Becoming sufficiently forearmed is the exceptionally difficult task of Bethany's socializing superstructure of church, school, and home. It is realized in the main, but still imperfectly. Students slip through the ring of control, becoming deviators from the norms, rather than deviants. Most do not want to break free in any total sense. Taken together, students can be classified on a continuum of conformity ranging from true-blue believers, at the one end, to outright rejectionists, at the other, who mean to leave BBA at the earliest opportunity. Between these extremes—and there are significantly more at, and bordering on, the true-blue end—are many who reject some of the rules and violate some of the doctrinal standards. Save for those few at the rejectionist pole, all other students mean to savor the rewards available from some combination of orthodoxy and heterodoxy.

The more orthodox the students are, and the closer they come to fulfilling Bethany's expectations, the greater are their institutional rewards, epitomized in Matthew 25:21: "His lord said unto him, Well done, thou good and faithful servant . . . enter thou into the joy of thy lord." BBA's faithful servants may forgo the disputed pleasures the less faithful allow themselves. It is often a major test of character and conviction to set aside the cake of the world, if not of one's own past. Cake does not lose its appeal to dieters when they resolve to exclude it from their diet. The rewards and comforts of orthodoxy confront the rewards and comforts of heterodoxy; the scorners decide for themselves what combination they wish to pursue.

A consequence of the fact that most student scorners also adhere to Bethany's standards and norms is that they lead a somewhat schizoid life. Their split develops from a desire to win or maintain the approval of teachers, classmates, and relatives, who expect a type of performance and a degree of consistency that exceeds their capacity or wish to comply.

> My parents and relatives are leading people in the church. I'm expected to be this good girl that never gets in trouble. I think that I put on a front. I'm one way in front of the students and one way in front of my parents, relatives, and teachers.
>
> When they're giving their devotions, they always hit on

something and they'll ask you questions. You'll answer
something totally like, "I feel like this is the right thing."
And it might not even be you, but you do it just to impress
the teacher.

Like a pendulum, students swing one way when teachers are present, another way when they are not; one way with friends in school,
another way when they are out; one way when it is the school year,
another way when it is not. Because students are both deviators and
conformers, their behavior swings from one way to the other. What is
no struggle for some students who successfully contain their schizoid
parts, is indeed a major struggle for others who spend their lives within
the fundamentalist fold. As adults, they may choose to leave Bethany
for a denomination that somehow encompasses both behaviors, or they
may leave participation in a religious community altogether. In the
mean time, at BBA, we hear two voices. That of the scorner:

> You know you've been bottled up here at school for practi-
> cally nine months and during the summer it's like when you
> get home from school at night—you can let it all out.

And that of the conformer:

> It's a hard thing to say, really, if I'd want to change the
> academy or not. I could change it to the way that I would
> want it. But, then, it wouldn't be good for the school; you
> could be doing things against the school.

10

Bethany's Total Institution Truth's Organizational Structure

For us, this is a total life.
Pastor William Muller

Introduction

Erving Goffman's seminal essay "On the Characteristics of Total Institutions" (1961) has attracted the attention of many writers.[1] Drawing on the fact of the general "encompassing tendencies" of all institutions, he focuses his essay on a class of institutions intended to be encompassing to a considerable extent, some to the point of erecting physical barriers ("locked doors, high walls, barbed wire . . .") to provide an effective "barrier to social intercourse with the outside." Among his types of total institutions are "groupings" that include homes for the blind, the aged, the orphaned; mental institutions; jails; and convents and cloisters. A fifth grouping is one that he says is "established the better to pursue some worklike task." Goffman places army barracks, ships, and boarding schools in this category. I include in it the Christian school as Bethany conceives of it.

With the ensuing discussion of Bethany Baptist Academy as a total institution I begin a basic shift in voice from that of the researched—Bethany's students, educators, and parents—to that of my own. In a real sense, I have been heard all along, not directly by saying "Here is what I think or feel," but indirectly as I selected which Bethany voices would be allowed to speak. Up to this point, my personal charge has

257

been to portray Bethany within the context of its own structure and doctrine, that is, from their point of view. Hereafter, I will portray Bethany from my own perspective.

Bethany's students do not eat and sleep within academy walls. At the end of each school day, conformers and scorners alike return home to parents who willingly send them daily to Bethany's confines. Yet in my first week of full-time fieldwork at Bethany I saw indications that its educators intended that BBA operate as a total institution; the longer I remained in Bethany's world, the more convinced I became of the term's application there.

"Wherefore come out from among them, and be ye separate, saith the Lord, and touch not the unclean thing," students learn from 2 Corinthians 6:17. BBA emphasizes few messages more than this one. "If you want your child to grow up to be an outstanding servant of the Lord," writes the Christian educator Charles Walker in an official AACS publication, "it is absolutely necessary that you guard his mind so that it will be exposed only to those things that would be pleasing to Him" (1982:1). Walker's words convey one clear message: control the stimuli that touch your children so that you can control their minds. "What is the relationship between student and teacher in your school?" I ask a BBA teacher. "I feel closer to the kids because the Christian life is a total life. It's not just eight hours of school," the teacher answers. Separation, control, total life—given these elements of a total institution, the issue to consider here is not if BBA is a total institution, but what type of total institution it is.

I believe BBA's leaders mean it to be a total institution, for a total institution is the natural organizational outcome of a school based on absolute truth. To be sure, total institutions are viewed variously as necessary but unpleasant places, as places to avoid, and, at their worst, as truly dreadful places. But Bethany's school is—in their terms—a benign total institution designed to serve the purposes of Christian parents and students.

Bethany's Truth

As an alternative school, Bethany Baptist Academy is not meant to be a variant of American public schools. The purpose of public schools, according to a collective statement that several national organizations prepared,[2] "is to develop informed, thinking citizens capable of partic-ipation in both domestic and world affairs" (Butts 1980:84). According to Roland Barth, "A fundamental purpose of public education is to prepare children to live in a pluralistic society" (Barth 1980:239). The sociologist Christopher Hurn observes that "the continual expansion of human knowledge . . . will create further demands for understanding and learning-how-to-learn as the objectives of schooling. . . ." (1978:10). These ideas about schooling are consistent with Dennis Doyle's notion that "Good schools are not different in their fundamental purpose; they are good in that they are better expressions of a common form" (1980:18).

Bethany parents disagree with Doyle. When they choose the fundamentalist Christian alternative for their children, they knowingly send their children to a school that provides an intentionally deviant experience, one that is at odds with public schools and not "a better expression of a common form." McGraw said that the city of Hartney did not need one more school like its public, Catholic, and Lutheran schools. His church meant to establish a school with a difference. And so it did. The differences are not found in the school's ordinary moments; these they share with American schools everywhere, and they abound.

What is not ordinary are BBA's purposes. The academy, together with its fellow members of the American Association of Christian Schools, intends:

1. to bring children to salvation;
2. to inform children about the Word of God;
3. to keep children immersed in the Word of God;
4. to keep children separate from the world;
5. to encourage children to proselytize the unsaved;
6. to lead children to enter full-time Christian service as preachers, teachers, evangelists, etc; and,
7. failing this, to have children become full-time Christians, living their lives, whatever they do, wherever they are, always for the glory of God.

These purposes shape Christian schools, not "the development of informed, thinking citizens" (Butts 1980:84), concern for a pluralistic society (Barth 1980:239), or "learning-how-to-learn" (Hurn 1978:10). They are derived from scriptural doctrine as seen by the fundamentalist, not as metaphor, allegory, or the wisdom of sages, but as the direct Word of God. The Christianity of fundamentalists, John Dillenbarger and Claude Welch write, "is irrevocably committed to the inerrancy of the Bible. . . . To admit even the slightest amount of 'higher criticism' is to cast doubt on everything in the Bible. . . . It is all or none" (1954:227–28). Thus, Christian school purposes are based on scriptural Truth with a capital T, Truth that is absolutely known, universally applicable, beyond the claims of evidence, to be inculcated, and subject to questioning only to clarify, not to modify or interpret. Since the mood of doctrine is imperative, believers are expected to respond with obedience.

In ordinary discourse we frequently use the word "true" and its derivatives without qualification, as if the facts of the matter were established beyond doubt. If pressed, we probably would concede that though we sound absolutely certain, we can imagine a basis for qualification or doubt. Sounding absolutely certain, however, is normal behavior. For example, a dimension of absoluteness is present in statements such as these: "She was truthful when she said she expects to return home tomorrow." "It is true that tender house plants will die if exposed to freezing temperatures." Thus, it is misleading to assert that only Christians deal with capitalized Truth, and thereby to imply that non-Christians live in a world of clearly acknowledged relativism. In this juxtaposing of Christian and non-Christian domains, I contrast neither the confidence of absolute Truth with the confusion of relative truth, nor pit a single right source of solutions to world problems against a babel of competing, conflicting solutions. A dichotomous view exaggerates the distinctions between the fundamentalist's and the nonfundamentalist's view and use of truth.

In fact, an essential distinction exists: fundamentalists claim unequivocally to know the Truth. They organize their institutions—family, church, and school—to be fully congruent with it, confidently ignoring alternative notions, based, for example, on new evidence or on changing times. And they hope, knowing that such hope is futile until Christ returns, that the institutions now beyond their control also will incorporate their biblical Truth. Nonfundamentalists, more an aggregate than a group, are difficult to generalize about. If they behave as though some claims are absolutely true, they seldom can or do make claims to Truth like those of the fundamentalists. And they rarely have a single, consistent, uniform doctrine to direct every major aspect of their life.

Bethany's Truth does not answer unresolved questions of physics and chemistry, or thorny problems of international trade or Third World indebtedness. Scripture informs rather than settles such matters. Bethany educators do not view the Bible as an answer book that responds directly to every conceivable school-related question. However, since it does cover every issue and concern the school wishes to control, its educators speak with the true believer's full measure of certainty.

Their Truth pervades the students' lives. Having sacralized all of life, fundamentalist Christians see their way as fitting at the beach, on a date, or in a pizza parlor, as in Bethany's corridors. Their Truth provides a yardstick for judging music, art, literature, and dance; it defines both subordinate-superordinate and male-female relationships, and who is acceptable as close friend, spouse, and business partner; it establishes the acceptability of welfare, homosexuality, abortion, private property, gambling, drinking, dancing, and heterosexual activity; and it explains "the nature and character of God; the nature of the universe; the nature of man; the question of what happens to man at death; the basis of ethics; and the meaning of history" (Fountain n.d.:2). What else is there?

Bethany's Truth establishes the basis for heresy. To question such Truth, except within the framework of faith, is to question God himself. The Christian school, accordingly, is hermetic. Bethany's spiritual schoolhouse welcomes only those who believe or can come to believe. Dissenters and compromisers are unwanted guests. To those outside their fold, the Christian's all-embracing doctrine enslaves because it constricts one's options; to those inside, freedom lies in Truth's domain.

Bethany's Total Institution

My characterization of BBA as a total institution is structured by C. A. McEwen's excellent review of the total institution concept (1980). McEwen opens his essay with Goffman's own definition of a total institution as a place "of residence and work where a large number of like-situated individuals, cut off from the wider society for an appreciable period of time, together lead an enclosed, formally administered round of life" (p. 143). With the exception of a total institution as a place of residence, BBA fits every other aspect of Goffman's definition. McEwen continues by cautioning that the total institution is less totalitarian and less deserving of its usual status as an epithet than many writers have been aware. He quotes Nick Perry to show the term's use as a pejorative: A total institution is "a symbolic presentation of organizational tyranny . . . a closed universe symbolizing the thwarting of human possibilities" (p. 147). Applied to prisons and concentration camps, this conceptualization is generally apt; applied to other groupings, including Christian schools, it is debatable, as I will clarify below.

McEwen identifies several "dimensions of organizational variation" in order to demonstrate the variability of total institutions.

Shared Organizational Goals

McEwen identifies shared organizational goals as "the degree of staff coordination or consensus about work goals and practices"

(p. 157). In light of the data presented in previous chapters, we know that Bethany's teachers are in remarkable accord with each other about work goals and practices, accepting their school's preference to forgo dealing with conflict and ambiguity in the interests of insuring the successful inculcation of their Truth.

A critical indicator of an institution's degree of consensus is its capacity to sanction censorship. To succeed, censoring requires shared values and the belief that these values must prevail. Censorship naturally follows Truth. BBA's librarian describes her approved censorship practices:

> Some of the science books, if they have too much evolution or are too slanted in certain places, but they have a lot of good qualities in them, then I take them to Mr. Kruger [the science teacher]. I let him pick out what he can use.
>
> I can't deface encyclopedias. No one's told me I had to, so I just don't do anything with them. If students find a picture in them, well, that's an encyclopedia; you have them in your home. Everybody buys the same encyclopedias. I don't see why I have to go through them. It isn't that you're giving 'em to read for pleasure; they're there for finding facts. And the facts are there. What the evolutionists think about, that's there. If someone wants to write a book report on it, it's there. The *Almanac*, the *World Almanac*, the *Guinness Book of Records*, and those, I don't change them at all. I don't even think about those.
>
> I look for evolution. That's one of the things. I look for swear words. We take those out. I found a double page of monkeys developing into man and, of course, we don't approve of that at all, so I just sealed the pages together and it didn't bother the reading on either side. Then, in the beginning, there was a section on evolution. I bracketed that in black letters and wrote EVOLUTION across it so that anybody reading knows that it is evolution, rather than destroying the whole book, because a lot of it was good. If I find a naked person, I draw a little bathing suit on them or I put a little dress on, but just in a regular book that doesn't have anything to do with art. But in art, art is art, and if you find a person without any clothes on, that's what they drew. We had one storybook where the kids were all bathing in the nude. It was not anything, so I just put bathing suits on them.
>
> We just put out twenty new books on the value of hon-

esty and that sort of thing. I had each of the lower-grade teachers take four and read them through to see if they contained anything we should worry about. One of the books sort of made light of discipline and so we, instead of having a little frowning boy in there, you know, that had been punished and he didn't accept it, we put a sticker on there with a smiling face.

Then, of course, if there's anti-God, anything that's against God, those books we don't even put on the shelf. You see, it doesn't go with our philosophy. If something came through that sounded like it was for ERA, I wouldn't have that on the shelf because we're very much against that.

Bethany's teachers achieve consensus about work goals relatively easily, since goals are a matter of belief and belief is encased in the bedrock of Scripture. They implement their goals in a complex society where contradictory, competing goals exist in abundance; indeed, it is Bethany's triumph that its people remain as doctrinally pure as they do. For they do not enjoy the ease and luxury of groups like the Azande, which the Africanist Robin Horton describes:

> All their beliefs hang together. . . . In this web of belief every strand depends upon every other strand, and a Zande cannot get out of its meshes because it is the only world he knows. The web is not an external structure in which he is enclosed. It is the texture of his thought and he cannot think his thought is wrong. [1967:155]

If Bethany's educators know enough about the world to entertain the thought that some belief or other is wrong, they nonetheless strain toward spiritual purity, so that the unsanctioned thought becomes virtually unthinkable. As one teacher said, "Everything I do I do to honor the Lord, but I'm not saying I'm perfect, because nobody's perfect. I strive to be what the Lord wants me to be; every day I try. But it doesn't mean that I do it."

Like Scripture, BBA's goals apply equally to those who teach and to those who are taught. Each group is meant to be equally enclosed, and equally responsive to and shaped by Bethany's total institution, with certain allowances made for relative maturity. If diversity is permitted regarding personal taste and interests, doctrine prevails on matters that count. Accordingly, "work goals and practices" at BBA enjoy as much coordination and consensus as is humanly possible to achieve.

Voluntariness

Willingness to be a participant in a total institution varies. Prison inmates are placed there involuntarily; mental patients may or may not have a choice in the decision to be hospitalized; seminary postulants join voluntarily; and Christian school students differ in their degree of voluntariness.

Involuntary, if not coerced, participation stamps the nature of life in many total institutions, as certainly as drought stamps the nature of life in many subsaharan villages. At BBA, however, coercion seems only to apply to the 10 of the 114 students who said that their parents made them attend BBA and that if they could, they would leave and attend a public school. In the absence of coercion, institutions need not establish physical restraints, nor need they provide guards, custodians, or keepers. These roles imply watchfulness, safety, escape, and tensions of various sorts between guardians and guarded that do not apply to the role of BBA teachers as spiritual custodians.

Parents are not legally bound to enroll their children in BBA, but they may feel theologically bound to do so. Pastor Muller and Headmaster McGraw emphatically tell them that Christian children belong in Christian schools; they also tell parents that children are spiritually safe only at Christian schools. Though free to make a right or wrong choice, parents and children both know that if God prefers a Christian school, and if it is a sin to disobey God, . . .

A corollary of voluntariness is BBA's prerogative to expel students (see McEwen 1980:155). Parents may choose to send their children to BBA, but BBA need not keep them. Parents register their dissatisfaction with the school by withdrawing their children; BBA registers its dissatisfaction with students by expelling them. Both acts perpetuate institutional purity. While Bethany aspires to reach every student with Christ's message, it will not do so at the expense of its capacity to serve those students who are receptive to the Christian life. The sociologist Lewis Coser clarifies the necessity of a policy of expulsion: "Heresy derives from a Greek word meaning to choose or take for oneself. The sect defines as heretics all those who propose alternatives where the group wants no alternatives to exist" (1974:109). If Bethany's students or teachers "propose alternatives," they cannot remain at Bethany. Here, again, Bethany differs from coercive total institutions: it can reject participants who will contaminate or undermine its institutional order; the latter must retain participants until a specific time has transpired (a prisoner's sentence is served), or until the participant does not endanger society or self (a mental patient's health is recovered).

Finally, in regard to voluntariness, Bethany should be noted as a nonpublic total institution, contrasting with the more usual public institutions that Goffman and others describe. BBA is the result of private persons deciding to open a certain type of school. It differs, therefore, from those institutions which the state builds to establish organized means of controlling and shaping the lives of certain types of persons (criminals or the insane, for example). The state's coercive total institutions often contain people thought of as society's rejects (Wallace 1971:5). BBA was founded by those who reject society. Like many of its involuntary counterparts, Bethany has an instructional or "correctional" program to establish a "new identity" in its participants. Bethany claims its "new identity" as *the* ideal identity for all of mankind. Other total institutions, with their limited remedial purposes, do not make such claims.

The Extent of Totality

To call various institutions "total institutions" is to obscure the fact that they differ in extent of totality, both in intent and in practice.

Some total institutions, such as concentration camps, prevent inmates from having contact with the world beyond their walls. In the interests of control, they also restrict contact among inmates within their walls. Mental hospitals, as total institutions, may permit regulated contact between inmates and persons outside the hospital, and, in addition, permit the inmates to spend time outside the hospital. Mental hospitals, like prisons but unlike concentration camps, organize programs to socialize or resocialize their participants, while permitting a range of contacts with persons inside and outside the hospital. A fundamentalist Christian school is unlike concentration camps, jails, mental hospitals, and prisons in having no physical barriers to delimit its participants' physical movements. But within the boundaries of its nonresidential circumstances, Bethany establishes the broadest possible control of its students. Indeed, the Christian school's hoped-for degree of totality surpasses that of all coercive total institutions, as well as that of such comparatively noncoercive ones as English boarding schools, which do not have a strong doctrinal basis like that of the fundamentalists. Its aspiration to totality extends to most all behavior and thought, everywhere, at all times, throughout the entire life of everyone affiliated in any capacity with their total institution. That, indeed, is totality!

Do BBA teachers aspire to totality? To find out, I asked them to react to psychologist Jerome Bruner's statement that in the operation of schools he favors "diversity and openness, not trying to shape minds to one pattern." Representing the position of teachers is Art Swanson, BBA Bible teacher:

> My goal as a teacher *is* to shape students' mind to one pattern. I think that that one pattern would give society the freedom to be a free society. Individuals have the freedom to reject that system, to choose as they see fit. I can't make them choose; I can only teach them. I can try to guide and direct and give them that one pattern. If they don't accept what I teach, I feel they're making a mistake. But they have that freedom and I would defend their freedom to make that choice. I think God does, too. For a while he does. There is, ultimately, a consequence for being wrong, a severe consequence.

And the history teacher Frank Fortner:

> In a sense, we're trying to close students off from the world and to put as their goal holiness and godliness. The Bible tells us to bring every thought to the captivity of Christ. Now, if that's not shaping one's mind, I don't know what is. If students are left to their own discernment, their own wisdom, then they're going to go humanly, and we don't want that. See, we're in a battle: spiritual wisdom versus human wisdom. What Bruner is saying is let the child think what he wants to think, let him figure out his own problems, let him do this and do that open-minded type of thing. He's trying to say not to shape minds to one pattern, but we *are* trying to shape minds to one pattern. See, the Bible says that. Let the mind be in you which Christ uses.

Teachers and administrators affirm that their school, on principle, does not and should not offer alternative perspectives to its students. Interests, of course, are another matter—they permit of diversity; not so, however, the values and beliefs encompassed by scriptural Truth. Bethany educators reject what they see as the public school orthodoxy of anything goes, values are relative, and one person's truths are as good as another's. And they reject a view of teaching that encourages students "to think for themselves . . . to regard the world critically . . . [which] teaches, in short, a healthy skepticism" (Goldblatt 1981:34). Such teaching would spawn a diversity of organizational efforts that could threaten the institution's totality.

Does Headmaster McGraw aspire to totality? To find out, I asked him the following question one year after I began my study: "Do you try to establish a total atmosphere at the academy?" He had used the expression "total atmosphere" during the teachers' in-service week held a year earlier.

> Good question. We only can succeed in a total atmosphere when the home is in full cooperation. Roughly 50 to 60 percent of our homes are in full cooperation. By that I mean that we have the same goals as the home. Maybe another 25 or 30 percent, they are generally the same. And then the other 20 to 25 percent, probably their goal in the home is vastly different. What I would define as a total atmosphere is where the home is completely in line with our goals. Not that we are trying to control every breath that a youngster takes. We are trying to protect him. There are some who criticize Christian education because of the hot-house approach. Well, I don't think that's realistic. The very parent who may criticize us for that doesn't allow his children to ride their bikes everywhere. I mean, he has rules, not for their harm, but for their good.
>
> I sent a letter to all the parents at the end of the school year [see appendix K]. I put it in the report cards. That would be realizing the limited amount of clout we have in this area; we believe strongly that the ultimate authority is the home. We don't want to put ourselves in a position of controlling the home, but we sure think we can make strong suggestions. I would put that letter in the category of saying, "Please, don't fail to do these things this summer." It's trying to extend a little bit the umbrella of that [total] atmosphere.
>
> I spoke in Cleveland at a Christian school where they're having real problems. Their policy pretty much had been, "Monday through Friday, these are the rules. On the weekend, we have no control over you." Now, I have never taken that policy. I had a case a couple of years ago where four kids were smoking in the Pizza Hut parking lot on a Saturday night. Well, I knew it Monday morning before those kids ever got to school. I'd say dozens of people knew it. We handled that disciplinewise just as if it would have happened outside our parking lot Thursday afternoon. My rationale is that these kids are Bethany Baptist Academy students. We purposely make no distinction in our student pledge about time, because we ask these kids to commit to these standards, and we try to develop a way-of-life

approach. We don't want a Monday-through-Friday kind of Christian, any more than we want a Sunday-morning Christian when they get to be adults.

Our youth program is an important part of this atmosphere. Friday night and Saturday night youth activities, we see them as an important attempt to take that free time the kid has and fill it with Christian activities, rather than allow 'em to just go off with a gang and do anything. You know, it's the old saying that the idle mind is the devil's playground.

In the event that parents do not reinforce the school's doctrinal standards, students learn, albeit not in a direct and blatant way, that the Bible takes precedence over their parents' outlook. Thus, if parental behavior departs from scriptural norms, students know where to turn for guidance, as they heard one day in chapel:

As you get older, you must look more and more away from your parents and towards the Bible. If your parents don't read the Bible, at least you can try to read yours. Then, if you think of something, or get angry, or want something, you can think of a verse so you know how to react, how to believe.

Another way of expressing the point of institutional totality is by reference to an organization's scope, expressed as the extent of an organization's "barrier to social intercourse with the outside" (Goffman 1961:4), and as "the degree to which the organization sponsors or provides the context for its participants' social relationships" (McEwen 1980:154; also see Wheeler 1966 and Etzioni 1975). All of Bethany's educators, from its pastors to its administrators and teachers, unite in conveying the same point to their students—the Lord's Truth knows no limits. As Headmaster McGraw illustrates:

I might say to the kids, "Did you have a good weekend?" Or, "What are you going to do tonight after school?" I want to know what they're doing, and if I find out something is going on, I want to discourage it. But I'm not snooping.

The realities of the lives of students and teachers basically reflect the school's encompassing predisposition. Teachers say they have no life outside their church and school, that theirs is a twenty-four-hour job. Students, the few confirmed scorners aside, say, "If you break one of the rules here, you start to get a guilty conscience; you kind of let down on your convictions."

Convictions are the stuff of daily life at BBA. No Bethany Christian would be so naive as to believe that the school could ever dispense with its elaborate structure of control. Yet they deeply hope that Christians of any age will develop convictions about spirituality that will impel consistently right belief and behavior. One teacher's frank words communicate the difficulty of being consistently separate.

> It is hard for me every day. Many times I have to just buckle down and say, "Wait, I'm not going to do that." Immorality, I guess it's been that way down through the ages, but right now it's so blatant. It used to be that if someone dressed the way the average woman dresses in summer . . . I hate summertime for that reason, because it's an actual temptation sometimes for me to look at something I shouldn't look at. I think every red-blooded person is that way. Once I'm at home, it's easy, and once I'm here [at church or school], it's easy. When we get involved with activities here, we're kind of in our own world. Like at college, they controlled the environment and the whole thing. I'm not trying to be an isolationist, but we are so busy that we end up being isolationist.

The outside with which Bethany tries to bar social intercourse is not merely that of girls in their summer dresses or of taboo films and popular toe-tapping, hip-wiggling music, it is all that is unscriptural and tagged with the pejorative designation "worldly." "If you say something is worldly," observes Frank Fortner, "well, that's sinful."

In Goffman's total institutions, neither the inmates nor their custodians would exalt the contents of their institutional life; each may acknowledge its necessity, while wishing that the world was such as to preclude its necessity. Each prefers the outside world. Not so at Bethany. They reject non-Christian life outside their domain and wish that the world would join them in accepting Jesus Christ as personal savior. Bethany's educators are not linked to other societal causes, as, for example, seeking the good of the larger society by removing dangerous criminals, reforming lesser types, or developing the competency of the mentally ill to rejoin society. Bethany's linkages join them directly to others involved in Christian education; they have made common cause with each other. They believe—and this also distinguishes their total institution—that in their cause lies the entire world's well-being.

A junior boy, reflecting on the nature of his involvement in Bethany, expresses in overstatement what a majority of the students feel:

> My whole life, seems like, revolves around the church and the school. The only thing that I do that's not centered around the school is cut grass and go see my girlfriend. She says I'm always working at the school. Take the school and church away, she says to me, and I would be the boringest person on earth. She's right. I like it, but I haven't had it any other way.

And Bethany would like to keep it that way, for separation is not punishment to them; nor is it a transitional policy applicable to young Christians before they become mature Christians. It is an enduring state: "Be ye separate, saith the Lord." The more total BBA manages to be, the more fully separate will be its students.

In practice, Bethanyites apply the principle of separation differentially in different areas of life. Here is what BBA students are taught in ten different circumstances:

1. *Education*—attend Christian schools. Seek postsecondary education in non-Christian schools only after attending a Christian college and if no Christian college provides the desired course of studies.
2. *Friendship*—no close ties with non-Christians.
3. *Dating*—no dates with non-Christians.
4. *Marriage*—of course, never with non-Christians.
5. *The arts (dance, music, literature, painting, etc.)*—experience only those examples that measure up to doctrinal standards.
6. *Daily goods and services (shopping, doctoring, etc.)*—to my knowledge, there are no restrictions. Bethany does not support a Yellow Pages listing of Christian merchants, physicians, etc. My questions uncovered no support from BBA educators or parents for even a tendency to prefer Christians as the usual suppliers of their goods and services.
7. *Place of residence*—there are no restrictions. For convenience, many Bethany church families have moved to the vicinity of Bethany Baptist Church. However, residential separation, in the Amish fashion, gets no support. Living among non-Christians may create some hazards for raising one's children, but none of the approximately one hundred persons we interviewed saw virtue in a physically isolated life.
8. *Politics*—Christian candidates are preferable, but Christians must

deal with non-Christians while remaining true to scriptural standards in cases where doctrine clearly applies (e.g., abortion, women's rights, welfare, etc.).

9. *Jobs*—the ideal is full-time Christian service if one has been called by God. Absolutely rejected are jobs perceived as violating doctrine (such as bartender, gambler, projectionist in a movie theater, and rock musician). In acceptable non-Christian jobs the issue is to uphold Christian standards while working among non-Christians.

10. *Contact with non-Christians*—contacts are unavoidable, so one must learn to be polite, sociable, and distant. If properly inculcated with doctrine, students may acquire the view of non-Christians expressed by one of their teachers:

> I can't have confidence in a person if he's not saved. I have no right to expect anything, really, from them. I can't expect real understanding, because they don't know the God of understanding. I can't expect true compassion and love, even though they are very, very good people. They're just people; they don't owe me a thing. I have no right to really expect much out of them, but as for Christians, we are a family, brothers and sisters in the Lord.

These words underscore Bethany's ideal of limited contact with non-Christians and of enduring bonds with Christians.

Bethany's impact, unlike that of total institutions which lack an absolutist doctrinal foundation, is meant to be free of the constraints of time and place. Again, unlike other total institutions, BBA does not relax the grasp of its totality as a reward for good behavior. Indeed, one's capacity to exemplify total separation in one's personal life is a measure of personal and institutional success.

Mortification Practices

Goffman calls "mortification" those institutional efforts which reshape the self of inmates—break their spirit, so to speak—and remind them of the shift from their noninstitutional to their special institutional status, one that is more subordinate, dependent, and limited. These efforts are part of the process of institutional control. Goffman's graphic description of this process is too extreme to fit Christian schools. Yet so much of what he terms mortification has its counterpart at Bethany. To outsiders, to persons hostile to Bethany's scriptural foundation, Bethany's practices may mortify; I found little evidence to indicate that

Bethany parents and students perceive their school's practices as mortifying. This is so, I believe, because there is no disjuncture between what Goffman calls the "home world" and the institution. Here is his image of this disjuncture:

> The recruit [or student, ward, patient, etc.] comes into the establishment with a conception of himself made possible by certain stable social arrangements in his home world. Upon entrance, he is immediately stripped of the support provided by these arrangements. . . . he begins a series of abasements, degradations. . . . His self is systematically, if unintentionally, mortified. [1961:14]

Bethany is keenly mindful of its students' preinstitutional self, which is characterized either by the behavior of one who has not yet been born again or by one whose behavior is not directed by scriptural standards. Students who come up through BBA's elementary grades and those who come from fundamentalist Christian homes can see their school's expectations as natural; to new enrollees without this background these same expectations appear strikingly unnatural. Non-born-again enrollees, former public school students who enter BBA for the first time, may feel humiliated by the academy's disrespect for their present religious status, by its rejection of their normal behavior as "worldly," and by its demands that they change their appearance, their friends, their behavior, and their response to authority. If what stands out about their experience at Bethany is "the curtailment of self," the disruption of "role scheduling," or the "role dispossession" that Goffman notes as the outcome of the total institution's mortification process (1961:14), they probably will have a short stay at the academy. For, in fact, these processes do take place; they are the requisite efforts of an institution that is dedicated to the rebirth of its unredeemed youth. If, to the contrary, BBA's newcomers experience the rewards of rebirth, then they will focus on the positive aspects of the academy's behavior-changing processes and they may think of mortification as the necessary practices of a good cause.

The Subordinate-Superordinate Relationship

McEwen observes that the social distance between an organization's caretakers and those it cares for is another distinguishing feature of total institutions. Social distance is described as "the amount of spontaneous, open, potentially emotional, and relatively egalitarian interaction permitted" (1980:157). In schools of any type, the age difference between students and teachers is one basis for social distance. Another, with more profound consequences than age, is Bethany's view of authority. Deference to authority is the rule, with Scripture as the ultimate authority.

Therein lies a distinction of Bethany's as a total institution. All participants, subordinate and superordinate alike, draw their prescriptions and proscriptions from the same ultimate authority. They have one primary source of influence that shapes everyone's lives in the same way. Thus, the prevailing social distance between students and teachers coexists with an attachment to doctrine that joins both groups in a corporate life of shared ends and means. If definite status differences exist between the two, it still is true that both groups subscribe to and observe the very same rules (with minor exceptions relating to the restrictions on boy-girl contacts). No caste-like split characterizes the student-teacher relationship, of the type that Goffman identified (McEwen 1980:157).

McEwen indicates that institutions vary regarding the degree of participation of their subordinates. In some total institutions, inmates may become trusties and assist the custodians in running the organization. They lighten the custodians' load and, in the process, become associates of the custodial group. A trusty type of role also exists in the Christian school. Student leaders in each class, some elected and others self-appointed, play this role. They reap the benefit of grateful recognition from school authorities, and of greater freedom to move around the school or even to leave the school. As "trusties," students try to keep their class under control in a teacher's absence, caution fellow students who break big-demerit regulations (e.g., drinking and smoking), and inform the administration about potentially disruptive situations. We have already seen Bethany's endorsement of the role of brother's keeper; the world calls the same behavior snitching and condemns it. In fact, students playing the trusty role are apprenticing for the grander role of full-time Christian (and, possibly, for that of full-time Christian service).

Permeability to Extra-Organizational Influences

Finally, total institutions differ to the degree that they are, and must be, responsive to external forces that affect their operation. Some total institutions, such as prisons, are creatures of the state; they use state money, and their workers are state employees. Others, like private mental facilities, are subject to state laws that specify employee qualifications, health and safety regulations, and use of medication. Both types may be subject to media attention and public opinion which influence their organization and procedure. The presence of the state and of public opinion possibly, but not necessarily, moderates the totality of total institutions.

Though Christian schools are very much in the news and thereby exposed to public opinion, BBA can be upset by, but is generally unresponsive to, external influences. Why should an institution be open to ideas from any other source when it believes it has the Word of God to guide it? BBA and all of its fellow schools in the AACS struggle to stay free of all governmental ties, submitting only reluctantly even to the health and safety regulations that states apply to any school located within the state. As we have seen, the national office of the AACS and its state affiliates contest legislation that attempts to extend state control to anything beyond mere registration (which indicates that a Christian school exists) and health and safety requirements. In principle, Bethany is committed to resisting any influence from any source that could lessen its doctrinal commitment. In practice, in this and all other respects, it is amazingly true to its principles.

Conclusion

Though a formally organized round of church and school activities encompasses the lives of BBA students, their participation, albeit often strongly encouraged by parents, does not require coercion. And their total institution strikes neither them nor their parents as "sinister" (see Mouzelis 1971). This outcome is all the more surprising when we consider that Bethany's total institution is unrestricted in time and space, neither limited to a term or a sentence nor confined to a building or a particular setting. Its directives are always in season, never out of place. Unlike many total institutions, which resocialize their participants to conform with society's norms, Bethany socializes its participants to deviate from many of society's norms, while remaining, by some lights, exemplary Americans. Bethany's Christians comprise a minority that has stayed well within reach of historically cherished values. Thus they are recognizably American, even as the rigidity of their beliefs and behavior places them outside the mainstream of American life.

Clearly, the farther we move away from institutions whose subordinates are not properly called "inmates," and where degradation characterizes neither the intent of the organization's overseers nor the perceptions of most of its participants, the less the designation of total institution seems menacing. Still, Bethany's total institution is determined to isolate its participants in order to control the stimuli that impinge upon them. This is "organizational tyranny," a "closed universe," the "thwarting of human possibilities" (Perry 1974:353).

Bethany's total institution is the organizational means to achieve its broad purpose of serving, as they say, the glory of God. Given the nature of absolutist doctrine, it is a logical, fitting structure. Nonetheless, throughout most of our history, fundamentalist Christians did not feel impelled to act upon this logic. Pastor Muller, in his account of BBA's origin, suggests why they did not. His own children attended public schools; he sent them there without misgivings. His unease began when the social changes taking place outside the schools reached into classrooms in ways that upset and finally alarmed fundamentalist Christians. In the South, desegregation spurred flight from the public schools into church-based academies. Throughout the United States, public schools, once a safe preserve for conservative Christians, appeared increasingly unsafe in academic, physical, and moral terms. In short, for the logical connection between Truth and a total institution to strike home with force, fundamentalists needed an additional factor—a sense of threat from society in general and from public schools in particular.[3]

Now that the logical connection has been made repeatedly over a period of time, the inevitability of the Christian school seems normal. Even though the conditions of school and society may no longer carry the same degree of objective threat, fundamentalists have for too long excoriated public schools to reverse course and turn away from God's schools.

11

God's Choice
Costs and Benefits

Benign though their total institution may be to Bethanyites, and awesome their absolute Truth, total institutions and absolute Truth are nonetheless anathema to me. Thus, I continue to shift contexts from the *research I* who tried to stand in the shoes of others, becoming an as-if-Christian in order to see and understand the world as Bethanyites do, to the *human I* who, with personal dispositions intact, never ceased to be present.

Until now I have tried to control my personal dispositions—in a word, my subjectivity—in order to portray Bethany from its own perspective. Now I intend to analyze the meaning of what I saw there from my own perspective, capitalizing on my subjectivity (Peshkin 1985).

I will try to write with the constraint and respect due my Bethany hosts, whose cooperation throughout my contact with them was as absolute as their doctrine, and, more important, because their school is not merely a school like any other school: it is God's school, and I understand what this means to them. "We have a Christian school," said Headmaster McGraw in his address to parents and friends gathered to honor BBA's kindergarten graduates, "because we believe that God would have us teach his children." And the Reverend Gerald Carlson, writing in an American Association of Christian Schools *Newsletter*, congratulates Ohio for becoming the thirty-fifth member state of AACS and for "resisting the unconstitutional efforts of government to foist regulations upon God's schools." It is no small matter to take issue with what is believed to be God's choice. I do so in terms of my preferred pluralism, which I take with Darryl Baskin to be

the practice of a multiplicity of power centers [that] safe-
guards the associational variety necessary for man's requirement of a diversity of social means appropriate to the variety
of ends and purposes his human being is able to contain.
[1971:176][1]

The World's Pluralism

If, at present, many Americans feel ambivalent about their society's
ideological and social diversity, and if, historically, our courts, schools,
and legislatures often have been unfriendly to diversity, American
society still remains notably heterogeneous. Indeed, some observers
see a threat to our national integration in the proportion of non-
European to European immigrants who enter the country, and in the
possible impact of educational policies that engender respect for the
language and culture of these immigrants. Even if we set aside the
question of the extent to which our Asian, Hispanic, and Caribbean
newcomers will assimilate to the dominant Anglo-American model, we
know that our third- and fourth-generation eastern and southern European immigrants have resisted full assimilation sufficiently to undermine the old melting-pot theory (see Novak 1971; Glazer and Moynihan
1970; and Greeley and McCready 1974). Our pluralistic society rests not
only on distinctions derived from persisting ethnic differences, but also
on those rooted in the extraordinary complexity of our occupational,
denominational, organizational, academic, and class structures. Other
societies clearly surpass ours in terms of the political and economic
choices their national political parties afford them; our relative uniformity in these respects may be the basis for our general societal
integration. At our best, however, and, unfortunately, it is an intermit-
tent best, our laws enable the flourishing of political and economic
groups whose doctrines embrace the extremes of left and right, protected, for example, by an organization like the American Civil Liber-
ities Union, which defends the rights of American Nazis—to the dismay
of a populace less committed than it should be to our Bill of Rights.

I do not wish to depict a halcyonic splendor of a thousand flowers
blooming, all in equal glory, none enjoying more merit, respect, per-
quisites, entrees, or power than others. Our norms support inequities;
inequities are embedded in our institutions; laws are fashioned to
facilitate that which our norms fail to honor. Still, ours is a polyvalent
society, hard on orthodoxies, brimming with alternatives communicated and fostered by individuals, organizations, magazines, meetings, workshops, conventions, advertising, ad infinitum.

Our size, our complexity, our folk pride and belief in "it's a free country," our traditional "says who?" disrespect for authority, our watchdog organizations and media establishment—all these and more conspire to nurture doctrinal and ideological diversity. The result is a confusing, precious legacy: a society which finds it difficult to establish constitutionally the rights of women and homosexual males, but which is careful to define the rights of criminals; which debates the nature of truth and justice, taking them to be unsettled matters that never pop off the page neatly defined and readily translated into policy awaiting implementation. I value a society whose lack of orthodoxy encourages competing traditions in literature, painting, music, and sculpture to exist, if not flourish, with no academy, no panel of judges, no center able to stamp "success" on its favorites. I value a society whose judicial system struggles to define pornography, and which stubbornly guards parental rights to educate their children outside of formal schools, resisting the easy identification of the state's "compelling interests" that would, accordingly, favor a state's educational prerogatives. I value a society which encourages national unification, but where the imperatives of unity must always compete with those of diversity and its concomitant disunity. Herbert Muller's final words in his fine volume on freedom capture well my general outlook:

> The whole faith in a free society remains literally a faith . . .
> one that implies fallibility and ultimate uncertainty by its
> very stress on tolerance and open-mindedness, that always
> invites risk or further uncertainty through the uses and
> abuses of freedom, and that can never offer the promise of
> miracle or the guarantees of authority. [1960:170]

With this view of societal pluralism in mind, I will conclude my study with some comments on Bethany Baptist Academy's benefits to its students—from Bethany's perspective; on its costs to BBA students, to me, and to American society—from my perspective; and some final thoughts about the existence of such schools.

Student Benefits

Although my primary focus here is on a Christian school's contributions to its participants, I wish to begin by recognizing the possible benefits to the larger community of the school's existence. By their success in attracting and retaining students at a time of generally declining enrollments and financial hardship in public schools, Christian schools may spur public schools to change in ways that do not require a religious commitment. Of course, fundamentalist doctrine is the basis for much that Christian schools do that public schools might want to emulate—for example, regarding programs to promote improved student appearance, discipline, safety, moral standards, etc. But such doctrine is not the only foundation for these developments. Seeing a Christian school with these programs could inspire public schools to find the means to introduce or restore policies that would benefit their own students and teachers.

That public interest in such programs exists is clear from the Gallup Poll results of recent years (see Elam 1978 and annual reports in the *Phi Delta Kappan*). Moreover, the *American Educator*, journal of the American Federation of Teachers, in 1981 approvingly quotes both the research of K. Marshall Clayton, who found considerable support for a return to mandatory dress codes (5:8), and the plan of the Modesto, California, school system to restore "standards of academic achievement and student conduct" (5:9). The following issue of the same journal had a special section called "Responsibility: A Selection of Materials for Teaching Traditional Values" (5:21–25).

All of Hartney's public school personnel can see traditional American values embedded in BBA's status quo. In addition, they can see attractive models of teacher dedication. BBA teachers exemplify hard work and caring; they do indeed teach as though teaching were their calling. We public school parents rejoice when our children encounter such teachers. To think what it be like to have an entire school of such teachers and administrators! Closer to public schools than the elite private schools, fundamentalist Christian schools are palpable models for changes that many parents would welcome; they could motivate public school neighbors located literally down the street. Perhaps, as Dennis Doyle suggests, "They are sending a strong message to the public sector" (1980:16).

Furthermore, Christian schools graduate youngsters who have been inculcated with attractive personal qualities. Their students may have been different when they entered BBA, but I am convinced they leave it as loyal, honest, hard-working, punctual, and reliable young adults. Add to these qualities their deference to authority and you have the makings of productive employees, a boon to Hartney's fast-food establishments and other employers of part-time student labor.

Finally, Christian schools, like other private schools, may simplify the work of public schools by freeing them of the pressure of serving many, diverse masters (Hazard 1980). Given the fact of local control, public schools generally cannot escape the demands of their constituents. When their constituency includes a group whose outlook diverges dramatically from that of its other groups, the schools may be unable to accommodate the resulting range of educational expectations. Kanawha County's textbook controversy, generated by fundamentalist Christians' rejection of books they believed violated their values, brought violence and split the community (Hillocks 1978). Given their views, the dissenters' demands were reasonable, but not in a public school. I do not believe that our typically diverse public schools can or should satisfy fully the needs and interests of the parents of all school-aged children. To do so reduces their operations to a level that, in not being repugnant to any one, can satisfy no one. Thus, Christian schools operate as safety valves, relieving public schools of the unreasonable challenge of presenting fundamentalist Christian values as an abiding fact in their classrooms.

Those who believe that classrooms must contain Christ are those whom Bethany benefits most directly.[2] However, since almost every school attracts clients who admire some but not all of its special features, BBA benefits families who do not necessarily share its doctrinal orientation. Some parents—neither they nor their children born-again Christians—seek a second chance for their children who "fail" in ways their public school seems unable to prevent; some want a physically safe school where they can feel secure about their children; some like a narrower curriculum, with emphasis on the basics; and some value an environment that is free of racial strife.

Whatever their parents' motivations, Christian school children are immersed in absolutist doctrine. All must respond to the school's particular Christian ways. Parents and children who do not subscribe to Bethany's doctrine can still use the school for their own ends and be reassured that their children are in a school that is recognizably American, but in a thoroughly, uncompromisingly spiritual setting. Bethany's students are the same as and different from their public school counterparts, just as their school is simultaneously the same as and different from its public school counterpart. To say the least, they cherish the differences.

Thus, at the same time Bethany satisfies its few non-born-again clientele, it pleases its large majority who seek a school pervaded by fundamentalist Christianity and its operational concomitants:

—yes, sir—no, sir behavior
—clock-ticking silence
—uncomplaining, committed teachers
—prelunch prayers with bowed heads and closed eyes
—obedient, Bible-toting students

—conservative dress and hair styles
—graffiti-free restroom walls
—kids on a fieldtrip-bound bus spontaneously singing religious songs for thirty minutes at a time
—seniors apologetically explaining their intention to attend a secular rather than a Christian postsecondary school.

BBA students get the moral education that many American parents say they want for their children. BBA parents can revel in a school that is explicitly, exultantly moral. Those who accept genetically sinful human nature as fact can find comfort in the doctrinal bulwark Bethany builds to withstand Satan's onslaught. Those who accept moral upbringing as the foundation for strength of character as an adult can find no less comfort, their belief supported by the distinguished psychiatrist Bruno Bettleheim: "Today . . . we hope mistakenly that somehow more and more citizens will have developed a mature morality—without having first been subject as children to a stringent morality based on fear and trembling" (1979:12).

At BBA, born-again Christian children can feel at home in a structure devised especially for them; since they are the norm, they can be themselves, free from the taunts and challenges of children not similarly oriented. Unlike public school youth, they endure little or none of the ambiguity and tension that can develop when teachers, peers, parents, and neighbors reinforce different values. Though they will live in a society replete with competing alternatives, Bethany's single-value domain provides them with a clear-cut identity. To be sure, BBA youth face critical decisions regarding the choice of vocation and mate. However, as long as they remain true to their faith, they have doctrinal bedrock for support. The questions "Who am I?" "What should I be?" "Where am I going?" are not unduly troublesome. Students know that they are depraved, that they should pattern their lives on the model of Christ, and that they should serve the Lord now in preparation for spending eternity in his mansion. "Thank you," prays BBA's science teacher during the preclass devotion period, "for giving us something that is true, that is perfect, that we can hold onto in a world where everything is changing so fast." Students find models and support to follow Truth's tough dictates in the combined force of church, school, peers, and family.

The shared doctrine that equips students with behavioral norms also joins them as brethren, responsible for and to each other. Daily they learn about the principles of faithfulness and spirituality that serve as criteria for popularity and peer-group formation, and daily they acquire the behaviors that prepare them for full participation in their Christian community. More than acquiring shared behavior and beliefs, students learn to accept as normal that their daily activities will be guided by their Christian community's plans. The academy functions as a community-maintenance institution, and its students develop both the habit of belonging and the expectation of receiving the support, the nurturance, and the comfort that are the gifts of community. Just as at ordinary public and private schools, BBA's students share a "this is my school" sentiment, replete with "remember the times" that link classmates forever. But Bethany students can also say, "These are my fellow church members" and, most significantly, "These are my people, my fellow believers in Christ."

The academy epitomizes the case of a community successfully projecting its idiosyncratic outlook onto its school. More than just a community school, however, the academy is a "communal" institution, as the term is ordinarily used in South Asian politics. *Communal* describes a community whose strong commitment to its own welfare inevitably places it in conflict with other communities that do not accept its doctrinal foundation. A communal school serves an internally integrative or community-maintenance function, and it also serves an externally disintegrative or defensive function (see Siegel 1970 and Schiff 1966). That is, it simultaneously links believers together and separates them from nonbelievers. In its defensive capacity, the academy shields its students and beliefs from competitors by promoting the dichotomies not only of we and they, but also of right and wrong. *We* follow God's Truth in God's preferred institutions; *they* are the unfortunates of Satan's false, dark, unrighteous world. The Christian school operates as a fortress vis-a-vis the rest of the world, albeit one that salvation opens to non-Christians. It sees other schools and other belief systems as rivals, while projecting its own school and beliefs as ideal for everyone. Bethany educators and church leaders are curious communalists, indeed, as they simultaneously scorn their non-Christian antagonists and extend them a welcoming hand.

The academy is a contemporary case of the formal initiation programs common in places like pre-modern Africa, whose tribes linked their rites of passage to group survival. The tribes intended to stamp each initiate with beliefs and behavior so that they and others knew precisely who they were and where they belonged—the integrative, community function (see Kraybill 1977); and who they were not and from whom they needed protection—the defensive, communal function. Many tribes marked their youth with distinctive scarification so that they could never be taken for members of any other tribe. Similarly,

BBA marks its students with behavior and dress in order to set them apart from non-Christian youth.

Does the school offer more than an opportunity to become and live as a born-again Christian? Is it a good school in conventional terms? Yes, if we accept as meaningful students' scores at or above grade level on standardized tests achieved without benefit of specific prepping for the tests.[3] Yes, if we accept as the attributes of academic effectiveness those that Rutter and his colleagues identify in their book *15,000 Hours*, and which Gerald Grant summarizes:

> Teachers regularly assign and mark homework . . . expected pupils to act responsibly and gave them an opportunity to do so . . . conveyed their expectations in the way they behaved themselves . . . [and demonstrated] consistency and shared norms. [1981:5]

And yes, if we accept the research findings on effective American schools that Edward Curran reports:

> The *qualitative* differences in schools . . . can be accounted for by five factors: strong leadership by the principal, an orderly school climate conducive to learning, emphasis on basic skills, teacher expectations of high student achievement, and a system for assessing student performance. [1982:11]

From the inside, where I tried to experience Bethany's world to the extent that my conscience and convictions allowed me, I could see a marvelous order, an enveloping sense of peace, an abundance of the meaning and sense of community that so often accompany a collective religious experience. When I left Bethany each Friday night to go to my own community, I felt I had left order for disorder, harmony for dissonance, and absolutism for relativism. To return, as I did each Sunday in time for morning services, was to be involved again with people whose distinctions of personality, taste, and interest were overlaid by their enveloping mantle of shared doctrinal commitment.

Bethany is an extraordinary haven for those who believe. Indeed, it is not farfetched to think about Christian schools as Bettleheim (1969) did about the kibbutzim: as special places, not for everyone, but surely of great value to many who seek the security of a particular type of value system and schooling.[4]

For me, learning about Bethany's world culminates a personal pursuit to understand the school-community relationship in circumstances where the community is basically homogeneous. Though Bethany is not a community in the geopolitical sense, like those towns and villages its church members reside in, it is a community in the fullest psychological terms: it is characterized by a sense of community. I marvel at the unity, the connectedness of Bethany's world. It takes no special powers of observation or imagination to perceive these qualities. I could never resist the thought—and it came frequently—"How nice it is to belong here. One can belong here in a deep and special sense."

A pretty picture, this, a reassuringly lustrous one. But for its luster to be more than merely observed, one must make that leap of faith that is prerequisite to becoming a born-again true believer. I did not, could not, make this leap. Thus I view Bethany from premises rooted in the world they reject. Based on these premises I ask: What is gained and lost by Bethany's students? What is the meaning of Bethany's school for American society? And because I am who I am, born a Jew and gladly remaining one, what is the meaning of Bethany to me? If I see Bethany's benefits and applaud them for believers and others who seek them, I still can not escape my "and yet" sentiments, with all the reservations they signal.

Student Costs

As a total institution, BBA logically indoctrinates its students, refusing to treat issues to which doctrine applies as matters for discussion. Indoctrination I take with Snook to be "Teaching an ideology as if it were the only possible one with any claim to rationality" (1968:76). He continues his definition by adding that "A person indoctrinates P (a proposition or set of propositions) if he teaches with the intention that the pupil or pupils believe P regardless of the evidence" (p. 80).

To be sure, fundamentalist Christian educators generally do not try to unsettle the settled matters of secular scholarship; they do not try to reconstruct their findings based on a completely different notion of fact and evidence. They are neither fools nor fanatics. Thus, what students read and how teachers teach is not basically distinguishable at BBA from the practices of any public school. Distinctions emerge at all those points that doctrine covers.

Indoctrination is not uncommon in public schools, notwithstanding the absence there of an articulated, accepted doctrinal basis to the indoctrinational stance of their teachers. The critical fact is not that one school never indoctrinates and the other one always does, but, rather, that most public schools have built-in diversity in the heterogeneity of their students and teachers, as well as the relatively unrestrained access to libraries and the media which they offer. Moreover, they do not make a conscious, planned, determined effort to control the employees hired, the students admitted and retained, the instructional and library materials available, and the operating rules and regulations according to the dictates of one, uncontested, overarching belief system.

On principle, BBA's students are beseeched to be separate. By internalizing this injunction, they acquire a means for sorting out the acceptable from the unacceptable in every conceivable behavioral domain. Their school is committed to circumscribing their behavior—whom they see, where they go, what they read and hear—in order to maximize its educative efficacy (Bohrek and Curtis 1975:105–9). Their teachers knowingly reject the ambiguity and freedom of choice that prevails beyond their conceptual boundaries. In doing so they claim the ultimate choice for themselves and their students, the one that ends choice by so enshrining belief that it is impervious to challenge (see G. K. Chesterton, *Orthodoxy* [1908] 1952:58).

BBA's success in circumscribing student experience is limited by its capacity but not by its right to do so. In contrast to the Christian schools' seemingly unlimited right to control students, public schools are constrained, for example, by the Supreme Court's 1982 decision in *Pico vs. Island Tree School District*. In this case, Justice Brennan's thoughts carried the day in a four-one-four split of opinion, a split that suggests that we will hear from the Court again on this subject. He wrote, according to Fitzgerald, that "the discretion of state and local school authorities must be 'exercised in a manner that comports with the transcendent imperatives of the First Amendment.'" A community's prerogatives to "inculcate community values" can operate in the classroom's compulsory setting but not in the library's voluntary setting (Fitzgerald 1984:78).

An essential power of private schools is their freedom from the First Amendment's "transcendent imperative." Bethany's mission can only be fulfilled if it has the right to control the socializing experiences of its children. At BBA, no settings comparable to the public school's library exist. The part of Justice Brennan's opinion that forbade school boards to remove library books if they did so with an intent "to suppress ideas" (Fitzgerald 1984:79) also has no place at Bethany. It means to suppress ideas in order to assure the ascendancy of its Truth, which by definition can have no rivals.

From my perspective, the costs BBA students pay can be variously expressed. Hofstadter characterizes an individual's or group's excessive "commitment to some special and constricting idea" as "dangerous to the life of the mind" (1966:29). Evans identifies the avoidance by conservative churches "of the ambiguity that is at the heart of the human experience" (1979:305). Dillon believes that "tolerance of ambiguity is a condition of survival" (1974:40). Neisser's study of perception and cognition leads him to observe that our "transactions with the world" do not merely inform us, they also transform us. "Each of us," he writes, "is created by the cognitive acts in which he engages" (1976:11). Compared to the relatively uncircumscribed world of public school students, including both their in-school and out-of-school opportunities, Christian students reside in a cognitively limited environment that provides fewer opportunities for Neisser's transactions and transformation. In keeping with their reading of Scripture, they and their mentors choose the promise of being transformed in the person of Christ. The artistic, literary, social, and religious riches of our society are a product of minds able to operate under relatively open conditions. As long as Bethany's students remain in thrall to fundamentalist doctrine, I believe they will neither contribute to nor appreciate these riches.

What BBA students do learn they learn well, and it is functional for survival in their own community and beyond. The price they pay is what they do not become, what they cannot enjoy, what they fail to comprehend. Indeed, everyone's choices are made at the expense of other possibilities: the investment of time and effort made in pursuit of these interests and that vocation must restrict one's opportunity to pursue other interests and vocations, if only because time and energy are finite. Bethany's constraints, however, are not the ordinary ones of time and energy, but the peculiar ones of specially conceived right and wrong, which place a vast sweep of experiences out of bounds to the faithful. Stigmatized as worldly, humanistic, or ungodly, these experiences are taboo. My data indicate that most BBA students are attracted to but usually avoid what they are taught is taboo.

Overall, do Bethany students gain more than they lose from their Christian school experience? Are they harmed in any way? Not only do the answers depend on the values of the responder, they depend on longitudinal data that do not exist. As I see it, if Bethany succeeds according to its aspirations, fundamentalists rejoice, while I and the world's nonbelievers mourn the loss of intellectual vitality and artistic creativity that are Truth's victims.

Personal Costs

During the years of my almost daily contact with Bethany I wished that they could accept me as fully OK and as a Jew, at the same time. I wished that being yoked to me would not constitute a case of unequal yoking. And I wished that their commitment to separation would not so irrevocably separate us. I wished all this not because of any personal need to be accepted by them, but because of my distress at the impact of their arrogance on them, on me, on all of us.

By couching the discussion here in personal terms, I continue to make explicit what is usually left implicit—that a particular I was present in the collection and analysis of these data. Since I was there, the costs I discuss are conveyed in the first person singular. In no way, however, do I mean to suggest that I alone, or only people just like me, Jewish or otherwise, bear the potential cost of institutions closed to intellectual diversity and inquiry. On the contrary, I readily imagine many others, inside as well as outside the world of Christianity, taking exception to the insularity of Bethany's fundamentalist outlook.

In the course of fieldwork conducted at great geographic distance from their homes, researchers may be alternately pleased and appalled by what they experience. Whatever their personal feelings about the group and events under study, they return home with their feelings intact and available to influence the shape of their writing. The events of their fieldwork are left behind, existing thereafter as memories, anecdotes, notes, and professional papers. In the course of fieldwork conducted near home, different circumstances may prevail. Geographic proximity to the field may well continue to make palpable the group and events studied so that they have an impact beyond the time of the study, not only on the researchers' writing but also on the researchers themselves.

Specifically, Bethany's Christians are not a group "out there" to me. Their collective doings—that is, as an assortment of fundamentalist-oriented groups and believers—are the stuff of the popular media and of professional books and journals. I read their letters to the editor, their leaflets admonishing me to repent, their protests against public school policies and practice, their newsworthy political activities. Because of their involvement with my world, I cannot simply leave them behind as I have done other subjects, my interests and concerns eventually subsiding as time passes. For they are here and I am here, right now.

Fundamentalist Christians make me aware of my existence and my potential nonexistence, or disappearance. When anyone believes that Jews are doomed, imperfect, incomplete, their prayers not heard by God, I hear the whispers of disappearance in these arrogant perceptions. What may appear as paranoia to non-Jews is anything but paranoia for a Jew: Someone *is* after me! At the risk of doing injustice to born-again Christians and their institutions, I voice my concerns, thinking that it is better to be noisy and wrong than to be silent and disappear (Steiner 1967).

The terrifying events of the past remain vivid. Destructive anti-Semitism, directing injury at Jews and their property, and rampant proselytizing, directing injury at Jews as part of a group labeled "un-saved," combine to renew for each generation of Jews the threats to their well-being as they define it. The real events of our world readily trigger our defensive instincts. Thus, I cannot consign to the dustbins of the past the anti-Semitic exhortations of Martin Luther:

> that their synagogues and schools be set on fire, and that those portions which will not burn be overheaped and cov-ered up with earth. . . . And this should be done to the honor of our Lord and of Christendom, so that God may see that we are Christians and have not knowingly tolerated nor willed such public lies, valedictions, and blasphemies against His Son and His Christians. [Quoted in Mensching 1971:38–39]

Many writers note the danger of joining religious orthodoxy to secular power (O'Dea 1967; Muller 1960; Mensching 1971), with the consequent persecution that empowered religionists might direct at so-called nonbelievers. In such circumstances, what religious doctrine supposedly dictates the force of government could bring to fruition. In general, we have avoided these circumstances. By any comparative measures, the United States has been unusually successful in estab-lishing a society that fosters religious freedom while maintaining a useful degree of separation between church and state. Despite notable lapses the First Amendment is intact, albeit forever under siege by religionists to erode this or that aspect of separation. Our historic separation of church and state has well served all of us.

The political activity of contemporary fundamentalist groups is fully legal unless they have tax-free status and thereby are precluded from partisan political activity. Their extensive involvement in politics, which peaked during the 1980 and 1984 presidential elections, lends credence to the thought that they wish to join the secular and the sacred. I worry that fundamentalists risk succumbing to "the subtle temptation" (O'Dea 1967:85) to put political power at the service of doctrinal ends. Bliven expresses well my fears: "Whenever men and women take belief seriously, orthodoxy and heresy emerge struggling, like Jacob and Esau, and spiritual disagreement becomes physical con-flict" (1979:116).

I experienced no bigotry at Bethany. Needing toleration themselves by governments and by groups that are not adherents of their doctrine, they fully subscribe—in the abstract—to the virtue of tolerance, of defending my right to disagree. In reality, however, they give little credence to the principle of toleration and considerable credence to the practice of evangelism. Headmaster McGraw told his teachers at their preterm in-service week, "The devil's crowd is after our kids." I believe that McGraw's fundamentalist crowd is after me and my kids—after the "world's" kids, in fact, whose lives and families and institutions the fundamentalists distort with the label of "secular humanists." In the fundamentalist's cant, secular humanists include the panderers of poor taste, those who exercise bad judgment, and the downright venal— lumped together with all nonfundamentalist others. The siege mentality they foster enhances their own social organization while blinding them to the realities of their host society.

Bethanyites and other fundamentalists baldly reject the integrity of non-Christians, unequivocally defining us as fair game for conversion. As long as I behave, they distinguish between me, the person, as OK, and my beliefs, which are not. What is the distance between judging my beliefs unacceptable and condemning me as unacceptable? Absolutism and universalism have a monumental dynamic, an imperious, implacable logic. Moved by such force, will fundamentalists be able to resist the temptation, should the occasion arise, to join secular power to sacred purpose?

I would be more reassured about the answers to these questions if Bethany Baptist Church's Pastor Muller had not reflected in these terms:

> We never will be in control of this or any other society until the Lord establishes his kingdom. . . . I can think of Christians taking over political life and pockets of power in certain communities like Greenville, South Carolina, Denver, Colorado, and little places up in Maine where Christians came out and took over the precincts. It can be done where there is a thriving church. If on the city council of my town the majority were members of Bethany Baptist Church and committed Christians, well, what would we do about liquor and liquor ordinances? I'd vote against them all the way. We'd be a dry town if I could control it. I guess I wonder if I'd be very tolerant of a non-Christian position. I would hope to believe that I'd be very understanding, but when my Christianity affects my whole life, it has to affect my politics. It has to affect what I'd do Monday night at a city council meeting.

I would be more reassured if he could ever say, as does the distinguished church historian Martin Marty: "It so often seems that a God
who cares about the humanizing of the world would bless churches that
care for wholeness and civility and not merely for aggressive pouncing
on prospects as possible converts" (1979:14–15).

The true believer's inflexible, inexorable doctrinal yardstick, which
so readily sorts out right from wrong and good from bad, is the basis for
an incivility which both denies and defies the social complexities of our
society. It is the antithesis of that live-and-let-live outlook which at its
best derives from genuine respect for, if not thoroughgoing joy in, the
diversity of others; this outlook enables a heterogeneous society to
survive free of the internecine strife of a Northern Ireland, a Cyprus, or
a Lebanon. I confess to seeing Bethany's doctrinal yardstick poised like
a guillotine to lop off dissenting heads, mine and others. I confess to
feeling profound unease when I hear Christian pastors and educators
speak—with the fervor of Muslim leaders exhorting the faithful to join a
jihad—in praise of Christian schools for "staying the hand of God's
further judgment" against America, as if to say that God's chosen
schools and people stand between him and the world's destruction. A.
C. Janney, national president of the AACS, expressed this view at a
huge meeting of Christian educators. Thus, I confess to worrying that
true believers may dismiss my precious right to dissent as the arrogance
of nonbelievers, an impediment in the path of Truth. Can those who
know God and have his blessing be far from concluding that I must be
constrained for my own good and that of the righteous brethren who
live in his will?

Fundamentalists and nonfundamentalists see each other across a
chasm that relativists always try to bridge with folk-wisdom variants of
"to each his own." From my side of the chasm I say, "OK, exist, even
thrive, but moderate your extremist perspective. Must you be so inexorably opposed to non-Christians and their world? Can't you relent?"
From their side they say, "Since we possess the Truth, we must obey it,
not compromise it. Can't you repent? By failing to accept our Truth,
your fate will be an eternity in hell."

Born-again true believers are my potential antagonists, notwithstanding their professed love for me and their concern for the final
condition of my soul. Unfortunately, true believers may never see my
differences as a source of strength for our mutual well-being, let alone
love me for, rather than in spite of, my differences. Their love for me is
the undifferentiated love I merit as unsaved mankind, a love, sad to say,
which never has protected me and other nonbelievers when transitory

moments of toleration give way to flights of anxiety and they challenge me: How dare I be different? How dare I reject Truth?

Before I lived among and studied Bethany's Christians I never understood the extent of the believer's love of and dedication to the Bible. Thus, I could read William Jennings Bryan's argument in the famous 1925 Scopes trial in the detached way one reads statements rejected out of hand, impervious to what was at stake for Bryan when he concluded, "If we have to give up either religion or education, we should give up education" (quoted in Ginger 1958:88). Grasping what is at stake for Bryan does not make his argument more cogent, but it does permit me to grasp the magnitude of the loss that he and others saw in the teaching of evolution. Understanding this loss does not make me wish that Clarence Darrow had less effectively countered Bryan's case, but it does add compassion to the civility that is requisite for survival in a crowded, heterogeneous planet. Without compassion and civility, I may too readily dismiss you and your claims for survival as a nuisance, as a barrier to progress, and thereby deny that your stripe of humanity deserves the voice, the time, and the space to be heard and acknowledged as worthy. Better the relative confusion and disorder of civility than the order of uncompromising true belief that defines my needs in its terms, not in my own.

Societal Costs

Beneath the common term of fundamentalism is a range of institutions which do not invariably see eye-to-eye on doctrine or public policy (Johnston and Wiles 1982). However, through its affiliation with the nationwide AACS, Bethany joins hundreds of churches and schools in supporting a lobby in Washington and in responding to requests from the association's leadership to pressure Washington legislators. Without benefit of a lobbyist, the Illinois branch of the association takes comparable action at the state level. Judging from their organized involvement in grass-roots politics in Hartney, their response to presidential election politics, and their general attentiveness to local, state, and national politics, Bethany evidences an awareness of and responsiveness to forces in the larger society that bear on its institutional health.

In chapter 1 I referred to fundamentalist Christian activity as having political, religious, and educational aspects. I mention this fact again here in order to make it clear that I see no conspiracy within or among these aspects. As the New Right, they ostensibly comprise a movement.

Those who reject the New Right often do so with some hysteria, and in sweeping terms, wrongly assuming that all who call themselves "fundamentalists" agree on religion and politics. They see peril in the behavior of groups such as Scientology, the Unification Church, and Hare Krishna, which, notwithstanding a pronounced similarity in proselytizing zeal motivated by absolutist doctrine, are a world away from Bethany Baptist Church and its school. It is wrong to commit the same error of overstatement that Bethany and its fellows do when they label and dismiss the nonfundamentalist world as "secular humanists," and thus the instrument of Satan.

In regard to American society, I see no basis for alarm in the activities of fundamentalist institutions such as Bethany's church and school. I do see grounds for deep concern, rooted largely, but not exclusively, in my aforementioned preference for pluralism.

Is Christian schooling divisive? If it is not, it is not due to a failure of intent: Bethany means to inculcate separateness; Bethany means to teach only one Truth; and Bethany means to control student contact with any competing doctrine. It does not contribute to divisiveness in the way feared by antipluralists who see danger in ethnic groups maintaining their native languages and not becoming loyal Americans. Born-again Christians are English-speaking super-patriots; they are God's people in God's church and school, living in God's blessed land.

When I questioned academy students and students from Hartney's public high school about their commitment to pluralism, the *overall* results were not drastically different. But on each item that related to a point covered by doctrine, the differences between Christian and public school students were enormous: Is interracial marriage OK? Yes, say 61 percent of public school students; yes, say only 30 percent of Bethany students. Should books written by Communists be available in public libraries? Yes, say 73 percent of public school students; yes, say only 29 percent of Bethany's. Is it good that America has so many different religious groups? Yes, say 82 percent of public school students; yes, say only 27 percent of Bethany's. And, finally, should homosexuals have the same rights as heterosexuals? Yes, say 58 percent of public school students; yes, say only 26 percent of Bethany's. Given the differences on these specific items, I conclude that the academy—abetted by its parental and church allies—communicates its beliefs and values to a considerable extent. If, by conventional standards, Bethany's students do not become deviant adults, the failure is not due to lack of effort or intent.

Fundamentalist educators represent themselves as a group besieged by the Internal Revenue Service and state departments of education.

Their struggle to stay the perceived intrusion of external control is consistent with our tradition of religious liberty, which is a cornerstone of American pluralism. Fundamentalists, accordingly, value the pluralism that underpins their existence, dreading the passage of laws that threaten their right to be and remain different. Pluralism is promoted when our courts interpret the Ninth and Fourteenth Amendments as assurance for the "right of parents to direct the education of their children" (Carper 1982:297).

Here, however, is the first rub: If Bethanyites cherish pluralism for its contribution to their survival, they nonetheless fail to make serious efforts to hold up the principle before their immature believers—BBA's students. One might reason that what fosters one's survival would get priority status, being presented in song, story, and sermon, just as these means are used year-round to glorify other cherished principles. I never heard a discussion, let alone an elaboration, of the concept of pluralism and its implications for their own survival as a group. On the contrary, I did hear Roman Catholics maligned, Mormons lumped together with Hare Krishnas and practitioners of Transcendental Meditation, and daily reinforcement of the scriptural Truth supporting these positions. Here is the second rub: As true believers, it is contradictory for them to advance a concept like pluralism. They want to thrive, but they do not want a multitude of competing doctrines to thrive. How could they if their Truth is singular? When they revel in "Blessed Assurance," sing out "All Hail the Power," and acknowledge "I Surrender All," they do so persuaded that while their doctrine has opposers, it has none with a leg of Truth to stand on.

Espousing pluralism is not functional to the cause of their monolithic Truth. Thus, while Supreme Court judgments secure their right to exist, their own doctrine does not move them to protect and preserve that network of ideas and practices which supports these judgments. This is a paradox, as is the fact that groups like Bethany's Baptists were instrumental during the American colonial period in fostering a religious individualism opposed to the intent of larger, more powerful churches to be recognized as the established church of their area. Bethany, an offspring of this individualism, is unsympathetic to its siblings. Based on what BBA instructs, its students cannot believe otherwise than that these rival claimants ignore and deny Truth.

And still another paradox is evident in the fact that the more vigorously groups like Bethany's Christians thrive, the more we know that American pluralism is healthy. Yet, the more successfully such groups proselytize, the more pluralism may be endangered. Furthermore, when I endorse pluralism I not only advance a principle that supports their existence, I also support other groups that are antithetical to Bethany. When they endorse one Truth, they foster conditions that are antithetical to American society as I value it. My logic sees them as an exemplar of pluralism's success in America; their logic sees me and others outside their boundaries as exemplars of their failure.

Fundamentalists charge that public schools propagate their own truths—those of humanism, relativism, godlessness, and unrestrained individualism. This characterization caricatures the public schools. Undeniably they have problems, but not those of this overdrawn picture. I cannot believe that children across the nation leave their public schools any more or any less godless or individualistic than when they entered. If public schools do not consciously espouse a pluralist outlook, they unconsciously foster it by the natural diversity manifest in the religion, politics, and morals of their students, teachers, and parents.

In contrast, BBA's selectivity succeeds in making it an extraordinarily homogeneous social setting. "The Word of the Lord is the source of our power," proclaimed the headmaster one Monday morning in chapel. "You are to be saturated with it, to sow it; and to know it always is the solution," he continued. Not a single adult within shouting distance of BBA's students could resist joining this alliterative chorus. The school has unfaithful students and misbehaving ones. Few or none are boldly heretical enough to utter a dissenting word about Bethany's doctrine, for to do so is to risk riding a yellow bus to the nearest tax-supported school.

Donald Erickson, an advocate for a robust private sector in American education, has advised state departments of education that their regulations "must encourage the pursuit of pluralistic goals" (1969:160) and "must encourage diverse approaches to the achievement of goals" (p. 165). His message: do not regulate private schools out of existence, particularly Christian schools, which see governmental regulation as a rejection of the separation of church and state.[5] I see merit in Erickson's advice. Henry Levin, an economist, writes in a paper prepared for a seminar on tuition tax credits:

> If a basic goal of public education in a social democracy is to reproduce a common core so essential to the effective functioning of democracy, then any system of choice ought to be evaluated with respect to whether it . . . supports such an objective or undermines it. [Levin 1982:24]

I also see merit in Levin's observations, though Erickson and Levin set up countervailing notions.

Erickson appeals to the ideal of pluralism in his opposition to the uniformity that characterizes public schools across the nation. Levin appeals to the ideal of democracy. He asks, "How can democracy function if students are socialized at every stage in the narrow and parochial views of their families, without exposure to competing viewpoints and values?" (1982:35). Were his views to prevail without qualification, BBA could not exist. Erickson supports pluralism without specifying the private schools' obligation to promote a common core; Levin supports a common core, while undercutting the possibility of such schools when he adds that their students should be exposed "to competing viewpoints and values." Since neither writer does justice to the concerns of the other, we are left with a dilemma.

Though BBA's instructional program does not endorse pluralism, is it divisive? That is, does it communicate facts and feelings that lead students to feel negatively toward other Americans? I conclude that it does, and, moreover, that it means to do so. Of course, Christian educators do not explicitly encourage this kind of divisiveness; they speak, rather, of separation, of not being unequally yoked with unbelievers, of going forth and bringing Christ to all nations. Thus, the same attributes of Bethany's institutions that I described as personally threatening apply equally to American society in general. Bethanyites may believe, as Headmaster McGraw states, that they would defend with their lives my right to utter thoughts they disapprove, but in their determined process of socialization, this fine sentiment gets lost. Moreover, if their doctrinal commitments became our status quo, we would be a radically different society. From the perspective of the pluralist America that I value I see that the more successful the Bethanys of America are, the less successful will be the ideal of pluralism which assures their survival. Their nonreinforcement of this ideal is a case of biting the hand that feeds you.

In addition to my concern for pluralism and the paradoxes engendered by Bethany's doctrinal stance, I believe that schooling at BBA contributes an intransigent element to American society. Intransigent behavior, defined as "refusing to compromise or budge from an often extreme position taken or held" (Webster's Third New International Dictionary), is the appropriate response if one has Truth. Placing God behind one's cause turns causes into crusades. When one's beliefs admit of no uncertainty, one thereby bars debate, bargaining, and compromise. If something is either this or that, true believers must reject solutions containing only a measure of this and that: purity of belief in doctrinal matters is Bethany's clear stance. As O'Dea observes, "by sacralizing the identity it provides, it [religion] may worsen and in fact embitter conflict, and build deeply into the personality structure of people a recalcitrance to come to terms with an opponent" (1966:101). I believe that Bethany's broad-scale, sacralizing disposition, which they see as instrumental to their success, can vitiate institutions that require

> flexible give and take dialogue if they are to function at all. This is particularly the case in democratic societies composed of people with both diverse religious faiths and no religious faith, in which widely divergent points of view must be accommodated in an on-going consensus of courses of action. [O'Dea 1966:105; see also Dahl, 1975:272]

I do not see how Bethany's ideal of Christian schooling from kindergarten through college can avoid promoting intransigence, since students neither learn the habit of compromise nor grasp its necessity in a diverse, complex society. Furthermore, I do not see students learning that dissent and compromise are critical attributes of healthy democracies, rather than unwelcome guests in the house of orthodoxy, the sort who ungratefully take your food, molest your children, and set fire to the upstairs bedroom.

My last example of a cost to society relates to Bethany's censorship. By allowing students only selective access to literary, artistic, and ideological expression they are being consistent with their commitment to doctrinal purity. Knowing that their depraved flesh is susceptible to un-Truthful temptations, BBA's librarian shamelessly censors; academy educators unapologetically denounce particular movies, books, and songs. With Truth at stake, they are unable to do otherwise. In this regard, Robert Nisbet speaks of "The essential barrenness of the creative impulse in the arts when, as in time of war in the democracies and the totalitarian states constantly, artists are made, in effect, to wear uniforms." (1976:26). When truth wears a uniform, as it does in BBA's classrooms, chapels, and corridors, the creative impulse is forced into the service of a single cause. In today's world, where orthodoxy prevails the arts languish; at all times, unmitigated orthodoxy fetters creativity. In a fundamentalist-dominated society, Henry Miller's books once more would be smuggled into the country and D. H. Lawrence's *Lady Chatterley's Lover* would return to its expurgated version.

Whither Light and Darkness?

> It is possible . . . that the culture of the future will be dominated by singleminded men of one persuasion or

another. It is possible; but in so far as the weight of one's will is thrown onto the scales of history, one lives in the belief that it is not to be so.

Richard Hofstadter

Christian schools offer an alternative to the public schools. As I eventually realized about schools I had studied in other communities, schooling at BBA was not meant to please me or my children. However, it does please those who find in such schools a haven from the perceived ills of public schools and contemporary America.

I was relieved to find that Bethany's children, even its most "spiritual" ones, are very ordinary Americans in many respects, far from the image of the automaton that critics of Christian schools present. I was further relieved to see that the desired inculcation of doctrine and obedience seldom attained a level of perfection sufficient to preclude personal, individualistic, independent judgment. Notwithstanding its indoctrinatory practices, Bethany's total institution is imperfectly total, perhaps inevitably so, because unlike the Amish, its adherents live mainly within the world it rejects. Its doctrinal blueprint is implemented amidst the marvels of modern society. In the end an abundance of invitations to backslide take hold, if only occasionally, so that Bethany's young people respond to doctrine with the variability of people on a weight-reducing or body-building program: they advance to exalted heights and regress to old norms, in a continuing series of advances and regressions. The promise of eternal, heavenly reward motivates imperfectly, as does the pleasurable vision of the perfect, healthy body.

Still, my data suggest that Bethany educators have a firm basis for feeling that their wards are faithful, spiritual Christians. The extent of their success argues for their potential contribution to divisiveness in American society. But however probable their divisiveness may be, I do not recommend state regulation of the sort that would vitiate their true distinctiveness.

Regarding the issue of divisiveness, no one has stated better than James Madison the proper response to what he calls "faction," that is, to groups whose actions are perceived to threaten national unity:

> There are two methods of curing the mischiefs of faction: the one by removing its causes; the other, by controlling its effects. There are again two methods of removing the causes of faction: the one, by destroying the liberty which is essential to its existence; the other, by giving to each citizen the

same opinions, the same passions, the same interests. It could never be more truly said than of the first remedy, that it was worse than the disease. Liberty is to faction what air is to fire. . . . The second expedient is as impracticable as the first would be unwise. . . . The inference to which we are brought is, that the *causes* of faction cannot be removed, and that relief is only to be sought in the means of controlling its *effects*. [Quoted in Wright 1962:130, 132]

Those who visualize Christian schools as locked in mortal combat with the good causes of liberty and pluralism (see Park 1980, and Nordin and Turner 1980) reverse Bethany's view of which side represents light and which side darkness. But, if they stir up extremist as opposed to informed reactions in those who personally oppose Christian schools and their supposed New Right allies, they do little to advance the cause of the basic principles at stake.

The existence of fundamentalist Christian schools creates a paradox of pluralism in the United States. Paradoxes of pluralism testify to our ideological health. I hope the day never comes when our society feels that Christian schools must be suppressed or curtailed in any way. I trust that the perceived cost of allowing Christian schools to flourish never exceeds the level of concern abolitionist Wendell Phillips expressed in his 1852 speech:

External vigilance is the price of liberty. . . . Never look . . . for an age when the people can be quiet and safe. At such times despotism, like a shrouding mist, steals over the mirror of Freedom.[6]

Studying Bethany Baptist Academy has rekindled my appreciation of Phillips's wise call for "eternal vigilance." I consider his view a sounder, more fittingly conservative reaction than proposals to contain Christian schools in ways that preclude their serving as appropriate educational means to a particular community's ends.

The essayist George Steiner wrote that "Men are accomplices to that which leaves them indifferent" (1967:150). I feel anything but indifferent to the orthodoxy of fundamentalist Christians. I confess to fearing those who know they have the Truth and are convinced that everyone else would do best to hold this same Truth. I further confess to fearing those who apply their Truth with an implacable logic unmoderated by a need to be pragmatic, to compromise, to see things in terms of degrees. But I prefer the anomaly of the Christian school paradox to the alternative of harassing them or unjustifiably constraining their right to survive.

The language of the Supreme Court is instructive. For example, the Court in its 1925 decision insuring the right of Roman Catholic schools to exist spoke of their necessity in terms of "additional obligations" Catholics may hold for the schooling experiences of their youth, obligations unfulfillable by public schools: "The child is not the mere creature of the State; those who nurture him and direct his destiny have the right, coupled with the high duty to recognize and prepare him for additional obligations" (Fellman 1960:5). This conclusion can be interpreted to mean that if it is acceptable in America to be Catholic, then it is acceptable for institutions to exist that make it possible to become Catholic. In the 1976 *State vs. Whisner* case, the Supreme Court of Ohio upheld the right of a Christian school to avoid state regulation, saying that the state's needs in this instance did not meet the "compelling interest" test which is necessary—according to the Fourteenth Amendment—to override parental rights to educate one's children (Hazard 1980 and Carper 1982).

Absolutists without a political arm are not deeply worrisome; with a political arm they acquire the power to legislate, to exercise police power, and to replace our many competing orthodoxies with their single one. The *potential* for abuse, however, does not establish the state's compelling interest to abolish either the political or the educational arms of absolutist Christian groups. To be sure, they may indeed become a "clear and present danger" to our open society, but until that time has been judged to exist, we must abide by the paradoxes Madison's liberty produces and remain mindful of liberty's effects. Meanwhile, their institutions must not be slandered, their leaders must not be vilified, their students and teachers must not be taken to task for what they *may* do. Their right to thrive is inviolable, at least until they overstep the line between safe and unsafe—an extraordinarily difficult issue to decide—and thereby signal that it is time for intolerance to replace tolerance. Tolerance, after all, is only a limited good. Sullivan, Pierson, and Marcus answer their own question, "Are the citizens of a democracy obliged to tolerate those who, if they prevailed, would destroy the practice of tolerance?" by saying, paradoxically, that the "defense of tolerance may require some degree of intolerance" (1982:9). "Totality breeds totality," states Samuel Wallace, "and each increment of its growth further corrupts our human environment. When will we begin to seriously fight this form of environmental pollution?" (1971:7). Not soon, or ever, I trust, will we deem that the time has unmistakably come to fight fundamentalist Christian schools.

Appendixes

7. Drama/Office Practice/
   Spanish II/S.H.
8. Band/Choir/Indus. Arts/S.H.

12th Grade

1. Drafting/Physics/S.H./
   Typing I
2. Bible/P.E. & Health
3. Chapel (M,W,F)

Journalism/Soul winning/S.H.
   (T,TH)
4. English
5. Lunch
6. Government/Economics
7. Drama/Office Practice/
   Spanish II/S.H.
8. Band/Choir/Indus. Arts/S.H.

B. *American Association of Christian Schools*
   Statement of Faith

We believe that the Bible, both the Old and New Testaments, was verbally inspired of God, and is inerrant and is our only rule in matters of faith and practice. We believe in creation, not evolution; that man was created by the direct act of God and in the image of God. We believe that Adam and Eve, in yielding to the temptation of Satan, became fallen creatures. We believe that all men are born in sin. We believe in the Incarnation, the Virgin Birth, and the Deity of our Lord and Savior Jesus Christ. We believe in the vicarious and substitutional Atonement for the sins of mankind by the shedding of His blood on the cross. We believe in the resurrection of His body from the tomb, His ascension to Heaven, and that He is now our Advocate. We believe that He is personally coming again. We believe in His power to save men from sin. We believe in the necessity of the New Birth, and that this New Birth is through the regeneration of the Holy Spirit. We believe that salvation is by grace through faith, plus nothing minus nothing, in the atoning blood of our Lord and Savior, Jesus Christ.

We believe that this statement of faith is basic for Christian fellowship and that all born-again men and women who sincerely accept it and are separated from the world of apostasy and sin can and should live together in peace, and that it their Christian duty to promote harmony among the Believers.

Membership will not be afforded to those associated with, members of, or in accord with the World Council of Churches, the National Council of Churches, the Modern Charismatic Movement, or the Ecumenical Movement.

Revised by the AACS Board
of Directors, October 6, 1977.

C. *The Academy Hymn*

From the mountains, hills, and plains, 'cross the ocean wide.
We can see that God in heaven cannot be denied.
He Who made the universe teaches us to be
Faithful servants of His Word. "Learn," He says, "of Me."

Knowledge of man's mind alone can't begin to give
Wisdom that is needed which will teach us how to live.
God's own Word directs our paths, that our lives might be
Satisfied through His own plan. Taught by God, we see.

Christ, the Lord of sacrifice, gave His life that we
Trusting in His full salvation might be saved to see.
We have come to learn of Him, give our lives that we
Might go forth, proclaim His name, that men's hearts be free.

D. Grass-Roots Christian Political Action

I. LEVELS OF POLITICAL INFLUENCE
  A. National Politics
    1. Presidential campaigns
    2. Executive branch politics
    3. Senatorial and congressional campaigns
    4. Federal legislation
    5. National political parties
  B. State Politics
    1. Statewide and legislative district campaigns
    2. State legislation
    3. State political parties
  C. Local Politics
    1. County/local political parties
    2. Local political campaigns
    3. Local legislation
    4. Precinct politics
II. PRECINCT POLITICS "Where the action becomes influential!"
  A. Organization of Political Parties at the Precinct Level
    1. Voter involvement
    2. Leadership involvement
    3. Volunteer involvement
  B. Political Action at the Precinct Level
    1. Voter registration and turn-out
    2. Campaigning for candidates
    3. Volunteer work for the party and candidates
    4. Impacting on the media
III. CHRISTIAN POLITICAL ACTION
  A. Educating the Christian Electorate
  B. Organizing the Christian Electorate
  C. Becoming Involved in Party Activity
  D. Supporting Worthy Candidates
  E. Monitoring Legislative Issues
  F. Mobilizing Christian Influence on the Political Process

Rev. Gerald B. Carlson, Field Director
American Association of Christian Schools

E. *Parent's Pledge*

Please read carefully before signing.

We, as parents who are accepting the challenge to "train up a child in the way he should go," do state that this training will be carried on in the home. We shall place *our trust* in the Christian school to extend that training more completely.

We recognize that for our child to make good progress in his work, it is essential that he have confidence in his teacher and school. Therefore, we will do all in our power to see that our child respects and obeys the school staff and rules.

We pledge that, if for any reason our child does not respond favorably to the school, *we will not try to change the school* to fit his needs, but will withdraw him quietly and that without delay.

We will not undermine the school administration or teachers. If we have suggestions, they will be made quietly and to the proper source.

We pledge that our child will bring to the school *a heritage of Christian culture*. We promise that the *home will provide a secure haven* of safety— free from the influences that are listed in the student pledge.

We grant permission to the school authorities to discipline our child and to allow whatever disciplinary measures are necessary. We understand that any student is subject to dismissal at any time.

We give permission for our child to take part and will cooperate in all school activities including fund raising, sports, and school-sponsored trips away from school premises.

We have read the dress code standards and agree to see to it that our child adheres to it.

We pledge our loyal support to the school and will cooperate in giving to its school extension fund as we are able.

We agree to pay the tuition according to arrangements that shall be made and to conclude all required payments on or before the last day of school.

We understand that assessments will be made to cover damage to school property (including breakage of windows, abuse of books, etc.).

We consider it a real privilege to have the opportunity to send our child to Bethany Baptist Academy, and shall endeavor to support and uphold the principles, practices and educational policies of the school in every way.

_____   _____

Date   Parent's Signature

F. Employee Contractual Agreement

I affirm that I am a born-again Christian believing the Bible to be the inspired Word of God without contradiction or error in its original languages.

I believe that every Christian should be separated from worldly habits such as smoking, drinking, dancing, and other such unacceptable activities, and I believe that a Christian should conduct himself/herself at all times as befitting his/her Christian testimony.

It is my desire to become a part of the church membership and to participate in the church program by my attendance at all services (Sunday School, Morning & Evening Services Sunday, Wednesday Mid-Week Service, and all special services). I will support the church with my tithes and offerings and use my talents in some specific way such as teaching a Sunday School class, bus work, children's church, etc.

Realizing that griping is destructive, I will not participate in this type of endeavor, but will instead if a question or suggestion arises, take it directly to the Pastor or Headmaster.

G. "Our Standard of Christian Leadership"

This standard is presented to every teacher and Christian educational worker of Bethany Baptist Church. It describes what the leadership and membership of our church expect of each person to serve as a teacher, worker, and leader of the congregation.

THE STANDARD

Faithfulness in Attendance—Every teacher and worker is *expected* to be faithful in attendance at the regular services of the church including the Sunday Morning, Sunday School, Sunday Evening and Mid-week Services. Faithfulness is also *expected* at Special Meetings, Revival Meetings, Committee Meetings, and Teachers and Staff Meetings. Each Teacher is expected to be in class or at Departmental Opening at least *10 minutes* early. Hebrews 10:25.

Faithfulness in Soul-Winning and Visitation—In as much as Christ *commanded* us to "Go" and disciple all peoples, and *commissioned* us to be witnesses and seeing as Soul Winning is the fruit of our Salvation, and seeing as Bethany Baptist Church has a weekly visitation program for this purpose, it is *expected* that every church educational worker and teacher participate regularly in the church visitation program. Matt. 28:19–20; Acts 1:8; John 15:16.

Faithfulness in Giving—Realizing the heavy responsibility we have to propagate the Gospel in this community and around the world, the leadership of the church is *expected* to tithe their income through the local church. 1 Cor. 16:2, 2 Cor. 8–9; Mal. 3:8–10.

Faithfulness in Christian Living—While it is understood that faith in Christ as personal Savior and Lord, followed by Believer's Baptism by immersion, and acceptance of the Articles of Faith of the Church are the basis for membership in Bethany Baptist Church, yet certain practices common in the world are detrimental to the Christian life and witness. As a leader and example for young Christians to follow, it is *expected* that you be separated from those activities which tend to hinder the work of the Holy Spirit, and which impair the capacities of body, mind and spirit which are gifts of God to be used for His glory. Such as:

1. The use of intoxicating liquor as a beverage. Prov. 20:1; 23:29–32; Hab. 2:15–16; Isa. 5:11,22
2. The use of tobacco. 1 Cor. 6:19–20
3. The over-indulgent use of television, thereby hindering your service for Christ. 1 Cor. 6:12
4. Attendance at the theater. 1 John 2:15–16
5. Dancing. 1 John 2:15–16; Rom. 13:14
6. Gossip. James 3:5–6

7. Pride. Prov. 16:18
8. Selfishness. James 2:8
9. Immorality. 2 Cor. 5:17; 1 Cor. 5:1–13; Tit. 2:12–14; Matt. 5:27–28
10. Profanity. Exod. 20:7; Matt. 12:36–37; Col. 3:8–9; Col. 4:6

Faithfulness in Dedication—Every worker, teacher and leader of Bethany Baptist Church is *expected* to be enthusiastic in his dedication and love for Jesus Christ and this His church. For a leader to inspire followership there must be a keen loyalty to Christ and the church. Luke 14:25–33; 1 Tim. 3:15

H. Teacher Duties

A. AFTERNOON HALL DUTY (3:10–3:25)

This teacher maintains school decorum in hallways of Junior High and Senior High School immediately following the 3:10 bell. The hall outside locker rooms should be immediately checked and a close watch kept on this area. Couples should not be permitted to loiter in any area. This is an important duty—teacher needs to be super-alert. The lunchroom area will be used for a student center. This will be the only area in which students can have refreshments. No students should play in the gym without permission. During basketball practice, no unauthorized person should be in the gym or entryway. Students should not be in any room without permission of a teacher. Students should not be in entryways unless it is raining.

B. NOON LUNCHROOM DUTY

Each fulltime secondary teacher will be given a time to eat lunch and will be on the duty schedule for that time in the lunchroom.

C. NOON LUNCHLINE DUTY

This teacher should be in the gym before the children start to line up. He should maintain a quiet and orderly lunchline, not allowing any horseplay, pushing, or loud talking and laughing. Couples should not be allowed any personal contact or close association. No students should be allowed in the kitchen and cooks should be given the greatest amount of respect. There should be no "budging line" or saving places. Demerits should be given for improper behavior or disrespect. Insist upon immediate obedience. There should be no mingling with elementary students.

D. GENERAL DUTIES OF TEACHERS

1. In all duty areas the teacher on duty is in complete charge. Students are to be made to obey and show respect. Teachers are to treat all students alike and be fair, not showing partiality.

2. Other rotating duties will be assigned in such areas as tournaments and basketball games, as the year progresses. Please make any changes or trades of duty through the office and with the permission of the headmaster.

3. Each classroom used is to be swept each Wednesday and Friday. Classrooms are to be kept neat at all times. This room needs to be kept as neat and sharp as your home.

4. Bulletin boards must be changed promptly the beginning of each month.

I. Student Pledge

Please Read Carefully Before Signing

I consider it a real privilege to have the opportunity to attend Bethany Baptist Academy and shall endeavor to support and uphold the principles and practices of the school in every way.

I promise my sincere effort to:

FIRST: Protect my mind, body and morals from evil companions by not making them my intimate associates.

SECOND: Be separate from the world in dress and grooming by adhering to the dress code of the school.

THIRD: Be separate from the world in the places I attend and the activities in which I participate. I will not attend the theater, dances, or other affairs prohibited by the administration of the school.

FOURTH: Treat my body as the temple of the Holy Spirit by not participating in such things as "Petting", smoking, taking drugs, or using alcohol.

FIFTH: Give honor, respect, consideration, and cooperation to all faculty and staff of the school. I will also obey and honor my parents.

SIXTH: Take correction and advice willingly, when it is deemed necessary by any member of the faculty or administration.

I will strive to obey all the rules of the school. I will completely back and support Bethany Baptist Academy as long as I attend school here.

SEVENTH: I will not willfully or deliberately inflict damage on school property. I will refrain from marring walls and lockers or mishandling books and classroom equipment.

EIGHTH: Select wisely and conscientiously the T.V. programs that I watch and turn from those programs which have vulgar jokes, immorality, and activity prohibited by the school. I will refuse to listen to music that creates a reckless spirit or words that suggest immorality or a turning against authority.

NINTH Refrain from lying, cheating, stealing and using obscene language.

TENTH: I shall seek faithfully to witness as a Christian by looking, acting and talking like a true Christian.

_____
Signature of Pupil

J. Hall Rules (extracted from the BBA Handbook)

1. No student is to be in the halls or restrooms, etc., without a permanent wooden pass.
2. No talking should be heard; whispering is permitted. Couples (any boy and girl) are not allowed to talk in the halls, at all.
3. All students and lines should stay to the right.
4. Lines should be single-file. Couples (any boy and girl) are not allowed to walk together.
5. Loitering and congregating are not permitted; couples (any boy and girl) are not allowed to stand and talk.
6. Loitering at entrances is not permitted; *girl students waiting, should not do so outside the locker rooms.*
7. Lockers need not be "banged"; books need not be dropped intentionally.
8. Absolutely no running, pushing, eating, chewing, loud laughing or yelling will be permitted by students.
9. Upper level students will gather in lunchroom until 8:25 when the person on duty will dismiss them to home rooms. They should not loiter in halls or restrooms or wander in and out of the lunchroom and through the halls. They should go directly to home room, after one trip to locker and restroom, and not leave without a pass.
10. Any disobedience or disrespect should be reported on a demerit slip.
11. Locker rooms are not to be used as restrooms; students may go in to deposit P.E. clothes and should exit immediately.
12. Students are expected to maintain a "hands-off," no-touching policy toward members of the opposite sex. A warning should be given in all home rooms and then infractions reported to the discipline committee.
13. No student is allowed in the kitchen, except those assigned for work duty, and then only during regular work hours.
14. No student is allowed behind the counter in the office unless he is in conference with the headmaster.
15. No student should be in the hall during class, except in extreme necessity.
16. Students are not allowed in the teachers' workroom for any reason.
17. Young ladies are not allowed in hall outside locker rooms after school.
18. Female students should use coat racks in north hall. Male students should use coat racks outside locker rooms.

K. *Leadership Pledge*

I consider it an honor and a privilege to be a leader in a school such as Bethany Baptist Academy. I understand that any place of leadership in a Christian school is a place of spiritual leadership, and I am determined to live the life of a spiritual leader. I have signed the Bethany Baptist Academy Student Pledge and in addition to living according to the promises I made therein, I also promise to:

FIRST—be an example in front of the other students in all points covered in the Student Pledge.

SECOND—if I have not already done so, follow the Lord's example by submitting to believer's baptism by immersion, as this is the first step in Christian obedience.

THIRD—if I have not already done so, join a local fundamental, Bible-believing church in obedience to God's Word.

FOURTH—attend all the services of the church to which I belong and also serve in that church in any way I am able.

FIFTH—be an active member of, and support all the activities of the youth group of my church.

SIXTH—actively participate in the visitation program of my church, or the bus ministry, or spend some time each week in witnessing for Christ.

SEVENTH—loyally support the pastor and youth pastor of my church and be a help and a loyal follower of the administrator of Bethany Baptist Academy.

Signature

L. End-of-the-Year Letter Sent to Each BBA Parent

Dear Parents,

At the risk of sounding pushy and presumptuous, I would like to suggest a few things you could work on with your child during the summer.

We've worked hard all year on your child, to teach him some things we know to be very important. It is possible to undo everything this summer by letting him slide back into old habits.

Not only will this help the child all summer, but it will make it easier on you (and us) when school starts next fall. This summer you are the teacher actively and by example.

Suggestion #1: Get *How to Rear Children* by Jack Hyles and read it. You can order it through the bookstore.

Suggestion #2: Practice the following "good manners" with your child:
— looking a person in the eye when speaking to him
— smiling at and speaking to people he passes
— standing when an adult enters the room
— using "Yes, Ma'am", and "No, Sir," etc., and calling a person by his name or title when addressing him
— sitting up straight in a chair, in church, etc.
— eating quietly and like a human being
— talking only pleasantly at the table
— refraining from loud laughter, whispering in front of others, making fun, and interrupting others
— refraining from "burps" and other improper noises

Suggestion #3: Encourage your child to show respect for others through his appearance and be a good testimony by:
— dressing appropriately for an occasion
— wearing clean clothes to start out the day
— keeping shirt tails in and belts on at proper times
— dressing modestly (girls), even wearing dresses occasionally
— keeping fingernails, hands and face clean
— keeping hair short (boys) and combed
— keeping underarms clean (some need deodorant)

Suggestion #4: Teach your child (and show him by example) how to be faithful to the Lord and the church.
— Have him with you at all the services, unless sickness or needed vacations prevent. You are hurting your child if you permit him to stay home while you come, and the damage is severe if you, yourself, are inconsistent in this area. If you and your child are

members of Bethany Baptist Church, your place is here; he will perceive a double standard of any kind—this is the most obvious area.

— Suggest, help, if needs be, push your child to attend V.B.S. [Vacation Bible School], Summer Camp, and youth activities. Some day you'll wish you had.

— Try to give Pastor and the child's youth director, the headmaster and teachers all the support you can by not criticizing them in any way in front of the child. You'll be sorry if you slight the character or teachings of a person you'll want your child to listen to later on.

— Encourage your child to have a daily quiet time with God.

In all Christian love and concern,

Headmaster Tom McGraw

Notes

Chapter 1

1. This is a pseudonym, as are the names of most other persons and places mentioned hereafter.

2. This is a book about Christians as Pastor Muller construes them. I therefore use the term "Christian" as he and his associates do, knowing that this does an injustice to the millions who comfortably view themselves as Christians, but not in Muller's terms.

3. The account that follows is composed of excerpts from Pastor Muller's responses to my questions. My questions are omitted, as are any indication of the succession of days on which he spoke.

4. *Growing Up American: Schooling and the Survival of Community* (1978).

5. *The Imperfect Union: School Consolidation and Community Conflict* (1982).

6. See, for example, Erickson (1964); Greeley and Rossi (1966); Himmelfarb (1974); Greeley et al. (1976), and Kraybill (1977).

7. It must suffice at this time (the point will be considered at length in chapter 10) to note that Goffman sees a total institution as "a place of residence and work [including places such as schools] where a large number of like-situated individuals, cut off from the wider society for an appreciable period of time, together lead an enclosed, formally administered round of life" (1961:xiii).

8. That at least one teacher believed my understanding was limited was made clear in these remarks at the end of my questionnaire: "I thought the questionnaire asked questions that required answers not listed. I believe that there is a lack of understanding about the need for Christian schools. The racial 'issue' is not important—holiness and

317

morality are. The make up of the work shows a nonsaved person's work. It shows lack of understanding," the teacher concluded, and ended with the full quotation of I Corinthians 2:14 about the "natural man."

9. And yet I do not mean to insert myself directly throughout the narrative, as do Belmonte (1979) and Slater (1976), although I am very sympathetic to Slater's comments: "Paradoxically . . . it is harder to extricate myself [from the study] than to preserve the totality as experienced. For there is a unifying link between the personal and the objective: the observer as tool, and a crude one never above suspicion, especially his own. Thus, to look 'inside me inside Africa' does not go counter to our experience but only to our conventions of reporting" (1976:12).

10. I had a third research assistant, Reverend David Housholder, mentioned earlier, who generously agreed to join us for one month of classroom observation during our first semester at BBA.

11. Robbins (in Robbins et al. 1973) describes an unexpected consequence of being empathetic in his study of Jesus Freaks. Misreading his empathy as acceptance of their beliefs, they became distinctly distressed with Robbins when he did not join them.

12. I use the word "movement" here and "conservative" in the next sentence with some reservation. "Movement" may suggest a degree of organization which belies the diversity of the contemporary groups whose activities derive from religious inspiration. Such groups may actually support the same ends (Reagan as president, creationism in schools, antiabortion, and opposition to the Equal Rights Amendment) without consolidating their efforts to achieve them. Moreover, their agreement on ends may mask the doctrinal differences which have given rise to separate organizational structures, in the first place, and which keep them separate, in the second. However, being lumped together as "conservative" not only places them in relationship to other religious groups in theological terms (they would tend to hold a fundamentalist, Bible-believing, born-again, evangelical outlook), but also to other religious and nonreligious groups in political terms (as indicated by their view of patriotism, gay rights, the women's movement, gun control, and abortion).

13. For example, from 1968 to 1978 Southern Baptists increased (15 percent) from 10.9 to 12.9 million while the United Methodist Church declined (4.36 percent) from 10.3 to 9.8 million (National Council of Churches, 1968 and 1978).

14. See *Digest of Education Statistics* for annual data on nonpublic schools.

15. Nordin and Turner "found that 72 percent of Kentucky and 50 percent of Wisconsin fundamentalist schools did not belong to any

national 'Christian' school organization" (1980:392), and Cooper and McLaughlin found that private schools were undercounted by as much as 35 percent (reported by Heard, August 24, 1981:4).

16. Important but lesser degrees of success are being experienced by other types of private schools amidst talk of vouchers that would afford parents the choice of public or private schooling for their children, and talk of James Coleman's instantly controversial study (1981), which purported to demonstrate the superiority of private schools.

17. On the one hand, there is the Creation Science Research Center, and, on the other, groups like the American Anthropological Association, which passes motions beginning: "Whereas evolutionary theory is the indispensible foundation for the understanding of physical anthropology and biology . . ." (*Anthropology Newsletter*, January 1981:1). Similarly opposed, Duane Gish of the Institute for Creation Research debates the famous writer-scientist Isaac Asimov in "The Genesis War" (*Science Digest*, October 1981:82–87).

18. Notwithstanding Jerry Falwell's and other fundamentalists' support for Israel, American Jews in the 1970s and 1980s were alert to and concerned about the signs of anti-Semitism associated with Christian fundamentalism. They were animated not only by the constant efforts to convert Jews, but also by the Reverend Bailey Smith, Southern Baptist Convention president, who within a two-week period informed a meeting of fifteen thousand people that "God almighty does not hear the prayer of a Jew" and then later said Jews have "funny-looking noses" (Champaign-Urbana *News Gazette*, November 15, 1980:8). Tom Driver of Union Theological Seminary coupled with "frightening irony" the pro-Israeli stance of Falwell and others and their anti-Semitism (Champaign-Urbana *News Gazette*, November 15, 1980:8). The same article quoted Rabbi Alexander Schindler, head of the Union of American Hebrew Congregations: It is "no coincidence that the rise of right-wing fundamentalism has been accompanied by the most serious outbreak of anti-Semitism since World War II." The fundamentalists' denials of anti-Semitism are weakened by statements such as the following by Bob Jones. He is editor of *Faith*, a family magazine published by Bob Jones University. Jones observes that Andrew Young, United Nations ambassador, did and said many unworthy things yet managed to keep his position until he "displeased Israel and her American supporters. . . . The point is, he has done and said other things just as detrimental . . . yet the President [Carter] smiled tolerantly and continued publicly to stand by this contemptible and unworthy man until the Israeli pressures were applied. It makes us wonder who, indeed, besides the Communists . . . is running America" (April 1980:2).

Chapter 2

1. Registration is the least that a state can require of its private schools. To register in Illinois is "to assure compliance with the federal and state laws regarding attendance, length of term, nondiscrimination and with applicable fire and health safety requirements" (State Board of Education 1978:1). At an IACS workshop, Headmaster McGraw advised his colleagues not to fight the state on its intent to enforce health and safety regulations: "Health and safety are Caesar's and should be rendered unto him." States that try to impose their customary standards for recognition incur legal resistance from Christian schools.

2. On the subject of outside funding, McGraw notes: "Our survival is tied to only one thing—the Word of God. It is not tied to any outside group. That's one of the reasons we fight so hard to refuse state or federal funds. We don't want our survival tied to allegiance to any outside group."

3. In 1978 tuition fees averaged $562 in fourteen Wisconsin Christian schools and $609 in seventeen Kentucky schools (Turner 1979:124).

4. The use of the male gender here and elsewhere in the book derives from the fundamentalist Christians' almost exclusive use of the male gender in both spoken and written language. They do not use plural nouns or a his/her construction to avoid dominance by the male reference.

5. Lester Roloff is so admired at Bethany that when he urged his audience to write letters in his behalf, Headmaster McGraw prepared a reminder to this effect and pinned it to the bulletin board in the teacher's room along with the duty assignment and the other announcements teachers should heed.

6. I heard numerous references to the heart during my interviews. Here is a sampling: "I pray if there is something [troubling] in my heart." "I think they've just hardened their heart against salvation." "I don't have to work at being separate; for a Christian it should be a condition of the heart." "Rebellion is a sign their heart is not right." "I gave the Lord a chance in my life and the Lord awakened my heart."

7. To Bethany's educators "sin" may function as an adjective, as in the term "sin nature."

Chapter 3

1. This chapter's data and teacher comments and quotations are drawn from interviews with all teachers but one part-timer. The interviews were conducted in forty-five-minute sessions begun five months after I started my fieldwork. Many of the questions in these interviews

are from the schedules sociologist Dan Lortie (1975) used as the basis for his outstanding study of school teachers.

2. Compare Lortie's teachers (1975:27–32) and what he identifies as their five attractors: "the interpersonal theme," "the service theme," "the continuation theme," "material benefits," and "the theme of time compatibility."

3. Lortie's teachers (1975:92–93) estimated that they spent four- to five-eighths of their time in school-related activities, somewhat less than Bethany teachers believed they devoted to school business.

4. Among Lortie's teachers (1975:95–98) 59 percent of the men and 4 percent of the women mentioned money as a major cost of being a teacher. Also, 36 percent of the men and 16 percent of the women believed there were no costs. Teacher isolation was a matter of concern to both men (22 percent) and women (42 percent).

5. Most of Lortie's teachers (1975:102–6) (76.5 percent), identify their rewards in the psychic realm, as opposed to the extrinsic (11.9 percent) or the ancillary (11.6 percent) realms. "It is of great importance to teachers to feel they have 'reached' their students—their core rewards are tied to that percept" (1975:106).

6. Lortie's teachers (1975:182) want smaller classes, less clerical and extra duty, fewer interruptions, better facilities, curriculum improvements, and better students.

Chapter 4

1. Note the 1982 case involving four New Hampshire nuns dismissed from their job as educators in a Roman Catholic school. To sue their bishop, they hired a lawyer and took their case to the civil courts. Superior Court Judge Joseph Nadeau dismissed the case on the grounds that he had no jurisdiction over the bishop, although he ruled that the nuns' contract was subject to civil law because it was drafted in terms of civil, not canon, law.

2. Here is a brief picture of BBA's organizational structure: Pastor Muller is, effectively, the superintendent of schools, but he does not actively participate in the school's day-to-day affairs. McGraw is headmaster of the entire school, K-12. Assistant Headmaster Russ Warren also has K-12 responsibilities, but he has a large high school teaching obligation. Donna Reynolds is the elementary supervisor, a principal-like position, and teaches English in the high school grades. Art Swanson is her counterpart for the high school and he, too, teaches only in the high school grades. Pastor Burt has primarily out-of-school relations with the students; he teaches only the class in soul winning.

3. The probability of this recurring is low because BBA has just about reached the point when all of its classes, kindergarten through twelve,

are composed primarily of students who began their formal schooling at BBA.

Chapter 7

1. For example, Greeley and Rossi (1966) studied Catholic schools; Erickson (1964) studied Christian schools; Johnstone (1966) studied Lutheran schools; Himmelfarb (1974) studied Jewish schools; and Kraybill (1977) studied Mennonite schools. Greeley and Gockel (1971) and Kraybill (1977) provide good reviews of the impact studies. The positive results of religious schools are tempered by the nature of the nonschool socializing forces at work in the students' lives. Greeley and Gockel conclude that "Religious education does indeed have an impact on the adult lives of its students, but only when the social context of childhood or adulthood supports and emphasizes the values learned in the school. Religious education apparently works when there is constant reinforcement from outside the school" (1971:279).

2. This section is the first of several in this chapter containing the report of my student survey. I do not report the findings here or elsewhere by sex, grade, years the respondents attended BBA, or number of years "saved," because in few instances did they produce significant results. For example, sex proved to be significant only in regard to external conformity; the girls were more outwardly conforming than the boys.

3. This response rate is disappointingly low. I sent each parent a questionnaire via his or her child. Parents complained to Headmaster McGraw, saying, among other things, it had too many questions about race. Much later, I rewrote the entire questionnaire and tried unsuccessfully to distribute it to parents, some of whose children had graduated or left the school. In the circumstances I probably was fortunate to get forty-seven completed questionnaires. Still, I am not certain that these forty-seven constitute a fair representation of parents' opinions.

4. For the purposes of this chapter, elementary school teachers were included in the sample.

5. A T-test of significance shows BBA students significantly more positive than Hartney students at the .02 level.

6. A T-test of significance shows Hartney students significantly more supportive of civil rights than BBA students at the .001 level.

7. A T-test of significance was applied to the three items answered by both BBA and Hartney students. The results show that Hartney students are significantly more supportive of religious diversity at the .001 level.

8. Alienation is represented here by a highly abbreviated scale used by the National Opinion Research Center (1974–75) and in my own

study (Peshkin 1978); the specific items are drawn mainly from the larger, more complex scales of Seeman (1959).

9. Factor analysis pretty much confirms the integrity of the three scales standing as separate scales. I see them as a reasonably coherent, logical set of scales that together indicate a person's sense of well-being about himself, his relations with others, and how he is getting along in the world.

10. A T-test of significance shows BBA students significantly less machiavellian at the .001 level.

11. T-tests of significance show BBA students significantly less alienated at the .03 level and significantly more certain at the .02 level.

Chapter 10

1. See, for example, Perry (1974); McEwen (1980); Wallace (1971); Mouzelis (1971); Hillery (1963); and Jose (1968). McEwen's bibliography is particularly good.

2. These organizations are the Association for Supervision and Curriculum Development, the National Council for Social Studies, the National Council for Teachers of English, and the National Association of Elementary School Principals.

3. The point in this paragraph was brought to my attention by Donald Erickson of UCLA.

Chapter 11

1. Pluralism clearly encompasses organizational pluralism (Dahl 1982) and cultural pluralism, in the sense of social diversity (Dahl 1980), and flourishes where, broadly speaking, power is decentralized.

2. Parental choice of Christian schools for their children is perhaps the most frequently researched aspect of Christian education. Among the studies bearing on this point are: Clerico (1982), Foreman (1982), and Stoms (1982). The most commonly cited reasons are: a preference for Christian-centered schooling and dissatisfaction with the discipline, values, and academic standards of public schools. For many parents, both a pull and a push operate in their decision.

3. Kienel (1977) and McDearmid (1979) report higher test scores for Christian school students. The analysis of this success by Stoker and Splawn (1980), Murnane (1982), and Willms (1983) points to Christian school selection and parental self-selection as explanatory factors.

4. I began my study thinking that people who needed the structure of an absolutist doctrine would be strongly dependent and insecure, certainly psychologically impaired. Though I did not intend to explore these expectations, I left Bethany believing they were basically untrue.

5. See Stephen Arons's thoughtful discussion of state regulation in his book *Compelling Belief: The Culture of American Scholarship*.

6. Although "Eternal vigilance is the price of liberty" is often attributed to Thomas Jefferson, the words in this form are Wendell Phillips's, and in the original are John Philpot Curran's, spoken in Dublin on July 10, 1790: "The condition upon which God hath given liberty to man is eternal vigilance."

Tables

Table 1
Bethany and Hartney Students on School Emphasis
(Percentages)

	School does emphasize		School should emphasize		Discrepancy: "Should" less "does"	
	Bethany	Hartney	Bethany	Hartney	Bethany	Hartney
Preparation for postschooling job	54	67	90	90	+26	+23
Intellectual development	65	58	83	83	+18	+25
Preparation for everyday life	56	55	90	89	+34	+34
Character development	84	39	89	75	+ 5	+36
Spiritual development	93	—[a]	82	—	−11	—

NOTES: Responses were made according to a four-point scale: Very much; Quite a lot; Somewhat; Not at all. In the table, percentages represent a combination of the first two divisions. For Bethany, N = 115 (grades 8–12). For Hartney, N = 100 (a sample drawn from the same grades).

[a]Hartney students were not asked to comment on this goal of schooling.

Table 2
Why Do Bethany and Hartney Students Like Their Schools?
(Percentages)

	Bethany	Hartney
Provides good spiritual experience	88	43
Provides good academic experience	92	87
Gives me a chance to graduate and get a good job	80	98
My friends are there	84	90
The school is safe	65	66
Gives me a chance to participate in sports and extracurricular activities	70	69

NOTE: For Bethany, N = 115; for Hartney, 104.

Table 3
Single Most Important Reason for Liking Their Schools
(Percentages)

	Bethany	Hartney
Good spiritual experience	58	3
Good academic experience	12	24
Chance to graduate and get job	11	48
Friends there	11	18
School is safe	3	0
Sports and activities	3	6
Total	98	99

NOTE: N as in table 2.

Table 4

Student Ranking of Attributes Important for Popularity of Female and Male Students (Percentages)

	Bethany				Hartney			
	Ranked first		Ranked first, second, or third		Ranked first		Ranked first, second, or third	
	Female students	Male students	Female students	Male students	Female students	Male students	Female students	Male students
Spiritual	51	57	71	73	1	3	8	15
Good-looking	28	16	49	33	54	37	83	65
Cares about others	8	6	71	62	22	26	52	66
Fun-loving	6	7	40	35	10	11	68	51
Intelligent	4	5	41	40	11	14	60	58
Right family	2	3	24	29	3	3	27	18
Athletic	1	7	40	28	1	6	7	33

NOTE: For Bethany, N = 115; for Hartney, 104.

Table 5

Conformity of Students' Beliefs with Bethany's Standards
(Percentages)

	Strongly agree	Agree	Dis-agree	Strongly disagree	No answer
If I know a student cheated, I should urge him to report himself.	39	34	18	9	0
If the cheater refuses to report himself, I should report him.	29	34	19	18	0
I should be close friends only with born-again Christians.	37	29	25	7	2
One of the most important lessons I can learn is to question authority.	7	18	30	44	0
It is a sin if I do less than my best.	64	28	4	3	0
I'm happiest when I live in the Lord's will.	68	19	9	2	3
I should live separate from the world, in it but not of it.	46	34	16	3	1

NOTE: N = 115.

328

Table 6
Conformity of Students' Projected Behavior with Bethany's Standards
(Percentages)

	Strongly agree	Agree	Strongly disagree	Disagree	No answer
If I marry, I'll marry a born-again Christian.	71	19	8	1	1
If I can afford it, I'll send my children to a Christian school.	63	25	8	3	0
When I'm an adult, the Bible will be the center of my life.	43	40	10	3	3
When I'm an adult, my best friends will be born-again Christians.	50	32	15	2	1
If I go to college, I'll go to a Bible-believing college.	56	17	14	11	2

NOTE: N = 115.

Table 7
How Important Is Earning a Lot of Money?
(Percentages)

	Bethany	Hartney
Very important	10	59
Fairly important	48	35
Fairly unimportant	25	1
Very unimportant	16	1

NOTE: For Bethany, N = 114; for Hartney, 103.

Table 8

Student Conformity with Bethany's Standards in Different Situations
(Percentages)

	Always	Most of the time	Some of the time	Never	No answer
At school	54	30	12	4	0
With parents	43	33	15	10	0
With strangers	30	32	25	13	0
Where nobody knows you	24	36	19	19	1
With friends	24	35	29	12	0
At weekend parties	29	26	16	23	6[a]
When shopping	24	31	29	16	0
On dates	12	13	19	8	48[a]

NOTES: The question was: "To what extent do your school's biblical standards *actually guide your behavior* in the following situations?" (N = 115.)

[a]The "no answer" responses for these two situations are explained by the fact that some students do not attend weekend parties and many more have not yet begun to date.

Table 9

Student Conflict with Bethany's Standards in Free-time Activities
(Percentages)

	Always	Most of the time	Some of the time	Never	No answer
Movies	6	23	46	24	0
Music	23	18	30	28	1
Television	3	21	56	18	2
Books and magazines	5	11	30	54	0

NOTES: The question format was (e.g.): "When you see movies (on TV or otherwise), how likely are they to be movies which are in conflict with your school's biblical standards?" Unlike tables 5, 6, and 8, responses here are tabulated in terms of conflict rather than conformity because of the language of the questions. See also note 2 for chapter 7. N = 115.

Table 10
Student Conformity with Bethany's Standards in Their Personal Behavior
(Percentages)

	Always	Most of the time	Some of the time	Never	No answer
Proselytize the unsaved	8	23	50	18	1
Reject friends who don't meet Bethany's standards	23	19	27	30	1
Try to get friends right with the Lord	16	34	34	14	2
Try to do best I can do	50	42	7	2	0
Ask Lord's help for important decisions	36	36	22	6	0
Turn off TV programs if they don't meet Bethany standards	15	34	30	20	1
Stop reading a book if it does not meet Bethany standards	31	25	18	24	1

NOTE: N = 115.

Table 11

Support for Positive Racial Attitudes by Student and Adult Groups (Percentages)

	Students			Adults	
	Bethany (N = 115)	Hartney (N = 104)	Rural public school (N = 47)	Roman Cath- olics[a] (N = 344)	Bethany teachers (N = 16)
Approves black family moving next door. (Agree and Strongly agree)	93	80	94	58	—[b]
Whites should be obliged to help end racial discrimination. (Agree and Strongly agree)	64	62	59	80	—[b]
Blacks shouldn't push where not wanted. (Disagree and Strongly disagree)	68	51	48	37	56
Blacks should respect the right of whites to live in all-white neighborhoods. (Disagree and Strongly Disagree)	63	59	45	25	—[b]
Interracial marriage is not OK. (Disagree and Strongly Disagree)	30	61	35	—[c]	—[b]

[a]"Roman Catholics" refers to a group of adults whose entire education was received in Catholic schools.

[b]These items were removed from both teacher and parent questionnaires at the request of Headmaster McGraw. The one item teachers answered was unintentionally omitted from the parent questionnaire.

[c]Data are not available.

Table 12

Support for Civil Rights by Student and Adult Groups (Percentages)

	Students			Adults		
	Bethany (N = 115)	Hartney (N = 104)	Rural public school (N = 107)	Roman Catholics[a] (N = 344)	Bethany teachers (N = 16)	Bethany parents[a] (N = 47)
People who don't believe in God should have the same right to freedom of speech as anyone else. (Agree and Strongly agree)	93	95	91	85	94	94
Everyone should have the same right to freedom of speech no matter how undemocratic his ideas are. (Agree and Strongly agree)	77	84	94	—[b]	94	83
Radical political groups should not have the same freedom as the rest of us. (Disagree and Strongly disagree)	77	80	85	—[b]	75	66
Books written by Communists should not be permitted in public libraries. (Disagree and Strongly disagree)	29	73	70	42	81	47
It is wrong for homosexuals to have the same rights as others. (Disagree and Strongly disagree)	26	58	64	—[b]	37	45

[a]Headmaster McGraw requested rewriting of the parent questionnaire, with the result that parents answered all the civil rights items either Yes or No.

[b]Data are not available.

Table 13

Support for Religious Pluralism by Student and Adult Groups
(Percentages)

	Students			Adults		
	Bethany (N = 115)	Hartney (N = 104)	Rural public school (N = 47)	Roman Catholics (N = 344)	Bethany teachers (N = 16)	Bethany parents (N = 47)
There are many different religions but no one absolute true religion. (Agree and Strongly agree)	17	50	42	—[a]	6	—[b]
One good thing about American society is we have so many different churches and religious beliefs. (Agree and Strongly agree)	27	82	83	—[a]	38	19
Only people who believe in God can be good Americans. (Disagree and Strongly disagree)	83	84	85	65	75	89
Catholics don't take religion as seriously as born-again Christians.[c] (Disagree and Strongly disagree)	64	—[b]	—[b]	70	31	17

[a]Data are not available.

[b]Response not solicited from this group.

[c]As administered by Greeley and Rossi to Roman Catholics this item read: "Protestants don't really take their religion seriously compared to Catholics."

Table 14

Machiavellian Outlook among Bethany and Hartney Students
(Percentages)

	"Strongly agree" & "Agree"		"Strongly disagree" & "Disagree"	
	Bethany	Hartney	Bethany	Hartney
It's smart to be nice to important people even if you don't really like them.	78	65	22	35
Criminals are just like other people except they're dumb enough to get caught.	18	28	82	72
It is better to be ordinary and honest than famous and dishonest.	96	90	3	10
The best way to handle people is to tell them what they want to hear.	22	30	78	70
It's hard to get ahead without cutting corners here and there.	33	72	67	28

NOTE: For Bethany, N = 115; for Hartney, 104.

Table 15

Bethany and Hartney Students on Alienation, Locus of Control, and Certainty (Percentages)

	"Strongly agree" & "Agree"		"Strongly disagree" & "Disagree"	
	Bethany	Hartney	Bethany	Hartney
Alienation				
There are exceptions but basically people can't be trusted.	30	35	70	65
I often feel lonely.	43	41	57	59
I often can't help wondering if anything is worthwhile anymore.	20	39	80	61
I can count on someone to help me when I'm in real trouble.	92	88	8	11
Locus of Control				
I can change what might happen tomorrow by what I do today.	90	89	10	11
Most of the time it doesn't pay to try hard because things never turn out right anyway.	13	23	87	77
One of the best ways to handle most problems is just not to think about them.	20	25	80	75
I believe that planning ahead makes things turn out better.	89	92	11	8
Usually when something is wrong, there is little I can do to make it right.	23	24	77	76
Certainty				
There are so many things expected of me, I'm not sure what I ought to do.	31	58	69	42
The way things are nowadays, I find it difficult to know just what to believe.	24	79	76	21
When I'm with people I don't know well, I'm uncertain about how I ought to behave.	34	60	66	40

NOTE: For Bethany, N = 115; for Hartney, 104.

Table 16
Evidence of Student Deviance from Bethany's Norms

Question or statement eliciting response	Deviant responses (%)
How spiritual is your best out-of-school friend? (Low)	36
How faithful is your best out-of-school friend? (Low)	32
I listen to music that conflicts with Bethany's standards. (Always)	23
Bethany's standards guide me in my behavior at weekend parties. (Never)	24
I obey the student pledge during summer vacations. (Never)	17
How often do you hold private devotions? (Never)	16
Bethany's standards guide me in my behavior on dates. (Never)	15
In general, do you obey the student pledge? (No)	14
Bethany's standards guide me in my behavior with friends. (Never)	12
The way I'm urged to act and think in school is different from the way I really feel. (Strongly agree)	10
If I could leave, I'd go to a public school. (Yes)	9
How spiritual is your best school friend? (Low)	10
How spiritual are you? (Low)	8
How faithful is your best school friend? (Low)	8
I should be close friends only with born-again Christians. (Strongly disagree)	7
I watch movies that conflict with Bethany's standards. (Always)	6
How important is it that BBA provides you a good spiritual experience? (Very unimportant)	5
I read books that conflict with Bethany's standards. (Always)	5
The people I'm with on weekends reject Bethany's standards. (Always)	4
When I'm an adult, the Bible will be the center of my life. (Strongly disagree)	4
I obey the pledge because I fear the consequences of sinning. (Very unimportant reason)	4
The most influential person in my life rejects Bethany's standards. (Strongly agree)	4
How faithful are you? (Low)	3
I watch TV programs that conflict with Bethany's standards. (Always)	3
I'm happiest living in the Lord's will. (Strongly disagree)	2
I will marry a born-again Christian. (Strongly disagree)	1

NOTE: N = 115.

References

Arons, Stephen. 1983. *Compelling Belief*. New York: McGraw-Hill.

Barth, Roland S. 1980. *Run School Run*. Cambridge: Harvard University Press.

Baskin, Darryl. 1971. *American Pluralist Democracy: A Critique*. New York: Van Nostrand Reinhold.

Belmonte, Frank. 1979. *The Broken Fountain*. New York: Columbia University Press.

Bernstein, Basil. 1975. *Class, Codes and Control: Toward a Theory of Educational Transmissions*, vol. 3. London: Routledge and Kegan Paul.

Bertocci, Peter A. 1971. "Psychological Interpretations of Religious Experience." In *Research on Religious Development*, edited by Merton P. Strommer. New York: Hawthorne.

Bettelheim, Bruno. 1969. *The Children of the Dream*. New York: Avon Books.

———. 1979. "Education and the Reality Principle." *American Educator* 3 (Winter): 10, 12, 33–35.

Bliven, Naomi. 1979. "Living at This Hour," *New Yorker*, 2 February: 116–18.

Bohrek, James T., and Curtis, Richard F. 1975. *A Sociology of Belief*. New York: John Wiley.

Bosk, Charles. 1979. *Forgive and Remember: Managing Medical Failure*. Chicago: University of Chicago Press.

Brothers, Joan. 1964. *Church and School: A Study of the Impact of Education on Religion*. Liverpool: Liverpool University Press.

Butts, R. Freeman. 1980. *The Revival of Civic Learning*. Bloomington, Ind.: Phi Delta Kappa Educational Foundation.

Carlson, Gerald B. 1982a. "Christian Schools are Different on Purpose." *AACS Christian School Communicator*. 2: 1.

————. 1982b. "Is the United States Government Discriminating against Christian Schools?" *Christian School Administrator* 2: 1.

Carper, James C. 1982. "The Whisner Decision: A Case Study in State Regulation of Christian Day Schools." *Journal of Church and State* 24: 281–302.

Cates, Paul W. 1975. "Christian Philosophy of Education." Hialeah, Fla.: American Association of Christian Schools.

Clerico, Donald R. 1982. "Searching for Peace of Mind: Parents' Rationales for Enrolling Their Children in a Christian School." Ph.D. dissertation, Syracuse University.

Coleman, James S. 1981. *Public and Private Schools*. Washington, D.C.: National Center for Education Statistics.

Coser, Lewis A. 1974. *Greedy Institutions: Patterns of Undivided Commitment*. New York: Free Press.

Curran, Edward. 1982. "NIE: An Agenda for the 80s." *Educational Researcher*, 11 (May): 10–12, 21.

Dahl, R. A. 1975. *Pluralist Democracy in the United States*. New York: McGraw-Hill.

————. 1980. "Pluralism Revisited." In *Three Faces of Pluralism: Political, Ethnic and Religious*, edited by Stanislaw Ehrlich and Graham Wooton. Westmead, England: Gowen.

————. 1982. *Dilemmas of Pluralist Democracy: Autonomy vs. Control*. New Haven: Yale University Press.

Demaret, Kent. 1981. "The House of the Two Gablers Helps Decide What Johnny Can't Read in Texas Schools." *People*, 5 October: 86, 88–89.

Digest of Education Statistics. Washington, D.C.: U.S. Government Printing Office.

Dillenberger, John, and Welch, Claude. 1954. *Protestant Laity Interpreted through Its Development*. New York: Charles Scribner's Sons.

Dillon, Wilton S. 1974. "E Pluribus Unum?" In *The Cultural Drama: Modern Identities and Social Ferment*, edited by Wilton S. Dillon. Washington, D.C.: Smithsonian Institution Press.

Doyle, Dennis P. 1980. "Public Policy and Private Education." *Phi Delta Kappan* 62: 16–19.

Drew, Elizabeth. 1981. "A Reporter at Large: Jesse Helms," *New Yorker*, July 20: 78–95.

Durkheim, Emile. 1915. *The Elementary Forms of Religious Life*, translated by Joseph Ward Swain. London: George Allen and Unwin.

Edgerton, R. 1976. *Deviance: A Cross-Cultural Perspective*. Menlo Park, Cal.: Cummings Publishing Company.

Elam, Stanley M., ed. 1978. *A Decade of Gallup Polls of Attitudes toward Education, 1969–1978*. Bloomington, Ind.: Phi Delta Kappa Educational Foundation.

Erickson, Donald A. 1964. "Religious Consequences of Public and Sectarian Schooling." *School Review* 72: 22–23.

———. 1969. "Freedom's Two Educational Imperatives: A Proposal." In *Public Controls for Nonpublic Schools*, edited by Donald Erickson. Chicago: University of Chicago Press.

Erickson, Donald A., et al. 1978. "Recent Enrollment Trends in U.S. Nonpublic Schools." In *Declining Enrollments: The Challenge of the Coming Decade*, edited by Susan Abramowitz and Stuart Rosenfeld. Washington, D.C.: National Institute of Education.

Etzioni, Amitai. 1961. *A Comparative Analysis of Complex Organizations.* New York: Free Press.

———. 1975. *A Comparative Analysis of Complex Organizations.* New York: Free Press.

Evans, Robert A. 1979. "Recovering the Church's Transforming Middle: Theological Reflections on a Balance between Faithfulness and Effectiveness." In *Understanding Christian Growth and Decline*, edited by Dean R. Hoge and David A. Roozen. New York: Pilgrim Press.

Fellman, David. 1969. *The Supreme Court and Education.* New York: Teachers College Press.

Fitzgerald, Frances. 1984. "A Disagreement in Baileyville." *New Yorker*, 16 January: 47–90.

Foreman, Chris. 1982. "Why Parents in Oregon Enroll Their Children in Protestant Christian Schools." Ph.D. dissertation, University of Oregon.

Fountain, Dennis. "Education for What?" Mimeographed (in author's possession).

Gallup, George. 1980. "Little Evidence of Shift to Right Detected in Nation." *Champaign-Urbana News Gazette*, November 14.

Ginger, Ray. 1958. *Six Days or Forever? Tennessee vs. John Thomas Scopes.* Boston: Beacon Press.

Glazer, Nathan, and Moynihan, Daniel. 1970. *Beyond the Melting Pot*, 2d ed. Cambridge: MIT Press.

Goffman, Erving. 1961. *Asylums: Essays on the Social Situation of Mental Patients and Other Inmates.* Garden City, N.J.: Anchor Books.

Goldblatt, Anne N. 1981. "The Magic Touch of Teachers," *American Educator* 5: 33–34.

Grant, Gerald. 1981. "The Character of Education and the Education of Character." *Daedalus* 110: 135–49.

Greeley, Andrew M., and Gockel, Galen L. 1971. "The Religious Effects of Parochial Education." In *Research on Religious Development: A Comprehensive Handbook*, edited by Merton P. Strommen. New York: Hawthorne Books.

Greeley, Andrew M., and McCready, William C. 1974. *Ethnicity in the U.S.* New York: Wiley.

Greeley, Andrew M.; McCready, William C.; and McCourt, Kathleen. 1976. *Catholic Schools in a Declining Church*. Kansas City: Sheed and Ward.

Greeley, Andrew M., and Rossi, Peter H. 1966. *The Education of Catholic Americans*, Chicago: Aldine.

Hazard, William R. 1980. "The Flight from the Public Schools: Myth or Reality." Paper presented at a Special Advanced Leadership Program Services Seminar, 31 July, at Atlanta, Ga.

Heard, Alex. 1981. "Study Discovers Many Overlooked Private Schools," *Education Week*, August 24: 4.

Hillery, G. A., Jr. 1963. "Villages, Cities, and Total Institutions." *American Sociological Review*. 28: 779–91.

Hillocks, George. 1978. "Books and Bombs: Ideological Conflict and the Schools." *School Review* 86 (August): 632–54.

Himmelfarb, Harold S. 1977. "The Non-Linear Impacts of Schooling: Comparing Different Types and Amounts of Jewish Education." *Sociology of Education* 42: 114–29.

Hofstadter, Richard. 1966. *Anti-intellectualism in American Life*. New York: Knopf.

Hoge, Dean R. 1979. "A Test of Theories of Denominational Growth and Decline." In *Understanding Christian Growth and Decline*, edited by Dean R. Hoge and David A. Roozen. New York: Pilgrim Press.

Horton, Robin. 1967. "African Traditional Thought and Western Science," pt. 2. *Africa* 37: 155–87.

Hurn, Christopher J. 1978. *The Limits and Possibilities of Schooling: An Introduction to the Sociology of Education*. Boston: Allyn and Bacon.

Jackson, Bruce. 1982. "Home Education." *AACS Christian School Communicator* 3: 3.

Johnston, A. P., and Wiles, D. K. 1982. "Christian Schools and Public Schools in Small Rural Communities of the Northeast." Report submitted to the Spencer Foundation.

Johnstone, Ronald L. 1966. *The Effectiveness of Lutheran Elementary and Secondary Schools*. St. Louis: Concordia.

Jose, William S. 1968. "Total Institutions: A Reconstruction." *Sociological Focus* 1 (Summer): 18–27.

Kienel, Paul. 1977. "Decade of Growth for Christian Schools." *Christian School Comment* 7: 7.

Kranendonk, D. L. 1978. *Christian Day Schools: Why and How*. Ontario, Canada: Paideia Press.

Krauthammer, Charles. 1981. "The Humanist Phantom." *New Republic* 185: 20–25.

Kraybill, Donald B. 1977. *Ethnic Education: The Impact of Mennonite Schooling*. San Francisco: R and E Research Associates.

Larson, Roy. 1980. "God and Politics 'From Sea to Shining Sea.'" *Chicago Sunday Sun-Times*, March 2.

Levin, Henry M. 1982. "Educational Choice and the Pains of Democracy." Stanford, Cal.: Institute for Research on Educational
Finance and Governance.

Lortie, Dan C. 1975. *Schoolteacher*. Chicago: University of Chicago Press.

Marty, Martin E. 1979. Foreword to *Understanding Christian Growth and
Decline*, edited by Dean R. Hoge and David A. Roozen. New York:
Pilgrim Press.

Mattingly, Terry. 1980. "Baptists Signal Right Turn in St. Louis." *Champaign-Urbana News Gazette*, June 14.

Matza, David. 1969. *Becoming Deviant*. Englewood Cliffs, N.J.:
Prentice-Hall.

McDearmid, Andrew. 1979. "Student Achievement in Accelerated
Christian Education Schools in Pennsylvania." Ph.D. dissertation,
Temple University.

McEwen, C. A. 1980. "Continuities in a Study of Total and Nontotal
Institutions." *Annual Review of Sociology* 6: 143–85.

McLoughlin, William G. 1978. *Revivals, Awakenings, and Reform: An
Essay on Religion and Social Change in America, 1607–1977*. Chicago:
University of Chicago Press.

Mensching, Gustav. 1971. *Tolerance and Truth in Religion*, translated by
H. J. Klimkeit. University, Ala.: University of Alabama Press.

Mitgang, H. 1983. "Publisher Rejects 3 Books for 'Offensive' Words."
New York Times, September 17.

Mouzelis, N. P. 1971. "Critical Note on Total Institutions." *Sociology* 5:
113–20.

Murnane, Richard. 1982. "Understanding Public and Private Schools."
Ph.D. dissertation, Yale University.

Muller, Herbert. 1960. *Issues on Freedom: Paradoxes and Promises*. New
York: Harper and Brothers.

Myerhoff, Barbara. 1978. *Number Our Days*. New York: Dutton.

National Council of Churches. 1968. *Yearbook of American Churches*. New
York: Council Press.

———. 1978. *Yearbook of American and Canadian Churches*. Nashville:
Abingdon.

National Opinion Research Center. 1974–75. *National Data Program for
the Social Sciences*. Ann Arbor: Interuniversity Consortium for Political
Research.

Neisser, Ulric. 1976. *Cognition and Reality*. San Francisco: Freeman.

Nevin, David, and Bills, Robert E. 1976. *The Schools that Fear Built:
Segregationist Academies in the South*. Washington, D.C.: Acropolis
Books.

Nisbet, Robert A. 1966. *The Sociological Tradition*. New York: Basic
Books.

———. 1976. *Sociology as an Art Form*. London: Oxford University Press.

Nordin, V. D., and Turner, W. L. 1980. "More than Segregated

Academies: The Growing Protestant Fundamentalist Schools." *Phi Delta Kappan* 61 (February): 391–94.

Novak, Michael. 1971. *The Rise of the Unmeltable Ethnic*. New York: Macmillan.

O'Dea, Thomas F. 1966. *The Sociology of Religion*. Englewood Cliffs, N.J.: Prentice-Hall.

———. 1967. "Sociological Dilemmas: Five Paradoxes of Institutionalization." In *Sociological Theory, Values, and Sociocultural Change*, edited by Edward A. Tiryakian. New York: Harper and Row.

Oliver, Donald W. 1976. *Education and Community: A Radical Critique of Innovative Schooling*. Berkeley, Cal.: McCutchan.

Park, J. Charles. 1980. "Preachers, Politics, and Public Education: A Review of Right Wing Pressures against Public Schooling in America." *Phi Delta Kappan* 61 (May): 608–12.

Perry, N. 1974. "The Two Cultures and the Total Institution." *British Journal of Sociology* 25: 345–55.

Peshkin, Alan. 1978. *Growing Up American: Schooling and the Survival of Community*. Chicago: University of Chicago Press.

———. 1982. *The Imperfect Union: School Consolidation and Community Conflict*. Chicago: University of Chicago Press.

———. 1985. "Virtuous Subjectivity: In the Participant Observer's I's." In *Exploring Clinical Methods for Social Research*, edited by David N. Berg and Kenwyn K. Smith. Beverly Hills, Cal.: Sage, 1985.

Robben, John. 1972. "Roaming Catholics." *New York Times*, February 24.

Robbins, Thomas; Anthony, Dick; and Curtis, Thomas E. 1973. "The Limits of Symbolic Realism: Problems of Empathic Field Observation in a Sectarian Context." *Journal for the Scientific Study of Religion* 12 (March): 259–71.

Rokeach, Milton. 1960. *The Open and Closed Mind*. New York: Basic Books.

Rose, Dorothy W. 1979. "Success Story of Christian Schools." *Good News Broadcaster*, September: 48–50.

Rosenberg, Harold. 1976. "Essay: A Meditation on Likeness." In *Portraits*, by Richard Avedon. New York: Farrar, Straus and Giroux.

Schiff, Alvin I. 1966. *The Jewish Day School in America*. New York: Jewish Education Commission of New York.

Seeman, Melvin. 1959. "The Meaning of Alienation." *American Sociological Review* 24 (December): 783–91.

Shanker, Albert. 1979. "Poll Shows Support for Education." *American Teacher* (November): 8.

Shipman, M. D. 1968. *The Sociology of a School*. New York: Humanities Press.

Siegel, Bernard J. 1970. "Defensive Structuring and Environmental Stress." *American Journal of Sociology* 76: 11–32.

Slater, Marian K. 1976. *African Odyssey: An Anthropological Adventure.* Bloomington, Ind.: Indiana University Press.

Smylie, James H. 1979. "On Growth and Decline in Historical Perspective." In *Understanding Christian Growth and Decline,* edited by Dean R. Hoge and David A. Roozen. New York: Pilgrim Press.

Snook, Ivan A. 1972. *Indoctrination and Education.* London: Routledge and Kegan Paul.

State Board of Education. 1978. *Policies and Guidelines for Registration and Recognition of Nonpublic Elementary and Secondary Schools.* Springfield, Ill.: Illinois Office of Education.

Steiner, George. 1967. *Language and Silence: Essays on Language, Literature, and the Inhuman.* New York: Atheneum.

Stoker, W. G. Fred, and Splawn, Robert. 1980. *A Study of Accelerated Christian Education Schools in Northwest Texas.* Canyon, Tex.: West Texas State University.

Stoms, William. 1982. "The Growth of Evangelical Schools: A Study of Parental Concerns and other Contributing Factors." Ph.D. dissertation, Rutgers University.

Sullivan, J. L.; Pierson, J.; and Marcus, G. F. 1982. *Political Tolerance and American Democracy.* Chicago: University of Chicago Press.

Turner, William L. 1979. "Reasons for Enrollment in Religious Schools: A Case Study of Three Recently Established Fundamentalist Schools in Kentucky and Wisconsin." Ph.D. dissertation, University of Wisconsin—Madison.

Wagenaar, T. C. 1981. "High School Seniors' Views of Themselves and Their Schools: A Trend Analysis." *Phi Delta Kappan* 63: 29–32.

Walker, Charles. 1982. "Influencing Your Child's Mind." *AACS Christian School Communicator* 2: 1.

Wallace, Samuel E., ed. 1971. *Total Institutions.* Chicago: Aldine.

Weissmann, Arnie. 1981. "Target McGovern." *Advocate* 15: 8–9.

Wheeler, Stanton. 1966. "The Structure of Formally Organized Socialization Settings." In *Socialization after Childhood: Two Essays,* edited by Orville G. Brim, Jr., and Stanton Wheeler. New York: Wiley.

Willms, J. Douglas. 1983. *Public and Private Schools: The Evaluation of Choice in Education.* Stanford, Cal.: Stanford University Institute for Research on Educational Finance and Governance.

Wrong, Dennis. 1961. "The Oversocialized Conception of Man in Modern Sociology." *American Sociological Review* 26: 183–93.

Index

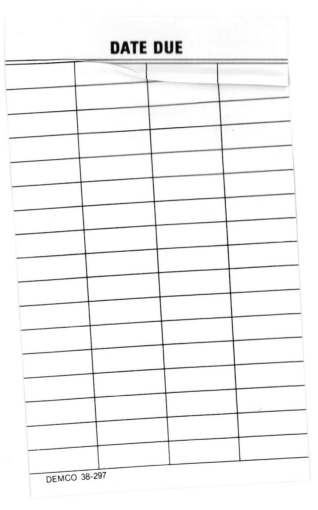